STONEWALL INN EDITIONS
KEITH KAHLA, GENERAL EDITOR

ALSO BY MICHAEL BRONSKI

Culture Clash: The Making of Gay Sensibility

Flashpoint: Gay Male Sexual Writing,
editor

Outstanding Lives: Profiles of Lesbians and Gay Men,
consulting editor

Taking Liberties: Gay Men's Essays on Politics, Culture, and Sex,
editor

The Pleasure Principle

Sex, Backlash, and the Struggle for Gay Freedom

MICHAEL BRONSKI

St. Martin's Press
New York

Design by Ellen Sasahara

Library of Congress Cataloging-in-Publication Data

The pleasure principle : sex, backlash, and the struggle for gay
freedom / Michael Bronski.
    p. cm.
    ISBN 0-312-15625-1 (hc)
    ISBN 0-312-25287-0 (pbk)
    1. Gays in popular culture—United States. 2. Gay rights—United
States—Public opinion. 3. Homosexuality—United States. 4. Gays—
United States—Public opinion. 5. Public opinion—United States.
    I. Title.
HQ76.8.U5B76   1998
306.76'6—dc21   97-7983
                                                    CIP

First Stonewall Inn Edition: February 2000

10 9 8 7 6 5 4 3 2 1

Acknowledgments

IN MY ACKNOWLEDGMENTS to *Culture Clash,* I suggested that books are the product of the complex intellectual and emotional interplay between friends and colleagues: community. The same is true for this book. While I take full responsibility for all ideas included herein, they have benefited enormously from the nurturance and sustenance of community. Earlier incarnations of some of these ideas surfaced in my earlier work, most notably in articles and reviews in *Gay Community News.* I have had the good fortune to publish—to think out loud, as it were—in this and other venues in the gay and lesbian press. The constant feedback from editors and readers is not only intrinsic to the development of any writer and thinker, but a luxury that many authors lack. It is also one of the embodiments of community, without which this book would not have been written.

I would like to thank my agent, Jed Mattes, and my editor, Keith Kahla, for their constant insight and attention. Many friends, including Gail Epstein, Alison Pirie, Craig Lucas, Chris Bull, Michael Roberts, Kevin Cathcart, Richard Voos, Jerry Cabrera, Ken Feil, Jason Moore, Linda Lowenthal, and Neale McGoldrick, read early versions of these chapters. Their comments informed and challenged my thinking and writing.

During the two years I spent writing this book it was impossible for me to keep it contained in a distinct sphere of my life. Much of my thinking and reading spilled into my everyday relationships and conversations. Will Leber, Christopher J. Hogan, Urvashi Vaid, Patrick Carr, and Neil Miller kindly and patiently refined my ideas. Sue Hyde was an invaluable source of information and critical thinking about the gay rights movement. As they have been for more than twenty-five years (when we first worked on *Fag Rag* together), Charley Shively and John Mitzel were unending sources of intellectual inspiration and support.

Five people were central to the evolution of *The Pleasure Principle.* While all critiqued the manuscript with insight and care, they also bestowed upon me their own singular gifts. From Christopher Bram I received the benefit of his incredible range of knowledge and empathetic commentary. I drew upon Joseph Canarelli's unique understanding of culture and politics as well as his intense and loyal friendship of more than thirty years. Michael Lowenthal gave me not only his invaluable friendship but his editing expertise. Sarah Schulman is an inspiration for living and writing with integrity and love. And Joshua Oppenheimer sparked a renewed sense of intellectual excitement and an idealistic commitment to truth—a pleasure as vital and important as that of the flesh—that I had barely realized was missing from my life until we met.

Contents

Introduction

*T*HE *PLEASURE PRINCIPLE* is an exploration of themes and ideas that I have been writing about over the past three decades: homosexuality, gay culture, gay politics, the meaning of popular culture in people's lives, and the role that gay culture plays—not only in the lives of gay people but in those of heterosexuals as well. This exploration, in both general themes and cultural and political specifics, is often bold and intentionally provocative, but it is proposed with the desire to stimulate thought and encourage discussion. By drawing upon a wide range of historical and cultural topics and sources—Freudian theory, *Pee-wee's Playhouse,* African slave culture, the blood libel against the Jews, the Marlboro Man, the *Bowers v. Hardwick* decision, the Harlem Renaissance, the writings of urbanologist Jane Jacobs, the Dreyfus Affair, essays by Hannah Arendt, Orientalism, early-twentieth-century ethnic theater, the political theories of Lani Guinier—I have tried to map out and illustrate a new way of imagining gay culture and gay history.

The Pleasure Principle has two main concerns. In its first five chapters it examines the role pleasure plays in our society. In the broadest sense it is about how pleasure is constructed, used, and regulated. Specifically, it is about the inextricable and unavoidable connection between sexuality and pleasure. It is about how we view sexuality—the ur-pleasure—and how our attitudes about sexuality construct our basic definitions of pleasure. Most significantly, it is about how the regulation of sexuality shapes our ideas about pleasure.

At first glance *The Pleasure Principle* might appear to be primarily about homosexuality and gay culture. Actually, it is as much about heterosexuality and mainstream culture's highly ambivalent relationship to homosexuality and gay culture. Institutionalized heterosexuality—reproductive intercourse, gender roles, the family, and the traditional raising of children—is the dominant culture's primary means of regulating sexuality and sexual activity. The social mandate of heterosexuality also prohibits all forms of homosexual identity and behavior, which are viewed by the dominant culture as emblematic of sexual license and erotic freedom— a freedom that has become increasingly apparent with the rise of the gay movement. At its heart *The Pleasure Principle* is an exploration of the tension that exists between heterosexual fear of homosexuality and gay culture (and the pleasure they represent) and the equally strong envy of and desire to enjoy that freedom and pleasure.

Chapters six through eleven of *The Pleasure Principle* are a series of investigations of the effects of gay culture on mainstream culture showing how the more pleasure-based arrangements of gay culture have consistently provided heterosexuals with viable alternatives to the restrictive structures of mainstream culture. This is interwoven with an examination of the problems faced by gay people in gaining basic civil rights and becoming full citizens—problems that raise the profound question of what it means to be an "American" and the increasingly contentious question of who is able to become an "American." These questions have as much to do with culture as with politics.

One of the aims of *The Pleasure Principle* is to remove gay culture from the historical vacuum in which it is often placed as though it were a discrete entity. By situating gay history and politics in broad historical and cultural context—the history of popular culture, the struggles of other subcultures for independence, the growth of U.S. cities, the rise of feminism—*The Pleasure Principle* attempts to locate them in the material world, inseparable from the ebb and flow of everyday life.

I began writing *The Pleasure Principle* at a unique time in gay history and culture. The social and political advances made by the gay rights movement over the past twenty-five years have secured for gay people greater visibility and more legal protections than ever before. This advance, however, has been accompanied by two, not unconnected, phenomena: a broad-based backlash by political conservatives and the religious right, aimed at countering the visibility and gains of the gay movement; and a growing sentiment within the gay community promoting the "assimilation" of gay people into the dominant culture.

The right-wing antigay agenda is part of a larger political movement that—as lesbian writer and activist Sarah Schulman has pointed out—has as its aim the eradication of the progressive social and political change that began with the New Deal. Thus it serves as a reminder that the struggle for gay freedom is inseparable from other struggles for social justice. Gay "assimilationism" is, to some degree, a self-protective response to this backlash. But it is also anchored in the belief that homosexuality is a minor human differentiation, and that, if gay people were less demonstrative, or obvious, in their social or sexual affect—less publicly homosexual—they would be accepted by heterosexuals. The assimilationist position is predicated on a deeply held belief in the worth of such basic social structures as traditional sexual morality, monogamous marriage, accepted gender roles, and the nuclear family.

The Pleasure Principle is an argument against both conservative and assimilationist positions. It does not argue that homosexuality (as a sexual activity) is in any way "better" than heterosexuality, but rather that institutionalized heterosexuality as a fixed—indeed, entrenched—worldview is deeply flawed and does not suit the needs of its detractors or adherents. While my first book, *Culture Clash: The Making of Gay Sensibility* (published in 1984), charted the evolution of a distinct gay male culture, *The Pleasure Principle* examines not only the complicated relationship between that culture and the dominant culture, but the political and social ramifications of that interchange.

While the book comes from my experiences as a writer, political activist and organizer, critic, cultural maven, reader, moviegoer, and general consumer of culture, it also has very specific political and theoretical roots. My formative years were spent in the antiwar movement, the early years of gay liberation, and the counterculture of the late 1960s. I have been enormously influenced in my thinking by Herbert Marcuse's *Eros and Civilization,* Kate Millett's *Sexual Politics,* R. D. Laing's *The Politics of Experience,* Shulamith Firestone's *The Dialectic of Sex,* Paul Goodman's *Growing Up Absurd,* and Norman O. Brown's *Life against Death.* These works may seem, in our postmodern times, slightly antiquated or even naïve but, I feel, they still offer profound insights into how civilization is organized and how we live our lives. These writers offer a vision of personal liberation that focuses upon the importance of sexuality and pleasure in human existence. More important, however, this vision of personal liberation forms the basis of a far broader social vision of human liberation. This vision is profoundly centered on the idea of community and an almost utopian desire to remake the world in a way that would prioritize freedom over repression, and to understand that pleasure and sexuality are vital tools in creating a society and culture that is humane, celebratory, and life-sustaining.

If this vision feels utopian—and it may be—I have no excuses except for the fact that any other vision seems shortsighted, repressive, or outright destructive to the enormous potential humans have to create a civilization in which they can flourish instead of languish in chains of their own making. It may also be utopian because it presumes that the seeking of pleasure—the pleasure principle—is a fundamental human need not only positive but useful, not only possible but necessary.

One

_____

The Making of Americans

1.

During the 1992 Republican National Convention, right-wing columnist and demagogue Pat Buchanan declared that America was in the midst of a cultural war that imperiled the country's moral and political well-being. This caused a huge media furor, but it was not news. Conservatives had been decrying the decline of American morals and values for at least a century. Recent culture wars have centered on National Endowment for the Arts funding of "pornographic" artists such as Robert Mapplethorpe, Tim Miller, Holly Hughes, and Karen Finley; past battles involved censorship laws, reproductive rights, sex education in the public schools, and sexual freedom for gay men and lesbians.

Buchanan's stand—which many secular and religious conservatives supported—came at a time when the culture wars were proliferating and becoming more ferocious. The progressive social-change movements of the 1960s had created, with considerable struggle, a social climate that promoted greater political and personal freedom, but a backlash had quickly followed. By the early 1980s, a new wave of conservatism had polarized U.S. culture and politics. Race, sexuality, and popular culture erupted into social battlegrounds. By 1992, issues as diverse as government funding for the arts, AIDS, abortion, pornography, the rights of immigrants, access to safe-sex information, welfare, Afrocentrism, drug use and rehabilitation, bilingual education, the "protection" of children, the academic canon, and a whole spectrum of gay rights concerns—from gays in the military to federally funded studies of gay-teen suicide—had became flashpoints for conservatives determined to impede progressive politics. In this broad range of topics there were two common threads: the parameters of personal identity and the limits of collective freedom. The social and political implications of these

5

themes, however, were far greater. Specifically, the culture wars were—and are—an ongoing series of acrimonious debates about two larger questions: "Who is an American?" and "Who has full rights of citizenship?"

These are not new questions. The idea of the "American" is essentially a mythic construction that is constantly shaped and reshaped, through a complicated historical process, as a traditionally white, Anglocentric political and social culture (which has implicitly been male, heterosexual, and capitalist as well) and is constantly challenged by those who do not fit those criteria.[1]

This contentious process of redefining the national identity has been at the core of U.S. history and culture. The United States, after all, began as a country of interlopers and immigrants, most of whom were intolerant of other religious and ethnic groups; the Anglo-British character of the early North American colonies was itself the result of victory over competing French and Spanish claims. After independence from Britain was established, waves of Irish and other European immigrants challenged the Anglocentric nature of "American" culture. As for African slaves and their descendants, they were integral to the nation's social, economic, and political fabric, but their status as "Americans"—whether they were slaves or free—was always in question. The same was true of Native Americans, Asian residents, and, to a lesser degree, Jews and other non-Christians.

"American" identity is determined partly by legal citizenship, but being an "American" is more than that: it implies a level of acceptance by mainstream culture that protects against marginalization and discrimination. This acceptance is, in turn, predicated upon the assumption that "Americans" believe and uphold what are commonly called "American values." (The definition is circular since the nebulous category of "American values" is central to the definition of the "American" identity.) These "American values," which usually reflect the most conservative aspects of the dominant culture, shift over time as the economic, political, and psychological needs of "Americans" change. When these issues are up for debate—in a culture war—a renegotiation process occurs and the specifics of "American values" can change. Even the language and definition of membership can change. During the Vietnam War, for example, the category of the "real American"—one who supported the war—emerged to signify a split in national identity and values.

The relationship between being an "American" and having the full rights and privileges of legal citizenship is complicated. White women in the nineteenth century, for example, were considered American citizens even though they did not, in many states, have the right to own property, or to hold office, or even to vote. On the other hand, even though African Americans were released from slavery by the Emancipation Proclamation in 1863 and the Thirteenth Amendment in 1865, granted citizenship by the Fourteenth Amendment three years later, and (in the case of males) enfranchised by the Fifteenth Amendment in 1870, they still faced enormous legal and legislative battles to exercise those rights fully. And even full legal citizenship has not changed a prevailing attitude among many white citizens that whiteness is a prerequisite for being an authentic "American." Native Americans and residents of Asian descent, as well as African Americans, have suffered from this perception.[2]

In fact, the common definition of citizenship—as a relationship between an individual and a nation whereby individuals are granted clearly defined rights in exchange for certain duties, such as obeying laws, paying taxes, and serving in the military—is deceptively simple and inexact. Children, for example, are legally citizens but are denied the vote because their age is seen as an impediment to making informed decisions. White women had citizenship but were, for more than a century, denied basic rights. African Americans had citizenship rights they were barred from using. Yet both groups were expected to pay taxes, and black males were liable for military service.

This limited vision of citizenship has been an effective mechanism for curtailing minority groups' cultural and political freedom. While it secures rights and protections for some groups, it does not necessarily provide legal recourse when those rights are abridged. More important, it does not include the ability to live without the fear of violence or discrimination, or be assured of personal safety in public as well as private. It does not provide for minorities the same rights to public assembly, access to information, and self-expression that majority groups have. Ideally, full citizenship would mean the creation of a national social and political environment in which the cultural self-expression and determination of all minority groups would be respected.

The struggle over defining who is an "American," or a full citizen, is, at its heart, about power. It is about the power of the majority to set and maintain a political and cultural agenda and to create and regulate codes of personal, social, and sexual behavior that conform to the majority's standards. It is also about the struggles of those with less power to secure and protect their individual autonomy and dignity, as well as their right to a distinct, nonmajority identity.

2.

THE culture wars, in all of their manifestations, are the public forum where issues of what it means to be an "American" and a citizen are being debated and decided. Although many of the contemporary culture wars concern issues of race and ethnicity—immigration rights, bilingual education, Afrocentricism—a majority of them involve issues of sexuality and gender. Specifically, they revolve around reproductive rights, alternative definitions of the family, children's rights, feminism, pornography, and homosexuality. All of these issues are targeted by conservatives and the religious right as antithetical to "family values."

To the extent that this is true, these culture wars are actually about the restabilization and reaffirmation of heterosexuality and traditional gender norms in U.S. culture. Over the past century myriad factors have decentered or radically altered the institution of heterosexuality: increased freedom for women and children, the ability to regulate sexual reproduction, the effects of industrialization on the family, and the breakdown of established gender roles. But none of these are as deeply disruptive to the institution of heterosexuality as the emergence of homosexuality as a public identity and a political agenda—a "coming out" that forced the dominant culture to deal with homosexuality.

To understand why homosexuality is at the heart of the contemporary culture wars, it is important to examine the actual and metaphoric role that homosexuality plays in Western societies, and then to explore how mainstream culture's fear of homosexuality is constructed and manifested.

One of the most persistent myths of the gay rights movement, and of liberal thinking, is that the dominant culture's fear of homosexuality and hatred of homosexuals—what is commonly called "homophobia"—is irrational. This is untrue: It is a completely rational fear. Homosexuality strikes at the heart of the organization of Western culture and societies. Because homosexuality, by its nature, is nonreproductive, it posits a sexuality that is justified by pleasure alone. This stands in stark and, for many people, frightening contrast to the entrenched belief that reproduction alone legitimates sexual activity. This belief, enshrined in religious and civil law, is the foundation for society's limiting gender roles and the reason why marriage, traditionally, has been the only context recognized by society and by law for sexual relationships between men and women. It is the underpinning for the restrictive structure of the biological family unit and its status as the only sanctioned setting for raising children. It is the hidden logic determining many of our economic and work structures. In profound, if often unarticulated ways, this imperative view of reproductive heterosexuality has shaped our world.[3]

Although heterosexuals individually, throughout the centuries, have engaged in sex for pleasure, attempts to unseat the ideology of sex-as-reproduction have continually been resisted. Until recently, explicitly sexual material (that which portrays sex as simply pleasure) has routinely been censored, medical information about birth control has been banned, and access to contraceptives has been limited by law. Only in 1965 did the Supreme Court rule that married adults had a constitutional right to privacy in marriage that allowed them to use birth control. Even for heterosexuals, securing personal and sexual freedom has been a long and difficult battle.

The imperative of reproductive heterosexuality has had enormous effects on homosexuals as well. It is the basis for the labeling of homosexual activity as "unnatural," sinful, and sick. Historically, it has been the rationale for executing, castrating, and otherwise physically punishing male and female homosexuals—assaults that continue today under the rubric of "queer-bashing." It has prompted contemporary measures to curtail, regulate, and punish homosexual behavior and deny homosexual people such rights of citizenship as free association, freedom of expression, and the right to join the military or form legal marriages. It has fueled and inflamed attacks on gay people who fight for these freedoms.

These attacks occur because homosexuality and homosexuals present attractive alternatives to the restrictions that reproductive heterosexuality and its social structures have placed upon heterosexuals. The real issue is not that heterosexuals will be tempted to engage in homosexual *sexual* activity (although the visibility of such activity presents that option) but that they will be drawn to more flexible norms that gay people, excluded from social structures created by heterosexuality, have created for their own lives. These include less restrictive gender roles; non-monogamous intimate relationships and more freedom for sexual experimentation; family units that are chosen, not biological; and new models for parenting. But most important, homosexuality offers a vision of sexual pleasure completely divorced from the burden of reproduction: sex for its own sake, a distillation of the pleasure principle.

The threat of homosexuality is thus so tremendous, and affects so significantly the basic structures of Western societies, that the sustained and often vicious antihomosexual response is not surprising. The construction (and manifestation) of antihomosexual fear and hatred, however, is a more complex phenomenon.

In his provocative analysis *Anti-Semite and Jew,* Jean-Paul Sartre argued that the fear and hatred of Jews was not a political or social "opinion" but a "passion," meaning not that it is emotional or irrational, but simply that it is the basis for a cohesive, sustained view that is held independently of material reality. It is "the *idea* of the Jew" that incites the anti-Semite, not necessarily any specific action or person.

So it is with homosexuality. It is the *idea,* the concept of homosexuality—that is, sexual pleasure without justification or consequences—that terrifies the gay-hater. As with Sartre's explanation of anti-Semitism, gay-hating derives less from a feeling about particular people than from a profound attachment to maintaining the existing social order. This helps explain why vocal antigay politicians are sometimes capable of maintaining cordial relationships with gay friends or family members.

The institutionalized hatred of homosexuality serves clear social functions. It brings together people of various races, religious beliefs, classes, and backgrounds in a unified vision and identity as heterosexual. In this way, it actually performs the function that traditional ethnic and religious "assimilation" has never achieved in the United States, uniting divergent groups, no matter what their genuine conflicts, under a common identity: heterosexuality. This identity then comes to delineate "American." Consequently, when homosexuals are denied specific legal rights and social opportunities, heterosexuals are then defined as authentic, full citizens.[4]

Like anti-Semitism, the hatred of homosexuality serves the function of valorizing the "normal"; it bonds heterosexuals, rallying them against a collective, and by implication more powerful, enemy. The creation of the "homosexual menace," not unlike the fantasy of a worldwide Jewish conspiracy, transforms the average man into a valiant defender of the "normal"—a process that celebrates and reinforces the sexual status quo while at the same time granting enormous importance to sexual differences. Just as the mythology of anti-Semitism magnifies the power of the Jew, gay-hating recasts the homosexual as sexually and socially dangerous. Yet because this fantasy homosexual also embodies a sexual freedom that stands in sharp relief to the restrictions of institutionalized heterosexuality, he is an object of envy as well as scorn.

But the creation of the homosexual menace—at once a threat and a temptation—is complicated by the fact that gay culture actually does, if its alternatives to institutionalized heterosexuality are embraced, present a threat to basic social structures. This poses a difficult dilemma for the dominant culture. If homosexuality is accepted, it challenges the status quo overtly; if it remains demonized, it presents a seductive vision of alternative possibilities.[5]

3.

WESTERN societies have dealt with this dilemma by curtailing and punishing homosexual behavior, by limiting the citizenship rights of homosexuals, and by creating a social milieu that rewards the closet and punishes visibility. In the United States, homosexuals' full citizenship is denied in many ways: from the denial of marriage rights to discrimination in the workplace, to physical violence. But these limitations on citizenship, which homosexuals share with other minority groups and subcultures, are indicative of a lack of standing as "Americans" as well.

The national debate, as manifested in the culture wars, raises the profound question of what it means to live in a pluralistic democracy. How are people of varying races, ethnicities, classes, sexual orientations, religions, and values all to live together? The ideal of "America" as the ultimate melting pot able to "assimilate" all difference and produce a unified national identity—the "American"—is a myth. Although U.S. culture is often split along ethnic, racial, and other identity lines, this is not a new phenomenon. The fantasy of a cohesive "American" national culture is a strategic, right-wing argument against minority and subcultural groups demanding full citizenship. The divisiveness of the culture wars is a replay of what has occurred throughout all of U.S. history.

The religious and conservative right have used the culture wars as a rallying cry for the establishment—or, more precisely, reestablishment—of traditional standards. Often the battles take place within the academy, focusing on the emergence of multicultural curriculum, the critique of "Western civilization" as Eurocentric, and the debate over the traditional canon and the alleged banishment of Dead White Male writers from reading lists.[6]

The conservative drive to reaffirm a secure national identity also manifests itself in the battles over Black English, Ebonics, and Spanglish. The tension over defining an official "American" language moved out of the classroom as states passed English-only laws and some workplaces mandated that all employees speak English even on breaks and personal time. These battles over language resonate with the larger conservative political agenda of limiting all non-English-speaking immigration to the United States and even withholding traditional educational and welfare benefits from legal immigrants and their children.[7]

Culture wars also manifest themselves in educational settings when conservatives object to the introduction of safe-sex and AIDS-education programs in public schools. Classroom diversity and sensitivity programs and materials that focus on gay, lesbian, and sexual issues—from books like *Heather Has Two Mommies* as a resource for grade-school teachers to condom distribution in secondary schools, to the establishment of gay and straight student alliances and support groups—are, for the right, further examples of declining moral values.

The energetic, often rabid, campaigns of the conservative and religious right to reassert traditional moral standards are a response to the once gradual, now inevitable unraveling of the social, political, and sexual status quo: The question of who is an "American" is more hotly contested than ever before. Over the past century, and particularly the last fifty years, social standards have undergone enormous changes. The struggle for racial and gender equality has fundamentally transformed Western societies, upsetting once rigid hierarchies. But although these social changes have radically altered how most people live, they have not brought about a society in which social justice is a reality or even a goal. Most of these transformations continue to be resisted, or accepted only reluctantly, by those in power. Equality has rarely been won by arguments of fairness, justice, or compassion.

The culture wars have reached a new intensity because both sides experienced them as decisive, even final conflicts. The progressive changes of the last decades have rendered the right furious over its decline of power, panicked about the possibility of further social change, and determined to prevent it. The popularity among conservatives of the slogan "I'm mad as hell and I'm not going to take it anymore" in the late 1970s and the 1980s is a gauge of how far they felt they had been pushed.

The current culture wars provide a map of the dominant culture's discomforts and fears. Race, gender, and sexual orientation are hotly disputed factors in the exploration of the mostly unspoken question "Who is an American?" But for the dominant culture there is another, more frightening and complicated question lurking beneath this unarticulated inquiry: "Who are we?"

Still, although struggles for gender, ethnic, and racial equality have produced mixed results, an ongoing public debate has established these concerns as central to the broader discussion of social justice. This has been far less true of homosexuality, for several reasons. Whereas race and gender are seen as immutable, physically determined, and publicly discernible characteristics, sexual identity and behavior have historically been perceived as personal traits or decisions. Also, it is easier for homosexuals to "pass" than it was for minorities or women. And it was far more difficult to "pass" out of the strictures of race or gender, but relatively simple for homosexuals to "pass."

As a result, the threat that homosexuality poses to the dominant culture is substantially different from the threat posed by demands for racial and gender equality. The latter challenges come from outsiders whose otherness is clearly and physically defined. Homosexuality, on the other hand, is a far more complex, protean identity. It is rare that people are confused about their race or gender, but anyone can be a homosexual or engage in homosexual behavior. This ambiguity, combined with the homosexual's ability to "pass," challenges the presumed cohesion of mainstream heterosexual culture.[8]

The struggle over citizenship rights for homosexuals comes at a critical point in U.S. history. Campaigns for racial and gender equality have progressed far enough that the dominant culture believes that it has made enough concessions (or, from a conservative viewpoint, sustained enough losses). The dominant culture has become increasingly hostile to minority demands. While this animosity has affected the gay rights movement, particularly in the 1980s and 1990s, it accounts for only part of the antagonism that homosexuals face in the culture wars.

Struggles over racial and gender equality have deeply shaken the power structures in the United States, but the rise of a public and politicized homosexuality—in an organized gay rights movement and a visible gay culture—has proved even more threatening. Homosexuality offers a clear critique of the ideology of heterosexuality and attractive alternatives to heterosexuality as an institution. It challenges accepted ideas about sexual activity, gender roles, relationships, marriage, family, work, and child rearing. Most important, it offers an unstinting vision that liberates sex from the burden of reproduction and places pleasure at the center of sexual activity. This is what frightens Pat Buchanan and what is at the heart of the culture wars over sexuality, sexual orientation, and related issues.[9]

For the dominant culture, the threat of homosexuality is that it embodies and prioritizes the pleasure principle—the denial of which, we have always been told, is necessary for civilization, as we know it, to go on.

The question is this: Do we *want* civilization as we know it to go on? Or do we want to change it to meet our most basic needs?

Two

The Pleasure Principle

PLEASURE IS A great paradox. At first glance contemporary society seems obsessed with it, constantly encouraging us to enjoy ourselves, to let go, relax. "Double your pleasure, double your fun," claims the Doublemint chewing gum slogan. Good food, good wine, good company, and good sex all hold out the promise of pleasure. Yet as highly touted as pleasure may be, American culture has largely viewed it with suspicion and alarm. H. L. Mencken's definition of Puritanism as "the haunting fear that someone, somewhere, may be happy" recognizes this long antipleasure tradition. We are, conservative social critics quickly remind us, a society so obsessed and perverted by pleasure that we have lost sight of the important priorities of hard work, moral righteousness, and traditional moral—i.e., "family"—values.

The tension between the pursuit of pleasure and its repression is a defining element in contemporary culture and politics. On one hand, pleasure is used as an incentive. The promise of pleasure functions as currency for shaping socially appropriate behavior. If you behave correctly, dress nicely, and don't challenge accepted authority, you will be compensated with pleasure. Pleasure is also a reward for hard work; it is always just around the corner—one more cigarette, one more purchase, one more vacation away. We have been taught to conceptualize pleasure as something with which we are rewarded in small doses, as something that is granted by an external source, not as an innate potential. The idea that pleasure might exist unrationed in its own right, without apology and without justification, is considered radical, almost unnatural.

In the endless cultural debates over pleasure that go on today, and have in the past, it is homosexuality that most clearly embodies the paradox of pleasure in U.S. culture. Conservative political forces have targeted homosexuals, gay rights, and gay culture as threats to "family values," and yet, in so many ways, society is obsessed with gay people and gay culture. The specter of homosexuality haunts the mainstream imagination in a way that is persistent and unique. This specter is at once phantasmagoric and real. It is conjured from the actual lives of gay men and lesbians, from fears of homosexuality, from the real or imagined details of gay sexual activity, from historical prejudice, and from existing but archaic legal codes. Most important, it arises from the imaginations of heterosexuals who find homosexuality—and everything it signifies—both frighteningly lurid and very titillating. A placard carried by a lesbian in Manhattan's first Gay Pride March in 1970 said it all: "We Are Your Worst Fear. We Are Your Best Fantasy."

In relation to pleasure, homosexuality signifies many things for the mainstream popular imagination: It is a sin, a crime, a disease, a failure of willpower, an escape from responsibility. In spite of endless negative connotations, homosexuality also carries with it the possibility of escape from the constraints of heterosexuality.

The cultural fear of homosexuality is not so much the fear of "perverted" or "unnatural" sexuality as it is the fear of a sexuality unfettered by biological consequences or social responsibility. While the Hebrew Bible endorsed reproductive sexual activity with the injunction to "be fruitful and multiply," much early Christian teaching linked sexuality and sexual pleasure with weakness and sin, which deserved punishment. Reproduction came to be viewed, especially for women, not simply as a natural consequence of sexual activity, but as chastisement. Roman Catholic and Protestant fundamentalist arguments that birth control is contrary to natural law are predicated on the understanding that you cannot have pleasure without responsibility. Such arguments, however, have deeper roots: the idea that sexuality and sexual pleasure cannot exist for their own sake but must have some justification.

In the popular imagination there has long been a strong connection between nonreproductive, uninhibited sexuality and the decline of the social order. The idea that Rome's fall was caused by homosexuality (as well as a host of other nonreproductive sexual behaviors) began with St. Augustine and is reflected in such diverse forms as the 1920s biblical epics of Cecil B. DeMille and the rhetoric of today's Christian fundamentalists. This same theme is sounded by democratic historians about the ancien régime of eighteenth-century France, and by leftist historians about prerevolutionary Cuba. Animosity toward "decadent" sexuality was integral to the political ideology of the Third Reich. Ironically, recent right-wing attacks on gay rights like Scott Lively's book *The Pink Swastika: Homosexuality and the Nazi Party* have claimed that male homosexuals ran the Nazi Party and engineered the Final Solution. The concept of the decadent society—one about to fall in on itself because of moral decay—is usually connected with its toleration of male homosexual behavior.[1]

Contemporary ideas and stances about homosexual behavior are an outgrowth of a long history of deeply entrenched, often contradictory, beliefs. While many premodern societies had legal statues that punished forms of homosexual behavior, those prohibitions existed in a broader context of laws forbidding other forms of nonreproductive sexuality. For example, passages in the Hebrew Bible that condemn homosexual behavior, including Leviticus 18:22 and 20:13 and, in popular interpretation, the story of Sodom and Gomorrah (Genesis 19:1–26), are no more or less emphatic than comparable passages forbidding other nonreproductive heterosexual activity. Perhaps the most noted of these is the story of Onan (Genesis 38:8–10), which technically condemns coitus interruptus, but has been generally interpreted to also forbid masturbation.

Attitudes toward homosexual behavior itself in these premodern societies ranged from moderate or circumscribed acceptance to outright condemnation. Pederasty, for example, was prevalent, even prescribed, in Attic Greece, while Persian Zoroastrians considered it a serious offense against morality. Laws forbidding certain types of homosexual behavior (and other forms of sexual activity), such as those enacted in classical Greece and Rome, were prohibitions about crossing social or class lines; their objective was to preserve basic social, economic, or class structures.[2]

During the early Christian era, particularly in the codification of laws under Theodosius and Justinian, attitudes toward homosexuality had an overtly theological basis, but their purpose was also to preserve social order. In A.D. 538, Justinian issued an edict enjoining those participating in homosexual behavior to cease because of the possibility of divine retribution in the form of earthquake, famine, and pestilence. While all nonreproductive sexuality had always been viewed as unnatural in Judeo-Christian thought, homosexual behavior eventually became emblematic of nonreproductive sex. It embodied, and highlighted, all of the social and moral dangers and ramifications of that behavior.[3]

Historically, prohibitions against homosexual behavior (and other nonreproductive sexuality), as well as attitudes about sexual pleasure, are inseparable from prevailing attitudes toward reproduction and the social status of women. The patriarchal character of most Western social organization has ensured men greater permission to seek and experience sexual freedom. Because womanhood was defined by the bearing and raising of children, sexual reproduction was securely separated from nonreproductive sexual pleasure. This separation led to a social structure in which women's capacity for sexual pleasure was denied, vilified, and punished. Women were then divided into two groups: "good" women whose sexuality was inactive or used only for reproduction, and "bad" women whose capacity for sexual expression and pleasure made them seductive, predatory, and dangerous. The constructions of the "virgin" and the "whore" run through Western culture from the Virgin Mary and Lilith to such recent incarnations as predivorce Princess Diana and the ironically named Madonna. Like the "degenerate" nonreproductive homosexual, the "evil" woman who enjoys sex without the responsibility of children is seen as a source of social harm.

The more social and legal power women have in any given culture, the more likely that culture is to encourage, allow, or celebrate sexual pleasure, including the toleration or acceptance of homosexual behavior and identity. This is evident in the Roman Empire, where women of independent means and social position had the autonomy to own property and instigate divorce, as it is in eighteenth-century France, where a relaxation of traditional sexual morality in the upper class was accompanied by feminist thinking, and in Germany's Weimar Republic, where the struggles for homosexuals' and women's freedom were conceptualized in similar terms. Not surprisingly, conservative historians have labeled each of these historical instances as "decadent" because of the freedoms offered women and gay people and the lack of adherence to strict religious precepts.[4]

The rise of secularism since the Enlightenment has shifted the language while essentially keeping the deep-rooted fear and mistrust of sexuality and pleasure found in Judeo-Christian beliefs. Often these antipleasure ideas were given profound expression in the material world. The Protestant Reformation of the sixteenth century, for example, revolutionized conceptualizations of spirituality, work, sex, and the material world. Rejecting traditional Roman Catholic concepts of collective identity, the new Protestant "ethic" strongly reinforced the idea of the individual. Whereas Catholic thought focused human energy toward the afterlife, deemphasizing the importance of the temporal world, Protestant thinking was concerned with the temporal world, and consequently with material success.

This new emphasis on the individual, along with the emergence of a postfeudal mercantile and later capitalist economy, encouraged the accumulation of private wealth and redefined, economically, the need for a strong, heterosexual family unit. This new Protestant ethic quickly conflated (hetero)sexuality with work, reproduction with production, and financial success with spiritual worth. The pragmatic equation of sex with mercantilism has had enormous influence on Western thinking about sex, and by the Victorian era the language of capitalism had completely merged with that of sexual metaphor—"saving yourself" for refusing to partake in sexual activity, "doing your business" for engaging in sexual intercourse.

During the Scientific Revolution, pleasure—as a nonquantifiable entity—received little attention. While the Enlightenment was preoccupied with the life of the mind and rational thought, the idea of pleasure as a philosophical question was never a primary concern. As the Industrial Revolution altered the physical landscape of Europe, psychological, emotional, and sexual changes occurred as well. The pressures of work and the hardships of urban living created environments that, by necessity, focused on survival, not on evaluating the merits of personal pleasure. The emergence of Darwinian theory in the latter half of the nineteenth century clearly positioned the instinct for survival over the instinct for pleasure.

The deprioritization of pleasure throughout this time span contributed to the codification of rigid gender roles, the reaffirmation of the heterosexual nuclear family as the sole site of sexual activity, and the further stigmatization of homosexual behavior. While there were culturally specific periods such as the Italian Renaissance or late-eighteenth-century Great Britain and Germany where pleasure was regarded as important and socially beneficial—and where women had more freedom and sexuality was less regulated—these exceptions highlight the reality that personal pleasure, in Western societies, has not been seen as a right or a necessity.

Pleasure does not, and cannot, exist independent of experience. The gradual emergence of a concept of distinct personal identity—separate from a class, caste, or religious identity—was an important evolutionary step toward our contemporary understanding of being and of the role that pleasure plays in our lives. This concept of personal identity both engendered and augmented the invention, in the early twentieth century, of psychology as an intellectual discipline. The theories of Freud and his disciples radically altered how we conceptualize the mind, identity, interpersonal relationships, and an individual's relationship to all aspects of the world. These developments encouraged, more than ever before, an inquiry into how the erotic shapes our lives. Freud's theories opened important, revolutionary new ways of understanding the phenomenon of being human—especially the role that sexuality and pleasure play in our lives. Their social and intellectual impact was tremendously positive. Yet as radical as much Freudian theory is, it was also, paradoxically, a reflection of preexisting ideas of pleasure and repression.[5]

Underlying all of Freudian thought is the tension between the pleasure principle" and the "reality principle." Simply put, the instinct toward pleasure or Eros (including, but not limited to, sexuality) must be constantly mitigated and constrained ("repressed" or "sublimated," in Freudian language) by the need to place order and structure on human lives—in short, by civilization. In Freudian theory, the absence of the repressive, organizing mechanism of the reality principle would result in civil disorder.

> Civilization has been built up, under the pressure of the struggle for existence, by sacrifices in gratification of the primitive impulses, and it is to a great extent forever being recreated, as each individual, successively joining the community, repeats the sacrifices of his instinctive pleasures for the common good. The sexual are amongst the most important of the instinctive forces thus utilized; they are in this way sublimated, that is to say, their energy is turned aside from its sexual goal and diverted towards other ends, no longer sexual and socially more valuable.[6]

In concrete terms Freud's theory addresses the central organizational patterns of how we live: work, sex, order. Freudian philosopher and critic Herbert Marcuse states succinctly the implications of Freud's thought: "Free gratification of man's instinctual needs is incompatible with civilized society: renunciation and delay are the prerequisites of progress. Happiness must be subordinated to the discipline of work as a full-time occupation, to the discipline of mongamic reproduction, to the established system of law and order. The methodical sacrifice of libido, its rigidly enforced deflection to socially useful activities and expressions, *is* culture."[7]

While much of Freudian theory has been reevaluated, reinterpreted, or dismissed by contemporary psychologists and philosophers, his construction of civilization in terms of sublimation continues to inform how we think and live today. This is partly because Freudian thought has so profoundly influenced how we categorize and evaluate experience—the notion that the unconscious is an active force in our everyday lives is simply undisputed today—but also because many of Freud's theories, while seemingly radically new, actually reflected, and reinforced, preexisting cultural prejudices and social structures.

Freud posited his theory of "civilization" as universal. Because his social theories were inextricably intertwined with his theories of psychological development, the social tensions between pleasure and repression are depicted as mirrored in—indeed, as coming out of—the tensions between the id (the instinctual force of life) and the superego (the governing force) within each individual's personality. Freud's view was that these tensions were inevitable, beyond the influence of history or established culture.

Freud's theory is self-referential, and self-sustaining. Belief in it simply forecloses any discussion of the nature or desirability of the work ethic, institutionalized heterosexuality, or existing social structures. Discussions of alternative structures—socialism, non-capital-based production schedules, homosexuality, nonreproductive sexuality, nonhierarchical social structures like anarchism, or collective or communal living—are also rendered impossible. Freudian analysis of civilization not only does not prioritize pleasure, but actively warns against it.

Because Freud's basic premise was biased against the "pleasure impulse," the Freudian conceptualization of pleasure works on the scarcity principle: While we desire pleasure we must forgo it for the sake of order and civilization. But the pleasure impulse is not simply about gratification, Eros, or even happiness. The basis of the pleasure principle is freedom—personal, intellectual, artistic, and imaginative. The constant tension between pleasure and repression takes very real forms. Freud was quite specific on the role of liberty in the lives of individuals: "The liberty of the individual is no gift to civilization."[8]

The tension between personal, individual freedom and the need to control pleasure-seeking behavior has been at the center of most of the culture wars that have been the hallmark of social and cultural changes in the last hundred years of U.S. history. When progressive political and cultural change occurs—change that increases personal freedom, most particularly in regard to gender, sexuality, freedom of expression, and encouragement to use the imagination—it is met with repressive resistance from mainstream culture.

The late-nineteenth-century campaigns for social purity—including temperance, antiprostitution, and antiabortion movements—arose in response to the emergence of the first wave of U.S. feminism as well as to agitation for immigrant workers' rights. The rise of conservative Christian evangelism was a response to the new economic, sexual, and artistic freedoms of the 1920s. Most recently, this backlash response was seen in the conservative "law and order" response of the federal government against the perceived political and sexual excesses of the 1960s and 1970s. This well-organized government response included massive surveillance by the FBI, infiltration of suspected "radical" groups, reinstigation of censorship campaigns, and an all-out media war against those who pursued personal freedom over the prioritized values of patriotism, family values, and tradition. The current culture wars—over gay rights, multiculturalism, safe-sex education, arts funding, school curricula—are extensions, specific as well as metaphoric, of the battles that were fought during Reconstruction, the Reform era, and the New Deal.[9]

Western societies have historically conceptualized the tension between the state and the pursuit of individual freedoms—particularly sexual freedoms—as inevitable. Freud's hypothesis that repression is necessary for civilization has been accepted as a truth so self-evident as to be indisputable. It has reinforced already existing suspicions about pleasure to such a degree that the repression of pleasure seems natural, not even unfortunate. There is another way to view Freud's hypothesis, however, one that shifts the burden of living and creating a culture from the reality principle to the pleasure principle.

Philosophers Herbert Marcuse and Norman O. Brown both argue that such a reinterpretation of Freud's theories is necessary to effect change in the world today. Marcuse notes: "[T]he fact that the reality principle has to be reestablished continually in the development of man indicates that its triumph over the pleasure principle is never complete and never secure. . . . What civilization masters and represses—the claim of the pleasure principle—continues to exist in civilization itself. The unconscious retains the objectives of the defeated pleasure principle." In other words, in the struggle between pleasure and repression, pleasure, even if it doesn't always win, always rebounds; it is never defeated.[10]

Freud understood the complexity of human existence and allowed for a complication of the "eternal" tension between the pleasure principle and the reality principle by introducing the notion of "phantasy": the ability, and proclivity, of the human mind to imagine. "Phantasy" always functions within the "pleasure principle"; it provides an alternative to reason and reality. And even within Freud's constricted view of the human psyche and civilization, imagination and phantasy provide a trapdoor, a way to see past the inevitable, overpowering need to constrain pleasure by reality.

The role of the imagination for humans—the appreciation of "beauty," the creation of art, the ability to conceptualize alternative modes of being—is enormous. It allows the pleasure principle to manifest itself, but more important it gives us the ability to envision change, to see alternatives. Freud himself commented on the strong connection between sexual instincts and phantasy.[11]

The power of the imagination in providing an alternative to the Freudian model is illuminated beautifully by late-eighteenth-century playwright and critic Friedrich von Schiller in his 1795 treatise *Letters on the Aesthetic Education of Man*. Schiller posits an approach that is the reverse of Freud's theory that civilization must be built upon repression, that the reality principle must win out over the pleasure principle. Schiller argues that it is possible to remake culture by following "the order of sensuousness" over the "order of reason." Schiller even proposes that the conflict between the two forces be mediated by a third, the "play impulse," whose aim would be beauty and freedom. Marcuse notes that such a situation would result in "a genuinely humane civilization, the human existence would be play rather than toil, and man would live in display rather than need." Schiller's intention is not to explore an abstract aesthetic theory of freedom but to create a material world in which each human would have "freedom to be what he ought to be."[12]

Schiller's theory—which was echoed in the twentieth century by Freud's critics—provides a new framework for conceptualizing pleasure. Schiller privileges pleasure over the "toil" of building "civilization," and claims that following "the order of sensuousness" will lead to authentic freedom. As abstract as his theory sounds, frequent manifestations of it can be found in history and culture: in various utopian, communitarian experiments that flourished in nineteenth-century America; in the "free love" philosophies and experiments promoted by such diverse people as Victoria Woodhull, Emma Goldman, and John Humphrey Noyes, who founded the Oneida Community; in the cooperative movements of the late nineteenth century and early twentieth century, particularly those of Josiah Warren and Stephen Pearl Andrews; in the "art for art's sake" movement spearheaded by Walter Pater and Oscar Wilde; and most recently in the counterculture movement of the 1960s.[13]

These alternative manifestations of the pleasure principle were frequently ridiculed. Often, after their social importance was understood and their liberating effect accepted, they became accepted as part of mainstream culture. The language used in attacking them was historically specific. In the latter part of the nineteenth century, when there was fear of a largely Catholic immigration wave and a soon-to-be-organized labor force, derogatory words like *papist, anarchist,* and *un-American* were prevalent. In the early 1920s, in the face of the Russian Revolution and the enormous cultural changes that were happening, the charges were "Bolshevik," "red," "free-lover," "antibusiness" and "unpatriotic." During the 1950s and early 1960s, at the height of the black civil rights movement, communist witch-hunts, and new sexual freedoms, the code words were "race dilution, " "race traitor," "mongrelization," "smut-peddler," "un-American," "communist," "beatnik," and "degenerate." In the late 1960s, with the emergence of a vital political, sexual, and artistic counterculture, the charges were "women's libber," "hippie," "homosexual menace," "hedonist," and "anti-American."

What mainstream culture finds most threatening are attempts to create more gender and sexual freedom, questioning of the current definition of patriotism, challenges to the current status of ethnic and race inequities, and efforts to expand existing limits of artistic expression. The impulse for pleasure is closely tied to impulses for creativity and personal freedom—what Schiller called the human being's "freedom to be what he ought to be." When the pleasure principle manifests itself, it is often as a critique of the existing culture.

Political repression occurs because those in power in mainstream culture fear activities that they believe could radically alter the social order. This is why the unbounded imagination—an embodiment of the pleasure principle—is intrinsically political, and why it is always in danger of being repressed. While there are many threads in the complex fabric of the manifested imagination, it is the sexual that is the most consistently under attack. The sexual instinct is at the heart of the pleasure principle—the ur-pleasure—that we experience first as infants and are taught to deny and avoid. The regulation of sexuality is also at the heart of our social organization. It is the underlying impulse of marriage, the "natural" organization of heterosexuality and child raising. It is the unspoken assumption of traditional gender arrangements, of how "men" and "women" are and act. Entrenched gender roles inform the most basic structures of work and economy, which are constructed to reinforce institutionalized heterosexuality as well as gender behavior and activity. To a large extent, everyday basics of life such as shelter, transportation, and even food are sold and packaged to fit the needs of heterosexual family units, still seen as our basic form of social organization.[14]

The specter of homosexuality—male and female—strikes directly at the heart of how culture and society are organized. Same-sex eroticism and relationships break down accepted social structures; the model of the nuclear family is irrelevant. Appropriate gender roles are not applicable: butch women and nelly men destroy the two-gender dichotomy. Questions of gender and the workplace are challenged: What is "women's work"? What is a man's job? There is no need for consumer items seen as a basic part of the mythic American fabric: split-level suburban homes, roomy station wagons for the kids, family-pac frozen vegetables. But the greatest threat posed by homosexuality is that sexuality can—and in this case, has to—exist without reproduction. For a culture so wedded to the idea that sexuality must be justified by the "responsibility" of having children, the idea of nonreproductive sexuality is deeply frightening. Sex, in the past two hundred years, has been seen as a form of labor, a utilitarian exercise in the production of children and the continuance of "civilization." The idea of sex without reproduction moves it from the realm of work to that of play: Freud's unfettered pleasure principle combined with Schiller's play impulse. Sex for pleasure is the ultimate form of play, a nonutilitarian exercise of imagination and creativity.

For decades conservative psychoanalysts, religious leaders, and politicians have charged that homosexuality is about nothing more than having sex; that homosexuals are "obsessed" with sex; that homosexuality is a "flight" from the responsibilities of "mature" sexuality. And they are right. If you define sexuality as "about" reproduction, if you insist on "justifying" sexual activity by reproduction and the replication of existing social and economic order, if you define "mature" sexuality as being about more than just pleasure, then homosexual activity is an aberration.

But if you view homosexuality, as well as other forms of nonreproductive sexual behavior, as a much-needed challenge to the existing system of social and sexual conformity that curtails personal freedoms and undercuts humans' realization of potential, then it is not only a permissible behavior but a necessary one.

Three

Popular Culture

1. Pleasure and Culture

HOMOSEXUALITY, IN WESTERN societies, has come to symbolize intense and forbidden pleasure. The overt fear and covert desire that homosexuality engenders can be understood only by looking at how, in the broader scheme, society deals with pleasure—both in and of itself, and particularly as it is manifested in popular culture.

Pleasure and repression are constant, shifting tensions. Our myriad impulses to experience pleasure are countered by the social injunctions to act "responsibly." Many of these injunctions are common sense: Don't eat too much food, you'll feel bad later; make a living so that you'll be able to afford shelter. Others are more restricting: Don't value sexual pleasure over work or you will lose your moral standards; don't engage in homosexual fantasies or activities or you will be ostracized.

We negotiate these tensions by engaging in a variety of compromises. Often we compartmentalize our pleasure impulses, separating them from the routines of everyday life: the eagerly awaited two-week vacation, the boy's/girl's night out, the occasional "tying one on." These clearly delineated periods of release allow pleasure in lives overcontrolled by socially enforced codes. They also provide a safety valve, a socially engineered mechanism that permits the pressure created by social repression to be regulated. The tension between pleasure and repression in our personal lives is reflected—writ large—in our social organization, where similar regulating mechanisms are also at work.

Humans find pleasure in many ways: sexual activity, eating an enjoyable dinner, exercising our bodies. One of the primary ways pleasure is allowed to manifest socially is through popular entertainment: movies, plays, concerts, television. These entertainments, particularly when they are enjoyed communally, are public sites of pleasure, where people congregate simply to be pleased. Even when the underlying intent of the entertainment is more serious, or educational, the impulse for pleasure is still present. (Reading also falls into this category, but as a private, solitary action it does not provide the communal experience common to other forms of popular culture. On the other hand, since books communicate so directly with the mind, their ability to spark the imagination is even greater.)

In an essay celebrating the liberating, and sexual, power of the imagination, Brigid Brophy postulates that fiction, and by extension all serious and popular art, is simply a structured extension of the daydream: the imagination unchecked by the reality principle.[1] In Freudian terms, the daydream is an extension of the masturbatory dream or sexual fantasy; thus one could argue that the origin of all art and popular culture, indeed of the artistic imagination, is the sexual drive. Our emotional responses to popular entertainment are often related to sexual feelings, not only erotic stirrings felt during a depiction of sexual activity, but also the sentimental responses to a romantic moment, or the excitement at watching a chase scene. Public entertainments present audiences with stories about sex, love, emotional intrigue, and physical action: what film critic Pauline Kael calls "kiss, kiss, bang, bang"—emotional and sexual catharsis.

Popular entertainment allows, even encourages, us to experience pleasure we are normally denied. That is why going to the movies or attending a concert feels like a treat, a release from busy or emotionally restricted lives. More important, while these forms of popular culture allow us to experience pleasure, they also put very distinct time and place restraints upon it. We can laugh, cry, get sexually excited or ecstatic in these contexts, whereas such behavior would be inappropriate at other times and places. In this way, popular culture both encourages and contains pleasure.

This is not new. Human cultures have long recognized the sexual underpinnings of pleasure and the social necessity of encouraging and containing it, often through public events. The planting festivals and harvest feasts of peasant cultures were celebrations of fertility as well as means of promoting and rewarding hard work. Greek theater, originating in the Eleusinian and Dionysian mystery cults, also had roots in the sexual and religious; and its very dramatic structure acknowledges the erotic impulse. The Aristotelian concept of catharsis, an emotional release, corresponds psychologically to the idea of sexual release. Even the medieval mystery and morality plays, which began as liturgical ceremonies, quickly evolved into public pageants that included bawdy humor and satirical burlesque.

The vicarious engagement of emotions through popular culture can help clarify personal feelings that are otherwise unarticulated. We can be moved by theater because we relate to the plight and feelings of the characters: Aristotle's concepts of terror and pity. With film, our fantasies and feelings are literally *projected*—as if from the unconscious—as huge images for public display. Listening to a song in concert can move a whole audience to tears or laughter, allowing emotions, usually kept quiet, to be felt.

Popular entertainment also allows us to contemplate aspects of our lives we may normally not feel permitted to address: sexual desire, pleasurable impulses, forbidden fantasies, confusions over what it means to be a man or woman. We are permitted for the moment to experience what we are not allowed to experience—or often even think about—in what is fancifully called "real life," where the reality principle gives way, if only for a time, to the pleasure principle.

This ability of popular culture to produce pleasure and incite the human imagination to new levels of freedom exists as an ideal, all too often underrealized. In postindustrial Western society, much popular culture is a prefabricated commodity that, while manufactured to bring pleasure by inciting the senses, also has as its goal the reaffirming of basic traditional, even reactionary, social norms. Thus, a Hollywood romantic comedy may also confirm and justify gender and sexual roles that are limiting and destructive; an action thriller may also seek to promote conservative political tenets. The use of pleasure in popular culture to reinscribe the status quo stands in sharp relief to the more radical function of pushing or transgressing the boundaries of social thought and experience. For example, the influence on the mainstream of jazz and later rock shows how popular culture can contest, and ultimately break down, conservative social positions concerning the expression of sexuality and emotion.

Roland Barthes, in *The Pleasure of the Text,* distinguishes between these two functions of pleasure by labeling the more conservative function "pleasure" and the transgressive function "bliss." Popular culture that corresponds to the Barthian notion of bliss—that liberates, rather than reinforces conformity—operates as an instigator of more emotional, psychological, and political freedom. This is especially true in regard to how issues of sexuality, sexual behavior, and gender have changed over the past two hundred years.

2. Gay Sensibility

BY expanding our capacity for imagination—a radical act in a society that attempts to curtail this capability—entertainment has often been a site where criticism of the dominant culture might occur. Since popular culture, as a pleasure generator, provides a place to "be different," to express nontraditional and nonacceptable desires, it has historically attracted those already outside the mainstream: gay people, women and men who did not fit gender expectations, other groups defined as not part of the cultural mainstream.

Popular entertainment, even in a commodified form, has often provided a public forum for examining the complexities of sexuality and gender. Even the mystery and morality plays of the Middle Ages became important vehicles for frank depictions of sexuality. Sexual frankness has always been valued on the stage and in popular entertainments. The bawdiness of the Elizabethan stage and the sexually driven revenge tragedies of the Jacobean, as well as the excesses of Victorian melodramas, illustrate how popular entertainment provided outlets for a continuing and ever-evolving public sexual discourse.[2]

The history of theatrical cross-dressing is a prime example of this. Elizabethan and Jacobean theater barred women from the stage and male actors, usually boys or young men, cross-dressed to play female roles. While theatrical cross-dressing was an accepted—indeed, enforced—convention, it also consciously manipulated accepted ideas of gender. Shakespeare's use of double cross-dressing—young male actors playing women who disguise themselves as men in *Twelfth Night* and *As You Like It*—betrays an investment in gender and sexual politics that is far deeper than simple adherence to stage convention. A measure of the anxiety male cross-dressing could raise is obvious in a program note in a 1660 production of *Othello* that featured, for the first time on the British stage, a female Desdemona: "The woman plays today; mistake me not: / No man in gown, or page in petticoat . . . / In this reforming age / We have intent to civilize our stage."[3] Often the stage has been the only place where certain topics might be broached, if only obliquely. Questions about children and sexuality must have been raised when boys played passionate female roles like Juliet, Beatrice, Lady Macbeth, and Volumnia.

After women were allowed to perform on the Restoration stage, male cross-dressing became largely comic and satiric. Conversely, a strong tradition of women's cross-dressing began. In the eighteenth century, "roaring girls," actresses in breeches, became a London theater craze, and in the nineteenth century the appearance of trousered women on stage was considered shocking and highly erotic. The spectacle of female cross-dressing has been enduring and resonant: Sarah Bernhardt's Hamlet, Marlene Dietrich's tuxedo drag in the 1930 film *Morocco,* Mary Martin's Peter Pan. The image of woman-as-man has gripped the public imagination in cultures in which women had less power or were valued for their fragility. The female cross-dresser engages and titillates because she mimics the socially approved erotic power of the male, whereas, historically, the theatrical male cross-dresser took on traditionally devalued "female" qualities for comic or mocking effect. Recently the proliferation of cross-dressing and drag queen films—*Tootsie*; *La Cage aux Folles*; *Victor/Victoria*; *To Wong Foo, Thanks for Everything, Julie Newmar*; and *The Birdcage*—reflects the confusion about and ambivalence toward the breakdown of traditional gender roles caused by feminism and gay liberation.[4]

The evolution of popular culture as a venue that raised sexual and gender issues dovetailed with the emergence of a distinct gay and lesbian identity. The fusion of these two developments brought a strong gay and lesbian presence to entertainment. By the late seventeenth century a gay male subculture—including a coded language and male cross-dressing—was evident in London. This newly visible gay identity and culture created enormous social change. The possibility of a visible social identity gave men and women attracted to their own gender a clearer sense of themselves and their relationship to the world around them. This included an acutely defined sense of being an outsider and the necessity of finding institutions that would tolerate, or even support, this identity. The theater and other forms of popular entertainment became places where sexual outsiders could feel safer.

The connection between homosexuality and the theater was not new. The Elizabethan stage was often associated with sexual license; theater managers might even be brothel keepers. By Puritan times, the theater was seen as attracting homosexual performers and patrons. The male frequent theatergoer was viewed as a sodomite "who is at every play and every night sups with his ingles [catamite]." Theaters were understood to be cruising grounds where "everyone brings another homeward of their way, very friendly, and in their secret conclaves covertly play the Sodomites or worse."[5]

As British cities grew, popular entertainment became increasingly organized and socially established. The theater, along with traveling shows,

fairs, and circuses, provided homosexuals, those who did not fit traditional gender roles, sexually active women, and even people of non-
British ethnicity a degree of safety and the possibility of self-expression.
Women and men who chose to remain outside of the strictly defined
world of marriage, children, and home life found comfort in the looser
social structure of theater. It was possible for women to be more independent, and often to make their own living. Charlotte Charke, a noted
actress, performed male parts on the stage and was a theatrical producer,
playwright, tavern keeper, open lesbian, and cross-dresser. The "immorality" of the theater also created an accepted, if frowned-upon, alternative to sexually repressive mainstream culture. Women could maintain
sexual lives outside of marriage—sometimes getting paid for sex—without undue prohibition. For homosexual men, the theater provided a
sense of community with other homosexuals as well as an excuse not to
take on the expected responsibilities of family and children.[6]

This dialectic between popular entertainment and alternative sexual
subcultures was doubly reinforced. As women and men who were denied
self-expression in mainstream culture gravitated toward the entertainment professions, these professions fostered experimentation with ideas
about sexuality and gender. And the more the entertainment venues tolerated nontraditional lives the more they became sites of increased sexual freedom. More important, they became places where mainstream
culture, particularly ideas about sexuality, might be challenged.

The critiques of mainstream culture present in the entertainments of
preindustrial society never caused large-scale social upheaval, although
they were vital in exploring and pointing to the possibilities of change.
The alternative visions of freedom and pleasure generated by popular
culture were enjoyed but remained contained. The British "masquerades"
of the eighteenth century are a clear example of how "entertainments"
both rebelled against and reinforced the status quo. The masquerade—a
fancy-dress party where masked anonymity promoted sexual license and
blurred class and gender differences—came to London from Italy and
quickly gained enormous popularity. Commercial masquerades, produced at the Haymarket Theater beginning in 1717, drew up to eight
hundred people weekly. Elaborate costumes and masks hid the identity,
the class status, and sometimes the gender of the revelers. This frequently promoted the breakdown of social and sexual prohibitions.[7]

Harriet Wilson, an upper-class woman who attended these parties as
an Italian or Austrian peasant boy, wrote in her journal: "I love a masquerade because a female can never enjoy the same freedom anywhere

else." Wilson, of course, is right. The masquerades provided the illusion of freedom and the temporary acting out of freedom, but as soon as the ball ended, her position as a woman in mid-eighteenth-century London society was as circumscribed as before. The church, the conservative press, and government morality-watchers associated the masquerades with homosexuality, sexual depravity, and social decline. The masquerades—no real threat to established sexual, class, or gender status—were considered dangerous because they embodied, if only for the evening, the possibility of what might happen. The utopian political implications of the masquerade were so apparent that, as social historian Terry Castle notes, one commentator claimed they were the image of a "perfect Commonwealth."[8]

All societies have created limited, specific sites for the release of sexual and emotional repression: burlesque, the carnival, the fraternity party, Mardi Gras, Fasching, Purim. Up until the mid-eighteenth century, in the United States, Christmas was more often marked by public rowdiness and violence than by religious observation. April Fools' Day, in many European countries, is traditionally understood as a day in which "the world is turned upside down." These sites exist within historical contexts shaped by social factors ranging from economic and class structures to prevalent gender roles and religious practices. The contexts change over time, often changing the limits of permissibility. The ribaldry of the Restoration stage was unacceptable to Victorian audiences two hundred years later; the sexual innuendo of 1930s pre-Code Hollywood movies was unfilmable by the early 1940s. The radical potential of popular culture rests in delicate balance. When viewed as nothing more than "entertainment"—even "naughty" or ribald entertainment—it is tolerated. When its alternative visions of sexuality, gender, and emotional freedom (as well as racial, economic, and social freedom) appear too seductive, too possible, popular culture is seen as dangerous and subversive.

3. Repression and Reaction

POPULAR culture thrills and excites its audience while making conservative culture-watchers ill at ease; this is at the heart of how we construct and experience entertainment. Labeled "escapist"—and it is hard to think of a better word—by supporters and detractors alike, the fantasies provided by movies, novels, television, and other forms of entertainment remove us from our everyday, constrained lives.

The lure of popular entertainment entices everyone. It is especially resonant for outsiders, who often experience it as a refuge from a hostile world, and who frequently draw upon it for self-expression. When entertainment—whether in commodified or more authentic versions—seems to offer escape or resistance, those invested in upholding traditional social and moral structures perceive it as dangerous. Yet the desire to uphold the established social order does not preclude individuals from enjoying the pleasure provided by popular culture. The result can be a conflict between the desire for pleasure and the need for repression—a friction often reflected in mainstream culture itself.

The monitoring of popular entertainment is frequently promoted by government, church, and political groups—groups that historically have been invested in maintaining the status quo. Mainstream political culture has two strategies for dealing with the threat posed by popular entertainment. The first is to regulate or, if need be, repress it. The second is to devalue it culturally and make it seem unimportant and negligible. In either case, the core issue rests not only on the explicit content of the entertainment, but also on the issue of who has the power to control it.

The regulation of entertainment includes zoning and licensing laws, nongovernmental rating systems, governmental regulations, extraordinarily high pricing, and overt seizure and destruction of printed materials that are deemed pornographic or socially unacceptable. In almost all cases, censorship is imposed to "protect" or control public morals, usually the public morals of women, the young, the lower classes, or sexual outsiders. From the closing of the British theater during the Commonwealth to the outcry over "teen rebel" movies in the 1950s, from complaints against Elvis and the Beatles to the current claims against gangsta rap and violence on television, the impulse to censor has been based in the fear that displays of nontraditional sexuality, gender affect, and morality, and even civil disorder, will ultimately lead to the same in the body politic: that life will imitate art, that imagined immorality will lead to actual immorality.

"Protection of the public good" is a concept involving complex issues of social and political power: who gets to ban and who gets to be protected. Women were often prohibited from reading books or viewing stage shows and films deemed "not suitable" for them; children still are. Class is often a divide, the implicit argument being that working-class viewers and readers would be unable to control their sexual urges if allowed to view sexual material. Before the mid-nineteenth century there were few large-scale attempts to officially suppress explicitly erotic material, because it was available only to the upper classes. Once printed erotic materials could be produced cheaply, and purchased by the average wage earner, censorship became an imperative. Not all censored material, however, is erotic. Medical pamphlets explaining venereal diseases and birth control methods were banned by the U.S. postal system until the mid-twentieth century. Progressive political materials, particularly concerning labor issues, have also been banned. The "protection" of individuals or groups is never for their benefit but is intended to reinforce social power structures as much as traditional ideas about sexuality, gender, and behavior.

The idea that certain groups need "protection" is a creation of political forces. While women, children, and the working class were traditionally "protected," a new, less distinct group emerged in the first half of the twentieth century. In his celebrated 1933 ruling allowing the U.S. publication of James Joyce's *Ulysses,* Judge John M. Woolsey claimed that the word "obscene" (defined as "tending to stir the sex impulses or to lead to sexually impure and lustful thoughts") must be judged by its effects "on a person with average sex instincts." Thus Woolsey excludes persons who lack "average sex instincts"—a category so undefined that it is meaningless—from common social and legal discourse.[9]

The concept of "average sex instincts" does not simply presume some nonexistent standard of erotic desire and behavior but implicitly mandates that one be constructed and enforced. Thus, anyone who does not fit the prevailing cultural/sexual norm of reproductive heterosexuality is automatically labeled culturally suspect. The legal implications of this are evident in a 1956 federal district court decision prohibiting the homophile magazine *ONE* from being sent through the U.S. mails. The court wrote: "An article may be vulgar, offensive, and indecent even though it is not regarded as such by a particular group . . . because their own social or moral standards are far below those of the general community. . . . *Social standards are fixed by and for the great majority and not by and for a hardened or weakened minority* [italics added]."

The idea that culture must be uplifting dates back to the mid-eighteenth century. By the Victorian era, it was a commonplace belief that art had to useful, utilitarian. Culture that was merely pleasurable, that refused to instill some sense of goodness or morality in its audience, was suspect. New ideas in aesthetics and technology seriously contested this notion.

Aestheticism, as defined by the art for art's sake movement, espoused by Oscar Wilde and Walter Pater, promoted the idea that beauty was justification unto itself: Art need not be useful. Modernism in literature and art fostered a far more complicated view of human experience. Advances in inexpensive printing, photography, and phonographic recordings, and the just-invented motion picture, brought popular culture to an ever wider audience. Traditional moral values and social structures were challenged more intently than ever, and dominant political forces responded with stricter censorship, which in turn was contested.

As battles against censorship were increasingly successful, particularly on the legal front, institutions invested in maintaining the status quo developed new strategies to deal with popular culture that challenged traditional mores. One of the most effective methods was to devalue its importance, to claim it was negligible because it was simply enjoyable. To some extent, this worked. Popular culture, particularly mass-produced entertainment, became more suspect, and was held to closer scrutiny. (Ironically, the idea of popular culture as bad became, in time, its attraction: it was pleasurable because it was bad.) Despite the attacks on it, popular culture thrived.

Attempts to disparage popular culture to audiences or diminish its importance were doomed to failure. The charge that popular culture failed to be uplifting, to instill moral virtues, missed the point. It was popular precisely because it was *not* uplifting. The lure of popular culture is that it gives us pleasure, it excites our senses, it is popular because, like sex, it turns us on. This connection between sex and popular culture is made explicit by Roland Barthes in *The Pleasure of the Text,* when he describes the overtly sexual nature of transgressive popular culture as *jouissance,* which is usually translated as "bliss." A more accurate and appropriate translation of *jouissance* is "coming." Like the unregulated imagination or unfettered sexuality, popular culture can be a threat to repressive mainstream values.

It is this threat that places popular culture in a difficult double bind. We live in a society that promotes entertainment as one of the few places we can find sanctioned, and seemingly uncomplicated, pleasure. But we are simultaneously told that such pleasure, like its source, is bad, or at least unimportant. Pleasure is promised as a gift and a relief, and then our experience of it is viewed as a personal foible or failure. We feel that we never have enough pleasure, yet we know it is vital to our lives. This is the tension that pleasure—and popular culture—must sustain in our society and our lives.

The content and importance of popular culture has shifted radically over the past fifty years. The relaxing of official and informal censorship has permitted popular culture to more honestly reflect the enormous changes—in sexual behavior, gender roles, and racial identity—that have occurred in this time period. These political changes have generated backlash and a desire to reinforce traditional mores and social structures from conservative political and religious movements. Popular culture, however, not only reflects social and political change but is also part of it. The threat popular culture—as a pleasure generator—already poses to the status quo is escalated when it becomes a venue for manifesting newly claimed freedoms. As a result, conservatives respond with increased attempts at regulation and control.

The question of who controls popular culture has become a primary battlefield in the fight between those looking to reinforce traditional social structures and morality and those looking to expand personal freedoms. In this fight for control, popular culture representing or portraying new social freedoms has become highly and overtly politicized. From the brazen female sexuality of Madonna to the overt homoeroticism of Calvin Klein advertising, from the agitprop politics of gangsta rap and Spike Lee films to federal funding of gay and lesbian artists, the culture wars have dragged popular culture into the forefront of political debate. The politics of popular culture is the politics of pleasure and personal freedom.[10]

Four

Subculture and Dominant Culture:
The Limits of Assimilation

T O UNDERSTAND THE current culture wars with regard to homosexuality, it is vital to understand how subcultures and mainstream culture interact, and particularly the process of "assimilation." Mainstream culture responds in similar ways, often with repression, to the tensions and resistances raised by various subcultures. By placing gay culture in a broader historical and political framework, and by discerning the connections between it and other subcultures, we can better understand the role that gay culture plays in mainstream culture.

Mainstream history and sociology have, by and large, promoted assimilation as a positive, culturally unifying mechanism. This ignores a darker side of the process. In its common usage, "assimilation" describes the mode by which subcultures merge with or are absorbed into an intact mainstream culture. But the reality is far more complex. To begin with, the sociological use of the word "assimilate" has two meanings—distinct but often conflated—describing events that are frequently at odds. The first meaning refers to the act of mainstream culture accepting as part of itself aspects of a subculture (e.g., "Mainstream culture assimilated the culture of Italian immigrants"), thus casting the dominant culture as the active participant. The second meaning refers to the desire of people in a subculture to become part of the dominant culture (e.g., "many Italian immigrants wanted to assimilate"), thus casting the subculture as the active participant. While these two positions might be congruent with one another—the desire by a subculture to assimilate is matched by the dominant culture's wish to have them do so—they do not have to be. As much as newly freed African Americans might have wished to assimilate after the Civil War, they were not allowed to do so. Some European immigrant groups discovered, to varying degrees, that their desire to assimilate was not met with an equal desire by the dominant culture.

A further complication is the idea that subcultures are assimilated into an intact, unified mainstream culture. The commonly accepted concept of a cohesive national U.S. culture is a fallacy: a prophecy that can never be fulfilled.

The United States had always been composed of disparate ethnic, religious, national, and cultural groups continually at odds, if not at war, with one another. Building upon the enforced colonization and subjugation of Native inhabitants, English Puritans, Spanish Catholics, Dutch Protestants, French Catholics, and English Catholics, both Roman and Anglo, all brought strong cultural identities that often allowed little room for negotiation with or tolerance of those who were different. By the mid-nineteenth century the colonies had become a republic with a coalesced cultural, religious, and social identity: overwhelmingly white, Anglo-European, Christian, and patriarchal. America was able to absorb a wide range of cultural differences as long as certain ground rules were observed, the most basic being that those looking for a new life in the Untied States—the "wretched refuse" of Emma Lazarus's poem—must be ready to give up aspects of their old identities to meld into their new one: the American.

Cultural and religious conflicts present in the earlier years of the colonies were minimized either through overt aggression—violence against Native populations or English driving French or Spanish settlers out—or through historical erasure. Frances FitzGerald, in *America Revised,* charts how producers of history texts, in response to increased European immigration at the end of the nineteenth century, invented a purely Protestant, Anglo origin for the country, downplaying or writing out the contributions of non-Anglos and Catholics. The Spanish-Catholic influence, prominent in the Southwest and Florida, is all but ignored in favor of that of the Pilgrims and other English colonists of the Northeast.

As immigration to the United States increased, a new paradigm was needed if the semimythical "American" identity was to be sustained. That paradigm would explain how the dominant culture could expand without diluting its unique character. The solution was the "melting pot." Merging an industrial image (resonant of the steel mills in which many immigrants labored) with one of a homey kitchen (food plays an enormous role in the conceptualization of assimilation), the melting pot metaphorically brought together the workplace and the home as sites where, through slow heating, careful science, and attention to flavor, "American" identity might accommodate difference, though never enough to radically change the overall character of the brew. The original idea of the melting pot was that white European subcultures would be completely subsumed into a cohesive "American" culture. Immigrant cultures, however, made a distinct impact on mainstream culture, so the idea of the "melting pot" was moderated to explain that new subcultures (usually much older than "American" culture) might retain their "flavor" while adding to the dominant culture. The metaphor of the melting pot conceptualized for the dominant culture their ability to assimilate—in the first meaning of the word—ethnic and foreign subcultures in a way that decreased their implicit threat to a unified American character. As immigration increased so did this threat.

The national and religious mix of immigrants grew over the years. Polish, Swedish, and Irish immigration occurred early in the twentieth century and was followed by large waves of German immigration and both Christian and Jewish immigration from Eastern Europe and Russia. Assimilation did not happen without tensions. Immigrants experienced enormous violence in the late nineteenth century and early twentieth century. American Nativist movements campaigned—with tactics including legislation and violent vigilantism—to keep the United States a white, Anglo-Saxon, Protestant country. The stigma of not fitting in was great. Job and housing discrimination, public harassment, and lack of access to public education were all realities immigrants faced on a daily basis. Often, "assimilation" meant becoming "American" as quickly as possible.[1]

Assimilation was, for the most part, not an equitable exchange. Ethnic, religious, and national subcultures often lost their most defining, salient, and vital characteristics when they assimilated. A more honest paradigm for the interaction between dominant culture and subcultures is not the melting pot but the protection payoff. Immigrants were allowed into the Untied States for a variety of reasons, the most important being to supply cheap labor needed to fuel the enormous industrialization of the times. Many immigrants, coming from poverty-stricken rural areas in Europe (where some also faced ethnic and religious intolerance), were happy to take their chances in a land of imagined opportunity. But the cost of opportunity—of assimilation—was high. To become an "American" you had to pay a price. Immigrants brought their own cultures: names, languages, religious beliefs, foods, dress, family patterns, ethical behaviors, entertainments, customs, and social structures. The immigrant experience was one of constantly figuring out what was, and was not, acceptable to be an "American": what one had to give up in order to fit in. For many immigrants, receiving (by bureaucratic fiat) a new name was necessary; learning English (and often giving up your first language) was mandated; dressing in non-European clothes was helpful; moderating religious practices was often required. To not "fit in" or not be a "real American" often meant facing ostracism, denial of social and economic opportunity, and even violence.

Of course, some immigrants were eager to make these tradeoffs. It was not unknown for some immigrant to "pass"—hide his or her ethnic, national, or religious origins and simply be "American." Often the advantages of living in the United States made the immigrants' lives better than in Europe. For some, life in the United States offered economic independence, political involvement, and more personal autonomy. While there were real reasons for immigrants to assimilate—in the second meaning of the word—for self-protection as well as to secure a better life, the reality was that they were not always welcomed, encouraged, or allowed. The limits set by the dominant culture regulated potential changes in that culture and also helped keep in check any incipient political and social power that individual subcultures might seek or attain.[2]

The experience of European immigrants contrasts sharply with the interactions between nonwhite subcultures and dominant "American" culture. The concept of "assimilation" (whose Latin root, *similis*, means "like") is used in describing the interaction between European immigrants and the dominant U.S. culture. Nonwhite subcultures are generally not thought of as able to assimilate because "whiteness" is one of the major components in how the traditional "American" identity is constructed. Moreover, members of some European subcultures, such as Slavs, were viewed as less "white" than other subcultures. The vast majority of Jews who spoke Yiddish, despite their country of origin, were also viewed as not "white."

"Whiteness," however, was a construct protean enough to adapt to circumstance and necessity. Often these reconfigurations of "whiteness" reflected and influenced shifts in social, economic, and political power. Assimilation was dependent upon keeping some form of racial and social hierarchy in place. In *How the Irish Became White,* historian Noel Ignatiev traces the "assimilation" of despised Irish immigrants—not considered "white"—who established a base of economic, political, and social power by actively working against increased freedom and independence for African Americans. While the standards of who could be "white" or a "citizen" shifted for European immigrants, nonwhite subcultures were always excluded from full citizenship, thus preventing them from assimi-lating—entering into the mainstream of U.S. culture—in the way that European immigrants did.[3]

Native Americans who did not die in the U.S. government's genoci-dal campaigns were colonized on reservations as second-class citizens, their cultures obliterated or treated as regional folklore and art. Native Americans were not guaranteed the right to vote until 1975.

The lives of Chinese immigrants, who also arrived in the mid-to-late-nineteenth century, were radically different from those of their European counterparts. As non-Caucasians the Chinese faced greater discrimina-tion, less access to social and economic mobility, and more violence. They were often prohibited from entering the political process. The 1868 Burlingame Treaty encouraged Chinese immigration but forbade Chinese-American citizenship. In 1870, the Nationality Act stated that only "free whites" and "African aliens" could qualify for U.S. citizenship. In 1906, the San Francisco School Board segregated all Chinese students to "Asian schools" in an attempt to limit Chinese assimilation and integration. Of-ficial policies refused non-Caucasian immigrants the option of the melt-ing pot, although the United States had no trouble using them as cheap labor without political or social enfranchisement. This exclusion of non-Caucasians from the "American" identity served to reinforce its "white" character. As a result, Chinese immigrants had far less control over their material lives than did European immigrants. Another consequence of this disenfranchisement was that Chinese culture remained intact in the United States for a longer period of time.[4]

The position of the African slave and the evolution of African-American culture in the United States represent a third model of interaction be-tween dominant culture and immigrant subculture. African slaves came from a variety of distinct Central or West African cultural backgrounds: Yorubas, Akans, Ibos, Angolans. But in Caucasian America they were treated as—and eventually assumed the characteristics of—a single cul-tural force.

Sterling Stuckey, in *Slave Culture: Nationalist Theory and the Foundations of Black America,* speculates that shared horror of the Middle Passage and the slave ship "were the first real incubators of slave unity across cultural lines, cruelly revealing irreducible links from one ethnic group to an-other, fostering resistance. . . ." Forced to live and work side by side in a hostile new environment, slaves from differing African cultures formed alliances with one another, learned strategies for survival, and discovered forms of resistance. Their cultural differences were made negligible by the harsh reality of oppression, and shared cultural customs became more important. By the mid-nineteenth century, Africans and African culture had coalesced into a social unit with its own shared customs, language, history, and religion.

The position of African subculture *vis-à-vis* the dominant white culture stands in sharp relief to the European and Chinese situations. Black slaves, legally considered property, lived intimately with their white owners. The two cultures existed in a tightly bound, often contentious, symbiotic relationship that profoundly shaped both. This is not to say that African culture was *merely* reactive, but rather that reaction *and resistance* were integral to its evolution.

The evolution of U.S. African culture (the basis for contemporary African-American culture) took many forms. African language, dress, song, religion, and work habits were the basis for how African slaves lived in their new country. Most slave owners forbade the presence of any African culture except song and dance, which were thought to improve work. But slaves found ways to preserve their heritage, often keeping it hidden. Work songs sung by groups of field-workers were patterned after West African group choral singing—a call-and-response pattern—but adapted for new circumstances. The reliance on this shared cultural attribute was vital for forging a new unified culture. The singing was a manifestation of communal pleasure as well as an expression of an emerging social—and ultimately political—identity.[5]

The intricacies of interaction between the African subculture and the dominant culture are elucidated beautifully by Roger D. Abrahams in *Singing the Master: The Emergence of African American Culture in the Plantation South*. Abrahams charts the evolution of the harvest celebration that centered on the shucking of corn every autumn. The festival was a carryover from Anglo-European harvest celebrations, but soon became a place in which slaves were encouraged to perform and to express themselves. Songs based upon African rhythms, with lyrics invented—often on the spot—for the occasion, were sung. The festival performed several functions: vital agricultural work was completed; the white slaveholders were entertained, thus reinforcing their dominant status; and the slaves, inventing the entertainment, gained some autonomy.

What emerged was something quite surprising. The slaves, forced to adopt a celebration from white culture, used the opportunity to slyly criticize and mock their "owners," composing satirical lyrics that ridiculed individuals as well as the injustice of the social system. The slaveholders often did not realize the subtext of the humor. Thus the

corn-shucking festivals became a dual celebration for the slaves: a celebration of work completed and a celebration of psychological independence over their "owners." The creation and celebration of minority
culture as a form of resistance is intrinsic to this evolution as a social
force for change and as a threat to the status quo.[6]

The intense interplay between the coexisting African and white cultures continued after slavery was abolished in 1865. While the Fourteenth Amendment, ratified in 1868, granted full citizenship to all
U.S.-born or -naturalized residents, and the Fifteenth Amendment, ratified two years later, granted all citizens the right to vote regardless of
race or former slave status, African Americans were never fully allowed
into the dominant culture. The nativist movement—including the newly
formed Ku Klux Klan—that persecuted European immigrants also targeted freed slaves. Antiblack racism in the South and the North, through
overt and covert discrimination, deprived African Americans of job opportunities and security, access to housing, and even freedom of association. At times widespread institutionalized violence was perpetrated
upon black people and communities. Between 1890 and 1920 there were
four thousand lynchings of black men by whites, none of whom were
ever brought to trial. Most pervasively, legal segregation—which found
its most sophisticated expression in the "separate but equal" doctrine of
the Supreme Court's *Plessy v. Ferguson* decision of 1896—in both the
North and South kept black and white individuals and communities separated.

The enforced separateness of segregation perpetuated an environment in which African-American culture coexisted with the dominant
culture, yet remained apart from it. While many aspects of European
immigrant culture were assimilated into mainstream culture, this was
not true of African-American culture (and was even less so of Native-
American or Asian-American culture). The dominant culture perceived
"race" as so insurmountable a difference that any ethnic group defined as
nonwhite was not admitted into it. While the construct of "whiteness"
was malleable, at times even ostracizing certain European cultures, it *always* excluded those of African, Asian, and Native-American descent, and
often those of Latin descent as well.

Since these groups could not assimilate, they existed in an uneasy association with the dominant culture. While there were many ways in
which members of these subcultures were useful to the larger social
ecology—most obviously as underpaid industrial labor, as a servant class,
and as consumers—one of the most vital functions of their status as

outsiders was to define, particularly in regard to race, the construct of the authentic, real "American."

In the absence of assimilation, these outsider groups were tolerated, albeit with overt discrimination and persecution. While the dominant culture acknowledged their existence and exploited their usefulness, it was willing to grant them full citizenship as "Americans" only under duress. When that occurred, these groups were seen as "integrating" rather than assimilating—and even this has been a fairly recent development. The use of "integration" to define a movement toward a more equal interracial society was first noted in the United States in 1949, after decades of organized struggle by African Americans to attain full social and political equality under the Constitution.[7]

The struggle of African Americans to attain basic constitutional rights did not automatically bring with it a desire for African-American culture to assimilate, or lose its unique character. If anything, the struggle for full citizenship occurred in conjunction with a desire to continue to invent and maintain a distinct African-American culture. This vision of cultural autonomy took many forms. In the extreme, it was the basis for Marcus Garvey's nationalistic "back to Africa" movement. It was also the impulse that fueled the flourishing culture of the Harlem Renaissance and newly recognized black arts movements. As Langston Hughes wrote in "The Negro Artist and the Racial Mountain": ". . . there is a mountain standing in the way of any true Negro art in America—this urge within the race toward whiteness, the desire to pour racial individuality into the mold of American standardization, and to be as little Negro and as much American as possible."

The desire on the part of African Americans for an autonomous culture, as well as the refusal of the dominant culture to assimilate aspects of that culture, created an alternative dynamic to traditional assimilation. While aspects of European immigrant cultures became part of mainstream U.S. culture, African-American culture exercised an enormous influence, but never became accepted as part of it. Frequently the influence of the subculture is never acknowledged as such; this is called "appropriation." Both "assimilation" and "influence" are predicated upon, and implicitly acknowledge, the reality of limits in how the "American" identity is constructed. The first signifies a degree of acceptance by the dominant culture, the second only varying degrees of toleration.[8]

The political intricacies of assimilation (in the most general sense of the word) and cultural influence are complex. We see the effects of various subcultures on mainstream culture every day in the United States:

Italian food, salsa music, Jewish humor and Yiddishkeit, jazz, Black English, reggae, sushi. Even celebrations like St. Patrick's Day or Columbus Day, once uniquely ethnic, are now observed on a much wider scale. Issues, ideas, foods, and artifacts that were once located in distinct subcultures have become assimilated—accepted or integrated—into the dominant culture. This complex series of processes, often simply accepted and not examined or discussed, is part of the culture wars being fought over the construction of the "American" identity.

In the late 1960s Levy's, a small East Coast bakery with limited national distribution, began a New York–based print and billboard campaign featuring different "ethnic" types—an older Native-American man, a young Chinese student, a thirty-something African-American woman with an Afro—all eating deli sandwiches on thick slices of rye bread. The captions read: "You Don't Have to Be Jewish to Love Levy's Rye Bread." The campaign was an instant success because it acknowledged, with humor, two ideas that most viewers understood but might not have articulated. The first is that, in our pluralistic society, we all have conflicted attitudes toward ethnic stereotypes. If we are a member of the group depicted, we may view the representation as positive (seeing it as a form of visibility) or negative (feeling that it limits a complex understanding of our identity). If we are not a member of that group, we have to examine, at least cursorily, our responses to those images. Whatever the reaction, viewers had to acknowledge that the contradictory feelings these images engendered were emblematic of deep-seated ambivalence toward ethnic identities in a "melting pot" society.

The ad campaign, after raising anxiety around ethnicity, humorously resolved it. The success of the "You Don't Have to Be Jewish" campaign resided in the acknowledgment that the enjoyment of food—pleasure on its most elemental and visceral level—could bridge cultural gaps. This insight is at the heart of how assimilation (in the broadest sense) of subcultures into mainstream culture functions. The elements of subcultures that manifest themselves in dominant culture after "assimilation" are those that are most likely to give pleasure: food, theater, music, inventive and original language, humor, clothing, even the more elusive notions of "style" and "fashion." The Levy's campaign played upon our deep-seated ambivalence about differences—ethnic, religious, national, physical, gender—and told us that while they may not be easily reconciled, a common ground of compatibility might be attained, especially when personal or shared pleasure becomes a common denominator.

This makes sense in the "melting pot" model: unique aspects of individual subcultures become accepted, or tolerated, and maintain their integrity when they enhance the quality of the dominant culture. How does this fit into the "protection payoff" model? All subcultures bring into the dominant culture a wide range of customs, artifacts, and social patterns, many of which are rejected as too extreme, foreign, or dangerous. They cannot be assimilated because they challenge basic structures and belief systems. But the dominant culture is very willing to take, or tolerate, from subcultures anything that produces pleasure, and to allow those pleasure-generators to become part of popular culture.

Most people experience pleasure as a scarcity in their lives; since the pleasure drive (the id) has to be repressed (by the superego) to further civilization, they are always left wanting more. Therefore pleasure is always being sought, but with ambivalence. This connection is so pronounced that ambivalence even shapes what we define as pleasurable; often it is connected with "the other," something that is outside of our experience and life. As a result, a "pleasure" offered by a subculture becomes even more desirable. This is partially because the pleasure of "the other" is, by its nature, "displaced." This displacement—the idea that pleasure resides elsewhere, that it has nothing to do with us—is a distancing mechanism that makes us feel safer. But more important, "the other" becomes the forbidden—that which is not safe—and as such its potential for pleasure becomes greater.

Many of the elements that the dominant culture is eager and willing to embrace from subcultures manifest themselves in popular culture: song, music, theater, movies, art, dance, public dining, cultural celebrations, dress, sports, and even public presentations of self or identity. A major route of assimilation in the United States has been through entertainment and the entertainment industries. Not only has this type of assimilation allowed aspects of various subcultures to manifest themselves in more mainstream venues, but it has encouraged and facilitated economic mobility.

This assimilation through popular culture that highlights aspects of subcultures and gives the appearance of a relatively high degree of tolerance also presents problems. Often it is a tolerance that selectively promotes visibility without necessarily providing complete citizenship, that promises economic mobility without any control of economic resources. It also frequently places those seeking acceptance into the dominant culture in vulnerable social and political situations where they are open to attack because of backlash to their perceived progress. The supposed tolerance might more realistically be labeled "fake visibility," or, in Sarah Schulman's phrase, "fake tolerance."[9]

This fake tolerance allows minimal, nonthreatening visibility for subcultures, yet often simply functions as a means of obfuscation and erasure. Similar to Herbert Marcuse's "repressive tolerance"—controlling political resistance by allotting small amounts of freedom— fake tolerance promotes measured amounts of cultural assimilation and visibility but never permits the full range or impact of a subculture to be acknowledged. The "assimilation" promoted by fake tolerance also creates cultural containment and even disempowerment by partially appeasing, but never really fulfilling, the needs of the subculture to express itself.

Another aspect of fake tolerance is cultural appropriation. Often, the pleasurable attributes of subcultures that influence mainstream culture without recognition of their origins are "appropriated"—in essence, stolen. The history of African-American music is rife with such appropriation. In the late 1940s and 1950s black musicians and writers could not find adequate industry support for their work. Recording studios and distribution networks were closed to them. Yet white musicians often recorded the work of black composers—with little, or sometimes no, remuneration to the original artists—and became famous.[10]

There are other limitations to cultural assimilation. Social tensions can arise when subcultures are forced to bear the burden of creating, providing, or representing pleasure for mainstream culture. Popular culture provides us with pleasure that is both highly desired and viewed with deep suspicion. Those who create this popular culture are viewed through the same double, conflicted lens.

Mainstream culture's attitude toward African-American-inspired music—from jazz to rhythm and blues to rock—is a clear expression of this phenomenon. Experienced by many white listeners as overly emotional and overtly sexual, these musical forms were denounced as a threat to public morals when they first appeared. This stance was clearly as much a response to an imagined black sexuality—dangerously unfettered and enticingly uncivilized—as it was to the music itself. Yet the white listening public's desire for pleasure was so great that, despite the criticism, each of these musical forms flourished. The desire for the pleasure provided by this music (as well as the sexual freedom it signified) eventually won out, but not without a fight. Mainstream culture's reaction to gangsta rap, a product of inner-city black experience, has been slightly different. Gangsta rap's use of violent, sometimes sexual, images, and its underlying critique of the state's violence against black people, incurred the wrath of conservative mainstream culture. At the same time it engaged young white suburban listeners who, while they may have related to its message liberation through violence, also used it to reaffirm their fantasies of black violence, outlaw status, and social disruptiveness.

The reduction of a subculture to an acknowledged pleasure-manufacturer can also lead to social and political backlash. The linkage of Jews to Hollywood in the popular imagination has often produced resentment in the mainstream culture, and sometimes this has spilled over into other subcultures. The myth that "Jews control Hollywood" is persistent in our culture. Neal Gabler, in *An Empire of Their Own,* examines the complicated history of how Jewish immigrants like Samuel Goldwyn, Louis B. Mayer, and Adolph Zukor "invented" Hollywood. Because many Hollywood studios were owned or run by identifiably Jewish businessmen in the industry's heyday, morality watchers and conservatives in the dominant culture were quick to blame every industry problem—from the mistreatment of individual stars, to "immoral" film content, to the social role of the industry itself—on Jewish influence. Joseph Breen, who enforced the industry's own censorship mechanism, the Motion Picture Production Code, attributed immoral films to "those lousy Jews . . . the scum of the earth . . . whose only standard is the box office."[11]

Anti-Semitism aimed at Hollywood was also present in East Coast artistic and intellectual circles. In 1938, *Vogue* printed a drawing by acclaimed British artist Cecil Beaton illustrating the clash between the old and new cultural elite. On a newspaper within the drawing, Beaton had lettered the headline "Mr. R. Andrews' Ball at the El Morocco Brought Out All the Damned Kikes in Town," and a telegram in the drawing read PARTY DARLING LOVE KIKE. Marginalia in the drawing asked: "Why is Mrs. Selznick such a social wow?" "Why Mrs. Goldwyn?" "Why Mrs. L. B. Mayer?" Beaton was exiled from *Vogue* for three years after columnist Walter Winchell called attention to his comments.

The irony of this is that early Hollywood moguls, fearful of not being accepted because of their ethnic and religious backgrounds, did everything they could to disguise or play down Jewish elements in the industry. This included forcing stars like Sylvia Sidney (Sophia Kosow), Edward G. Robinson (Emanuel Goldenberg), and Paul Muni (Muni Weisenfreund) to change their names to "pass" as gentiles. When a Jewish executive at Warner Brothers wanted to change Julius Garfinkle's name to James Garfield, the actor protested that it was the name of a U.S. president. "You wouldn't change a name to Abe Lincoln, would you?" he asked. "Of course not," the executive agreed, "because Abe is a name that most people would say is Jewish and we wouldn't want people to get the wrong idea." They split the difference, and the New York actor became the Hollywood star *John* Garfield. The paranoia behind the fear of a Jewish-controlled Hollywood was that the economic control of Jewish executives would translate into representations of Jewish life, or display itself in some other cultural agenda, such as anti-Christian sentiment. The pervasive anti-Semitism of mainstream culture mandated that Jewish executives "fit into" the dominant culture to such a degree that they would avoid any indications of Jewish heritage or identity.[12]

Anti-Semitism is so ingrained in U.S. culture that the Jews-control-Hollywood canard remains with us today. In 1988, right-wing Christian protesters against Martin Scorsese's *The Last Temptation of Christ* directed their anger at a "Jewish-controlled" Hollywood, ignoring the fact that Scorsese is an Italian-American Roman Catholic, and that the film was based on the novel by Nikos Kazantzakis, a Greek Orthodox Catholic. This anti-Semitism is so culturally entrenched that it is expressed from a broad range of political perspectives. Leonard Jeffries and other Afro-centrist theorists have blamed the lack of black representation in Hollywood films on the influence of Jews.[13]

The capacity of subcultures to produce entertainment and pleasure can also be used as a form of resistance and need not always result in backlash. Self-expression and the potential to critique the dominant culture are always possibilities in artistic production. The evolution of corn-shucking festivals is only one model of subcultural resistance. African-American culture has a long history of using ironic humor to subvert mainstream oppression. Mel Watkins, an historian of black humor, notes: "African-Americans became the arbiters of a reversed joke in which others' assumptions of their ignorance became the source of humor." Thus "Sambo"—the foolish, dimwitted, but ingratiating slave, a staple of racist humor and stereotyping—was also used by African Americans to make fun of the "master." The humor was often satiric. An 1855 slave narrative recounts the following dialogue:

> "Pompey, how do I look?" the master asked.
> "O, massa, mighty, you looks mighty."
> "What do you mean, 'Mighty,' Pompey?"
> "Why, massa, you looks noble."
> "What do you mean by noble?"
> "Why, suh, you looks just like a lion,"

"Why, Pompey, where have you ever seen an lion?"
"I saw one down in yonder field the other day, massa."
"Pompey, you foolish fellow, that was a jackass."
"Was it, massa? Well, suh, you looks just like him."[14]

The double-meaning wordplay is reminiscent of the "trickster"—a nimble-witted survivor whose intelligence and double-dealing help him survive. The trickster was a staple character in West African as well as European cultures who became established in African-American and, ultimately, mainstream humor. The Sambo character is a variation on the trickster. The trickster can twist language, logic, and circumstance to enlarge his limited range of freedom and satirize dominant culture. The trickster appears in animal folktales like those in the 1880 *Uncle Remus: His Songs and His Sayings,* authentic slave folklore retold by white writer Joel Chandler Harris, and continues on through the *Amos 'n' Andy* shows in the 1940s and 1950s and *Sanford and Son* in the 1970s.[15]

The use of comic personae has taken three main forms in popular culture. The first, usually used by those outside of an ethnic group, is to ridicule. Mean-spirited comic ethnic stereotypes began as a reaction to late-nineteenth-century European immigration. Skits like "The Sport and the Jew," "Irish by Name but Coon by Birth," "The Merry Wop," and "Two Funny Saurkrauts," performed by non-ethnics, were common. Variants of these, albeit diluted and coded, exist in popular culture today.

In the second form, ethnic stereotypes constituted a whole genre of early-twentieth-century novelty songs produced by Tin Pan Alley. Using corrupted African-American, Irish, Italian, and German dialects, these songs, usually humorous, had a gentler, empathetic tone and were enormously popular. The African-American song—called the "coon song"— was often performed by a white performer in blackface. While "coon song" referred to any musical number with a black protagonist, such numbers were often "rags," which used a syncopated beat that drew directly from African and slave traditions. In the second half of the nineteenth century, blackface was the province of Irish entertainers; in the twentieth century the convention was used almost exclusively by Jewish songwriters and performers. Cultural historians see Jewish performers' use of blackface as having two, perhaps contradictory or conflated, primary meanings. It may have been a way for the singers to express their own outsider cultural status through the use of a black persona, or conversely, a way for them to "prove" their whiteness by parodying and thus distancing themselves from a group who would never have the option of whiteness. Whatever the reason, the appropriation of the African-American persona and music was for European immigrants an important and meaningful aspect of their learning how to be an "American."

The third form of ethnic stereotype, usually used by members of that group, attempts to speak the truth and actively resist the mainstream culture's pressures to conform. This allows the performer a degree of honesty and at the same time entertains the audience. Irving Berlin wrote popular Yiddish dialect songs that both celebrated and poked fun at Jewish immigrants. "Sadie Salome (Go Home)" pokes fun at an upright young man who is angry his girlfriend has become an exotic dancer; "Becky's Got a Job in a Musical Show" hints that its heroine is finding financial rewards off as well as on the stage.[16]

In the early 1900s Jewish comics began presenting authentic ethnic humor. But it could be satiric and socially aggressive as well. Fanny Brice, who first performed onstage singing Berlin's "Sadie Salome" and was one of the most popular performers in the first half of the century, consciously used her Jewish identity and immigrant background in her presentation and material. Her Baby Snooks routines, in which she played an obstreperous, precocious upper-class child, were clearly mocking of goyim and their culture.

Fanny Brice was professionally and financially successful. She was able to integrate a distinctly Jewish image into her art, but she was still caught in a cultural bind. Ethnic humor worked for comedy, but Brice had aspirations to be a serious actress. In 1923 Brice had a "nose bob"—one of the first plastic surgeries on a public performer—an event so noted that *The New York Times* covered it in five articles over a two-week period. Brice claimed that the operation was simply a career move to improve her appearance as a "dramatic" actress, but many felt her motivation was to look "less Jewish." Wit Dorothy Parker quipped that Brice "cut off her nose to spite her race."[17]

In the process of negotiating the demands of assimilation, distinctive, ethnic-based cultures and the popular entertainment they produce—particularly when formed in resistance to mainstream culture—often manifest a unique "sensibility." Susan Sontag points out in her 1964 essay "Notes on Camp" that "a sensibility is almost, but not quite ineffable. . . . Any sensibility which can be crammed into the mold of a system, or handled with the rough tools of proof, is no longer a sensibility at all. It has hardened into an idea. . . ."

A sensibility is a way of looking at the world that reflects a complex mixture of "taste," moral response, and learned experience. The collective responses of an ethnic group—immigrant Jews, African Americans, Chicanos—when examined in their entirety often constitute a sensibility. In spite of its elusiveness to those outside of the subculture, a sensibility is immediately identifiable to those who share a common experience. As a character in Spike Lee's *Do the Right Thing* explains: "it's a black thing, you wouldn't understand."

The emergence of a sensibility is the triumph of a subculture: the sum of the experience used collectively as a lens through which the world is viewed. A sensibility also allows a subculture to become more visible, to mark out a place in the world. As soon as you can say, "It's a black thing"— however that "black thing" is defined—it creates a new, more cohesive category of cultural identity and thus of potential influence. Conversely, a sensibility, perhaps because it is difficult to define, is subversive; its ability to infiltrate the dominant culture can go unnoticed, as unremarked-upon as it is unmistakable. The gradual appearance of Black English phrases into common usage—"weed," "dig," "cool," "man," "dis"—from the 1930s to the present occurred with only minor public notice, and now the phrases are often used without recognition of their origin. This subcultural infiltration can occur simultaneously with a process of appropriation, in which the dominant culture takes on, in a more conscious manner, aspects of the subculture.

Subcultures, unless they are completely eradicated through political violence or genocide, always engender cultural change in the dominant culture. During that process they also change, either by forced assimilation or by a more organic form of independent evolution. Is it possible for a subculture, after this interaction with dominant culture, to maintain its individual identity and autonomy? More important: Do members of a subculture want to see themselves as members of a distinct group or would they rather be seen as an integral part of the dominant culture?

There is no one answer. Some members of ethnic groups pinned their hopes on assimilation—on becoming "real Americans" with no discernible difference between them and the dominant culture— but often discovered that there were limits to how much acceptance would be offered. Other members of the same group demanded acceptance on their own terms, refusing to compromise their ethnic identity.

African Americans had no choice but to see themselves as a distinct subculture with no immediate chance of being assimilated into the dominant culture, even though aspects of black culture influenced mainstream culture or were appropriated by it. There was, and is, a strong African-American cultural tradition that resisted assimilation and was intent upon preserving and celebrating a uniquely black culture, and racial pride.

The complexities of interaction between mainstream culture and subcultures are myriad. Questions of ethnicity, religion, race, economics, identity, culture, and power shape individual and group situations. Historically, cultural battles flare up when a subculture insists upon visibility and autonomy, a demand that increases the ever present tensions between sub- and dominant cultures.

Five

Gay Culture

GAY CULTURE, in its widest definition, is simply how gay people live their lives: how they have sex, where they socialize, how they dress, how they create extended-family and social networks, how they regard themselves in relation to heterosexual society, how they express themselves artistically. Since the gay community is composed of women and men with a wide range of other identities—racial, national, class, ethnic, religious—its boundaries are open-ended. Because gay and lesbian identity is defined by sexual attraction to members of the same gender, sexuality is, necessarily, at the heart of gay culture.

It is unclear when same-gender sexual behavior began to constitute an "identity." Historian John Boswell, in *Christianity, Social Tolerance, and Homosexuality,* argues that this coalescing began to happen in thirteenth-century Europe; Michel Foucault contends that the emergence of distinct sexual identities is a product of a nineteenth-century urge to classify and contain sexual experience. The presence of molly-houses (taverns where homosexual men could meet), as well as commonly known public cruising places, in early-eighteenth-century London indicates that the beginnings of a solid social identity of male "homosexuality" was forming. This identity entailed self-definition as someone whose sexual attraction to the same gender placed him outside of the accepted norm, and the acknowledgment that others—a community—shared these desires.[1]

Homosexual populations congregated in urban areas because cities offered anonymity and the critical mass of people needed to form a community. Historically, in the United Kingdom and Europe, rural and agricultural life was centered around the biological family. Individuals who decided, for whatever reason, not to fit into that mold could find a new life in the city. This was easier for men, who had more economic and social freedom, but was possible for women as well.

The evolution of a contemporary gay identity and community is complicated. Its manifestations reflect the cultural differences of individual members. Like African slave culture, gay culture was, and is, formed by the coalescing of disparate groups and individuals who often have only one factor in common. Homosexual desire cuts across race, nationality, class, ethnicity, and religion. The coming together that occurs is instigated by a shared sexual desire and a rebellion against oppression. An individual's sexual identity may evolve over time, and it is only one aspect of a conglomerate of personal identities. As a result there is no single "gay identity"—just as there is no single African-American, Jewish-American, or Italian-American identity. What those identities do have, however, is a connection to visible, public communities.

Because gay communities do not have the kinship patterns that sustain other communities, structure must be easily discernible to those who need know about it. At the same time it must be secretive enough to protect itself: it must be simultaneously visible and invisible. Over the years special codes developed—language, dress, mannerisms, specific interests—by which gay people could recognize one another. The gay male practice of referring to other, absent, gay men with female names or as "she" and "her" began in eighteenth-century London. This was, in part, a protective device that allowed men to appear heterosexual in their public lives. Dress was also a way for gay men and lesbians to recognize one another. In Victorian London, some gay men wore green-tinted carnations to indicate they were homosexual, and in early-twentieth-century New York wearing a red scarf was an indication of male homosexuality. For lesbians in the 1930s wearing slacks or "sensible" clothes might be a sign of more than simple nonconformity in dress. In the 1950s, wearing chinos, crewneck sweaters, or loafers were all ways for gay men to recognize one another publicly. Lesbians with DA haircuts, or wearing men's shirts, might be recognized as nonheterosexual.[2]

Gay codes existed on a thin line: obvious enough to be read by gay people, but sufficiently obscure to remain invisible to straights. As it became safer to be more open about being gay, coded clothing or styles would often cross the line and become "gay fashion." The line between perceived tolerance and incipient violence was always shifting, and the need to be mindful of the code was important. To overstep or misperceive the line could lead to harassment or physical attack.

The need to create codes and alternative realities is a major component of a gay culture and sensibility. The image of the male homosexual as "creative"—a stereotype ranging from serious novelist to interior decorator, from filmmaker to dress designer, from renowned stage performer to drag queen—is well established. Indeed, a great deal of gay male culture has been centered upon the creation, cultivation, and appreciation of the arts. One explanation of gay male culture's impulse to creativity is that it is predicated upon imagining and acting out alternatives to the restrictions of the closet. While this still occurs now, it is, historically, part of a complex legacy of invention and subversion that both formed and continues to inform gay culture today. Gay people have had to learn, by necessity, how to perform—to be who they were not and invent personae and scenarios acceptable to the straight world.

Gay culture was formed largely in reaction to mainstream society's repression. Its evolution and creativity were shaped by resistance as were those of African slave culture. While the hidden nature of gay culture allowed a degree of safety for gay people who were able to "pass" as heterosexual, it also permitted gay culture to be more subversive. Unlike African slave culture, which was always clearly identifiable, gay culture often coexisted, invisibly, within the larger culture. The power of gay culture is the power to critique mainstream culture, particularly in areas of sexuality and gender, to be able to speak the "truth" or offer an alternative model.

The character of the West African trickster in slave culture has a gay corollary. In Western culture, the roots of the trickster were in the European tradition of the fool and the court jester. Like the fool in *King Lear* and the medieval jester, the trickster challenges and deflates prevailing authority and culture. The Mattachine Society, one of the first gay movement organizations in the United States, derived its name both from the Société Mattachine, a secret medieval French society of unmarried men who wore masks to perform masques and rituals, often as a form of social protest, and from the Italian *mattaccino,* the court jester who was able to speak the truth while wearing a mask.[3]

The idea of the mask that protects the wearer while allowing him to speak truthfully is resonant in much of gay culture. The most obvious contemporary incarnation of the trickster is the quick-witted, sharp-tongued drag queen. Never without a retort and frequently exposing hypocrisy, the drag queen critiques with wit and the perceptiveness of an outsider. The act of "drag" itself is a comment on prevailing gender roles. The gay trickster is embodied in the high-profile visibility of RuPaul, the performers in Jennie Livingston's documentary film *Paris Is Burning,* Mae West's jokes at the expense of male vanity, and working drag performers in gay clubs.[4]

Using verbal wit and wordplay, the trickster is able to take the ordinary and expose hidden meaning, as in this classic drag monologue from the 1950s:

> I was walking down the street the other day with my friend Flora. We were all gussied up and ready for a night on the town, and maybe a little business. Suddenly on the corner of Seventh and Christopher a cute cop comes up and stops us. "What are you ladies doing here?" he asked. "Why, officer," I replied, "we're just two girls out on the town." "Well," he replied, "you better be careful. There are a lot of prostitutes around here. But I guess it's fine, as long as you know what you're doing. You don't want anyone mistaking you for what you're not." "Don't worry, officer," I said. "I've never been mistaken in my life."[5]

While the secretiveness of gay culture protected homosexuals, it also helped create a paranoia about them in mainstream culture. If homosexual identity was detectable only through public self-disclosure or being caught in homosexual activity, it was possible that *anyone* might be a homosexual.

If the idea of overt homosexuality was threatening, the notion of the "hidden homosexual"—and a hidden culture—was more so. A secret subcultural world organized around an antisocial sexuality was seen as a grave threat to the heterosexual status quo. This threat was even more dangerous because, culturally, homosexuality had come to represent sexual pleasure without the burden of reproduction—a forbidden, but attractive, alternative. On a personal level, the idea of the hidden homosexual was threatening because it implied the possibility of a hidden homosexual in everyone. Both popular and psychoanalytic literature of the 1950s were rife with the notion of the "latent homosexual."

The threat of gay culture is not simply that it celebrates sexual nonconformity and pleasure, but that, by its very existence—particularly since gay liberation—it offers critiques of the more repressive strictures of organized heterosexuality. The dominant culture, while strongly drawn to gay culture, is terrified of it precisely because it represents, on some level, such a compelling alternative. If it weren't so seductive, it wouldn't be such a threat.

The discomfort mainstream culture feels with gay culture is amplified by the closet. The "hidden" homosexual becomes the "secret" homosexual: the fugitive becomes the schemer. This is the same as the long-lived fantasy that there is a secret Jewish conspiracy running the world's economic system. A palpable social fear of gay cultural control began to surface as homosexuals were becoming more visible in the late 1950s and early 1960s. Conservatives saw homosexuals and Communists, often one and the same, infiltrating the U.S. government and even the army. (This fear fuels the overheated rhetoric of the current gays-in-the-military debate. The federal government's "don't ask, don't tell" policy is a tacit admission that it is not homosexuality but homosexual visibility that is the problem.)

Because gay sexuality, like race, was seen by the dominant culture as an insurmountable barrier to an authentic "American" identity, gay culture could not "assimilate" along the same lines as certain European immigrant models. Its impact upon the mainstream culture occurred through "influence" rather than assimilation. This influence, when detected, was seen as culturally corrosive and destructive. Psychoanalysts blamed a gay-run fashion industry for publicly humiliating women. Heterosexual theater critics worried that Broadway was in the grip of gay playwrights and directors who were promoting a homosexual agenda. Conservative morality campaigns of the 1970s and 1980s followed this lead and accused gay men of having too much influence in cultural endeavors: in music, publishing, design, fashion, and the art world. In the mid-1990s, the "velvet mafia"—a gay network of influential men in the entertainment industry—has been "exposed." Yet like the Jewish executives who closeted Jewish performers and avoided specifically Jewish content in films, most of these homosexual power brokers—some of whom, like Barry Diller or David Geffen, are openly gay—actively avoid promoting gay themes in their projects.[6]

The discomfort with gay culture grew as the gay movement brought about legal and social reform. The concept of inappropriate gay cultural power appears in right-wing propaganda videos like *Gay Rights, Special Rights* and *The Gay Agenda*. It has even surfaced in Judge Anthony Scalia's dissent in *Romer v. Evans,* a 1996 Supreme Court decision that upheld the right of the state to prohibit antigay discrimination. Scalia describes homosexuals as a group that "enjoys enormous influence in American media and politics."

While there are similarities between gay culture and other subcultures, there are also important differences. One of the reasons gay culture could maintain its protective, camouflaged status within mainstream culture was that it did not conform to traditional definitions of a subculture. Shared identity, experiences, styles, and customs are the traditional hallmarks of a subculture, as is the ability to pass these down through biological family networks and community institutions. Members of a religious denomination may not share the religion's exact beliefs, and a national identity may be fractured by sharply defined subgroups within it, yet there are acknowledged parameters by which these subcultures are delineated and acknowledged. Gay culture is far less defined in its structure.

Gay men and lesbians do not discover their sexuality or their identity through the biological family. Much of the time, biological families resist accepting or even tolerating this identity. Gay culture is thus placed distinctly outside the family networks that nurture most other subcultures. Gay folk wisdom has it that gay men and lesbians are the only minority born into the enemy camp. In fact, much of the gay subculture is shaped in direct resistance to the institutionalized heterosexuality of the biological family. This situation, in conjunction with its hidden status, allows the gay subculture to evolve more quickly and with more dexterity than other subcultures.

Many distinct ethnic communities decrease in size during the process of assimilation. Second or third generations often identify themselves as "Americans," not as Italian Americans or Polish Americans. Marriage outside of the group also tends to weaken identification with the subculture. The gay community, on the other hand, is always expanding as more and more people discover their homosexual identities and come out. This resembles not the assimilation model of European Americans but rather the African-American model, in which racial identity is reinforced as the differences between subculture and mainstream culture are reinforced.[7]

The protean nature of gay culture comes, in part, from its being defined by sexuality. Human eroticism is fluid. It encompasses not only the heterosexual and homosexual but a wide range of desire from the most banal to the most transgressive sexual actions. Desires may exist as nascent "feelings," often not even admitted, or may manifest as full-fledged fantasies. If desires are strong enough, and social attitudes permit, acting upon them is possible.

The fluidity of sexuality is both real and theoretical to most people. They may acknowledge a range of sexual desires or fantasies but decide to limit themselves to one identity. Gay self-identification—"I am a homosexual"—is an act of determined willfulness in a culture that promulgates heterosexuality as the only normal, healthy sexual identity. The threat of gay culture is that it destabilizes the presumption of a heterosexual norm.

One of the ways that gay culture in its broadest sense—how gay people live their lives—clearly manifests itself to mainstream culture is through the production of art, both high and popular. This art can realistically depict the lives of gay people—Radclyffe Hall's *The Well of Loneliness,* John Rechy's *City of Night*—or it can reflect the realities of gay experience in terms not explicitly gay. Critics often describe the paintings and sculpture of Michelangelo, the plays of Oscar Wilde, the writings of Gertrude Stein, and the work of Tennessee Williams as coded representations of gay experience. In both cases, art that is produced about, from, or within gay culture destabilizes the heterosexual norm. This is particularly true when the art is identified as the work of an openly gay artist. Such an identification mandates that homosexuality, simply by being discussed, becomes visible.

The emergence of a once-hidden heterosexuality as a material reality generates a cultural crisis for mainstream culture: if homosexual desire can "inspire" a great piece of art, it must have some intrinsic worth. Yet if we view art and culture, either high or low, as an expression of the creator's inner life/emotions/thoughts/imagination, logic insists that homosexual desire is going to manifest itself in the creative process. If some, or all, of the artist's erotic imagination is homosexual, that is going to be an influence.[8]

The literary and political ramifications of the connections between sexuality and creativity are complex. While art can and may be judged on its own merits, its creation is inseparable from the experience of its creator. Most critics have no trouble discussing a distinct heterosexual artistic process: how male artists were "inspired" by great love or, in a misogynistic reversal, how women artists created art because they had lost, or were denied, a great love.

Many subcultures have supplied mainstream culture with venues of pleasure, but the relationship of gay culture to various culture industries makes it unique. Susan Sontag has noted that "homosexuals have pinned their integration into society on promoting the aesthetic sense," and this is, to a large extent, true. By creating and promoting popular culture—style, design, and fashion as well as theater, film, and the visual arts—gay influence (as opposed to "assimilation") has had an enormous role in shaping mainstream culture. Other subcultures have made influential contributions to mainstream culture, but they have not had gay culture's wide-scale, concrete involvement in the production of popular culture. What happens when gay culture—the lives and artistic work of gay people—is labeled as such?

The first reaction is often to dismiss it. The overwhelming amount of "great art" and popular culture created by artists known to have experienced homosexual desire or behavior prohibits the wholesale dismissal of the work of gay and lesbian artists. Yet the impulse to dismiss or diminish the work of homosexual artists persists. In the popular imagination, homoeroticism, by its nonreproductive nature, cannot lead to creativity. Traditional psychoanalytic literature also reinforced the idea of the "noncreative" homosexual as it proclaimed homosexuality a stage of stunted emotional development.[9]

When an artist's homosexuality is known, mainstream culture will often dismiss the work as inauthentic. In the early 1960s, critics, blatantly misinterpreting the works of Tennessee Williams, William Inge, and Edward Albee, attacked these playwrights for "negative" portrayals of heterosexuality, marriage, and women, claiming that they were "likely to have an infective and corrosive influence on our theater." The attack was less on the plays than on the writers for their relatively open homosexuality: they were "gay playwrights."[10]

The marginalization by categorization of the art and culture of those outside the mainstream does not apply exclusively to works by homosexuals. Women, along with African Americans and ethnic minorities, have had their artistic creations deemed inferior—the strategies range from "She didn't write it" or "She wrote it but she only wrote one" to "He wrote it but it's only about life in the ghetto; it's not universal" or "It's pretty good for a novel by a . . ."[11]

Acknowledgment that homosexual desire can inform significant artistic achievement causes a panic reaction: appreciation of "homosexual art" carries the implication that the viewers/readers may be homosexual themselves. No man reads Emily Brontë and worries that he may be a woman, and no white person reads Richard Wright or Toni Morrison and worries that she or he may turn into an African American. The perceived boundaries of "the other" in gender and race are firm. This is not always the case with sexual orientation. It is the innate understanding that human sexuality has homosexual potential—no matter what someone's stated sexual identity might be—that lies at the heart of the great discomfort mainstream culture feels toward art and popular culture created by gay people.

Openly gay artists and their work continually provoke backlash. After Oscar Wilde was convicted of sodomy in 1895, his books were removed from bookstores, the up-until-then successful productions of his plays were closed, and his work was virtually unproducible for almost twenty years; legal proof of his homosexuality destroyed his career. Sir Thomas Inskip, the British Attorney-General, wrote of Radclyffe Hall's 1928 groundbreaking lesbian novel, *The Well of Loneliness,* "it is a missionary work, appealing for recognition of the status of people who engage in these practices, and there is not a word to suggest that people who do this are a pest to society and to their own sex." The outcry against the book was caused by Hall's unapologetic refusal to downplay her mannishness, a public display of her lesbianism, as well as by the book's content. In recent times, right-wing attacks on Robert Mapplethorpe's photography were fueled as much by his refusal to hide his homosexuality, sado-masochistic activities, attraction to African-American men, and HIV status as they were a response to the sexually explicit nature of the photographs.

All unmodified subcultures pose a threat to the perceived cohesion of the dominant culture. This threat is usually decreased through the process of assimilation, but when subcultures exert influence rather than undergo assimilation, the threat they pose may remain intact. Thus, subculture and dominant culture coexist in an uneasy truce, haunted by the possibility that underlying tensions will erupt: culture wars. Even when subcultural influence is acknowledged, it is usually in pejorative terms: i.e., as a bad influence.

While aspects of white European subcultures can be assimilated into U.S. mainstream culture, this is not true for gay culture, or even works of high or popular art that are labeled as gay or produced by openly gay people. Historically, openly gay culture has fallen outside the parameters of what has been construed as authentically "American." This has also been true of African-American and Asian-American cultures. Yet these cultures have had tremendous influence on mainstream culture. The impact of African-American music and language, for example, on mainstream U.S. culture has been incalculable. But this cultural influence does not carry with it the implicit social acceptance that accompanies traditional models of assimilation.

This paradigm is complicated by the dominant culture's schizophrenic relationship to the pleasure-producing elements of subcultures. While the dominant culture is attracted to and wants the pleasure-based alternatives of subcultures, it also realizes that they are a threat to the tightly controlled, repressive systems that define it. Yet the impulse to pleasure is so strong that the dominant culture, no matter how repressive, seeks new venues of pleasure and freedom.

The ever-present threat posed by "influencing" subcultures can be diminished in several ways. Appropriation—which can be seen as assimilation under duress—allows the dominant culture to enjoy the pleasure-generating aspects of subcultures without acknowledging their origins. While African-American culture is always identifiable as such, its influence on rock, for instance, can be ignored or misrepresented. In this sense, appropriation is a form of enforced "closeting."

The position of gay culture is more complex because, while it can be appropriated by the dominant culture, it can also self-closet, hide itself, to gain a degree of safety as well as be more palatable to the mainstream. The self-closeting of gay culture complicates the paradigm of "influence." Because much gay culture is not labeled as such, its influence is less overtly detectable. This makes it both more likely to infiltrate mainstream culture and, at the same time, more threatening.

Gay culture, because it is predicated upon nonreproductive sexuality—pleasure for its own sake—strikes at the heart of how mainstream culture is organized. The burden of representing pleasure in a repressive culture has made homosexuality and gay culture a lightning rod for all of mainstream culture's ambivalence and anxiety about sexuality and pleasure. While gay culture remained hidden, it was possible for the mainstream to ignore it while still enjoying its benefits. When homosexuals insisted that they and gay culture be more visible, this was no longer possible.

The growth of a gay movement that not only encouraged visibility but politicized sexuality forced the relationship between gay culture and mainstream culture to a new level of conflict. As gay men and lesbians demanded legal rights and acknowledgment of their lives, mainstream culture found it increasingly problematic to deal with the once-hidden gay culture. As the tensions between gay culture and mainstream culture rose, they erupted into the culture wars. As gay men and lesbians come out in larger numbers than ever before, manifesting their political and cultural presence, they raise the vital question of who can be an American. For the problem for mainstream culture is not gay culture, but openly gay culture; not gay artists, but openly gay artists; not gay people, but openly gay people.

Six

Gay Freedom,
Gay Movement, Backlash

THE TRUCE THAT bestowed "safety" on homosexuality in exchange for invisibility—and granted mainstream culture new venues of pleasure whose origins they did not have to acknowledge—was irrevocably broken with the advent of gay liberation and the explicit demand for gay freedom.

While the evolution of gay identity and community began in the early eighteenth century, it was not until the early twentieth century that gay men and lesbians began to organize for basic civil rights. In 1869, Károly Mária Kertbeny (who coined the term "homosexual" that same year) wrote an open letter protesting the reinscription of a Prussian law that criminalized male homosexual behavior into the new penal code of the North German Confederation. Kertbeny's argument included a list of famous homosexuals—Henry II, James I, Pope Julius II, Michelangelo, Shakespeare, Molière, Isaac Newton, and Byron—who had made important contributions to Western culture. He also noted that the persecution of homosexuals created an easy scapegoat upon which the dominant culture could displace its own sexual anxiety. Despite these arguments, the Prussian law entered the Confederation's penal code and in 1871, with the unification of Germany, was reinscribed again as Paragraph 175 of the German penal code.[1]

Paragraph 175 was the new manifestation of a long legacy of German laws that not only curtailed and criminalized personal freedom but also created categories of people who were excluded from full citizenship. The most infamous and pervasive of these, beginning in the Middle Ages, were legal prohibitions that regulated where Jews could live, work and socialize. Jews were thus defined as separate from, and harmful to, the legitimate state. Paragraph 175 implicitly made this argument with regard to the homosexual. As early as 1830, Eduard Henke's influential *Hand-book on Penal Law and Penal Policy* stated:

> . . . sodomy damages the state [f]or it renders those individuals who practice it incapable of fulfilling their duties as citizens for the purposes of the state. This is due to several reasons: active sodomites waste their procreative powers instead of producing future subjects for the state. They weaken themselves through their debaucheries, whereupon, first, they cannot serve the state properly; second, they will finally be unable to take care of themselves and thus become an additional financial burden to the government. Furthermore, their bad example corrupts other citizens. The state must vigorously oppose this vice in the interest of its other citizens.[2]

The legal codification of who is awarded citizenship, as reflected in Paragraph 175, and the earlier anti-Semitic civic and social regulations, were the prototypes for subsequent "purification" laws passed under the Third Reich—the basic tools used to implement the Holocaust.[3]

In 1897 the Scientific Humanitarian Committee, based in Berlin, was formed by Dr. Magnus Hirschfeld to fight for the repeal of Paragraph 175 and to educate the public about homosexuality. The Committee's "yearbooks," distributed worldwide, discussed the rights of women, the importance of nonreproductive sexuality, and the connections between sex, pleasure, and creativity. In 1933, the Committee's library was attacked by one hundred young Nazis, who ransacked it in a National Socialist campaign to cleanse libraries of books of "un-German spirit." Later that day, storm troopers continued the attack and publicly burned over ten thousand books. By 1935, the first gay rights group was destroyed.

The German gay movement had a broader agenda than legal reform and civil rights. Hirschfeld and other theorists placed homosexual oppression in a larger framework of political repression. This was also the case with the early Mattachine Society, started in the United States by Harry Hay and a few other activists in 1950. Hay's background as a union and Communist Party organizer influenced his gay politics. In an early position paper, he described gay people as "an oppressed cultural minority"—a model used earlier by the Communist Party to organize workers and people of color. The "cultural minority" model presumed that homosexuals were part of a cohesive group, not simply individuals who shared a common sexual interest. The Mattachine Society placed homosexuals in a political context—citing Negroes, Mexicans, and Jews as "fellow minorities"—and worked toward a "higher ethical homosexual culture"; the organization did not emphasize sexuality or pleasure. As the Mattachine Society grew and attracted members who did not have the leftist politics of its founders, the group changed and became assimilation- and civil rights–oriented.

Other homophile groups—including the Daughters of Bilitis (DOB) for lesbians in 1955 and the Society for Individual Rights (SIR) in 1964— developed the political strategy of presenting homosexuals as "normal." Partly a response to mainstream 1950s thinking—the dominant culture was desperate to reestablish social norms, gender roles, and "the family" after the social dislocations of World War II—the strategy was also de- signed to desexualize homosexuality and thus make it less threatening.

The politics of the homophile movement was essentially a politics of privacy: if you kept to yourself, did not disrupt the sexual or cultural sta- tus quo, and worked quietly for change, things would get better. Sexual- ity was a private matter whose public disclosure could only hurt gay people. Individual freedom and autonomy were less important than group identity; public citizenship was possible only through privatizing the personal life completely.

Homophile groups emerged in the context of a growing, increasingly visible, gay subculture. Bars proliferated in large and small cities, com- plex community structures began to emerge, and the media became fas- cinated with the "hidden" gay life that signaled moral decay as well as provided titillation. The emergence of a visible gay life was only one of many disruptions occurring throughout U.S. culture in the late 1950s and 1960s, cracking the facade that posited the white, middle-class, nu- clear family as the American norm; a black civil rights movement was be- coming more militant; rock and roll was creating a new, rebellious youth culture; divorce rates were going up; institutionalized censorship floun- dered and books and films became more sexually explicit; Hugh Hefner, playing on heterosexual men's anxieties, created a financial empire based upon the "*Playboy* philosophy"; the birth control pill separated sexual ac- tivity from reproduction; the women's movement was demanding eco- nomic and social freedom for women; and there was a growing mistrust of the U.S. government, particularly with regard to the escalating war in Vietnam. By the end of the 1960s an important shift had occurred. Col- lective identity—the "organization man" of the 1950s—was diminishing in importance and was being replaced by a new sense of personal iden- tity: increasingly, the needs of the individual were being prioritized over those of the group, and U.S. culture was becoming pleasure-oriented. In Freudian terms, the discontents were taking over civilization.

It was in this context that the gay liberation movement was born. Just after midnight on Saturday, June 28, 1969, drag queens, street people, and patrons of the Stonewall Inn, a mob-controlled dance bar in Greenwich Village, fought back during a police raid. The riots continued for the next two nights and became a symbol of proactive gay resistance. This new sense of empowerment and individual autonomy, combined with the awakening sense that freedom for those outside the mainstream was possible, led to the formation of the gay liberation movement.

The politics of the movement were predicated on public visibility, exploration of personal growth, and understanding that oppression based on sexual identity took place in a broader social context. "The personal is the political," a slogan popularized by radical psychiatrist R. D. Laing, was a mandate of the late 1960s and informed both the gay liberation movement and feminism. Rejecting the homophile idea of the sacredness of privacy, as well as its effectiveness as a political strategy, gay liberation demanded that private lives become public. "Better Blatant Than Latent," a popular banner at gay pride marches read. This shift demanded two major changes in political strategy.

The first was that the forces of gay liberation could succeed only if they worked in coalition with other oppressed groups. Gay liberationists viewed all oppression as originating from the same source: a white, heterosexual, capitalist, male-dominated society. Effective organizing mandated making alliances. The Gay Liberation Front, a group of vaguely connected organizations across the United States (as well as in the U.K.), took its name from the North Vietnamese National Liberation Front (which, in turn, had taken its name from the Algerian movement for independence) and worked hard to do grassroots organizing and coalition-building with leftist, antiracist, and women's groups—outreach that was, for the most part, not reciprocated. Even on the casual level of pop lingo, the borrowings were obvious: "Gay is good" was coined from "Black is beautiful," "gay libber" from "women's libber," "Gay Power" from "Black Power."[4]

The second change in political strategy was to emphasize the power of the sexual. Gay liberation was as much a product of the sexual revolution as it was of the left, feminism, or the civil rights movement. The youth and drug cultures proclaimed a personal liberation through physical experience and expanded consciousness—sex, drugs, and rock and roll—that would revitalize the world. Gay liberation's early slogans displayed the same presumptions: "Turn on to gay sex," "Liberate your gay soul," "Gay Revolution."

While the homophile movement promoted the idea of private, responsible citizenship, the gay liberation movement called for public displays of identity but did not actively promote a civil rights platform that demanded full participation in the state. This was because, on a deeply political level, the movement deplored the state and its power. The question of who could become an "American" was, to these activists, utterly beside the point, since they did not profess belief in the commonly held ideal of "America." The GLF model of "citizenship" was less immediately civic, and not national but global, as indicated by the popular GLF slogan "Perverts of the world, unite."

The major organizing tool of the gay liberation movement was the consciousness-raising group (which came from feminist organizing). By talking, sharing, and understanding the importance of personal, especially sexual, experience, members struggled to make connections between personal growth and social change. A common chant in gay pride marches demanded: "Out of the closets and into the streets."

The utopian vision of gay liberation is summed up in Carl Wittman's "A Gay Manifesto," written just before the Stonewall riots: "An Outline of Imperatives for Gay Liberation: 1. Free ourselves: come out everywhere; initiate self-defense and political activity; initiate counter community institutions. 2. Turn other gay people on: talk all the time; understand, forgive, accept. 3. Free the homosexual in everyone: we'll be getting a good bit of shit from the latents; be gentle, and keep talking and acting free. 4. We've been playing an act for a long time, so we're consummate actors. Now we can begin *to be,* and it'll be a good show!"[5]

The idea of a good show was at the heart of much sixties organizing. Public demonstrations and protests functioned as guerrilla street theater and characterized the politics of the times. For gay liberation this was true of sex as well. Sex epitomized a resonant union of the personal and political, the individual and the group. It combined the visibility of coming out with the potential for an erotic revolution. Lesbian activist Rita Mae Brown wittily noted that "an army of lovers cannot fail": sex and pleasure had become a political act. Same-gender public kissing at rallies and demonstrations were an effective way to celebrate the public nature of sexuality and demonstrate the reality of gay love. Carl Wittman claimed sex is "both creative expression and communication: good when it is either, better when it is both. We already do better in bed than straights do; and we can do better to each other than we have been." Traditional structures like monogamy were suspect; sexual experimentation and permissiveness were praised. Promiscuity was seen as a form of personal liberation and social revolt and a vehicle for change.

Gay liberation completely turned around the idea of homosexuals as passive participants in their own oppression. Poet Allen Ginsberg remarked that the rioters at the Stonewall Inn "had lost that wounded fag look." It was a remark that echoed the words of Bob Moses, an African-American civil rights organizer of the early 1960s, who said, after looking at a photograph of young African Americans at a sit-in in Greensboro, North Carolina: "The students in that picture had a certain look on their faces, sort of sullen, angry, determined. Before, the Negro in the South had always looked on the defensive, cringing. This time they were taking the initiative." Gay men proudly holding signs proclaiming, "I Am a Faggot," in gay pride marches showed that even the most hurtful of epithets could be reclaimed. Change would happen from the bottom up and the redemptive power of sexuality was the beginning of all change.

The cultural and liberationist movements of the late 1960s eventually began to shift. The more militant aspects of the feminist and black power movements (as opposed to the black civil rights movement) lost ground to the more moderate in their ranks. The youth movement and the personal-growth movement gradually became commodified. Rock music and a blatant disregard for the niceties of middle-class dress, which epitomized the youth rebellion, were quickly repackaged by the music and fashion industries: grassroots impulses became products that banked on the *idea* of revolution without any of its *threat*. New Age spiritualities (some derived from popularizations of Zen Buddhism and other Eastern spiritual traditions) that had prompted the personal-growth movement became profitable "therapies" aimed at helping clients fulfill their earning potential rather than their personal potential. The "sexual revolution"—as it was called by the media—and the new sexual freedom for women were quickly put to use in marketing cigarettes ("You've Come a Long Way, Baby") and other products. Pornography was now widely available, but it reinforced traditional gender roles and offered few glimpses of actual "sexual liberation."

This process of social containment, presenting less-threatening forms of social change through commodification, developed for two reasons. As much as people wanted and enjoyed these new freedoms, they also viewed them as a potential threat to the existing social order. Caught between the desire for pleasure and the security of a tightly ordered society, they were comfortable with a compromise that allowed limited freedom without fear of disorder.[6]

The gay liberation movement gained momentum from 1969 to the mid-1970s, but its loose, non-leadership-oriented structure could not retain populist support. The changes brought on by gay liberation were great: it was easier to come out, bars were safer, public discussion of homosexuality was now permissible. As a result, the political climate was less pressurized than before. The gay liberation movement gave way to a less radical, more mainstream gay rights movement. This movement sought change through legislative and electoral channels and worked within the system to make gay people full American citizens. Demonstrations were acceptable, but they were intended to change a law, not the world.

Gay rights movement spokespeople did not reprise the homophile rhetoric of privacy and near-invisibility. They did, however, use "We are just like everyone else" as a strategy to promote assimilation and reduce the threat of homosexuality. "Gays are just the same as straights, except for what they do in bed" was a more tolerable line in a world frightened by the idea of "Gay revolution now" and gay pride march chants like "Two-four-six-eight: How do you know your wife is straight?" or "Two-four-six-eight: Smash the family, smash the state."

The gay rights movement's strategy was two-part: the desexualization of homosexuality, and the pitch that the fight for "gay rights" was the same as the fight for black "civil rights." Both had dire consequences for movement organizing.

The specter of homosexual sex had prevented gay people from being accepted into the mainstream. While the heterosexual erotic repertory included oral and anal sexual activity, these nonreproductive activities became "perverted" when associated with homosexuals. The gay rights movement downplayed homosexual behavior—sex—in an attempt to recast homosexuals as "normal" people. Gay sexuality was now a "private" activity.

This reprivatization of gay sexuality was, ironically, at odds with a new culture that promoted open discussion of sexuality. The age-old question, "What do homosexuals do in bed?" was being answered in a variety of clear, informed, and often graphic ways. Heterosexuals understood that what made homosexuals homosexual was that they desired and often *had sex with* people of the same gender: this is the difference between heterosexuals and homosexuals. The gay rights movement's attempt to hide, or downplay, gay sexuality was perceived by most heterosexuals as promoting a lie. Heterosexuals *knew* that gay people were not just like straight people: what they did in bed was antithetical to the traditional sexual and gender paradigms and values of mainstream culture, and *that* made a lot of difference.

The second part of the gay rights movement's strategy was to cast its fight for equal protection under the law as identical to the struggle of African Americans to gain full citizenship. While there are certain similarities between racism and antigay prejudice, the political and social situations of African Americans and homosexuals differ in crucial ways. Race in the United States is viewed as an immutable physical reality as well as an identity; homosexuality is seen as a behavior and/or an identity. Racism and antigay prejudice are structured very differently. The most obvious difference is that the "closet" allows some gay men and lesbians to avoid stigmatization; most people of color do not have this privilege of "passing." Racism has also created culturally specific economic realities for African Americans that are not shared by nonblack gay people, who, for the most part, are not necessarily penalized economically for their sexual identity. While there are parallels between racism and antigay prejudice, as well as the modes of resistance for fighting them, there is no exact political or social correlation.

The gay rights movement identified itself with the black civil rights movement chiefly for two reasons. First, the civil rights movement provided a ready model of political organizing for a movement that had very little history. Second, gay rights groups hoped to claim a moral authority similar to that which the black civil rights movement had gained in the dominant culture. But the equation between gay rights and black civil rights was problematic for some African Americans, who resented what they saw as the predominantly white gay rights movement's appropriation of black civil rights credentials. This resentment, informed to a large degree by homophobia, ultimately made it difficult for the gay rights movement to form strategic alliances with black political groups.

An enormous growth in gay and lesbian culture accompanied the shift from gay liberation to a more single-focus gay rights agenda. This growth signaled the emergence of distinct alternative cultures. While there was some co-gender political organizing and socializing, gay male culture and lesbian culture were, at this time, separate entities. Both cultures focused on creating gay art made by and for gay people. This art often exerted an influence on mainstream culture—a significant change, since before gay liberation only a limited number of books and a few "out" periodicals were published for gay readers.

The new alternative culture, with its two branches, was a complete break from the past: newspapers, magazines, small presses, record companies, bookstores, theater troupes, discussion groups, political action groups, social clubs, and singing groups all emerged to reflect the diversity and newfound strength and identity of gay men and lesbians. Much of this culture was outright celebratory.

Newspapers like *Gay Sunshine* and *Fag Rag* published writing and graphic art that exulted in the new sexual freedom and pleasure many gay men were experiencing, placing it firmly in a historical, radical-political context. This new gay male culture envisioned a world in which homosexuality—and sexuality itself—might form the basis of a more just and free society.

Sexuality and sexual autonomy were also at the center of the new lesbian movement, which was influenced as well by an emerging feminist culture. Lesbian culture demanded a woman's right to her own body, sexual autonomy, and freedom from socially mandated reproduction. Lesbian feminism defined lesbians as "woman-identified women," merging sexual orientation with a politics that prioritized the lives and concerns of women. Lesbian-feminist culture, celebrating women's power and independence, manifested itself in music, literature, and publishing. While sexuality was as important in lesbian-feminist culture as in gay male culture, it manifested itself less in graphic depictions of sexual activity than in discussion of sexual autonomy and values. In the early 1970s magazines such as *Big Mama Rag* and *Majority Report* were filled with debates over monogamy, sadomasochism, and the use of sex toys.

It was now possible to publish openly gay and lesbian material without fear of censorship. Gay male magazines featuring nudity such as *Mandate, Honcho,* and *Blueboy* were sold on newsstands and in bookstores. Avant-garde films of the 1960s, such as those by Kenneth Anger or Jack Smith, occasionally dealt with homosexuality, but the new, highly professionalized, gay-porn film industry began turning out full-length feature films with theatrical releases that received reviews in *Variety* and *The New York Times.*[7]

As more people came out, the market for gay consumer culture expanded. Mainstream publishers like Avon, St. Martin's, and Signet designed book lines that targeted gay men. *The Advocate,* started as a tabloid in 1967, was now a glossy feature and newsmagazine. More important,

The Advocate, along with the soft-core porn magazines, served as a sales network for a new gay male consumer culture—clothing, jewelry, bath towels, records, books, sex toys, party games. By the late 1970s gay male culture became a "consumer lifestyle."

The emergent "gay lifestyle" of the 1970s was an attempt by gay people to acquire a sense of community through consumption. "Lifestyle" magazines promoted the image of the white, male, middle-class gay consumer as a model citizen who had everything except a few civil rights. Gay consumerism never generated tolerance or made gay people and gay sexuality acceptable to mainstream culture. It did have the damaging effect, however, of promoting the idea that economic power, even for some homosexuals, was equivalent to political power and thus fuller citizenship. This was not the case.[8]

Concurrent with the rise of the gay consumer was the emergence of a less-closeted gay sensibility in mainstream culture. Rock performers Mick Jagger and David Bowie reveled in presenting themselves as androgynous, hypersexual bisexuals. Bette Midler's and Barry Manilow's careers began at the Continental Baths in Manhattan. The Village People, barely coded icons of gay male culture—the construction worker, the muscle builder—produced hit songs extolling the joys of sex in the "YMCA," enlisting "In the Navy" and simply being a "Macho Man."[9] *The Rocky Horror Picture Show*—with its transvestite hero and attack on traditional gender roles—had gone from stage to screen, attracting a huge, young, largely heterosexual cult following. Men's clothing advertisements, especially underwear ads, portrayed the eroticized male body in ways reminiscent of gay male porn. While gay people, and sophisticated heterosexuals, could see the obvious gay influence in these cultural manifestations, the effect on most people was more subliminal. They found these aspects of the new pop culture—the blatant sexuality, the eroticization of the male body, the expansion and subversion of gender roles—intriguing, unsettling, exciting, or overtly disturbing.

During this time the gay rights movement was becoming professionalized. The fight for gay freedom shifted from community-based groups to legal battles fought by lawyers—a radical shift from gay liberation's grassroots, consciousness-raising strategy. *The Advocate,* in a 1973 editorial slamming the gay liberation movement, stated that the gay rights movement must be run by "responsible, talented experts with widespread financial backing from all strata of the gay community." This working-within-the-system approach mandated a politics of respectability that reflected a basic trust in the social and political status quo. It also excluded anyone who was not deemed acceptable by mainstream culture, and full citizenship became inextricably bound up with socioeconomic and even sexual respectability.

On the local and national levels, legal and lobbying groups established a paradigm that prioritized legal reform over social and cultural issues. These groups laid the groundwork for legal change. Their work in traditional political venues identified them, in the mainstream media, as the most visible aspect of the gay movement. The American Psychiatric Association's removal of homosexuality from its list of psychiatric disorders in 1973 and the introduction of federal gay rights legislation in Congress in 1974 were signs of the movement's energy.

In spite of this, gay rights organizations played a very limited role in the lives of most gay men and lesbians. The groups remained small and were unable to garner much financial or organizational support from the community, a reality that says more about how Americans view politics than about how the gay community does. Gay men and lesbians, as did most heterosexuals, drew upon popular culture for recognition and validation of their existence. Magazines, movies, fiction, television, music, theater, fashion, and public socializing were where they saw their lives reflected and where they saw their fantasies enacted.

Gay culture was becoming increasingly visible. Mainstream coverage of gay community activities and gay life became commonplace. *Time* and *Newsweek* ran more, frequently favorable, stories on gay issues, although at times a deep-seated ambivalence surfaced. "The love that dare not speak its name," quipped one writer, "now can't seem to keep its mouth shut." More than ever, gay lives were in the public eye. This new gay visibility was part of a larger social trend that viewed the pursuit of personal and sexual pleasure—inseparable from the idea of legal and civil rights—as a worthwhile goal. Buttons and posters promoting this new alternative culture quoted the Declaration of Independence's promise of "life, liberty, and the pursuit of happiness" with particular emphasis on the last phrase. Conservatives and morals-watchers did not agree that "the pursuit of happiness" entailed easy divorce, day care, and access to sexually explicit material, and certainly not more social and legal freedom for homosexuals. They did not buy the gay rights slogan that gay people were "just like everyone else." While mainstream media seemed to be taking a more relaxed position on the visible emergence of gay people—particularly in popular culture, the bisexual, glitter rock personae of Bowie and Jagger, films like *The Rocky Horror Picture Show,* and celebrity-driven phenomena like Studio 54 provided good copy and were viewed tolerantly and with some envy—that emergence was making conservatives very nervous.

The specific backlash against the gay movement centered on legislative issues: the 1977 "Save Our Children" campaign headed by Anita Bryant to repeal a gay rights ordinance in Dade County, Florida, and California's 1978 Proposition 6 (the Briggs Initiative) that would have forbidden California schools to hire gay or lesbian teachers. Both pieces of legislation attempted to curtail homosexuals' full rights of citizenship by drawing upon entrenched fears of them as child molesters, and thus reinforcing the idea of homosexuality, per se, as outside the basic definition of what it means to be an American. These legislative attacks were the beginning of the all-out war launched ten years later by many of the same religious and political leaders, such as Reverend Jerry Falwell and fundraiser Richard Viguerie, in a new coalition of the religious right and the conservative wing of the Republican Party.

The small legislative gains of the first decade after Stonewall were developmentally important to the movement; they broke ground and indicated its growing influence. They also represented and concretized the growing visibility and importance of gay culture. Open homosexuality became a powerful symbol to those invested in maintaining traditional values. As issues concerning sex, family, children, and gender arose, conservatives were quick to focus, and lay blame, upon gay culture; the new open homosexuality—pictures of happy gay and lesbian couples holding hands in *Time,* or the popularity of films like *La Cage aux Folles*—became the visible emblem of what was wrong with America. Thus, modest legislative gains like the Dade County gay rights ordinance took on tremendous metaphoric meaning for conservatives; their cultural importance was as much symbolic as legal. The determined, zealous right-wing fight against these legal measures was fueled and aggravated by the anxiety that the new visibility and apparent media acceptance of gay culture produced. While gay people were not assimilating, in the traditional sense, their influence was becoming acknowledged and, more than ever before, openly enjoyed.

This anxiety increased tremendously in 1981 with the advent of AIDS. In the popular imagination, AIDS quickly became the physicalization of homosexuality: The psychological or moral disease had now become a physical one. For many right-wing evangelical Christians, AIDS was explicitly God's punishment for immoral behavior. It was the fire and brimstone of the biblical Sodom and Revelations' apocalypse, a sign that the social and moral order had truly broken down.

Although AIDS is not a "gay disease"—worldwide it affects far more heterosexuals than homosexuals—in the United States, and every other Western country, the gay male community was seriously, and disproportionally, hit. AIDS intensified long-standing struggles over public policy issues for the gay movement. Antidiscrimination legislation and confidentiality issues now involved HIV status as well as sexual orientation. Questions of access to new drugs, AIDS education, and funding for community AIDS-related services were all new issues to be faced.

AIDS changed concepts of public and private with regard to sexual orientation. Men who were once able to choose whether or not to come out now had little choice if they were ill. On a large scale, AIDS brought homosexuality out of the closet—it could no longer remain a hidden subculture. Equally important, the literal and figurative connection between AIDS and gay culture reintroduced into the popular imagination the idea that it was legal and appropriate to deny full citizenship to groups designated as disease carriers. Social and immigration policies from before the turn of the century to the 1930s stigmatized immigrant groups—particularly Jews, Italians, and the Irish—as unacceptable for citizenship because of both presumed and real health problems. While diseases like TB were a problem in crowded urban areas, nativist and anti-immigrant groups used the image of the diseased outsider as a threat to a healthy America.

By the 1980s, such blatant diseased-based stigmatization was still, if minimally, acceptable. Mainstream magazine articles detailing the "gay plague" promoted the image of homosexuality as a contagion, and right-wing political literature, as well as some politicians, called for quarantine (a tactic used earlier against immigrant groups) of those who were living with AIDS or were HIV-positive. Local campaigns to close down gay bathhouses, public sex venues, and sometimes even bars met with varying success. This attempt at public stigmatization and regulation was offset by the massive amount of media discussion about AIDS that was occurring simultaneously. Not only was explicit medical and safe-sex information disseminated—in both gay and straight venues—but phrases like "anal sex" and "intercourse without ejaculation" were spoken on afternoon television talk shows. Magazines routinely ran features about sex clubs, AIDS support groups, patterns of gay male relationships, and how AIDS was affecting the arts, business, and the fashion industry. This newly emerging portrait of the gay world ranged in tone from hostility to surprise to compassion.[10]

The barrage of mixed messages reflected the ambivalence main-

stream culture felt about gay life. This new attention was a mixed bless-
ing. The more conservative gay movement worried about "negative images" that portrayed gay men as overly sexual and irresponsible and that
exploded the myth of "We are just like everyone else." Other gay people
saw this as an opportunity to speed up the inexorable cultural trend of
uncloseting all aspects of homosexuality. AIDS made it impossible to
pretend that sexuality was not central to gay male lives. This position required an unapologetic defense of homosexuality, homosexual behavior,
and by extension, pleasure itself. This was a stance relished by the old gay
liberation movement, but not the more culturally conservative gay rights
movement, which was still wedded to the idea of privacy as the path to
acceptance and assimilation.

AIDS educators and prevention workers were caught in the middle of
this debate. While they had to convince private and state funders that gay
men were a responsible group who could—and deserved to—be educated about safe sex, they also had to design programs that addressed the
sexual realities of gay male lives. This entailed dealing forthrightly with
sexual practices like fisting, piercing, and scat, and admitting that many
gay men have multiple, anonymous sexual partners.[11]

The advent of AIDS altered the course and the context of gay movement organizing. AIDS service groups became central in providing direct
services, legal advice, and education. The AIDS crisis mandated public
policy evaluations on several fronts: funding for medical research, access
to drug protocols, and antidiscrimination laws. National gay rights and
legal groups, which had formed over the past decade, were helping to
shape these policies in tandem with government agencies or in the
courts. While the insider status of the gay rights groups, which had never
received widespread community support, allowed them some access to
mainstream venues, they were limited in what they could achieve.

AIDS had a profoundly politicizing effect on the gay community. Gay
men and lesbians, many of whom had little connection to the gay rights
groups, felt overwhelmed by the epidemic and frustrated by the constant
concern that not enough was getting accomplished by AIDS service
groups and public policy advisors. The need to publicly defend gay lives,
culture, and sexuality precipitated a new wave in grassroots activism that
moved beyond the more traditional models of gay rights organizing. ACT
UP (AIDS Coalition to Unleash Power) was formed in New York in
1987, and chapters soon spread to other cities. Larry Kramer, a founding
member of Gay Men's Health Crisis, one of the first AIDS service
groups, helped start ACT UP because he felt that GMHC and other

groups were unable to pursue an AIDS agenda as quickly or as directly as needed. ACT UP chapters created their own education campaigns, housing and care systems, drug research programs, and a direct-action agenda that challenged government agencies, the media, drug companies, and medical researchers for their refusal to deal with AIDS seriously. ACT UP used the nonhierarchical, shared-leadership model of the Gay Liberation Front and was predicated on promoting visibility. Their slogan was "Silence = Death." Like the gay liberation movement, ACT UP defined itself by rejecting the state, which it saw as grossly, even criminally, negligent in dealing with the epidemic. ACT UP posters, graphically displaying a red hand print, claimed: "The Government Has Blood on Its Hands: One AIDS Death Every Half Hour." They also explicitly voiced the idea that people living with HIV and AIDS were being treated as second-class citizens in posters that read:

LIBERTY AND JUSTICE FOR ALL*
*OFFER NOT AVAILABLE TO ANYONE WITH AIDS.[12]

Visibility was an impetus in the formation of direct-action groups: Queer Nation in 1990 and the Lesbian Avengers in 1992. Working outside of traditional political venues, these groups were fueled by a desire to destroy the closet. These grassroots groups' organizing and political work was predicated upon a rejection of all aspects of gay invisibility. Slogans like "We're here, we're queer: get used to it," public displays of sexuality such as kiss-ins, and demands for explicit safe-sex education were driven by the imperative to make homosexuality as visible and blatant as possible. Queer Nation even critiqued gay consumerism with their chant "We're here, we're queer, and we're not going shopping." To a gay political movement that had sought acceptance by downplaying or ignoring difference, these tactics were seen by many as shocking and wrongheaded. To a mainstream culture struggling with its own ambivalence about homosexual behavior, they were intriguing, titillating, and confusing.[13]

The emergence of gay and lesbian grassroots, direct-action groups was a response to the continued wave of conservative backlash begun by the Bryant and Briggs campaigns of the late 1970s. The rise of the right wing in the early 1980s was a clear response to the economic anxiety of the middle class, the impact of feminism and black civil rights upon the U.S. political scene, and the increased visibility of gay people and gay culture. The right-wing backlash has taken two forms, both defensive strategies to compensate for feelings of loss or deprivation.[14]

The first is a defense of "family values"—issues of marriage, children, gender, reproduction, and, ultimately, heterosexuality. This "defense" usually takes the form of controlling sexual behavior, access to sexual information and material, and even the sexual imagination. In the right wing's thinking, homosexuality has become a major, if not *the* major, symbolic threat to traditional sexual morality and social structure, as embodied in "family" and heterosexuality.

The second form that right-wing backlash takes is its attack on "special rights." The formulation of "special rights" is a conservative response to "special interest groups"—defined by race, gender, class, or sexual preference—seeking equal protection under the law. These "special rights," viewed as illegitimate and inauthentic, are portrayed as a threat to the social structure and moral standing of the majority.

The attack on "special rights" reinforces a clear-cut distinction between the majority and "the other." It also raises the question of citizenship, forthrightly addressing a subtext of the right wing's backlash: Who is a citizen? Who has rights in our culture? What does it mean to be an American?[15]

These questions have haunted the popular imagination and political discourse since the founding of the country. They have been at the heart of fights between mainstream culture and subcultures, between who has power and who doesn't. Citizenship is gained—slowly, painstakingly, sometimes hardly at all—by an aggregate of political and cultural initiatives. The process may include traditional lobbying and legislative action, but the ground is broken and the struggle moved forward by the more forceful political operations like direct action and civil disobedience.

Subcultures defined by race, nationality, ethnicity, religion, or gender have all developed strategies—some more successful than others—for confronting and overcoming prejudice and securing their place in the dominant culture. Gay people, however, are in a unique position in their struggle for freedom and full citizenship. Gay culture was often accepted and welcomed by mainstream culture as long as it was not labeled as such. When gay men and lesbians refused to hide their identity and sexuality and demanded equal rights, this social acceptance was threatened. To speak openly about gay lives and culture—to politicize them— threatens the unspoken truce between the dominant culture and gay culture.

When gay people and culture began coming out of the closet, mainstream culture found itself in a paradoxical bind, for it was only when gay culture was closeted—unacknowledged as such—that heterosexuals could enjoy it. If members of the dominant culture refused to accept homosexuals as full citizens, and continued to disregard the importance of now-uncloseted gay lives, they would also have to reject the pleasure granted by openly gay culture. This is the central irony of gay culture's relationship to the mainstream. As more gay men and lesbians come out and demand recognition and acceptance, mainstream culture has to respond. Those invested in maintaining traditional "family values" will continue to attempt to restrict and restrain gay visibility and autonomy, to deny gay people access to the identity of "American."

Gay people face two battles in their struggle for freedom and full citizenship. The first is to be visible, to destroy the closet in all of its myriad manifestations. The little tolerance that gay people did receive before was negotiated by trading invisibility for presumed safety, contributing to the mainstream culture without acknowledgment. To deny the importance of sexual activity in a gay person's life is to remain in the closet. Any movement for liberation or rights that does not include the acknowledgment of sexuality is going to fail.

The second battle is to convince the heterosexual mainstream not just that homosexuals have contributed to mainstream culture—that is already established—but that their unique position as sexual outsiders endows them with an unparalleled vision for cultural and social change. Most people understand, on some level, the enormous possibilities that may emerge from a fuller acceptance of pleasure in their lives: that is why they want it and why they are terrified of it. They see some of that potential in the lives of gay men and lesbians. That is why they envy and fear them. Once this is understood, the first step in the struggle for gay freedom will be taken. *We are your worst fear. We are your best fantasy.*

Seven

The Eroticized Male Body

T HE EROTICIZATION OF the male body over the past half century is a direct result of the influence of gay culture. The shift from the uptight man in the gray flannel suit on Madison Avenue to the long-limbed, well-hung Calvin Klein model adorning Times Square demonstrates how radically presentation of the male body has changed. From the strong, silent machismo of Clark Gable, Gary Cooper, and Humphrey Bogart to the fluid emotionality and vulnerability of Richard Gere and River Phoenix, American masculinity has gone from being emotionally reserved to emotionally relaxed, sexually restrained to sexually resplendent. Many factors have contributed to this change, but the most important has been a gay male eroticism.

1. In His Own Image

HUMAN anatomy has remained a constant throughout history: head, arms, legs, genitals, heart, stomach, liver all remain the same, the end result of millennia of evolution. While the body remains constant, attitudes toward it—conceptualization and presentation—change enormously over the centuries. Sometimes this is obvious: concepts of beauty, health, deportment, and the "natural" can mutate by the decade. Race and skin color are primary markers used to classify and categorize individuals and groups, creating and reinforcing power inequities. But there are more subtle transformations that occur, reflecting shifts in the broader cultural landscape.[1]

Institutionalized heterosexuality has shaped how the male and female body are perceived and conceptualized. Marriage, reproductive sexuality, and the raising of children are the determining factors that mold gender presentation. Men must be strong, impenetrable, and independent.

Women must be weaker, available, and subservient. In our two-gendered system, the attributes associated with male and female bodies are distinctly separate. Because of male supremacy, the male body has been granted primacy in the cultural hierarchy. God, we are told, made *man* in His own image. Women may be praised for their beauty (as defined by their attractiveness to men), but the male body is seen as inviolate and sacramental.[2]

There has been no standard idealized male body in Western societies, although whiteness has been such an unwavering measure of superiority and even humanness that it is universalized as part of what has become the *de facto* "classical tradition." The white male body has been portrayed in a variety of poses and presentations through Greek, Roman, medieval, Renaissance, and industrialized times. The male body has been used to portray "state," "honor," and "truth." Interestingly, the female body has been used to portray "justice" and "liberty"—qualities not always associated with men. The stature, positioning, musculature, dress and demeanor of the male body in Western culture and art have constantly equated maleness with power, masculinity with progenitivity.

Feminist theory holds that in art, as in the world, men are very often subjects and women objects: the looker and the looked-at. In contemporary culture the objectified—eroticized—male body is inevitably a passive body, a sexual display, a sign of weakness. By contrast, in the more openly sexual culture of ancient Greece, the male body was seen as a form of beauty and power. In statues like the *Apollo Belvedere, Silenus with Baby Dionysus,* and the bronze *Bearded God* (all fourth century B.C.), the male body connotes perfection, grace, beauty, and sexuality. The sexuality of Greek nudes seems at first minimized—penises are small, unobtrusive—but the erectness of the statues themselves suggests a phallus: strength, power, maleness. More overtly sexualized male nudes—with erect penises, engaging in sexual activity with men and women—can be found on Greek vases. These celebrations of sexuality are indicative of how eroticism and sexual pleasure were integral to the Greek conceptualization of being human. What makes them erotic is not simply the explicit display of genitals, but the implicit acknowledgment that the body is a vehicle of pleasure.[3]

Early Christian teaching emphasized the white body as a vessel of sin, and up through the Middle Ages, representations of the naked white body conveyed warnings of potential damnation. In contrast, Satan and his minions were portrayed as black, embodiments of evil and sin. As European culture rediscovered Greek classicism, this began to change. The work of Michelangelo and others during the Italian Renaissance reclaimed the white male nude as erotic and frankly sexual. The creations of erotic male nudes by male artists posed problems of interpretation for mainstream culture. If the male nude was eroticized by a male artist, what did this say about the artist? Was he simply appreciating male beauty, using it to render religious or classical motifs? Or was his work, on some level, a manifestation of his own sexual desire? This problem was replicated in the process of viewing. If a male viewed and appreciated the eroticized male form, was his experience erotic?

Michelangelo's love sonnets to men attest to his sexual love for men. It is also evident in his work, from the *David* to Adam on the Sistine Chapel ceiling to the *Dying Captive*. Michelangelo's work is considered among the greatest ever created, but the acknowledgment of his homosexuality creates a troubling situation for viewers or critics who do not wish to consider that his homoeroticism may have been an inspiration for his art. As late as 1975, as sophisticated an observer as Anthony Burgess could write that the *David* was "so epicene that it invokes unpleasing visions of Michelangelo slavering over male beauty." The male nudes of the Italian Renaissance presented the eroticized male body to a viewing public, but to avoid any implications of homoeroticism and the consequent cultural anxiety, it was vital that the sexuality of the artist remain invisible. Ironically, critical praise for Michelangelo's art is rarely presented in juxtaposition to his homosexuality, but is often an attempt to deny or closet it.[4]

In industrialized Western culture, public white male nudity could exist only in art; thus most eroticization of the male body occurred in social presentation: clothes, deportment, affect. (African and other non-white slaves were frequently subjected to public displays of undress in the Americas—a sign of their inferior, "nonhuman" status.) Male fashion has always been designed to exhibit the body. Since the Middle Ages men's clothing—from pantaloons, suits of armor, and tights and doublet to early versions of the "suit"—has been tailored to expose rather than hide. Various accouterments like the codpiece even accentuated the genitals. Formfitting garments allowed freedom of movement and the ability to present the body forthrightly. The eroticization of the male body was inseparable from the eroticization of power: what made a man sexy were his independence and ability to act boldly. Women's clothing, on the other hand, was designed to obscure, to cover, to limit activity. The process of eroticizing the "feminine" depended heavily upon concealing the human form and using adornments: jewelry, makeup, headdresses, and elaborate undergarments that restricted the body and hindered movement, while fetishizing the female form and body parts. The "civilizing" aspects of dress for European men and women were always contrasted to the more naked, and thus eroticized, representations of nonwhites.[5]

The tailored suit was invented between 1780 and 1820. The democratic aspirations of the Enlightenment and a return to the simplicity of classical design seemed to blend neatly in the stark, yet elegant, men's garment. The growth of urban centers, industrialization, and the rise of a middle class began to solidify gender roles. As dress became an important signifier of social status and gender for this class, men's clothing became more solemn, regulated, and determinedly "masculine." The suit reaffirmed a new concept of maleness: true masculinity was productive, influential, and nonflamboyant. Any deviation from this was marked as feminine and inappropriate. The suit also reinforced class distinctions, excluding poor and working-class men from the new conceptualization of proper "manhood." By the end of the eighteenth century men who did not conform to these stricter regulations found their masculinity in question.[6]

The "dandy," a man concerned almost entirely with style and public presentation, was a creation of the early nineteenth century. "Dandyism" was most closely associated with George Bryan "Beau" Brummell, a civil servant who rose in British society through determined self-promotion. Declaring himself an arbiter of taste and fashion, Brummell positioned himself as an infallible trendsetter. His social pose was idleness; he existed to exist. While Brummell's invention of "style" (surely a nonpragmatic ideal) enabled him to transcend class and social strictures, it also caused his social downfall. His refinement of dress and demand for elegance, as well as his unmarried status, placed him outside the realm of obvious "masculinity." The dandy deviated from the appropriate gender dress and behavior; he may have been, or was seen as being, sexually transgressive as well. The dandy's crime was twofold: moving beyond the socially set parameters of who was to look and who was to be looked at, and self-consciously refusing to participate in a world that required men to produce something. The dandy eroticized himself by presenting himself as an object to be viewed, and diminished himself as a man by insisting on being purely ornamental.[7]

By the end of the nineteenth century in industrialized European and U.S. culture, masculine deportment and dress were taken very seriously. For the middle and upper classes the black suit—combining the somber-ness of the clergyman, the productivity of the businessman, and the severity of the judge—became de rigueur. Standards of appropriate gender dress were socially dictated from the top down. Suits for men and elaborate clothing and ornamentation for women set the standard. The dress of working people was designed to be strictly practical. The uniforms of those in service, shopkeepers, and service employees imitated upper-class standards.

The nineteenth-century dress reform movements in both Britain and the United States was an outgrowth of feminism and various progressive social and political initiatives. Criticism of restrictive clothing for both genders was condemned by the mainstream press as a social threat. As Anne Hollander points out, "clothes are a social phenomenon; changes in dress are social changes." As early as 1850 in the United States, Amelia Bloomer and others advocated that modern women wear pants, called "pantelettes," or bloomers. In late-nineteenth-century England, Edward Carpenter, a gay male socialist who wrote early legal and scientific defenses of homosexuality, saw dress reform as part of a widespread social change. He advised wearing sandals, loose pants, and overshirts for social and political reasons. He saw dress reform as a strike against institutionalized heterosexuality. Dress reformers also claimed that clothing that was less "civilized" encouraged better health, as well as freedom of movement and imagination.[8]

"Effeminacy" in dress and deportment—a revolt against prescribed masculinity—and homosexuality were conflated in both the popular imagination and the gay community as early as the birth of the dandy. Public display of effeminacy denoted homosexuals as "less than masculine," while at the same time it provided a presentational style that redefined masculinity. In addition, it helped create a visible community: by dressing a certain way gay men could recognize one another. This display of homosexuality was eroticizing; it positioned the male form to be admired and desired. Gay men used it to make themselves sexually attractive to other men. This interaction between gender revolt and community building is the template for the gradual eroticization of the male body over most of the next century.

The emergence of an increasingly visible gay community and culture brought with it the possibility of public censure. The controversial career and trials of Oscar Wilde are examples of what happens when a gay sensibility becomes too evident. Wilde's arrest and imprisonment were, technically, for illegal homosexual activity, but he was tried as much for his vocal espousal of aesthetic theory and his flamboyant public persona.

As a major proponent of "art for art's sake," Wilde argued vehemently that beauty was an end in itself: neither art nor life had to have a utilitarian function. He praised the artifact over nature. Like Carpenter a utopian socialist, he argued against the value of "civilization." Like Brummell, he pinned his social success on inventing and dictating "style." Wilde and his wife, Constance, supported the British dress-reform movement—they appeared in public wearing matching green suits—but Wilde himself was more interested in sartorial display than sense. As a young man he favored scarlets and lilacs, in later years elegantly cut black velvet suits. It was not simply Wilde's ostentatious display of "effeminate" dress that got him into trouble but that such behavior, particularly in conjunction with his nonutilitarian philosophy, was increasingly seen as indicative of homosexuality. The scandal of the Wilde trials, especially in England, forced the new gay style and community to retreat underground.[9]

Within fifteen years the carnage and social upheaval of World War I had shifted cultural expectations of masculinity. The Roaring Twenties promoted pleasure as its own end, and gender roles began to break down. In the United States, dapper, close-fitting clothes for men emphasized the boyish male form; the Arrow Collar Man, a noted advertising image, radiated a sexuality not seen in men before. In the U.K., upper-class youth known as the "bright young things" staged a revolt against the status quo. A literary culture grew that challenged the old masculinity: poets Siegfried Sassoon, Rupert Brooke, and Wilfred Owen had written emotionally about male love in the trenches; writers Evelyn Waugh, E. F. Benson, and Noël Coward brought a flippancy and social critique to their work; designers Oliver Messel and Cecil Beaton encouraged "style" as a function of pleasure and as part of everyday living. The Bloomsbury Group experimented with new sexual and relationship patterns, and its male members were forthright about their homosexual desires. It was now possible for men from the upper and upper-middle classes to be emotional, artistic, even flamboyant. Manifestations of masculinity had changed, and it was possible to read in the social column of the conservative London *Daily Express* in 1927 that "The Honorable Stephen Tennant arrived in an electric brougham wearing a football jersey and earrings."[10]

If men were exploring new arenas of masculinity, women were also finding new dimensions of gender and presentation. The publication of Radclyffe Hall's *The Well of Loneliness* in 1928 established that women, too, could break from gender convention in experiencing sexual desire. The flapper startled moralists with her androgyny, but the emergence of the "mannish lesbian" was a distinct social threat. By imitating male style, dress, and presentation, and exerting social and economic independence, she became a competitor with heterosexual men for the attention and affection of women. The emergence of the mannish lesbian made clear that, to a large degree, gender was constructed by dress and presentation, and that the dichotomized system of two genders was not a fixed certainty.[11]

The emergence in the United States of a highly visible African-American culture—which found its first full manifestation in the Harlem Renaissance—produced images of black culture and masculinity that were viewed by white as well as African-American audiences. In mainstream culture, the black male image was defined strictly as entertainer or embodiment of brute strength. Count Basie and Duke Ellington presented suave, elegant sophistication, but perhaps the most common presentation of the actual black male body was in professional sports, particularly boxing, one of the few integrated games. Boxing displayed the semiclothed male body and emphasized physical force. In films and on stage the black male body was most often presented as either primitively masculine or comically ineffectual and emasculated. Even Paul Robeson, perhaps the most famous black performer in the world, was eroticized in his press photos with highly sexualized but passive and nonassertive poses. The display and eroticization of the black body was, for white audiences, a mechanism to reduce its perceived sexual power and make it less threatening.[12]

The United States' entry into World War II profoundly altered traditional gender roles and ushered in a vibrant new era of gay culture. With national peacetime conscription having been initiated in 1940, the U.S. armed forces swelled to more than four times what they had been during World War I. More than 16 million women and men enlisted or were drafted into the armed forces during the war. Most of them were young and single—35 percent of personnel in the U.S. Navy were teenagers. In line with the racial segregation that existed throughout much of the United States, the armed forces were segregated. As these young people left home, they also left many social and sexual pressures and expectations behind. Women and men already secure in their homosexuality found the armed forces free from the everyday social pressures of heterosexuality. Others discovered their gay identities in the armed forces, and homoerotic tensions were unavoidable in the gender-segregated settings. Men, living under the constant threat of death in battle, formed intense personal relationships. These relationships were not always sexual, but they opened up a new realm of same-gendered emotional closeness not granted to men in civilian life. Women who joined the Waves or the Wacs tended to be single, independent, and interested in breaking with the stereotypical restraints of femininity; this led to a high percentage of lesbians in the military. In the workplace, women took over jobs traditionally given only to men. The image of Rosie the Riveter—the female factory worker who was helping the war effort in her boots and overalls—was even promoted by the federal government.

Women's new role in the workplace and military, and the relationships men were forging on the battlefield, contributed to renegotiating of appropriate gender identity and behavior. Women danced with one another and "dated" for an evening out. The prevalence of drag in United Service Organizations (USO) shows indicates how dislocated traditional ideas about gender and sexuality had become. Ronald Reagan himself appeared in drag in the 1943 movie *This Is the Army*.[13]

2. Brave New World: New Bodies, New Visions

THE safety that many gay men and lesbians found in the armed services enhanced the freedom they had already found in breaking away from biological families and communities. After the war, many men and women who had left the isolation of small towns, farms, and rural areas never returned. They moved to large cities where they knew they would find other homosexuals. The emergence of the gay ghetto was vital in mobilizing a cohesive, increasingly visible gay community. As gay men and women began to move to New York's Greenwich Village, Boston's West End and Beacon Hill, and San Francisco's Tenderloin and North Beach, these locations became known as gay neighborhoods. That, in turn, made it easier for other gay people to find each other. This newfound security encouraged more recognizable public dress and deportment. It was now more possible to dress and "carry on" as open homosexuals. Strict personal surveillance could be suspended: lesbians could feel safer walking the streets in slacks and ducktail haircuts, gay men could camp or flirt with less fear of reprisal. While these new gay ghettos were largely white, gay people of color were often more welcome there than in many other settings. These neighborhoods allowed gay culture to flourish, and one of the most direct results was the emergence of distinct gay male fashions.[14]

The presentation of the male body in U.S. culture began to change after World War II. Men returning from the war felt more at ease with
their physical selves. Photos in *Life* and *Look* featured soldiers and sailors
(almost exclusively white) casually shirtless or displaying muscled bodies
while working on a base or at the front. Before the war, it was accepted
practice for men to cover their torsos at the beach, a fashion that changed
when the armed forces, in an attempt to conserve material, issued only
bathing trunks to the troops. Used at first only by servicemen, who also
wore them in public when they were on leave, bathing trunks quickly became accepted as standard male beachwear. This was part of a larger
movement in wartime fashion in which men's and women's clothing was
becoming more overtly revealing and sexual, a response to the more
relaxed sexual mores engendered by the war. Hollywood also began to
display the less-clothed male body. By the late 1940s stars like Victor
Mature, Guy Madison, Rory Calhoun, Kirk Douglas, and John Payne
were routinely appearing bare-chested in films. Not only had the war
made public male eroticism more acceptable, but Hollywood now perceived that female audiences were actively interested in looking at men's
bodies, a tacit acknowledgment of female (hetero)sexuality. There had
always been male movie stars, but postwar Hollywood now presented
men as overt sex symbols: male beefcake film-promotional photography
became a complement to the more accepted cheesecake shots of female
stars.[15]

The new gay male identity that flourished after the war manifested itself in two forms, each a revolt against gender roles. Determined not to
be trapped in the traditional male roles, some gay men loosened up the
masculine image. Others, refusing to be seen as less than men, were provoked to hypermasculinity. Both were deliberate and effective forms of
sexual display and male eroticism.

For many men, postwar clothing reflected the social mandate to join
the workforce and become good providers. Suits and hats were standard
office wear for middle-class men; working men, depending upon their
jobs, wore customized uniforms. Somber grays, browns, and blues were
the accepted colors, and both suits and uniforms were baggy, loose-
fitting garments that displayed the shape of the body but hid the details.

It was in this context that new styles in men's clothing began appearing: casual, formfitting, colorful, and even revealing, they broke down
traditional ideas of how men should look and, more important, be
looked at. Most new fashions for men that exposed, displayed, or orna-

mented the male body in the late 1940s and early 1950s were worn by gay men. Often these clothes could be bought, at first, only in gay neighborhoods. This reinforced the idea of gay men as arbiters of taste and fashion—a continuation of the "dandy" tradition that sought integration into society by promoting a sense of style.

The idea that men could dress sexily—to be looked at and desired—was just catching on, and gay fashions promoted the look. Casual wear like tennis shoes, sport shirts, and sweaters replaced the more formal afternoon and evening clothes for men. Loafers—which prompted the phrase "light in the loafers" as a code for "homosexual"—sporting tassels or "pennies" were common among urban gay men. Gay men—not unlike the dandies of the eighteenth century—reintroduced color into the male wardrobe. Sport shirts and knit shirts, both relatively new fashion inventions, could be bought in light blue, yellow, green, pink, and even chartreuse. Strapped T-shirts—the skivvy shirt of the armed forces—which displayed male musculature to great advantage, were popular and were sold in different colors. Chinos, Bermuda shorts, scarves, and flashy ties all began as gay fashions. Before the war, a watch, tie clip, and wedding ring were the only acceptable jewelry for men; postwar gay fashion promoted neck chains, bracelets, additional rings, flamboyant cuff links, even pendants. Belt buckles, more flashy than functional, were worn on the side for comfort.[16]

These new trends in men's fashion alarmed watchdogs of social morality, who saw them as eroding traditional gender roles and mores. Articles on male homosexuality in the popular press noted in often obsessive detail gay male dress and deportment. Tight-fitting clothes, colors, ornamentation—the perceived feminization of the male—were all signs of social breakdown. But social norms were also threatened by another gay male fashion influence: the hypermasculinization of the male image. Boots, jeans, leather jackets, and caps represented the gay man as rebel. Casual and informal clothing like jeans, rarely worn except by ranchers or farmers before the war, became an urban gay fashion. Robert W. Wood notes:

It wasn't just the wearability of the jeans which commended them; they were also sexy. Tight, cut low on the hips, rugged in appearance, different in style, able to be shrunk to form-fit, and the more worn and faded the better, they quickly became the costume of the homosexual who wanted to look trim, to be a bit revealing in the crotch and the rump, and to feel "butch."[17]

Ankle-high boots, adapted from military footwear, became commonly known as "fruit boots." Leather jackets and other variations on military clothing, such as pea jackets and fatigues, also became part of gay style. This look was soon taken up by heterosexual male rebels in motorcycle gangs, teenagers, and young men in trouble with the law (who were called J.D.'s—juvenile delinquents).[18]

In 1950s culture, the image of the J.D. was closely tied to the eroticization of the male body and homosexuality. The male rebel was a threat to gender, home, and social order. Single, too masculine, and without an attachment to a woman who might domesticate him, the male rebel could only cause trouble. In 1954's *The Wild One*—the epitome of the teen rebel movie—leather-clad, bike-riding Marlon Brando is asked by a frightened middle-class man: "What are you kids rebelling against?" His answer: "What d'ya got?" Brando's wild one was clearly mad, bad, and dangerous to know. The popularity of *The Wild One* was based not on its social insights but on its sex appeal—particularly the sex appeal of Marlon Brando. Reviewers gave a nod to the political implications of the screenplay, but spent most of their time describing Brando's smoldering performance.

For mainstream culture the image of the "wild one"—as well as the fear and excitement it generated—was connected to its implied homoeroticism. Pop-psychology texts of the 1950s made the connection between the social "rebel" and the homosexual. Kenneth Anger, in films like *Fireworks* (1947) and *Scorpio Rising* (1964), also explored this connection. The singleness of the male homosexual—his "predatory" and promiscuous sexual nature and his inability to form relationships—was a salient pathology in 1950s psychoanalytic writing. Men without women were dangerous men; the eroticized male body was a dangerous body. The social illness of delinquency became equivalent to the social illness of homosexuality. In the words of one psychoanalyst, homosexuals are simply "*frightened fugitives from women, fleeing in their panic to 'another continent'* [italics in the original]."[19]

Throughout the 1950s, mainstream culture was construing these images of male delinquency and the flight from women as highly erotic. The young, white male "outlaw" became the symbolic antithesis to the stifling security of institutionalized heterosexuality. Both a threat and a source of vicarious pleasure, the "outlaw" simultaneously broke the law and reaffirmed the presumed natural order of heterosexuality and home. Of course, in this paradigm, women were forced into the dichotomized and impossible roles of "protector of civilization" and "castrator."

If the homosexuality in *The Wild One* was subtextual, James Dean's 1955 star vehicle *Rebel Without a Cause* was gentler in tone, but clearer in meaning. In *Rebel,* Dean's anger toward his dysfunctional family and his confusions about what it means to be a man converged into a nightmare of sexy and emotional teen angst, and the film made connections between juvenile delinquency and homosexuality explicit. Sal Mineo's character Plato is clearly indicated to be homosexual—he keeps a photo of Alan Ladd in his school locker. Dean's relationship with Natalie Wood is less sexual than companionate; when left alone they don't have sex but playact being a middle-class family. Even Dean's character's home life is a classic psychoanalytic case history of homosexual development: close-binding mother, ineffectual father who wears an apron.[20]

The Dean and Brando performances were a revelation. Here was a whole new type of male acting: sensitive, emotional, vulnerable. Dean's character in *Rebel* explicitly rejects traditional male values: "You can't keep pretending you're tough, you know?" he explains to the audience as well as his fellow characters. Brando's wild one, for all his rough exterior, betrays a hurt child inside, afraid of the father who beats him. James Dean and Marlon Brando, along with Montgomery Clift, changed how men were portrayed in Hollywood. Their body language was fluid, their vocal range broader, and they had the ability to portray with strength and grace an eroticism that was pliant and full of promise. When Marlon Brando screamed a hurting "Stella!" in the stage and screen versions of *A Streetcar Named Desire,* decades of stiff, stunted male acting were erased. Not surprisingly, Dean and Clift were primarily homosexual and Brando was a self-proclaimed bisexual. All three actors were nurtured by Lee Strasberg's Actors Studio with its Method, and saw themselves as part of a new, deeply personalized revolution in performing. Their experience as sexual outsiders, and as part of a gay culture that promoted new ways of thinking and acting for men, placed them at the forefront of a new masculinity.[21]

By the end of the 1960s even the idea of what men should look like had altered radically. The bulky, cumbersome muscle-bound male bodies of Victor Mature and John Garfield had given way to the lithe angularity of James Dean and the gracefully fluid, defined musculature of the early Marlon Brando. The youthful—and ethnic—bodies of teen stars like Fabian, Frankie Avalon, and George Maharis began to appear on screen. Tab Hunter, Ricky Nelson, and Troy Donahue—all-American young men—also began to bare their chests, don swimsuits, and pose alluringly in glorious Technicolor. African-American performers were also being allowed more freedom in Hollywood, and while performers like Harry Belafonte and Sidney Poitier were not allowed the range of sexual display young, handsome white stars enjoyed, they were no longer trapped in the stereotypes of earlier years.

As the heterosexual male body in popular culture became more eroticized, criticism in mainstream magazines claimed that the "new" Hollywood males and pop singing stars were effeminate, that they lacked the hallmarks of conventional, no-nonsense heterosexuality. One of the traditional cultural markers of male heterosexuality had been physical bulk and strength: the macho, muscular man whose brawn and vigor created an imposing figure. This was in direct contrast to the stereotypical homosexual, who was boyish, slight, slim, and weak; whose body lacked will, force, and stature. As new, "softer" styles of masculinity became accepted, and its traditional physicalization was questioned, maleness itself was thrown into confusion.

Throughout the 1950s, comic books advertised a bodybuilding program promoted by former Mr. Universe Charles Atlas. In classic comic-book panels the ads portrayed the terrors of being a "98-pound weakling" who continually had sand kicked in his face while the larger, well-built man got the girl. "Let me make YOU into a NEW MAN in JUST 15 Minutes a Day. Yes Sir, that's my job. I 'RE-BUILD' skinny, run-down weaklings. . . . I turn weaklings like these into HE-MEN, REAL SPECIMENS OF HANDSOME, MUSCULAR MANHOOD." The message was clear: Get butch. For boys reading these magazines the *real* meaning of "98-pound weakling" was obvious. The power of the Charles Atlas advertisements was their appeal to queer hatred. Whatever you might be, you did not want to be the "98-pound weakling."[22]

Ironically, the drive to reinstitute traditional markers of heterosexual masculinity through body-building and "physical culture" were fraught with a clear homosexual subtext. The marketing of the muscular male body was not new. Eugene Sandow, world-famous strong man and bodybuilder, opened his Institute of Physical Culture in London in 1897. Two years later he started *Physical Culture* magazine. Since then, bodybuilding had proved to be a profitable business, and its focus was, by necessity, on mostly naked men.[23]

By the mid-1950s, the male body became the center of a cultural war. Professional bodybuilding magazines like *Strength, Iron, Muscle Power,* and *Iron Man* became associated with gay men and gay culture because of their intrinsic homoeroticism. While these magazines were not intended for a gay male audience, their presumed heterosexuality was constantly undermined by their focus on the male body and the invitation for men to look at and admire other men. The magazines, as well as the industry, became marked by a pronounced homoeroticism. Only by promoting bodybuilding as a clear path to heterosexuality—as the Charles Atlas ads did—could this obvious homosexual subtext be countered.

The popularity of bodybuilding magazines for gay men was so great that gay-oriented physical culture magazines—*Vim, Physique Pictorial, Adonis, Grecian Quarterly, TM*—began publishing with little or no health or exercise content. These new magazines substantially drove down the sales of the older ones—an indication of how strong the gay readership of the "straight" magazines was. The association of physical culture with homosexuals became so obvious that the more established, "heterosexual" magazines began printing explicitly antigay editorials, disclaiming any association with gay culture.

The explicitly gay *Vim* and *Physique Pictorial* highlighted the strong connections between homoeroticism and the new attention the eroticized male body was receiving in the 1950s. They also charted startling developments in the presentation of the gay male body. While the heterosexual male body—as represented in Hollywood films and advertisements for clothes—was becoming more pliable, less stiff and physically repressed, the traditional iconography of the gay body was also changing.

Photographs and drawings by gay artists and photographers like George Quaintance, Bruce of L.A., and Bob Mizer were inventing a new image for gay men by fusing the old hetero and homo stereotypes. Traditionally, mainstream culture dictated that "real" men had muscles and bulk, stern expressions, and little grace of movement, and that gay men were slight, slim-hipped, pretty, and swishy. The men in gay physique magazines combined both aspects. Stunning muscular definition and broad shoulders coexisted on bodies with slender hips, flighty hands, and a sense of physical grace. These figures were often engaged in butch activities like wrestling or horseback riding. Sometimes they were placed in rustic or classical settings to explain or excuse their nudity. When compared to mainstream media advertising or films of the time, this early porn is remarkably racially integrated; black and Latino models appear with some frequency. While nonwhite models are not feminized, they were often exoticized, arrayed in Nubian, Aztec, or Native-American attire that highlighted their "otherness." Because whiteness has been universalized, the nonwhite body is never neutral, and when eroticized it becomes, more than ever, "the other" by which the average is judged.[24]

This metamorphosing of the gay male body—an often ungainly amalgamation of straight and gay characteristics—was indicative of how gay men's self-image was beginning to change. Once told that they were sexually, psychologically, and even physically less than "real men," gay men were now gaining a new sense of self-worth and pride. The irony was that while gay men were relying upon a traditional masculine body type to express their new understanding of themselves, heterosexuals were making their own changes influenced by gay culture.

Shifting presentations of 1950s masculinity were a major contributor to the radical social changes of the 1960s. The evolution of a youth culture energized by young people's disillusion with the social and moral status quo, the imperative for more personal freedom, the new emphasis placed on raising and expanding consciousness, and the advent of the second wave of feminism all coalesced in transforming the male body. As the counterculture took root in mainstream culture, traditional gender expectations were quickly vanishing. Women were no longer mandated to wear the codified emblems of femininity: dresses, bras, hats, hosiery. Men began dressing more casually. Personal ornamentation was now acceptable for men, and rings, bracelets, and necklaces were appearing on the new male body. By the late 1960s, the earring—once worn only by women and pirates—began to dot the ears of young, heterosexual men. These seemingly cosmetic changes were emblematic of deeper cultural shifts that underlay enormous anxiety about gender and sexuality.

One of the most resonant images of this anxiety in the late 1960s was long male hair. The young white man's struggle to wear his hair long was a major issue in the 1960s. Clergy, moralists, and concerned parents saw long hair as a sign of rebellion. They were right. Editorials in newspapers and national magazines fretted that this rebellion was against "authority"—a vague concept that included parents, home, school, the military, and the "system." But the actual threat of long hair was its outright rejection of traditional masculinity.

The most common complaint against men's long hair—unceasingly articulated in the media—was that "you couldn't tell if it was a boy or a girl." In the postwar years, short hair was the accepted, even mandated, style for men. The crew cut, a holdover from military regulations, was neat, unexpressive, and hygienic. Long hair on men, a sign of nonconformity since the Victorian age, was still a potent symbol. The Beats of the 1950s sported collar-length, unkempt hair, and the Beatles popularized a working-class British "mod" cut. Long hair had also been fashionable with men in urban gay neighborhoods since the late 1950s. By the mid-1960s, the elaborately constructed pompadour gave way to the freer shag cut. In the early 1960s, gay parlance for men with long hair, or those who were overly concerned with their hair, was "hair fairies." In the popular imagination, long hair and elaborate hair-care were associated with effeminacy and homosexuality.[25]

By the late 1960s, hair became *the* symbol of youth rebellion, and beneath this the specter of homosexuality was always lurking. Antiwar protestors with long hair were attacked for being "girls" by prowar advocates. In 1968, *Your Own Thing,* a contemporary musical version of *Twelfth Night* in which long hair "explains" Shakespeare's gender confusions (you couldn't tell if it was a boy or a girl) was an off-Broadway hit. That same year *Hair,* replete with references to sodomy, fellatio, masturbation, drag, drugs, and group sex and containing a shocking nude scene, moved from downtown to become a Broadway hit.

The cultural crisis of men wearing their hair long was not simply a white phenomenon. As the Black Power movement grew in the 1960s, African Americans, both men and women, began wearing the natural Afro, a revolt against what was seen as imitation white "processed" hair, and a symbol of racial pride. For black men, the Afro was a sign of anti-authoritarian revolt, but its gender meaning was almost the reverse of what it was for white men. The Afro established or reclaimed a masculinity that had been denied black men by white culture; it secured gender identity rather than rendered it ambiguous.

This was the cultural context in which the Stonewall riots of 1969 occurred. The attack on traditional gender and sexual expectations was in full force, and mainstream culture was fighting back. By the mid-1970s, gay liberation and gay rights were being taken seriously by the mainstream press. In 1971, *The New York Times Magazine* printed "What It Means to Be a Homosexual," an article by noted novelist Merle Miller, in which he came out. (Miller was told by his editor that he could be personal but not "proselytize.") Gay rights bills were being introduced in cities across the country, and openly gay men and women were being quoted in news stories as gay men and women.[26]

The media were even beginning to recognize the role that gay culture played in setting trends. Bette Midler acknowledged on *The Tonight Show* and *The Mike Douglas Show* that her career had been started by her gay following at the Continental Baths. Disco was being described in the mainstream press as a gay phenomenon that crossed over to mainstream culture. Nowhere were these changes more evident than in the reshaping, packaging, and marketing of the male body.[27]

Images of the eroticized male, almost always white, became prominent in advertising. Cigarette advertising was one of the first to use the newly eroticized male, often with a homoerotic subtext. Since the 1920s, most cigarette advertising was traditionally aimed at a female audience. When men were targeted they were presented as "sophisticated" (i.e., effeminate). In 1964, Marlboro began its "Marlboro Country" ads. With his sexy, rugged but expressive face, the Marlboro Man told men that smoking and mature masculinity were compatible. The Marlboro ads had a seriousness about them. Wearing western clothes, a Stetson, and often on horseback, this lone man on the prairie invoked the butch masculinity of Hollywood westerns as well as the isolated existential condition of modern man.

By the mid-1970s ads for men's underwear, sporting sexy half-clad men, began appearing. Advertising for men's underwear had traditionally been aimed at women, who were thought to purchase such items for their husbands. While those ads appealed to women viewers, men were now a targeted audience as well. A B.V.D. ad featured a handsome man in T-shirt, B.V.D.'s, and a cowboy hat shaving in front of a mirror in a redwood-paneled bathroom. The caption read: "The Great American Fit for the Great American Male: America Discovers Living Colors by B.V.D." An ad for Great Looks, a sub-brand of Fruit Of The Loom, was even more sexually explicit. Over a photo of a handsome man wearing only tight jockeys and looking alluringly into the camera, the copy read: "Because a Man's Life Should Be Filled with Adventure." In smaller print the ad continued: "It's a style that won't be tamed. Colors that command attention. And the kind of fit that feels fantastic. . . . And it's a whole new spectrum of styles, colors, and fabrics. Just invented for adventure. So slip away from life and into Great Looks." Until then public images of the scantily clad male body had been rare, but sexy underwear ads in mainstream magazines and on billboards radically changed that.

The Marlboro Man and sexualized underwear ads would have been inconceivable ten years earlier. Before male presentation became increasingly eroticized, the older male was not an erotic image, and underwear for "real men" was white and utilitarian. Concern over colors, fabrics, and style reflected the new impulse to uncover and display the male body. These ads also promoted the idea of the solitary, butch man— on a horse in the idealized West, in his redwood-paneled bathroom— who had escaped from the restraints and repressions of "civilization."[28]

The absence of women in these ads is striking. To reinforce a "masculine" atmosphere, the advertising constructs an all-male world. Winston cigarettes ran ads of butch men in workplace situations like construction sites lighting one another's cigarettes and looking into one another's eyes. "This Is Your World. Nobody Does It Better," the ad copy read. The men's posture and proximity create a distinctly homoerotic subtext. An advertisement for Macy's men's department that ran in *The New York Times* in 1980 featured butch-looking forty-year-old men dressed in leather and Western gear—complete with hats—standing at the bar staring straight at the viewer with the caption "East Meets West: Macy's Rugged Western Wear Makes a Lot of Horse Sense." The photo resembled advertisements for gay leather bars like New York's Mineshaft and San Francisco's Ramrod.

These new sexy, butch men were complemented by another image of eroticized masculinity: the sophisticated, European look. The continental, suave male had surfaced earlier in U.S. culture but was viewed by the mainstream as suspect. Well built, but never masculine enough, and displaying too much "style," the European man was reminiscent of the dandy. This image of European maleness, modified by a more rugged, traditional American look, could be seen in the Arrow Collar Man advertising in the first decade of the century. Created by gay commercial artist J. C. Leyendecker, the Arrow Collar Man was square jawed, patrician, strong featured, well built, educated, and elegant. The Arrow shirts fit his body so tightly that his musculature was perceptible. His pegged pants showed off his lower torso and legs. As the U.S. economy became more urban and business-centered, the image was perfect: an upwardly mobile middle-class male who needed ready-made shirts that had class and style. It was a rejection of the ruggedness that had, until now, defined American masculinity. Leyendecker's men were always in a domestic or office setting, sitting on sofas together, reading books or magazines. They were men's men: educated, sophisticated, and sexual.[29]

This version of the Arrow Collar Man faded from advertising during World War II. In the 1950s, he became the company man: middle-class, on the way up, but no different from anyone else. Men's fashions standardized; they did not glamorize. The European male image came into fashion in the 1960s. Foreign films and European designers introduced a new type of masculinity to the United States: beautiful, manicured, aloof, and unashamed to be looked at; his sexiness was in his ability to withhold rather than project attention. Like a precious object in a museum, he was on constant display. This less-aggressive male image resonated with U.S. stereotypes of male homosexuality. The 1967 paperback edition of John Rechy's novel *Numbers* featured a nude French model famous for underwear ads. By 1980, Calvin Klein underwear ads epitomized the Americanized version of this look. Photographed by Bruce Weber, the ads were to define, over the next decade, a gay male aesthetic. The models radiated an effeteness that was contrary to traditional U.S. masculinity, and their overt sexuality reformatted the gay subtext as text. These models conveyed a distinct gay male urban affect, even if their homosexuality was not publicly proclaimed.

The clear emergence of a "gay male look" announced a new stage in the eroticization of the male body: it was promoted in media advertising as a standard, not simply an influencer, of beauty. Nowhere was this more evident than in *Playgirl* and *Viva*. Conceived as a cross between *Cosmopolitan* and *Playboy,* they were lifestyle publications that featured male nudity and were marketed for heterosexual women. Their monthly nude centerfolds, almost always of white men, were patterned after gay male softcore porn. The personality profiles of the male centerfolds also reflected a major shift in U.S. masculinity. The *Playboy* centerfold profile was a juxtaposition of traditional male and female qualities: she wanted to study engineering and help the disadvantaged, and she was a good listener. The men in *Viva* evidenced a similar stitched-together set of desires: he loved cooking, rode horses, and was a good listener.

In many ways, the new heterosexual man was similar to the stereotypical old homosexual: emotional, sensitive, not afraid to explore his "feminine" side, aware of his body, and in touch with his sexuality. Three factors influenced this change. Women, tired of being treated as inferiors, began to demand that men change. Heterosexual men started to realize that their lives were less stressful, more enjoyable, and more fulfilling when they broke the old patterns of masculinity. Gay men and gay culture provided mainstream culture with new alternatives and possibilities for what it meant to be a man.

3. A Crisis of Transfigured Bodies

As mainstream images of heterosexual masculinity changed, so did gay men's images of themselves. Told by mainstream culture they were less than "real men," gay men continually reinvented themselves. Denied access to a traditional gender identity, they improvised and imagined new gender possibilities. Through style, imagination, and wit, gay male culture has always sought new ways of presentation. These shifting styles and shapes are responses to mainstream culture; they are often critiques, and sometimes parodies.

The concept of "drag" has come to mean men cross-dressing as women (and occasionally women dressing as men), but it can be used in a much broader context. Gay men and lesbians in the 1960s would refer to their suit-and-tie or skirt-and-blouse office clothing as "drag." Gay culture has traditionally viewed many aspects of gender presentation as a form of drag. Gay men pretending to be women was drag, but gay men pretending to be "men" were in drag as well. Susan Sontag, in "Notes on Camp," states that camp sees life not "in terms of beauty, but in terms of the degree of artifice, of stylization . . . camp sees everything in quotation marks." This insight into an element intrinsic to gay culture is a productive way to think about gender.

Feminists have asserted that "femininity" was a social convention. As early as 1949, Simone de Beauvoir wrote: "One is not born a woman: one becomes a woman," and contemporary feminist theory claims that all "gender" is socially constructed. Gay men understood this and, in the context of gay culture, had no trouble inventing and reinventing new ways to be "men." The gay stereotypes of the 1950s and 1960s—the swishy queen, the nancy-boy—were fast disappearing. Miss Thing, a nelly, sharp-tongued cartoon character, appeared in *The Advocate* from the late 1960s to 1975, when it was replaced by Big Dick, a likable, not-very-bright, well-hung hunk. Swish was on the way out. This was partly a response to the idea that older "stereotypes" were socially forced upon gay men: that being nelly was the only way to be gay before Stonewall. This idea was reinforced by the homophile and gay rights movements in their quest to present homosexuals as "normal." The cultural power of the stereotypes was enormous: not all gay men were effeminate, but the reigning image of the "queen" took precedence in the mainstream and gay imagination. The queen presented three problems for the gay rights movement. His unmistakable public persona was overtly gay and sexual; he was not like everyone else; and his effeminacy reflected a "femaleness" which, in a misogynistic culture, was designated inferior. Gay liberation, which advocated visible extravagance, understood and valued the threat that stereotypes posed to the mainstream; it valorized the queen as a hero and an outsider. (The tension between sexual visibility and respectability would resurface in the late 1980s with the advent of a more confrontational queer politic.)

In the 1970s, the gay rights movement was not alone in wanting to marginalize the queen. Mainstream culture, realizing that homosexuals were not going to keep quiet or go away, was conflicted. The overt queen caused discomfort, but could be seen as ludicrous or laughable: an imitation man and second-class citizen. The queen was clearly identifiable and thus a source of comfort for mainstream culture. This is why drag shows were (and to a large extent remain) popular with straight audiences. Whatever unease the queen engendered was generally outweighed by the fact that he embodied homosexuality, and thus marked the boundaries of heterosexuality. The existence of "normal-looking" homosexuals was more disconcerting to mainstream culture, since they blurred the lines between looking "straight" or "gay" and created a paranoid fear of the "hidden homosexual"—"the other," who is lurking undetected.

Until the 1970s, the queen was the primary manifestation of a gay public persona. While the butch motorcycle-riding loner and the body-builder often signaled a homoerotic subtext, they were not identified by the mainstream as uniquely gay. By the mid-1970s, homosexuals began to manifest new personal, highly identifiable public images that were understood even by the dominant culture as specifically gay. The softer style of maleness that marked gay life before and just after Stonewall was replaced by gay versions of more traditional images of masculinity. These changes in gay male style were noted even by those hostile to homosexuality and the concept of a gay community. In a 1981 piece in *Commentary*, neoconservative apologist Midge Decter wrote about her history with gay men. In the 1950s she knew many gay men when she summered on Fire Island: "The largest number of homosexuals had hairless bodies. Chests, backs, arms, even legs, were smooth and silky. We were never able to discover why there should be so definite a connection between what is nowadays called their sexual preference and their smooth feminine skin. Was it a matter of hormones?"

Now, Decter wrote, she saw only bearded, rough-looking, and angry gay men walking the streets of Greenwich Village. Interpreting this new image as a form of self-hatred and self-destruction, Decter blamed the gay movement for making easy acceptance of gay identity a real option for people. "What indeed," she writes, "has happened to the homosexual community I knew . . . who only a few short years ago were characterized by nothing so much as a sweet, vain, pouting, girlish attention to youth and beauty of their bodies?"[30]

The joke, of course, was on Decter. The rough, bearded, leather-clad men in the Village probably *were* the harmless, sweet queens of ten years earlier. These men took the butch look of the 1950s and early 1960s and enhanced it, turned it into butch drag. But what Decter observed was also a community breaking out of certain forms of socially prescribed behavior and finding new ways to exhibit self-esteem, and growing up: gay boys becoming gay men. The obvious corollaries were women's refusing to dress and act "feminine" and African-American men's refusing to straighten their hair and wearing Afrocentric clothing.

While the queen still existed, he was now one of several modes of gay presentation. The radical change in the queen's position as an emblem of public gay culture was due to at least two factors. As homosexuality was becoming more acceptable, some gay men wanted to establish themselves as more masculine to partake more easily in the social privileges available to all men (often without considering or understanding how this would affect their individual or collective relationship with lesbians). At the same time, feminism was claiming that women did not have to play the socially constructed version of "femininity," and many gay men understood that this might apply to them as well. In the 1950s and 1960s, the queen was a threat to mainstream culture because he flagrantly violated gender expectations. The new butch gay male images were a threat because, while they adhered to traditional gender presentation, they heavily emphasized male sexuality. While Midge Decter was, on some level, reassured that gay men were still identifiable, the aggressive sexual persona of the leatherman was far less comfortable to her than the less-sexual queen.

By the 1980s, these new images of masculinity, pioneered by mostly white gay men, were evident in gay publications, pornography, bars, neighborhoods, and bodies. (As gay porn and "lifestyle" publications became more commercialized, the images of men of color, more frequent earlier, disappeared.) From the mid-1970s on, the "butch queen," "clone," "leatherman," and "daddy" became common images in gay male life. These new images were blatantly sexual. Black jeans, tight-fitting T-shirts, flannel shirts, leather chaps, vests, harnesses, ripped jeans, and boots were all designed to show off the sexualized male form. A complex scheme of sexual semiotics added to the overtly sexualized nature of gay male presentation. Men who wore their keys on the left were indicating a desire to be sexually "active," keys on the right indicated a desire to be "passive." A detailed "hanky" code—colored handkerchiefs worn in the left or right back pocket—indicted everything from active or passive desires for fucking to bondage to water sports. The attention to detail, nuance, and meaning of clothing and the fetishization of ornamentation signaled an intense need and willingness to construct a new, visible, unavoidably blatant language of masculinity. As intricate as the details of the Victorian woman's boudoir, this evolution in gay masculinity—for all of its aspirations to "natural" maleness—was completely constructed: hypermasculine drag.

The clone look of the mid-1970s—tight jeans, construction boots, flannel shirt, short hair, and regulation mustache—was a manifestation of gay male visibility. It publicly identified men as gay to one another and, because they all looked alike (they were, after all, "clones"), part of a community. In some urban neighborhoods, clones were identifiable as gay men to nongay people as well.

As the last of the baby-boom generation came of age and came out into a world made safer by the gay movement, they needed a style that reflected their sexual desires, as well as their social and economic aspirations. Clones evolved when gay men were finally able to see themselves, socially and psychologically, as "men." The neat, clean, short-hair-and-mustache, and lean-body look was a middle-class, socially acceptable version of the frontiersman. The clone was a nice, safe outlaw, able to express his sexuality in public, but with minimal threat.

The object of gay male desire has changed radically over the last half century. Pre-Stonewall gay male life dictated that the socially sanctioned, culturally appropriate objects of desire for gay men were straight trade, hustlers, and young boys. We see this reflected in the pornography, novels, and personal accounts of those years: *Physique Pictorial* photos, Gore Vidal's *The City and the Pillar,* and the first two volumes of Donald Vining's *A Gay Diary,* all idealize nongay over gay male sexual objects. Of course, gay men loved and had relationships with other gay men, but in a world that denigrated gay men, it was "the other" who had to be idealized. One of the profound changes wrought by gay liberation was the permission granted to gay men to like themselves. It was when gay men—as a group—realized that they were worthy of love that they could love one another, desire one another as appropriate sexual objects.

The clone look, with its emphasis on a gay-specific masculine image and new community identity, set the stage for the emergence of a widespread S/M subculture in the gay male community. There had been a small but dedicated gay male S/M subculture that began in the postwar years. Its existence is detailed in Robert W. Woods's 1960 *Christ and the Homosexual,* William Carney's 1968 novel *The Real Thing,* and Larry Townsend's 1972 *The Leatherman Handbook,* but it was a covert subculture. By 1975, with the publication of *Drummer* magazine, the leather scene was institutionalized in gay culture. The leatherman and S/M culture became quickly visible for two reasons. The first was that the blatantly sexual outfits made S/M shockingly visible: these fantasy costumes made the clone look like he was on his way to a church meeting. The second was that S/M culture was quickly commodified: there was so much to buy. The commodification of "lifestyles" is nothing new, but for gay men—looking for ways to increase visibility—the acquisition of clothing and objects promoting a sense of communal and sexual identity was important.

The social, sexual, and psychological disenfranchisement of the pre-Stonewall years denied homosexuals a sense of entitlement and power. The advent of gay liberation changed this. But the new heady sense of power was often overwhelming, confusing. The widespread popularity and emotional resonance of S/M subculture was due, in large degree, to its roles, rules, and determined desire to "play with" power. These provided gay men with a psychological and communal structure that dovetailed neatly with the need to deal with this newly discovered social, sexual, and emotional freedom.

The "daddy"—an experienced older man who takes tender, loving care of his son and provides discipline when necessary—was a sexual fantasy that evolved into almost archetypal status by the early 1980s. Films like the Gage Brothers' *El Paso Wrecking Corp.* and Arthur J. Bressan's *Daddy Dearest* were emotionally resonant for many gay men. Later, *Drummer* and other porn magazines, including *Daddy,* which catered explicitly to this image, capitalized on the phenomenon. Personal ads from men in their late forties were looking for "daddies" in their twenties; others were from younger men looking for men older than their own fathers, or even their own age.[31]

"Daddy," like drag or leather, was a sexual persona donned at will. The cult of the daddy is the cult of the older man, even if that man is younger. For gay men it is a complicated scenario. Fathers, in our patriarchal culture, represent power and authority. Gay men, by refusing to participate in reproductive sexuality and the replication of the family, have implicitly repudiated the cultural role of the father. On a primal level, male homosexuality is a tremendous rupture in the presumed father-son relationship. Traditional thinking and anecdotal evidence hold that gay men have more difficult relationships with their fathers than their mothers, and much gay liberation theory called for a rejection of fathers, of patriarchy. Why would the daddy—or the older man, even if he's not labeled "daddy" as such—become such a potent fantasy for many gay men?

Gay people have always been in the forefront of reinventing kinship patterns. Excluded from the web of biological family life, they made up their own. "Daddy" is gay male culture toying with the more benevolent aspects of "father" and "family structure": this is the new father—the kinder, gentler, always accepting and loving daddy. On a deeper level, the daddy represents an attempt by gay men to come to terms with their estrangement from their biological families. Many psychologists argue that the process of learning to love begins in the family; for many men, loving the daddy is a way to reimagine and reexperience that love of the father.

The daddy and the eroticization of the older man is also an attempt by gay men to deal with aging. As the baby-boom generation grew older, its choice of sexual object evolved. Baby boomers learned not only to love themselves but also to love and desire men who were like them. While youth continues to be idealized in aspects of gay male culture, as it is in mainstream culture, the impulse to deal with male aging through sexualization is unique to gay culture. Older heterosexual men in mainstream culture often garner respect through money or power, but gay culture's purposeful and active sexualization of the older man is predicated upon an expanded notion of beauty and attractiveness, not material status. It is an example of how the eroticization inherent in gay culture provides a lens through which many aspects of human existence can be viewed.

While the eroticization of the white heterosexual male body brought pleasure to mainstream culture, it also began to cause anxiety. By the late 1980s, male flesh seemed to be everywhere. Advertisements in newspapers and magazines were more explicit than ever. A popular print ad campaign for Johnson's baby powder portrayed young, cute, and mostly naked fathers changing their (naked) babies' diapers. Zest soap ads featured naked men showering, their heads thrown back in ecstasy as the shower head sprayed their faces. Television ads for Fruit Of The Loom showed a young father and three-year-old son in briefs on their morning trip to the bathroom. Tommy Hilfiger ads focused on the knees-to-navels of young men wearing trendy shorts. Gap ads routinely portrayed shirtless teen-boys wearing low-slung pants that exposed their boxer shorts, and, in 1982, Calvin Klein placed above Times Square a huge billboard that featured a sultry model naked except for his well-filled briefs. The Klein billboard—large, imposing, and looming over the most famous urban site in the United States—seemed to symbolize how far the eroticized white male body had come into mainstream culture. The eroticized black male continued to be too threatening, too "sexual" for mainstream viewing.[32]

The commercialization and omnipresence of this new male body also presented problems. As the explicit sexuality of the male model increased, it became necessary to articulate a clear heterosexual context. In the early 1990s, the original Calvin Klein underwear campaign featuring Marky Mark Wahlberg pictured him alone, caressing his body, longing to be gazed upon: the classic pinup of sultry male sexuality. The iconography of the advertising was indistinguishable from the poses of gay male porn: male body as object. Wahlberg became a gay poster boy and gave interviews to *The Advocate* and other gay magazines. He also did solo dance shows in gay clubs. It was telling, however, that while Wahlberg encouraged a gay male audience, he would not remove his shirt when performing in gay venues, although that was a major part of his act in straight clubs. In response to questions raised in both the gay and straight media about Wahlberg's sexual orientation, the second part of the Calvin Klein underwear campaign featured Wahlberg with a woman. While Wahlberg's body and sexual allure appealed to gay men, as well as straight women and men, it was the explicit acknowledgment of the former as an audience that caused cultural anxiety. The old question "Is it a boy or is it a girl?" had now shifted to "Is it a gay or is it a straight?"[33]

While commercial advertising was publicly refiguring the male body, it was "The Perfect Moment," a retrospective of Robert Mapplethorpe's photography—including male nudes and explicit depictions of S/M activity—scheduled to open at the Corcoran Gallery of Art in Washington, D.C., in July 1989, that created a full-scale cultural crisis.

The Corcoran Gallery had received National Endowment for the Arts funding to mount "The Perfect Moment" but canceled the exhibit two weeks before the opening in response to a public-relations scare campaign by Reverend Donald Wildmon, head of the right-wing American Family Association. Wildmon's organizing was so effective that thirty-six senators signed a letter demanding changes in the NEA's decision-making process so "that shocking, abhorrent, and completely undeserving art would not get money." The Mapplethorpe flap continued, and, in April of 1990, law enforcement officials in Cincinnati closed down the Contemporary Arts Center before "The Perfect Moment" opened, to collect evidence for an obscenity charge. Seven photos were deemed "obscene." Six months later, a jury cleared the Center of any wrongdoing.[34]

Mapplethorpe, who had died of AIDS-related complications in March 1989, had specialized in combining highly detailed photographic techniques and blatant homoeroticism. Early collages used hard-core gay male porn. By 1977, he was noted for his studio portraits of socialites, studies of flowers, male nudes—primarily of African-American men— and erotic photos detailing S/M activity.

While the Mapplethorpe controversy focused upon the nudes and S/M images, it was the artist's entire body of work and unapologetic, openly gay life that generated enormous cultural anxiety. Mapplethorpe's public acclaim and mainstream acceptance indicated that many of the traditional restrictions surrounding open homoeroticism and the uncloseting of gay art were disappearing. Mapplethorpe's unabashedly open homosexuality dictated that all of his work—particularly the male nudes—had to be viewed through this lens. The emphasis on the highly eroticized black men in Mapplethorpe's work brought to the forefront the cultural anxiety surrounding the black male body, because while it celebrated that body, it also echoed traditionally racist ideas about black male sexuality. Mainstream white audiences, used to more covert displays of black male sexuality, were made deeply uncomfortable—and even more so because the images appeared in a gay context. Some African Americans, like poet-playwright Ntozake Shange, found the images celebratory because they depicted black men as beautiful. Essex Hemphill, however, claimed Mapplethorpe's photos sexually "objectified" and dehumanized their subjects.[35]

The Mapplethorpe S/M photos, with their nipple piercings, anal penetrations, and bloodied penises, were shocking to many viewers. More disturbing, however, were the classic male nudes and eroticized flowers viewed through the lens of the artist's homosexuality. Here were everyday forms and items transformed, by the removal of the closet, into something new. The threat of Mapplethorpe's artistic vision was that it clearly and decisively influenced all of his work, not just the explicitly sexual material, but the commonplace as well. It was not simply the juxtaposition of the eroticized male nudes and ethereally pure lilies that disconcerted, but the unapologetic implication that the artist's homosexuality influenced both photographs. This was seen by the right wing and cultural moralists as a dangerous sign of the times. The attack on the National Endowment for the Arts was as much an attack on gay visibility and the advances made by gay culture as it was on specific artists and works.

The emergence of the sexualized male body—particularly the gay male body—had become identified by political conservatives and the religious right wing as a primary threat to the social and moral order. Images of drag queens and leathermen participating in gay pride parades appeared in late-1980s, right-wing-funded, antigay documentary films like *Gay Rights, Special Rights* and *The Gay Agenda*. As mainstream entertainments like *Cruising, Tootsie*, and *La Cage aux Folles* popularized images of leather and drag, the right wing was attempting to reinforce the stigma on homosexuality. The public, sexualized gay male body, presented without apology, but rather with unabashed pride, embodied the primal fears of mainstream culture.

The right wing was not alone in its discomfort with the display of such blatantly sexualized gay male images. Conservative gay spokespeople and some mainstream gay rights groups were also critical. They saw the display of drag, leather, and scantily clad bodies as the work of a small homosexual fringe intent on presenting a "bad image" to mainstream culture. As Bruce Bawer noted: "The marchers who make the Gay Pride Day march embarrassing to many homosexuals and disgusting to people like my mother's friend represent the same small but vocal minority of the gay population that has, for a generation, played no small role in shaping and sustaining most heterosexuals' notions of what it means to be a homosexual."[36] This fear that the public sexuality of "blatant" homosexuals would hurt the community echoes editorials of *The Mattachine Review* and *The Ladder* forty years earlier. The politics of assimilation promoted by the homophile groups and parts of the gay rights movement mandated that gay and lesbian sexuality be kept private. Even when simply seeking legal equality, the gay rights movement viewed the politics of privacy as necessary if not mandatory.

This concept of privacy was now no longer possible. By the mid-1980s public discourse had been so transformed by gay liberation and gay culture that open, celebratory displays of gay sexuality and the gay body were not only possible but welcomed. The public, sexualized gay male body was now widely perceived by the gay community as a symbol of freedom and pride.

This emergence of a new, distinctly gay body is only the latest step in a long evolution of transformations that have moved the male body from a rigid symbol of power to one that is more vulnerable and the object of sexual desire. This enormous change was due to the influence of a gay male sensibility that encouraged the overt display and sexualization of the male body. Most important, it decentered a long tradition of power residing in the heterosexual male body and allowed heterosexual men more freedom, and it granted homosexuals the agency to control their own bodies and images.

Eight

Suffer the Little Children

THE STORY IS simple and well known: The town of Hamelin is over-run by rats. A strikingly handsome young man, dressed in multi-colored garments and playing a silver flute, comes to Hamelin and claims that, for a sum, he will rid the town of rats. Rats follow him as he walks through the town playing the flute, and he leads them into the river, where they drown. When the Piper requests his payment, however, the Burghers stall and make excuses. They tell him to return the next day, then once again do not pay him. On the third day, they simply refuse to pay his fee. The Piper explains that unless he is paid he will leave town but will return for the children of Hamelin. The Burghers scoff at his threat and the Piper departs as the townspeople mock him. A year later, the Piper returns and walks through the town playing his flute. Children run into the streets singing and dancing and begin to follow the Piper through the town. As he leaves the town's gates, followed by laughing and dancing children, the townspeople plead with the children to stay, but the children cannot hear them and they follow the Piper into the mountains.

"The Pied Piper of Hamelin" is one of the most lasting and resonant markers of mainstream culture's ambivalence about children and the threat of the homosexual. It can be read and understood in a variety of ways: Is it a frightening myth of the mysterious, single man with unnat-ural powers "stealing" children from their parents, or a cautionary tale of what happens when parents place greed before love? Or is it about the in-nate and understandable ambivalence parents feel toward their children and the parents' simultaneous projected fears and desires to be rid of them?

The tale of the Pied Piper is best known from Robert Browning's 1842 poem—in which all the children, except for a lame boy who can-not keep up, disappear into a mountain that magically opens for them—but it dates back to 1450. Folklore commentators link the tale to the

Children's Crusade of 1212, in which, during two separate drives in France and Germany, seventy thousand children were recruited to march to the Holy Land. Many died, and others were captured by pirates and sold as slaves.

The most striking elements of the Piper tale are the archetypical image of the Piper and the refusal of the townspeople to take seriously the Piper's threat to enchant their children. The Piper is usually pictured in the multicolored clothes of the court jester or fool. Apparently without family or home, he is free to wander. In all versions, he means no harm to the children, who are happy, under his spell, to go with him; his actions are simply to punish the townspeople. As a fool—a medieval trickster—he is the outsider who retaliates against the wrongs of mainstream culture; but he is also the truth-teller, a moral center. Given his unnatural powers, his single status, and the associations of the jester and fool with homosexuality, the Piper can be read as the archetypical homosexual who seduces—recruits—children.

The Piper's image as homosexual seducer or enchanter is mitigated by the ambiguousness of the situation and the fact that the townspeople care more about their money than their offspring. Their ambivalence toward their children causes their loss. This may reflect the history of the Children's Crusade, when parents willingly sent their children away, less out of piety than a desire to shed a financial burden during desperately hard times. But it also reflects a deeper truth. The tale of the Piper highlights Western culture's deep-seated uncertainty toward children and, by extension, the burdens of heterosexuality.

Seen in this light, the sexually ambiguous Piper, with his unnatural powers and freedom, is the projected menace who "steals" the children from their safe homes. He is the personification of everything the parents are not: carefree and unencumbered by family and parental responsibility. The children are happy to leave their parents and be in his company.

But it is also possible to see the Piper as a gay male redeemer who embodies alternatives to institutionalized heterosexuality and its trappings. This liberation of children is clear in the Browning version. The lame boy who is left behind is consumed with sadness because he knows the other children are having fun and he is doomed to remain in Hamelin; for him, the Piper represents freedom and pleasure. And what of the parents? In the standard versions of the tale, they are punished for their greed and distraught with grief. But isn't it possible that they are also liberated? Freed of their children and their parental responsibilities, they are now able to explore new lives.[1]

1. The Innocent Child

THE Piper as seducer is a resonant image. The social and sexual tensions between mainstream and gay culture manifest themselves in many areas, but nowhere do they reach such a volatile point as when children are involved. The image of the predatory homosexual pervades European and American culture. It has been used by psychoanalysts and educators, the Christian right and the far left to demonize gay sexuality for at least a century. It is a deeply ingrained, irrational fear that justifies violent retribution and preemptive legal action. It is a threat that keeps children in their place and reinforces adult control over them.

Religious and social codes have historically viewed children as the justification, and sometimes the punishment, for sexual pleasure. This belief is often obscured, and its essential harshness mediated, by a culturally entrenched sentimentalization of children: they are "blessings," "gifts from God," "bundles of joy." While some children were always wanted and loved, it was the advent of birth control that allowed them to be chosen. Symbolically, children were made to bear the weight of justifying institutionalized heterosexuality. In actuality, children were—and are— experienced as a burden. They take enormous time, energy, money, resources, responsibility, and sacrifices (especially from mothers). Even when chosen and loved, children are a lot of work. Western societies allow little or no room for acknowledging ambivalence over the arduous process of parenting. The burdens of parenting are so significant and pressing that, without social, moral, and legal safeguards—reinforced by sentimentality—the welfare of children would be threatened far more than it already is.

In the past century, mainstream culture's ambivalence toward children has been manifest. Victorian Britain praised the sanctity of children while promoting child labor. A popular genre of late-nineteenth-century U.S. literature written by women and clergymen sentimentally enshrined the sadness and purity of infants' and children's deaths. This literature increased in direct proportion to enormous declines in child mortality rates, indicating, some historians argue, a collective wish for child-death. In the 1950s, the happy images of "Dick and Jane" coexisted with popular fascination with the murderous "bad seed." Campaigns to "save" children from homosexuals, hippies, drugs, and other social menaces in the 1960s and 1970s were balanced by a plethora of popular entertainments like *Rosemary's Baby* and *The Omen* in which children were evil incarnate.[2]

The fears associated with homosexuality and children have many sources. The most socially powerful of these is the fear of sexual abuse. While all studies show that physical and sexual abuse of children is far more likely to occur within the heterosexual biological family, the fear of the homosexual molester is persistent and powerful. The charge of child molestation was used not only against homosexuals but also against other unpopular subcultures.

From medieval times, Jews have been accused of killing, and often sexually mutilating, Christian infants and children, and of using their blood in witchcraft and to make traditional Passover food. This myth is a variation on the "blood libel," the charge that Jews were collectively responsible for the murder of Christ. The theory was that, after killing Christ, Jews still hungered for Christian blood that only the most innocent—children—could provide. The first recorded instance of Jews being accused of murdering Christian children occurred in 1144 in Norwich, England, but the charge remained a major justification for Anglo and European anti-Semitism, resulting in countless pogroms across Europe and Russia.[3]

While these charges against Jews were the most notable examples of child molestation's being used to stigmatize an unpopular minority, other groups have faced accusations. Jesuit missionaries in Japan were accused of child molestation by the Imperial Palace in the late seventeenth century. In the United States, a mid-nineteenth-century campaign by Protestant fundamentalists accused Roman Catholic immigrants of a wide range of sexual abuse, including the molestation of children and use of the confessional for seduction of young people. The charges were so lurid that the books and pamphlets in which they appeared were occasionally banned as pornographic. In the late nineteenth century, Chinese immigrants in California were routinely accused of sexually molesting young girls, a charge so established in the popular imagination that it was the basis for D. W. Griffith's 1919 film *Broken Blossoms.*[4]

In these instances and others, such charges were instigated less by the fear of sexual abuse—which had radically different meanings in various time periods and cultures—than by what the "abuse" and the "victims" symbolized. The dominant culture's fear of "the other" takes many manifestations, and one of the most significant, and illuminating, is the positioning of "the other" as a direct threat to the "innocence" of children, and the consequent need to "protect" children. Because childhood innocence is defined in sexual terms, the threat of "the other" is imagined, by a fearful mainstream, as actual sexual activity. Yet since sexual molestation by "the other" is a myth, discussions about the "abuse" and "protection" of children tell us more about the symbolic position of children in the culture than about their actual standing.

While the charge of child molestation is no longer used against most other groups, the stereotype of the predatory homosexual still exists. The charge continues to resonate, and can only be understood in juxtaposition with the idea of the sexually innocent child. The concept of childhood as being "innocent" of sexuality has emerged only recently in modern thought, but it has become rooted so securely that it now informs much of our thinking about children.

Our current, Western, concept of the child originated in the early seventeenth century, and was firmly entrenched by the late nineteenth century. Previous to this, adults treated children as miniature versions of themselves who had the same needs and duties as their elders. Children may not have had the sexual desires of adults, but they were fully aware of sexual behavior and reproduction. Industrialization, the growth of urban centers, and the rise of the middle class began changing social and gender relationships, and the result was the hierarchical structure of the modern nuclear family. In this new family arrangement, especially for the middle class, children were treated less as equals and more as possessions. By the Victorian era, children of the middle class were conceptualized not as small adults but as preternaturally innocent versions of adulthood: little angels, to be seen and not heard, and, most of all, to be protected from harm.[5]

The evolution of the "child" occurred in tandem with the codification of the categories of heterosexuality and homosexuality. Each of these categories evolved as a means of restricting and classifying sexual pleasure. Heterosexuality was defined by its reproductive capacity. Homosexuality was unrestrained, nonreproductive, immoral pleasure. Childhood was innocent pleasure, devoid of any sexual implication or threat. Children became fantasy projections of "innocence"—humanity uncorrupted by sexual desire.

The innocence of children—their naturalness—is predicated on their not having been socialized to behave in a "civilized" manner. Adults sometimes view this as a positive attribute, the ability to see through social sham, as in "The Emperor's New Clothes." But children's lack of socialization—especially in sexual matters—is also deeply threatening. Unhindered by morality, convention, or even good manners, children are more in touch with, and able to act upon, their pleasure principle than adults. The infant's polymorphously perverse sexuality—the ability to find pleasure in its body without internal or social censoring—is part of what makes children frightening to adults. It is also an ability that is eradicated as the child "matures." The unsocialized child, like the homosexual, is mainstream culture's worst fear and best fantasy.[6]

The main threat posed by children is that they have the potential to grow up differently; that is why so much child-culture has been compulsory indoctrination of the values of church, state, and family. Children have to be taught to be like their parents; it is not a lesson they learn easily.

The potent scare of homosexual child molestation emanates from heterosexual fears that the very *existence* of homosexuality disrupts the heterosexual indoctrination of children. A cartoon in *Christopher Street* in the late 1970s, during the Anita Bryant campaign, ironically summed up the paradigm. Under a banner proclaiming "Recruitment" one smiling queen says to another: "Straight people have to reproduce, they can't recruit." Heterosexuals' fears that a child might become gay, or even *be* gay, are based less upon explicit sexual activity than upon the profound understanding that the homosexual alternative—nonreproductive, unrestrained pleasure—undermines the repressive social structures of institutionalized heterosexuality.

The heterosexual culture's fear of children's becoming homosexual extends to their being sexual at all. The surveillance of children's sexuality is intertwined with the evolution of the concept of "the child." Childhood "innocence" was historically defined as a natural state, but one that needed to be guarded and molded at every turn. For almost a century, child rearing—from Victorian antimasturbation devices to contemporary concerns about children's having access to sexual images on the Internet—has focused on keeping children unaware of their own bodies or sexual impulses.[7]

The fear of the sexual child in our culture is a reflection of how conflicted adults are about their children's, as well as their own, sexuality. Children are often blank screens on which adults project their fantasies. As supposedly presexual or sexless humans, children are viewed by adults as in constant need of protection. Yet, at the same time, they are made to reflect the desires and the sexual and emotional longings of adults. From the emphasis on children in Victorian pornography to designer jeans ads from the 1970s featuring a blatantly sexual Brooke Shields to Calvin Klein advertisements using children today, children have been eroticized, depicted not simply as sexual, but as having the sexuality of adults. The eroticization of children in our culture serves two purposes. The first functions as part of the larger project of heterosexualization, a complicated process that attempts to control or repress the frightening polymorphous perversity of childhood—the unchecked pleasure impulse—and make them "normal." But the eroticized child is also a manifestation of the reverse, the dark side of the fantasy of children's sexual innocence. Having denied children an authentic sexuality with a false idea of innocence, adults then construct a hypersexuality of children to negate that "innocence" and give themselves permission to enjoy their own sexual desires.[8]

2. Father Ritter

I stepped on his foot just a little and said I was really glad he was here, and walked over to the stove to stir the mashed potatoes.

The boy got up, walked to the stove, and bumped into me, except that he didn't move away. We stood there, his right side to my left side, foot, calf, thigh, hip, shoulder pressed together. I stirred the carrots and peas, said I hoped he was hungry, and moved over to the broiler to check out the hamburgers.

The boy walked around the table and into me, bumping me, and did not move away, his left side to my right side, foot, calf, thigh, hip, shoulder pressed together. I stuck a fork into the hamburgers, pronounced them ready. It was great having him around.

There was a blond kid, about 15, leaning next to the wall of a porno theater. Next to him was an overflowing garbage can. He gave me that unmistakable, speculative look, inquiring look. The boy was still there when I passed back the same way at 6 P.M.

I went out again around 2 P.M. to get a bite to eat; there were 17 (I counted them) prostitutes across the street, moving slowly back and forth. It was a warm night, and the streets were crowded with hundreds of night people, washing up and down the littered sidewalk. There was an indescribable sense of violence and electric tension, a fascination, the anticipation of something about to happen.

The boy was still there. We nodded at each other. I walked down 42nd Street and saw seven kids hanging out by one of the porno bookstores. The oldest was 16—obviously a runner for a pimp.

The older kid, the runner, touched me on the arm. "Which one do you want?" he said. "You can have anyone you want for $20."

I said I wasn't into that, but he didn't believe me. He called over one of the kids. "Take this one." he said. "You'll like this one. His name is Nandy. He's 11."[9]

In January 1990, Father Bruce Ritter, the founder of Covenant House, the most famous nonprofit shelters for street kids in the country, was ordered to take an open-ended leave of absence pending the outcome of inquiries into sexual abuse charges leveled at him by Kevin Kite and Darryl Bassile, former male Covenant House residents. The young men asserted that Ritter instigated sexual relationships with them and took them on trips under the guise of counseling, allegations that the priest vehemently denied. The allegations, after thorough investigation by the New York City district attorney's office, were proven true. The media, as well as elected and church officials, professed shock. But more shocking was the fact that charges such as these against Ritter were not new. As the story unfolded, it was revealed that complaints of sexual abuse by teenage male clients against Ritter had been routinely ignored by church officials, coworkers, and the media for more than two decades. How had this happened? And what does it tell us about how mainstream culture deals with sexuality and children?

In 1968, Father Bruce Ritter received permission from his Franciscan superiors to start a ministry to help homeless teens. Working out of two deserted tenements on New York's Lower East Side, Ritter began a homeless shelter for runaways and, with the help of volunteers—with whom he formed a "covenant"—began to provide outreach services to street youth. By 1977, Covenant House had flourished and Ritter, with the help of the Archdiocese of New York, volunteer labor, and fundraising, was able to open a large facility in Times Square to deal with what Ritter saw as the epicenter of teen homelessness and prostitution.

During this time, Ritter perfected a highly effective fund-raising technique. Using personally written newsletters that detailed everyday life at Covenant House and the horrific street lives of his young charges, Ritter also explained how sexual liberation, divorce, and attacks upon the family were destroying America. It was in these letters that he created a public persona that defined himself and Covenant House. Ritter was the lone, embattled street-priest not only fighting pimps, pornographers, and drug dealers, but also waging a war against the destruction of traditional morality and the American family.

Covenant House expanded because of Ritter's efforts. Profiles in *The New York Times* and on *60 Minutes* portrayed him as a paragon of virtue in a world gone crazy with sin and sex. In 1984, then-President Reagan hailed Ritter as "an unsung hero of America" in his State of the Union Address. Ritter was so successful that, by 1990, Covenant House had sixteen homeless centers, a staff of 1,600, and a $90 million budget, over 90 percent of which came from private funding. The rise of Covenant House was inseparable from the emergence of political and social movements of the late 1970s and 1980s, movements which were, in large degree, a backlash against the social-change movements of the 1960s, including the gay movement.

Ritter's fund-raising for Covenant House was predicated not simply on "saving"—in Ritter's words—"throwaway kids" but on establishing a social and political context for the problem. Ritter's fund-raising newsletters were blatant defenses of the nuclear family, chastity, and established morality. These kids were in trouble, Ritter argued, because America had betrayed them by giving in to sexual freedom, divorce, pornography, drugs, and homosexuality. The image of the frightened, crack-addicted, fifteen-year-old hustling johns on a bitter winter night in Times Square was a symbol of the breakdown in traditional family values.

Covenant House's fund-raising material was deliberately aimed at its white, middle-class donors, to the point of dishonesty. The waifish teen destroyed by sex and drugs featured in Covenant House's fundraising material was middle class, white, and under sixteen. Most of the foundation's clients were underclass, black or Latino/Latina, and over eighteen.

Ritter's provocative but sentimental portrayal of children as innocent victims of a world gone sex-mad dovetailed with the emerging religious, right-wing, moralistic tone of U.S. politics: Nancy Reagan's "Just Say No" campaign, Jerry Falwell decrying the collapse of the nuclear family, and Pat Robertson's attacks on militant homosexuals. Ritter became a favorite of the political right wing, soliciting and receiving donations from conservative power brokers who approved of his morality message. Charles H. Keating, Jr., a right-wing funder, antipornography crusader, and the banker who bore much of the blame for the S&L scandal of the late 1980s, lent Ritter and Covenant House $40 million during that decade. Ritter's conservative message helped establish him in mainstream politics. In 1985, he was appointed to the Meese Commission on Pornography, a federal inquiry to determine "the nature, extent, and impact on society of pornography in the United States." The Meese Commission was convened because of pressure from the right wing, in particular Jerry Falwell's Moral Majority and Keating's Citizens for Decency through the Law. Ritter's stand on the commission was decidedly conservative. While other members felt nudity alone was not pornographic, Ritter worried about close-ups of the genitalia of Michelangelo's *David*. He also demanded that the commission take the stand that homosexuality was less "normative" than heterosexuality. He lost the vote 8–2.

Ritter's morality and adherence to strict Catholic doctrine informed the policies of Covenant House. Ritter was a vocal and active opponent of the New York City lesbian and gay rights bill throughout the long history of the fight for its enactment. He spoke out repeatedly against the gay movement as a force that had broken down conventional morality and the American family. These politics were reflected in Covenant House policies. No birth control or safe-sex education was allowed in Covenant House, even though more than 10 percent of the residents were HIV-positive and many worked as hustlers. *The Village Voice* reported that some runaways were refused shelter at Covenant House because they handed out safe-sex material. Condoms were never available to residents.

For all of its fame, Covenant House was seen by many social work professionals as an extremely ill-considered model of youth services. By emphasizing simple overnight shelter over training programs, counseling, and ongoing medical care and education, Covenant House failed to change the lives of its clients. Its bigger-is-better approach countered the prevailing professional thinking that small, neighborhood-based shelters were more effective. Covenant House also broke another strict social services axiom, which was that troubled street kids should be moved out of the neighborhoods they frequented. Ritter felt it was important to keep the shelters in Times Square and similar areas.

Ritter's career and Covenant House were built upon the myth of the abused, throwaway child, a myth readily believed by the dominant culture because it reinforces the ideal of childhood sexual ignorance and innocence by promoting children as victims of out-of-control adult sexuality. The reality of the throwaway child is, however, quite different from what Ritter's fund-raising letters or right-wing figures show.

Covenant House and conservative groups like the National Center for Missing and Exploited Children (NCMEC) used scare statistics that claimed that over 1.5 million children "disappeared" every year. Huge media campaigns, like the "Have You Seen Me" milk cartons instituted by the NCMEC, were launched to promote the idea that huge numbers of children were being abducted. It was often implied that they were forced into prostitution and the making of pornographic movies. The NCMEC statistics made headlines, were unverifiable, and completely at odds with reports from law enforcement agencies. In 1984, for instance, when NCMEC stated that there were fifty thousand cases of stranger-abduction in the United States, Federal Bureau of Investigation records listed only 67. Outcry in the press against the inflated numbers was so strong that the following year NCMEC substantially lowered their estimates.

The plight of runaway teens and the victimized child were real, but the facts were radically different. Contrary to Ritter's assertions that the decline of the American family, divorce, pornography, or homosexuality caused teen runaways, most social service experts claim the cause is sexual, physical, and emotional abuse within the nuclear family.

The ambivalence that the right wing and conservatives in general feel about children, and the family, is made clear in their public policies. As the Republican Party and right-wing fund-raisers decried the neglect of American children and the decline of the family, in the mid-1980s they pushed for cutting programs that helped teens: family counseling, job training, and drug rehabilitation programs, and alternative shelter and housing arrangements. Even as they bemoaned the decline of the family, they were pursuing an economic agenda that placed lower-middle-class, working, and below-the-poverty-line families under more stress. Attacks on welfare and on public relief programs—even those that supported children—and cuts in public education made life increasingly hard on the family. For conservatives, the solution to the problem of runaway teens was a return to traditional morality and supporting social service programs with private funding. Ritter found support for Covenant House by espousing conservative ideas about morality and funding.[10]

The success of Covenant House's fund-raising was based upon Ritter's complicated use of images of the neglected, abused teen who is overtly sexual. Ritter's teens reflect mainstream culture's ambivalence toward "innocence," sex, and children. In Ritter's newsletter, he writes of meeting a fourteen-year-old boy in Times Square: "'I'm a hustler,' he said, and watched me carefully with a total awareness that made me afraid. I liked him a lot. I mean I really liked him. I felt the electricity, the chemistry operating between us. He knew it before I did." Other stories detail Ritter's dealings with pimps, with boys coming on to him sexually, and with the sexual activities of male hustlers.

Ritter's fund-raising technique appealed to the prurient interests of his readers. Most of Ritter's fund-raising stories are about attractive, usually blond, boys and are filled with detailed descriptions of their bodies, facial features, and clothes. In tone and content they are not very different from soft-core pornography. Covenant House staff were often critical of Ritter's eroticized approach to fund-raising, and there were even complaints from donors about the sexual suggestiveness of the material. Ritter felt that this was the best way to raise funds for Covenant House, and, for the most part, he was correct.

Father Ritter's success at promoting both himself and Covenant House was predicated on his ability to simultaneously titillate and moralize using the symbiotic images of the innocent and the sexual child. He understood the ambivalent relationship adults have toward children and sexuality and preyed upon it. Ritter personalized this ambivalence and offered himself as both a model and a solution, and in doing so, he directly addressed the contradictory emotions many of his funders felt in their own lives.

When Ritter's relationships with Kevin Kite and Darryl Bassile were publicly disclosed and he was forced to step down as the head of Covenant House, the mainstream press did not play up the homosexual implications of the story. Ritter, the staunch conservative, never "came out" and thus was never labeled a "homosexual." Editorials in the gay press focused upon the hypocrisy of his antigay public persona and the reality of his personal life, but his numerous personal and organizational stances against homosexuality make sense as the logical continuation of his closeted life.[11] Like J. Edgar Hoover, Roy Cohn, and other right-wing closeted gay men who attained social and political power, Ritter understood that the closet grants access and opportunity and is made more secure by one's supporting conservative social and political positions. But Ritter, in his blatantly sexualized fund-raising approach, manipulated the closet even further by covertly (and not so covertly) revealing his own sexual interest in young men. This allowed his audience to be titillated by eroticized youth while simultaneously appearing respectable and giving the appearance of "protecting" innocent children. Among his other talents, Ritter knew how to work the closet.

In many ways, Father Ritter embodied the mainstream's fear of the "hidden homosexual." He was the secret pedophile who abused power and trust. It is telling, however, that when Ritter's secret life was exposed, the mainstream media greeted it with dismay and sympathy rather than indignation and anger. *The New York Times,* which had supported Rit-

ter until the very end, ran an editorial that spoke of "sadness" and "heal-
ing," and other media presented Ritter's story as a personal tragedy
rather than an outrage. Even after his fall from grace, Ritter retained
goodwill because he continued to voice a belief in traditional moral and
social standards.

But the Father Ritter story conveys another, more complex message.
The wide-scale denial, or excusing of, Ritter's sexuality and actions is indicative of the reality that society's vocalized concern for children, particularly around sexuality, is largely posturing. The state, church, and
other social service agencies cared more that Ritter was giving the appearance of doing good, than that he was actually doing it. Father Ritter
promoted himself as a mythic figure: the crusader against immorality and
savior of innocent children. Unlike the Piper, who rescues children from
uncaring parents, Father Ritter was going to "save" them by reestablish-
ing the moral order and the status quo. But this salvation was devastat-
ingly false, predicated on fantasies of the innocent and sexualized child,
not on the actual lives of children themselves, and it ignored the brutal
reality of family life for many children.

3. Pee-wee Herman and the Gay Playhouse

THE anxiety surrounding gay men and children can be seen even more
explicitly in the media coverage of the 1991 arrest of Paul Rubens, better known as his television persona, Pee-wee Herman, and star of the hit
children's show *Pee-wee's Playhouse.* Rubens and several other men were
arrested and charged with indecent exposure in a porno theater showing
The Naughty Nurse, a heterosexual porn film, outside of Sarasota, Florida.
The immediate fallout, for Rubens, was that the next five scheduled re-
runs of *Pee-wee's Playhouse* were canceled by CBS. The show itself had
been canceled several months before, after a highly successful run of four
seasons.

The news coverage was moralistic and reporters never questioned
why the police were arresting men in the relative privacy of a dirty-
movie theater, where, one might imagine, the exposure of genitals is a
common, even expected, activity. (Nor did anyone mention that gay men
often go to nongay porn theaters to cruise.) *The Boston Globe* referred to
the arrests as a "sting" operation—code for entrapment. The news coverage of the arrest was replete with sly innuendo: "Pee-wee was caught
playing with his pee-wee" was the tag line that one Boston radio host

used. The news coverage implied a perversity about Rubens's situation that would not have been implied if Tom Cruise, Keanu Reeves, or Hugh Grant were discovered in a similar position. The immediate consensus in the media was that Rubens's career was ruined.[12]

Within days the media had taken a new tack. National newspapers and radio and television talk shows like *Good Morning America* began counseling parents on explaining the "Pee-wee Herman scandal" to their children. Suddenly a simple, probably unlawful, case of police entrapment had become a large-scale crisis for America's children.

What caused this media hysteria? Rubens's Pee-wee character began as a comedy club novelty act, was the basis for two full-length films, and ended up as the linchpin on the Emmy-winning *Pee-wee's Playhouse.* There was, however, a sneaking suspicion among media critics and others that there was something not quite right—not quite *healthy*—about Pee-wee and, by extension, about his creator, Paul Rubens.

Pee-wee Herman was a brilliant creation. In his two-sizes-too-small gray suit and his slightly made-up face, Pee-wee was a grotesque man-child, caught between childhood "innocence" and adult sexuality. He was a subversive parody of the epitomical fifties nerd, overly fastidious, uptight, and sexually repressed. It was this repression that shaped Pee-wee's character, for it could barely suppress his sexual energy that kept erupting in nervous giggles and snide, childish quibbles. His most frequent response to any criticism—"I know you are, but what am I?"—was a defensive taunt that betrayed enormous hurt and anger, as well as his own carefully constructed sexual enigma.

Pee-wee's sexuality was neither explicitly heterosexual nor homosexual, and his neither-macho-nor-effeminate affect rendered him less than manly, but not stereotypically homosexual. Because his sexual impulses manifested themselves through innuendo and childishly sniggering jokes, he palpably embodied the tension between mandated "good behavior" and sexual energy. Even when he would ask Tito, a well-built friend who came by to visit the Playhouse, if he could feel his muscles, the effect was less overt homosexual than repressed homosexual. Pee-wee Herman was a perfect comic manifestation of sexual repression. It was both funny and frightening, and not surprisingly adult viewers often found Pee-wee—a living example of how repression distorts sexuality—unsettling. But the irony, and the problem, was that children *loved* Pee-wee. Part of the appeal to children was that Pee-wee mirrored their own anxieties about living in a grown-up world, as well as their fears of assuming and negotiating the burdens of ill-fitting sexual and gender identities.

The *Playhouse* was a world of unlimited imagination. It presented a world where anything was possible, and where nothing had to be justified as productive or useful. In some ways *Pee-wee's Playhouse* was a perverse parody of traditional educational programming. While the typical children's show would try to increase vocabulary by having a special word to be learned on each show, the *Playhouse* also had a "secret word of the day." The twist was that this was a commonly used word and viewers were encouraged to scream wildly whenever it was used. Not only wasn't this instructional, but it was probably highly annoying for parents. *Pee-wee's Playhouse,* not limited by didacticism or ideology, was unique in encouraging children to act out their impulses and question or even mock the world around them.

Gender, on the *Playhouse,* was nonheterosexual and nontraditional: The mail carrier was a young African-American woman named Rheba; one of Pee-wee's best friends was the unbearable Miss Yvonne (whose high-1950s prom gown outfits made her look like a drag queen); Cowboy Curtis, an attractive African-American man in a fouffy Western outfit, looked more like an inexperienced Midnight Cowboy than a children's show character; and Tito, a Latino bodybuilder, would occasionally stop by just to flex his muscles for Pee-wee. With its multiracial cast, *Pee-wee's Playhouse* was the most integrated children's show on commercial television.

Pee-wee's Playhouse was also infused with an overtly sexual sense of humor unheard of on children's TV. Once, after Pee-wee showed an extreme interest in Curtis's boots, the cowboy replied, "Well, you know what they say, Pee-wee. 'Big feet, big boots.'" This was a reference to the old folk wisdom, "Big feet, big meat." In another episode, Pee-wee and Cowboy Curtis go camping and end up arguing about who was supposed to bring the "hot dogs, buns, and mustard." Even Jamby the Genie (a detached, highly made-up face in a box, with a stereotypical "queeny" voice) became sexualized when, during a slumber party, he wished up pajamas for Curtis and, after being thanked, replied seductively, "Anytime . . . cowboy." Every now and then, "Chairy"—Pee-wee's talking chair— would say, "Sit on me, Pee-wee, sit on me." The sexual material on *Pee-wee's Playhouse,* combined with the nontraditional gender affect, the emphasis on male sexuality, and the coded references to gay male culture, gave the show a distinctly gay sensibility.

One of the reasons that *Pee-wee's Playhouse,* and Pee-wee himself, caused such disconcertment among adult viewers was that the world his characters inhabited was supposedly childlike and innocent, which traditionally means not sexual. But Pee-wee displayed that "innocence" as little more than sexual repression. He created a Freudian nightmare world in which traditional developmental stages and appropriate behaviors were thrown askew and mocked. Children, being keen observers of adult hypocrisy and sham, related to the show's subversive subtext. Pee-wee acted out in the way that they wanted; he was constantly struggling against what was expected of him.

It was no surprise, then, that after the first reports of Rubens's arrest the media began dispensing advice to parents about how to deal with questions from children about it. Most of the advice took a decidedly anti–Pee-wee slant. In a *Boston Globe* piece, a child psychologist told parents to tell preschoolers: "He was doing things that were inappropriate. He went to a place that Pee-wee Herman shouldn't have gone to and he did something wrong." National television shows like *Good Morning America* followed suit. The undercurrent to all of this was that "innocent children were being traumatized by Pee-wee Herman." Suddenly, in shocking reversal, it was "innocent children" who were now the victims of Pee-wee Herman rather than Paul Rubens being the victim of police entrapment and an antigay media.

In all of the news reports about Rubens's arrest, however, the issue of his sexuality was completely absent. The mainstream press may not have wanted to discuss Rubens's sexuality because the year before it had taken such a vehement stand against "outing." But the decision was not an ethical one based upon his right to privacy; if that was the issue, they never would have publicized the news of his arrest. The media's decision to "in" Rubens was the result of cultural ambivalence, in which protecting the heterosexual status quo was more important than punishing a gay person. It also dispensed with Pee-wee and the *Playhouse,* while avoiding the more difficult discussions about children, homosexuality, and popular culture.

Pee-wee's Playhouse was an extremely popular show that spawned a whole line of Pee-wee–licensed toys and games. If the mainstream media were to openly conjecture that Paul Rubens was a homosexual, most of America's parents would have to explain to their children that their idol—or rather the creator of their idol—was a gay man. Rubens may not have been a model straight man, but even an imperfect heterosexual was preferable to a beloved homosexual. But while Rubens was not labeled a homosexual, it was important to address the discomfort Pee-wee's *Playhouse* caused many adults. The ultimate aim of the news reports and the use of psychologists to "explain" the Pee-wee scandal was to prove to the public at large that they were right to be made uncomfortable by Pee-wee Herman and *Pee-wee's Playhouse*—that he was, in some unspoken way, unnatural and perverted.

The backlash against Paul Rubens was, in part, a response to the popularity, especially among children, of Rubens's nontraditional imagination. The threat of *Pee-wee's Playhouse* was that it encouraged children to resist the socially mandated rules of good manners, gender affect, and even prescribed sexual behavior. Paul Rubens—and Pee-wee Herman—hit an emotional and sexual nerve. If Father Ritter was the Pied Piper who played by the rules of the system, Pee-wee Herman, with his unfettered imagination, was closer to the threat of the original Piper who offered to take children to a different, less restrained, less repressed life.

4. The Molestation Libel

THE discomfort caused by Pee-wee Herman and the *Playhouse* was, to a large extent, the simple association of children with homosexuality. Whether explicitly expressed or left unspoken, the "molestation libel" runs on a continuum and takes many forms. At its most extreme, it charges that gay men are physically raping children. A less violent version posits that gay men seduce children to have sex. Mainstream culture is always, and vigilantly, suspicious of the homosexual's intentions toward children.

The charge of child molestation in any form carries such weight in our culture that it has effectively prohibited the gay movement from dealing openly and efficiently with the molestation libel. But the molestation libel is not about sexual abuse. By posing homosexuality as a threat to children—a population culturally defined by its innocence and vulnerability—mainstream culture stigmatizes it. The molestation libel is a mechanism of social regulation used to reinforce the closet. This has been incredibly effective. Lesbians or gay men who deal with children in any capacity—as parent, teacher, camp counselor—are immediately suspect. The sexuality of gay or lesbian parents has been, and still is, an issue in child custody cases. The circular construction of the molestation libel makes it unavoidable: The charge is so grave that any gay person charged with it is undefendable; it is so widespread that any person presumed to be homosexual is open to accusation.

How did the molestation libel become so potent and pervasive? The neglect and abuse of children is rampant in our culture. Children are beaten, maimed, and murdered at an astounding rate. Statistics show that this occurs, overwhelmingly, within the nuclear and extended heterosexual family. Child abuse has historically been denied, kept secret, or—when practiced in "moderation"—even approved of as appropriate discipline. Because the family is perceived, and lauded, as the site of safety and nurturance for children, the reality of wide-scale abuse within it has been practically inadmissible. Recently, however, the existence of such abuse has become so clear as to be undeniable. Children are also sexually abused—coerced into sex by adults—and this happens as well, overwhelmingly, within the biological and extended family network.[13]

The acknowledgment of all this abuse has not, however, led to a critique of the traditional family itself. Neither has it called into question the cultural system that mandates reproduction as the justification for sexuality, marriage as the only venue for sexuality, and the nuclear family as the only arrangement for raising children—stifling, repressive conditions that are at the root of child abuse. Because prevailing structures of sex, gender and reproduction go unquestioned, it is necessary to displace or project the blame onto some other group. Homosexuals, who are seen to exist outside of the accepted system of sexuality and reproduction, become the obvious scapegoat.[14]

As a way of containing the threat of homosexuality, mainstream culture constructs it into the most menacing scenario available: sex with children. In the same way the blood libel led to the belief that Jews killed Christian children because they represented the purity of Christ, homosexuals are thought to abuse children sexually because they represent sexual innocence.

Despite all evidence to the contrary, the myth of the homosexual molester persists. The power of the molestation libel is so strong that many gay people would rather hide the importance of sexuality in their lives than risk being seen as molesters. The problem is compounded by the gay movement, which has taken a defensive position and downplayed sexuality as central to gay identity. By denying the obvious differences between heterosexual and homosexual activity, the gay community appears duplicitous, because mainstream culture knows that "We are just like everyone else" is a lie.

This defensive position denies the importance of sexuality to gay identity, and has had enormous ramifications for the gay movement. Foremost has been the reaffirmation of the social paradigm in which gay people are encouraged, in obvious and subtle ways, not to be open about their sexuality, particularly in any situation that concerns children. A striking example of this is seen in how the recent phenomenon of gay families has been presented in gay culture.

5. The Family "Reinvented"

IN the past ten years, openly lesbian women and gay men have increasingly chosen to be parents and raise families. Gay families were, by their nature, disruptive to the idea that "families" had to be heterosexual; for many conservatives, they were an assault on traditional family values. While there has been varying but steady success in securing the legal standing of gay parents, the cultural presentation of gay families in the media has been overwhelmingly positive. Newspapers and magazines have increasingly been covering gay families in lifestyle articles. These portrayals have been sympathetic to gay parents, their main message being that there is very little difference between "gay families" and the traditional heterosexual family. This eradication of difference can only happen in the absence of any discussion of gay or lesbian sexuality. The reality is that positive media portrayals of gay families are dependent upon hiding and closeting broader questions of gay sexuality.

This eradication of gay sexuality occurs in gay culture as well. The most visible manifestations of the new gay family here are gay-themed books produced for children of gay parents: *Gloria Goes to Gay Pride*, *Heather Has Two Mommies*, *Daddy's Roommate*, and *Uncle What-Is-It Is Coming to Visit!!* Books produced for children of lesbian and gay families, in an attempt to offset homophobic assumptions about the parenting abilities of lesbians and gay men, are glowingly positive in their depictions of gay family life. The problem, however, is that they also reduce the "gay family" to simply a replication of the traditional heterosexual family: except for same-gendered parents there is nothing unique about it.

In *Heather Has Two Mommies*, Mama Jane and Mama Kate, the title character's parents, are white middle-class women who live in an idealized suburban home complete with an apple tree in the front yard and a pet cat and dog named Gingersnap and Midnight. The conflict in the book centers on Heather's discovering that other children have fathers. Molly, her play-group teacher, helps her understand that there are many kinds of families and that one is not better than another. The emphasis here is on families being different but equal, although, except for the gender of the parents, there is no difference.

Gloria Goes to Gay Pride shares the same preoccupation with this idea of "difference." Little Gloria, her Mama Grace, and her Mama Rose all go off with their dog Butterscotch to the gay pride parade, where they meet friends, listen to speeches, and buy things. *Gloria* takes great pains to communicate the idea of difference here—Gay Pride is a holiday like Valentine's Day, Halloween, or Chanukah, and some of the characters prefer to eat their potato latkes with sour cream while others prefer applesauce. When Gloria, Grace, and Rose are confronted with dour Christian fundamentalists holding signs that say "Gays Go Away," the little girl is told: "Some women love women, some men love men, and some women and men love each other. That's why we march in the parade—so everyone can have a choice."

Like the idea of difference, "choice" here is presented in its lowest common denominator. It is as much a choice to use applesauce as a condiment for latkes as it is to be a lesbian. None of these books shows much physical affection between the gay parents. This stands in sharp contrast to the increasing depiction of heterosexual affection, and issues of sexuality, in other children's books. *Gloria Goes to Gay Pride* advocates giving women the choice to be "lesbians" but refuses to deal with what that choice is about. The presence of antigay fundamentalists potentially raises the serious, and ultimately unavoidable, issue of what it is about gay people that others find objectionable. But this is not discussed. Even the gay pride event is reduced to its most palatable. *Gloria* spends three sentences describing what the gay pride parade means, and three *pages* detailing things that you can buy at the event.[15]

These books are written for young children and have built-in limitations on complexity. They all, however, labor under the burden of attempting to salvage "family" from the New Right's ideological agenda. They do this by establishing and reinforcing the respectability and appropriateness of gay and lesbian families by casting them in a standard, mainstream media, white middle-class image. All of the families have two parents and are economically comfortable. While many gay families might fit this model, the existence of gay families should not have to be justified by the example of those most acceptable to mainstream culture.[16]

Books written for older readers convey these same messages, but in more detail. *Uncle What-Is-It Is Coming to Visit!!* presents readers with a scenario that replicates heterosexual and gender normality. It is as non-threatening as it is simplistic. Tiffany and Igor are a pair of middle-class white kids excited that their Uncle Brett is coming from London to stay with them. Igor asks a "boy" question: "Does Brett like baseball?" Mom explains, yes, he was on his high school team. Tiffany then asks the proverbial "girl" question: "Is he married?" Mom confesses that Brett is "gay." Before she can explain what that means she has to rush back into the kitchen. Igor and Tiffany wander the neighborhood until they are forced to tell the local bullies—Shelby and Waldo—that their uncle is gay. The two older boys, dressed in dirty and torn clothes, repairing a car—traditional signifiers of the working class—proceed to call Brett a "fag" and a "queer." With the help of a photo of a gay pride parade from the local newspaper, Shelby convinces Igor and Tiffany that all gay men want to be women and dress up like Carmen Miranda or wear black leather, dark glasses, chains, and chaps just like the Hell's Angels. Curiously, Waldo even knows that they are called "leather queens." That night the children's dreams are haunted by grotesque images of bearded muscle-men in dresses and Carmen Miranda clones in tight jeans and biker boots. When Brett appears the next day he is a well-dressed, pleasant-looking, clean-shaven guy who likes baseball, bakes cakes, and explains that gay men are "just guys who fall in love with each other instead of with women."

Of all of the books produced about gay families *Uncle What-Is-It Is Coming to Visit!!* is the most determined to present gayness as an insignificant difference, a difference all but eradicated by Brett's respectability and Tiffany and Igor's middle-class status, and reinforced by the dirty, working class images of the antigay Shelby and Waldo.

The gay images that Shelby and Waldo conjure up are accurate images of some gay men, but because *Uncle What-Is-It* is predicated on presenting respectable, "positive" images of gay men, the drag and leather queens become grotesques. And, in the world according to *Uncle What-Is-It,* they *are* grotesques.

Uncle What-Is-It is so determined to present the acceptable image that it is willing to ridicule the sexuality and dress of some gay men to bolster the proper, respectable middle-class belief that gay people are *just* like everybody else. Although *Uncle What-Is-It* is ostensibly critiquing how mainstream society uses outré images of gay sexuality to reinforce stereotypes, it uses those images in exactly the same way: to produce a sense of revulsion against what is not "normal." This is a pity, because *Uncle What-Is-It* might have incorporated these images in a charming and witty manner. Kids love to dress up, to make-believe, to invent alter egos and alternative lives. Imagine if—after being told about drag queens and leather queens—Igor and Tiffany invented their own dress-up fantasies, their own extra-normal identities. Instead, they merely reflect the same knee-jerk responses the straight world exhibits. *Uncle What-Is-It Is Coming to Visit!!* would have been a more inventive and challenging book if Igor and Tiffany were entranced by the drag and leather queen images and were sorely disappointed at how dull and ordinary their uncle was.

These books for children of gay families are a response to the right-wing attacks on the intrinsic sexual nature of gay culture and identity. They set out to prove that gay people are just like everyone else, and that sexuality is negligible. The books do, however, speak about love. Uncle Brett's explanation in *Uncle What-Is-It* is emblematic of how gayness is constructed in these books. The unnamed boy narrator in *Daddy's Roommate* learns that "being gay is just one more kind of love [and love is the best kind of happiness]." These sentiments are engaging and understandable to children, and the concept that relationships might be based upon "love" is an important one for children to learn. But the ultimate effect in these books for gay families is that "love" is not viewed as a complement to sexuality or even as an extension of it, but rather—in a culture that constantly denies children access to information about homosexuality—as something that eradicates sexuality. Ironically, this message of eradication leaves children even more vulnerable to the lies and misperceptions about homosexuality perpetrated by mainstream culture. Most children's books do not deal explicitly with sexuality—although more adventuresome ones do—but the sole portrayal of gay lives in these books is family bound. Only *Gloria Goes to Gay Pride* gives any indication that gayness can exist outside the family. By positing gay family life not only as another "choice" but also as the alternative to conventional images of gay culture, these books do not allow children to imagine a gay world outside the family. In an attempt to make homosexuality palatable—to their readers as well as to mainstream culture—these books privatize it within the context of the already privatized nuclear family.

Books for children in gay and lesbian families do not exist in isolation. The wealth of books and articles from the gay and the mainstream press also shows an almost universal refusal to deal with issues of sexuality and the new gay family. The gay family is presented as a new model for conceptualizing homosexuality. Often there is a masked hostility to a more visibly sexual gay culture: "We are about much more than barhopping and partying," states a gay man who has adopted two children with his lover. But none of the articles faces forthrightly the tensions between a newly constructed homosexuality that relies on the traditional structures of the family and one that acknowledges the centrality of sexuality to gay identity. One of the few attempts to examine these tensions ends in dismayed confusion. "I'm going to hold off on the explanations and finesse the situation a bit," writes a lesbian afraid her seven-year-old son might ask what a dildo is. "It may not be the most liberated approach, but, I guess for now, there's just going to be one more dildo that will remain a hot dog."[17]

The emergence of the child-centered gay family has not encouraged new or innovative discussion of the social constructions of sexuality and childhood, but rather has suppressed it. This is because the traditional nuclear family structure—even when populated by gay people—prioritizes children over personal autonomy, and reproduction (either biological or adoptive) over sexuality. The idea that gay men and lesbians raising children have "reinvented" the family is inaccurate. In many ways, gay and lesbian families have challenged prevailing notions of what a family is, socially and legally, but the family's basic structure is still in place. Bumper stickers like "Gay Families Practice Family Values" and "Family Values Are Gay Values" indicate an attempt to subvert the religious right's antigay language, but they also indicate the underlying conservatism of how gay families have been conceptualized.[18]

Beneath the discomfort with the gay family and the terror of the molestation libel is, for mainstream culture, a more primal anxiety: the fear of gay children. That children or teenagers might have homosexual feelings and might even—as youths or adults—admit these feelings and come out is unimaginable to most heterosexuals. The concept of the homosexual child completely disrupts the heterosexual model that informs so much of mainstream culture: gender, marriage, reproduction, family. Heterosexuality is construed as "natural" because it is reproductive: homosexuality is, by extension, "unnatural." The existence of the homosexual child indicates that heterosexuality may not be as natural as presumed. On a deeper level, the cultural presence of the homosexual child indicates a failure of heterosexuality to naturally reproduce itself.

The existence of gay children and young people has escalated the cultural war over homosexuality. If adults fear children because they are unpredictable and represent the possibility of difference, the gay child profoundly embodies the refusal to conform. Like homosexuality itself, the gay child represents a willful, radical break from the heterosexual model that underlies mainstream culture.

6. Recruitment

CHILDREN have been seen as a battleground by the religious right and conservatives since Anita Bryant's "Save Our Children" campaign and the Briggs Initiative in California in 1978. The response to the fear that children might be gay is twofold. The first is to blame gay people and the gay movement for "recruiting" children into homosexuality.

The idea that gay people "recruit" children to be homosexuals has a strong hold on the popular imagination. The word was not used to describe interactions between homosexuals and young people until the mid-1970s, when it replaced the more commonly used "seduction" and "corruption." The concept of recruitment was a response to the emergence of a gay movement—described by the mainstream press and then conservatives as "militant"—that promoted the radical idea that "Gay is good." The military implications of "recruitment" reflected the perception that the new gay movement had created a state of war between homosexuals and heterosexuals.[19]

In a sense the idea of recruitment was an improvement over "seduction" or "corruption" because it allowed the possibility that "recruits" might be won over by arguments, no matter how insubstantial, rather than tricked into homosexuality by sexual wiles. "Recruitment," by recognizing the existence of a gay movement, acknowledged a political facet to homosexuality that mainstream culture had not conceded until then. But the political context of gay "recruitment" escalated the social tensions generated by homosexuality.

While the concept of recruitment drew, almost humorously, upon a specific military image, its real agenda quickly became evident. Anita Bryant, in her "Save Our Children" campaign, proclaimed in a full-page newspaper advertisement that "the recruitment of our children is absolutely necessary for the survival and growth of homosexuality." For Bryant, the existence of openly homosexual teachers created the potential for such recruitment; she feared that gay and lesbian educators would "teach homosexuality." The concept of recruitment quickly broadened. The religious right and political conservatives saw any positive depiction of homosexuals in the media as proselytization. "Recruitment" came to signify the simple acknowledgment of homosexuality in a nonjudgmental context. The bottom line for those who considered homosexuality immoral was that any gay or lesbian visibility became synonymous with recruitment.

Mainstream culture's second response to the fear of the gay child is to step up the surveillance and control of children's lives and education. This is the reason behind the right wing's reaction to progressive attempts to institute progay curricula in public schools. In the last ten years, there have been attempts by school boards as well as gay grassroots organizers throughout the United States to promote organized, nonjudgmental classroom discussions of homosexuality, and to implement AIDS education programs that convey accurate, nonmoralizing safe-sex information.

Such programs have met with varying degrees of success. The most notable failure, however, was the 1992 attempt by Joseph Fernandez, then chancellor of the New York City school system, to implement "Children of the Rainbow," the first-grade portion of the multicultural Rainbow Curriculum, which dealt with, among other issues, gay and lesbian families. "Children of the Rainbow" acknowledged that a potential for homosexuality in students exists, and it was written accordingly: "Teachers of first graders have an opportunity to give children a healthy sense of identity at an early age. Classes should include references to lesbians and gays in curricular areas and should avoid exclusionary practices by presuming a person's sexual orientation, reinforcing stereotypes, or speaking of lesbians and gays as 'they' or 'other.'" "Children of the Rainbow" listed *Heather Has Two Mommies* and *Daddy's Roommate* as possible books to be read in the classroom.

While the curriculum was still in the recommendation stages, a coalition of right-wing community groups and the New York Archdiocese lobbied against it. A flyer from the Family Defense Council, a conservative group that opposed the curriculum, stated: "We will not accept two people of the same sex engaged in deviant sex practices as 'family.' . . . In the fourth grade the Chancellor would demonstrate to pupils how to use condoms . . . and refers to anal sex. . . . He would teach our kids that sodomy is acceptable but virginity is something weird." Despite support from the mayor, and the Multicultural Advisory Board, the Rainbow Curriculum was not implemented and Fernandez was forced out as chancellor.[20]

The fight over "Children of the Rainbow" was emblematic of similar fights in other school districts, but what distinguished the New York City battle was that the curriculum was written with the understanding that it would benefit young students who might identify as gay at some point in their lives. This radical stance articulated the worst fears of the conservative and religious opposition.

The gay community has always known about the existence of gay children and teenagers. Many gay people will admit to "knowing" they were "gay" or had gay sexual desires at a very young age, even if they did not come out until much later. Before there was a gay movement, informal networks of older gay men and lesbians helped and advised gay teenagers who had no other place to turn. In the past fifteen years, the gay movement has taken a more institutionalized approach to gay youth. Organizations like Manhattan's Hetrick-Martin Institute and Los Angeles's Project Ten have recognized the need for services and support for gay and lesbian youth. The increase of Gay/Straight Alliances and other support groups in high schools, and of curricula that recognize and discuss gay sexuality, are all important steps in acknowledging the presence of gay youth.

This new acknowledgment of gay teenagers is an important step for the gay community. In the past ten years, the emphasis on gay teens has established in the public imagination the idea that gay teenagers exist and have specific needs and problems. Advice columnists in the mainstream media, such as Ann Landers and Beth Winship, routinely answer questions from young lesbians and gay men, although their "advice" is usually to wait before having sex. The conservative and religious-right response to the acknowledgment of gay youth has been strong. Local school boards have been pressured to stop any educational programs that "promote" homosexuality. In Utah, the state legislature has forbidden the formation of all student groups in order to ban Gay/Straight Alliances or support groups for gay students in high school. The backlash to the Gay/Straight Alliance was so great that other students formed SAFE—Students Against Fags Everywhere. Other school boards have censured teachers for using "gay materials," including Nancy Garden's young adult novel *Annie on My Mind,* E. M. Forster's *Maurice,* and Shakespeare's *Twelfth Night.*

To a large extent, however, acknowledgment of gay teen identity has been divorced from the concept of a sexual identity. The Massachusetts Safe School program was instituted to combat violence against gay teens in schools but was expressly prohibited from influencing curriculum or discussing sexuality. Other programs have been focused upon the need for peer support but have been prohibited from discussing, or even allowing students to discuss, issues of sexuality.

This denial of gay teenage sexuality is, in part, a result of the gay movement's refusal to deal honestly with sexuality. And while some educators and health professionals in the mainstream are willing to admit the existence of gay teen identity, they have a much harder time with that identity manifesting itself in sexual activity. Books aimed at a gay teenage audience, such as *Two Teenagers in Twenty: Writings by Gay and Lesbian Youth*, edited by Ann Heron, have almost no discussion of sexuality. Even novels about and for gay teens almost never deal with sex, or depict their protagonists in sexual relationships. In the few that do, such as Aidan Chambers's *Dance on My Grave*, more often than not one of the partners dies. Even gay male sex manuals, safe-sex guidelines, and prevention pamphlets do not address the specific sexual problems of young people.[21]

The hesitancy of mainstream and gay media to portray gay teenage sexuality was shaped by the power of the molestation libel and the concurrent desire of some in the gay movement to project a desexualized image of gay culture—a politics of privacy—especially in relation to topics that would be likely to draw more criticism from the right wing. In the opening chapter of *A Place at the Table*, Bruce Bawer writes about seeing a fifteen-year-old boy in a bookstore in Grand Central Terminal furtively looking at gay magazines and newspapers. When Bawer sees him glancing at advertisements that feature drag queens and men in leather, he has the urge to tell the boy, "Don't think those pictures of leathermen and cross-dressers and nipple clamps are what gay life is all about. They're not." These images, Bawer adds, "had provided ammunition to gay-bashers, had helped to bolster the widely held view of gays as a mysteriously threatening Other, and had exacerbated the confusion of generations of young men . . . attempting to come to terms with their homosexuality. . . ."

Bawer's presumption is that the young boy—whom he has never seen before and does not know, but assumes is "shy and sweet-natured . . . the much-loved son of a decent family"—would be so frightened by images of overt gay male sexuality that he would panic and think, "But this isn't *me*." This conjecture is indicative of how readily the assimilationist trend in the gay movement would separate sexuality from gay identity and from manifestations of gay culture. For all Bawer knows, the young man might know exactly who he is, and be very interested in the various sexual photos in the newspaper.

The explicitness of sexuality in gay culture is emblematic of its importance in the formation of gay identity. It is also a lifeline to gay teenagers and children who have almost no access to materials explaining or promoting gay sexuality. While mainstream culture offers sexual materials to heterosexual teens, the sexuality of gay teens is rarely addressed. There is also much in mainstream culture that explicitly negates or vilifies gay sexuality. For gay children and teenagers growing up, often isolated within an un-understanding or hostile biological family, access to gay materials, including sexual materials, is crucial. Often gay and lesbian materials are unavailable in local stores or libraries, and often it is illegal to sell sexual materials to people under eighteen. (This barrier is augmented by the reality that most gay youth under the age of twenty-one also have no access to gay public meeting places like bars, clubs, and baths.) The politics of privacy, a hallmark of the conservative elements of the gay movement, runs the risk of damaging young gay people severely by depriving them of information that is crucial to their lives.

The culture war over the sexuality of gay children and teens is being fought on two fronts. The first is a battle for the freedom of gay children and teenagers to live unthreatened and productive lives. This cannot happen while the very idea of gay children produces a panic-and-fear response in mainstream culture. It cannot happen when gay culture and the gay movement refuse to take the lives and sexuality of gay teens seriously. But the fear of the gay child is a magnification of the fear and distrust generated by all children: that they will be different, that they will not conform, that they will not be accurate "reproductions" of their parents' lives and social norms.

The second battle is the fight for complete gay and lesbian visibility: to be able to portray gay culture and the lives of gay people openly—in the media, in politics, in schools. This exposure would mean that, by necessity, gay people and gay lives will simply be a public presence, an option. This is what a conservative politic would call "recruitment." If recruitment means offering an identity that will give the strength to fight back and assert oneself, if it means presenting an honest, reasonable, nourishing version of homosexuality and gay life, then the gay community does recruit. But the tactics of recruitment seem mild and fairminded when compared to those of heterosexual culture, which has consistently and with enormous pressure used what amount to impressment and the draft to force young people, often against their will, into the service of heterosexuality.

The conflict over children and homosexuality is predicated on the idea that the traditional nuclear family is an intact, nurturing place for both adults and children. Homosexuality and homosexuals are seen as destroying the nuclear family, as disrupting the natural order of heterosexuality, and as corrupting innocent children. Yet repeated studies show that physical and psychological violence has become a staple of nuclear family life, and that this violence is on the increase. Studies also show that parents in all economic classes experience, at various times in their lives, the responsibilities of family and children as burdens—a result of an emotionally and economically restrictive family structure. The traditional family as it exists today is not a safe place for children or, for that matter, adults.[22]

The Pied Piper—the enigmatic man who removes children from their biological families—has always been surrounded by ambiguity. The frightening, mysterious stranger who destroys the unity of the family, he is also a joyful free spirit. In the original tale, the children—whose parents have not cared enough for them to take the Piper's threat seriously—end up happy as well. The Piper today is gay culture offering an alternative to the strictures of the gender roles, the traditional family, and heterosexuality. The liberation of sexuality and children might well lead to the liberation of parents as well.

Nine

The Construction of a Pleasure Class and the Marketing of Homosexuality

1. Special Rights of the Pleasure Class

T HE RISE OF a public and politically aggressive gay movement engendered a defiant, well-orchestrated backlash from members of the conservative right, which viewed it not as a movement to secure basic civil rights but as an organized attack on traditional morality and the family. More important, in their eyes, the gay movement promoted nonreproductive sexual behavior—unlicensed pleasure—as normal, healthy, and socially beneficial. The right's attack on homosexuality and gay rights takes many forms, but its most potent and compelling organizing tactic is to make the argument that homosexuals, in seeking antidiscrimination legislation, are demanding "special rights."

Based on the claim that homosexuals are already protected by existing U.S. laws, the "special rights" argument was central to the 1992 passage of Colorado's antigay Amendment 2, which banned enactment of gay antidiscrimination laws and was convincingly used by right-wing operatives in Oregon and Maine, where similar measures failed by narrow margins in 1992 and 1995.[1]

The appeal of the "special rights" argument was driven by the idea that gay man and lesbians did not need "special rights" because, far from being disenfranchised, they already were wealthier, had better jobs, more leisure time, and more disposable income than almost any other group in the U.S. economy. This aggregate of images implied that homosexuals were a pleasure class with few responsibilities or burdens. A pamphlet produced by Colorado for Family Values (CFV), headlined "ARE GAYS OPPRESSED? YOU DECIDE!" served as a prototype for the dissemination of this idea of gay affluence and advantage:

Gays often claim that they need special rights in the workplace in order to have economic equality. But records show that even now, they already enjoy economic superiority over the rest of America.

On July 18, 1991 the Wall Street Journal reported the results of a nation-wide marketing survey about gay income levels. The survey reported that gays' average income was more than $30,000 over that of the average American. Gays were three times more likely to be college graduates. Three times more likely to hold professional or managerial positions. Four times as likely to be overseas travelers. These are people with tons of discretionary income!

Sound like an oppressed minority to you? Most minorities who rightfully enjoy civil rights protections would love to average $55,430 in household income. These statistics show that economic disadvantage—the smoking gun of oppression—simply isn't true of gays.

Line-graph comparisons of "gay income" to "average" and "disadvantaged African-American" income made the case even stronger: the average "gay income" was $55,430, that of the "disadvantaged African American" was $12,106; 66 percent of gay people had traveled overseas, fewer than 1 percent of African Americans had done so.

For many in the mainstream, the "privileged economic status" of homosexuals was conflated with their already established view of gay people as pleasure seekers and sexual libertines. (No distinction was made between gay men and lesbians, even though lesbians, as women, had far less earning power than men.) The statistics cited by the CFV to demonstrate gay people's economic advantage were not simply about earning power; they were concerned with leisure time and seeking out pleasure—number of vacations taken each year, number of concerts or Broadway shows attended, number of films attended, number of compact discs bought each week, the amount of designer clothing bought each month. In this scheme gay people were not only financially secure, as the survey results implied, they were also having a great time.

Right-wing strategists zeroed in on the image of homosexuals as wealthy pleasure seekers and made it the cornerstone of their attempt to galvanize animosity and resentment. The irony is that it was gay people themselves who originally constructed this image, which was now being used against them. The very statistics listed in the CFV pamphlet were derived from a survey conducted by Simmons Market Research Bureau and commissioned by the Rivendell Marketing Company—mostly from surveys of gay men with relatively high incomes—to sell advertising space in gay and lesbian magazines.

To understand how and why this happened we have to look at how gay identity, originally a private matter, became commodified into a "lifestyle."

2. From Gay Life to "Gay Lifestyle"

THE construction of a distinct social and personal identity through the acquisition of consumer goods is not unique to gay people. Thorstein Veblen, in his 1899 *The Theory of the Leisure Class,* demonstrated how patterns of consumption—as well as the invention of "leisure time"—define the "upper class" as a distinct, elite cultural group. In a consumer society, class, race, and gender identities are strongly shaped by what people buy and wear and how they socialize. For minority groups such choices are often an important way to establish a public identity as a means of separating and distinguishing themselves from the mainstream. Often this process began as an extension of an already existing identity, as with Italian-American immigrants buying foods or household items that reflected their national heritage. After a time, such items begin to define the minority identity in the mainstream imagination. The minority identity may connote not only visibility but also an ethnic or racial pride. The popularity of the dashiki, a traditional East-African tunic, and the emergence of the Afro, with all of its attendant hair care products, were material manifestations of African-American identity in the 1960s. Sometimes this commodification of identity can be as simple, and seemingly trivial, as T-shirts proclaiming "Kiss Me, I'm Polish" or bumper stickers that read "Happy to Be Irish."[2]

The use of material objects to define a cultural identity is common; when the identity becomes more codified it can mark the formation of a "lifestyle." The concept of "lifestyle" emerged as identifiable populations began defining themselves through their consumption habits. The emergence of an explicitly labeled, marketed "lifestyle" was first seen in 1953 with the publication of *Playboy* magazine. The "*Playboy* lifestyle" equated personal and sexual freedom with buying and possessing the accoutrements of an upwardly mobile, specifically male, middle-class life: the right car, the right high-fidelity system, the right clothes. The "*Playboy* lifestyle" was composed entirely of "leisure" items, which represented an alternative to—and relief from—the work-oriented lives of the 1950s married male. Additionally, those items were seen as enhancing sexual allure and prestige: a new car represented economic status as well as mobility from the home; a hi-fi system promised romantic music; hip clothes created a more sexual persona.

Although *Playboy* enticed its readers with photos of naked women, as well as articles and interviews, the real purpose of the magazine was to get readers to buy things that constituted the "*Playboy* lifestyle." Heterosexual men, burdened with the pressures of work and family, were drawn to the implied freedom of the "*Playboy* lifestyle" to find the pleasure they felt was missing in their own lives. While *Playboy* occasionally faced criticism from conservative morality watchers for its explicit sexual content, its consumer ideology was never questioned; and, in the end, mainstream culture happily accepted the idea that a masculine desire to buy the newest car was as "natural" as the desire to look at a naked woman.[3]

The idea of "lifestyle" is connected with the pursuit of pleasure in our culture; it offers material rewards to compensate for feelings of emotional deprivation. But it also functions as a form of social control by defusing the potential for cultural change. Positioned against the prevailing work-oriented, sexually subdued, family-centered ethos of the 1950s, the "*Playboy* lifestyle" seemed both an aberration and a revolt. Its actual social role, however, was to reinforce those structures. If men could find some relief by being part of the "*Playboy* lifestyle," the need to change their working habits or family arrangements was subverted, weakened.

The evolution of a "gay lifestyle" in the early 1970s was an attempt by some gay people to acquire a sense of community through consumption. Its roots can be seen earlier. As gay culture began emerging from the closet in the 1950s and early 1960s, it manifested itself in ways discernible to gay people but invisible, and thus not threatening, to mainstream society. A visible, urban gay identity emerged, composed largely of wearing specific fashions and owning distinctive books or household items that signified a homosexual identity. Magazines such as *ONE* and *Physique Pictorial* offered mail-order sales of books and clothing for the "gay man." *The Ladder* featured a popular book review column to inform lesbians of new titles that were of interest.

How and where people socialized also helped constitute the definitions of this almost entirely urban "gay world" as well. Certain restaurants and coffeehouses became known as gay meeting places. Gay men or lesbians might meet one another and socialize at the opera, certain Broadway shows, or concerts. Resort areas such as Provincetown, Fire

Island, and Key West also catered to a gay population. For many gay people, partaking in a clearly defined "gay world" was attractive and comforting. It reinforced group identity and visibility, and, because it implied a heightened class status attached to buying power, gave the appearance of enhanced social standing, which sometimes compensated for the stress and lack of self-worth gay people often experienced. Inevitably, personal and group identity manifested itself through a consumer identity. This new consumer identity was more possible for gay men than lesbians, not only because, as men, they had higher incomes but consequently because various markets began to cater to their buying power.[4]

There was not, however, at this time enough gay visibility or social support to sustain a widespread phenomenon of a "gay lifestyle," and these markers of gay identity functioned only in certain urban areas. This changed after the advent of gay liberation and the gay rights movement. As more gay people came out, the possibilities for marketing to a clearly defined population became self-evident. While the early post-Stonewall gay press tended to be noncommercial and community oriented (and for lesbian publications remained so), by 1974 a new national gay press, aimed mostly at gay men, became the main promoter of the "gay lifestyle." Glossy magazines for gay men like *Mandate* ("The International Magazine of Entertainment and Eros"), *Playguy* ("The Magazine for Men Who Like Things Manly"), and *Blueboy* ("The National Magazine ABOUT Men") followed the lead of *Playboy* and promoted themselves with photos of naked men and articles about entertainment and travel, but really existed to sell a "gay lifestyle." Advertisements for book clubs, jewelry, clothing, sex toys, records, nightclubs, and sea cruises alerted readers to what they needed to buy to partake in this lifestyle. The concept of a "gay lifestyle" was concretized in 1978 when *The Advocate,* a national news and feature magazine, instituted a new advertising campaign: "*The Advocate*— Touching Your Lifestyle."[5]

The commercial construction and potential of the "gay lifestyle"— defined essentially as "gay male"; lesbians and lesbian culture were outside of this paradigm—was quickly recognized by magazine publishers and the business world. Gay consumers were quickly targeted as the "gay market." What gay people bought, what they wore, how often and where they socialized, what they drank, where they vacationed, and how they spent money were of great interest to mainstream businesses, which perceived the gay market as enormously profitable. This was not an entirely new idea. In the mid-1960s, *After Dark* magazine, which catered to an almost entirely gay readership but never identified itself as a gay publication, drew advertising from the entertainment industry, which targeted a homosexual audience. By 1974, *After Dark* had a circulation of 100,000 and described it as 98 percent "single, male, and affluent." *After Dark* resisted being labeled a gay magazine, and instituted strict advertising regulations that prohibited use of the work "gay" in advertising copy.

Other magazines were less shy about acknowledging the existence of a self-identified gay market. By 1975, *The Wall Street Journal* could report: "Campaigns to Sell to Homosexual Market Are Being Launched by More Firms." Gay male publications understood that they could increase revenues by convincing potential advertisers that their readerships possessed sizable disposable incomes and had generous buying habits. In the April 1976 *Advertising Age,* Donald N. Embinder, publisher of *Blueboy,* ran a full-page ad headlined "Now You Can Reach America's Most Affluent Minority . . . The Male Homosexual." He received 488 responses from potential advertisers and felt that the fashion, liquor, and hi-fi industries were his best prospects. Subsequent advertising in trade magazines noted that readers of "homosexual periodicals . . . are young, educated, and well off. Not only do they make good salaries, but they have lots of discretionary income. They do not have wives, they do not have children, they usually do not have mortgages."[6]

The gay lifestyle had ramifications beyond magazine publishing and business. For *The Advocate,* and its publisher David B. Goodstein, the "gay lifestyle" was not only a measure of the economic ability of gay men to partake in consumer culture, but a political barometer as well. A 1977 editorial by Goodstein noted that the social and political standing of the gay community had progressed, as evidenced by the "large numbers of well-lit bars, clean bathhouses, and fashionable restaurants that now cater to gay people." Goodstein noted that the economic clout and the buying power of the gay community (by which he meant gay men) positioned it for social acceptance.

Goodstein's theory of social acceptance was based on the idea that increased consumerism—particularly the amount of money spent on non-necessities—automatically equates to increased social status. This was important to gay people because the perception was that disposable income purchased not only more comfort and pleasure, but safety and privacy as well. In reality, however, the ability to spend money does not necessarily grant privileged status to the spender. For example, people making middle-class incomes, if they are seen by those firmly accepted as middle-class as exhibiting working-class affect, are still viewed as socially inferior; an African American may not be able to move into a neighborhood, even though she/he can afford it, because it is segregated; a woman, no matter how wealthy, is in danger of being raped; a gay man or lesbian, no matter his or her financial standing, runs the risk of being queer-bashed.

Despite Goodstein's theories, the reality was that neither gay and lesbian people nor their sexuality was accepted in mainstream culture. Aspects of the U.S. economy were willing to seek an openly gay male market, but this was not the same as real social change. While *The Advocate*'s ideology of liberation by accumulation made for good consumers, it failed to make substantive political change.

3. The Gay Market

THE emergence of a distinct gay market mandated the need to further define and assess its potential and parameters. While advertising in the gay press was mutually beneficial to gay publications and mainstream businesses, the gay market remained, to a large extent, undefined. It was the use of marketing surveys that finally established, quantified, and codified the idea of the gay market as we know it today.

In 1968, in its first year of publication, *The Advocate* did a marketing survey to promote the idea that its readership was middle-class and affluent.[7] In 1988, *OUT/LOOK* magazine, a San Francisco–based gay and lesbian cultural and political quarterly, commissioned a marketing survey of its readership that placed gay male annual incomes at between $25,000 and $29,000, within the national male median income of $27,352. Lesbian incomes, at $20,000 to $24,000, were somewhat higher than the average female income of $18,825. In 1989, a survey done by the *San Francisco Examiner* showed similar results. It was a landmark 1988 survey by Simmons Market Research Bureau, however, that began to establish the image of the affluent gay consumer. Based upon the readership of eight national gay and lesbian newspapers, it showed the average annual gay male/lesbian income to be $36,900. The survey, which was 86 percent male, claimed that gay/lesbian respondents made 35 percent more than the average national income—figures substantially higher than those of earlier studies.

In 1992, Simmons Market Research Bureau was hired by Rivendell Marketing Company, a national advertising firm, to study gay and lesbian consumers. This time they polled the readership of fifteen gay and lesbian magazines. The Simmons study, in conjunction with surveys conducted by Overlooked Opinions, a Chicago-based marketing firm specializing in gay and lesbian community issues, provided the data that now form the basis of many corporate marketing strategies targeting lesbian and gay populations.

The statistics generated by Simmons Market Research and Overlooked Opinions were significantly higher than those in the 1988 study. They were a revelation to companies looking for new lucrative markets. According to the Simmons report, the income for the average gay male household was $63,700. Education levels were also very high, with nearly 60 percent of respondents having a four-year college degree, and 27 percent having a graduate degree. Employment figures were also very high, with 92 percent of respondents currently holding jobs, and more than 50 percent of those in a professional or managerial position. Overlooked Opinions discovered from its data that the average gay or lesbian consumer was more likely to spend money on personal improvement or leisure activities: 81.1 percent of gay men had dined out more than five times in the past month; 17.2 percent of lesbians had spent some time daily reading a book in the past month; 20.1 percent of gay men had attended a fitness club ten times in the past month. According to Overlooked Opinions, there were 18 million gay and lesbian adults in the United States with a collective annual income of $514 billion.[8]

The formulation of a well-heeled, lucrative gay market was quickly promoted by market researchers, the gay press, and the corporate world, although it was rarely made clear that these statistics applied only to a readership of a specific set of mostly gay-male-centered, urban-based, lifestyle-oriented magazines and newspapers. Articles appeared in *Ad Week, The Wall Street Journal,* and *The New York Times* promoting the homosexual as the ideal consumer. The concept of the "gay lifestyle" soon found its perfect manifestation as Benetton, Absolut, Levi Strauss, Columbia Records, Seagram's, Miller Beer, and Calvin Klein began to target the gay market, their products becoming emblematic of, and inseparable from, the "gay lifestyle."

Gay visibility is a rare enough commodity that it is usually welcomed by gay people in any form. The positive feelings many in the gay community experience from seeing ads directed at a gay audience are reinforced by gay consumers supporting those advertisers. The growing visibility of the gay and lesbian community in the past decade has been largely a direct result of the emergence of the gay market and the commodification of gay life.

In a world in which antigay discrimination is rampant, some gay people found comfort in the idea that gay people's material and economic lives seemed secure and successful. More important, however, for some gay people, the gay consumer—usually personified as a gay male, not a lesbian—was intended to project a less threatening, more appealing image to mainstream culture. While in the past homosexuals were portrayed as socially disruptive and dangerous sexual deviants, the new gay consumer was financially secure and more concerned with supporting the existing economic and social system than with changing it. As early as 1978, David Goodstein claimed, when he was looking for mainstream advertising, that *The Advocate* was being "desleazified." Since that time, *The Advocate* and other gay lifestyle magazines have marginalized their sexual content and advertising. Any threat of overt gay sexuality was diminished since the persona of the gay consumer was essentially nonsexual—more concerned with buying a comfortable lifestyle than exhibiting any conspicuous sexuality. The sexuality associated with the gay consumer was privatized and often coded by the use of "sexy" consumer items like leisure clothing or romantic dinners. This image dovetailed neatly with the gay political movement's desire to downplay the importance of sexuality in gay culture.[9]

4. The Gay Constituent

Promoting the image of the affluent gay consumer in the media and the public imagination had another important consequence. As gay issues began to play an increasingly large role in national politics, the gay consumer was undergoing a transformation into the gay constituent. When politicians began courting the gay vote, marketing research companies were busy determining the voting—and political donation—patterns of gay and lesbian voters. Marketing surveys painted a picture of the gay constituent that was almost identical to the gay consumer: highly educated with a large disposable income, more than 90 percent registered to vote (and more than 60 percent registered as Democrats), and very concerned about gay-related public policy issues. The gay constituent was a Democratic politician's—and a fundraiser's—dream.

The coemergence of the gay consumer and the gay constituent was a pivotal moment: both were responsible, and invested in the existing social system, and both emphasized the importance of personal privacy over public sexuality. This reflected a gay rights agenda that promoted the idea that gay people were just like heterosexuals. The increased social standing implicitly promised by the gay market was equated with access to political power. The gay vote was now being courted by politicians the same way that the gay consumer was targeted by large corporations. It was a small step from seeking gay social legitimacy to seeking political access through buying power.

The media hype around the new gay constituent was similar to the hype surrounding the gay consumer. It reached its peak in the 1992 presidential election when Bill Clinton's campaign aggressively pursued the gay vote. Fund-raisers and organizers in the gay community, using the marketing statistics, promised to deliver gay money and gay votes. David Mixner, a Clinton adviser and gay organizer, claimed to have delivered more than $3.5 million to the Clinton coffers. The payoff for this was the promise that Clinton would "by a stroke of the pen" sign an executive order that would change the military policy that discriminated against gay men and lesbians. Like the social visibility promised by the gay market and gay consumerism, the new gay conflation of money and political power was seductive, and many gay donors and power brokers felt that they had purchased access to real political power in Washington.[10]

But despite the active participation of mainstream gay activists and very successful fund-raising efforts in the gay community that helped Clinton's election, the military policy did not change. Democrats and gay activists had underestimated the fight that Republicans and the right wing would wage against the policy change. Gay constituents discovered that money could not, in the end, buy the power they had been promised.

More disastrous, however, was the way images of the gay consumer and the gay constituent were used by the right wing to promote antigay referenda. Instead of granting the gay community prestige and clout in mainstream culture, these images engendered a backlash. By positioning homosexuals as wealthy power brokers who were buying "special rights," the right wing established in the popular imagination the myth that homosexuals were not disenfranchised, but were a powerful and self-serving minority, as disdainful of traditional value as they were eager to foist their own morality upon mainstream society. Furthermore, the association of homosexuals with high levels of disposable income used for personal pleasure reinforced the image of gay people as nonproductive sexual hedonists.

5. *False Images and the Burdens of Heterosexuality*

IT is no surprise that the promotion of an affluent gay community as a political force backfired. The concepts of the gay consumer and the gay constituent were myths created by means of market research and, when used
without explanation of their context, they created a false public image of
the entire homosexual community. The 1992 Simmons Market Research
study surveyed only those gay people who read the selected gay periodicals. Of those surveyed, only 10 percent were women, and a statistical
breakdown on race was either not done or not disclosed. The Simmons
survey sample may have been an accurate reflection of the income and
buying patterns of the periodicals' readership, but it did not, and was not
intended to, reflect the statistics of the larger community. According to
the Simmons Market Research Bureau, corresponding figures for the
African-American community show that readers of *Essence* and *Ebony*
earn 41 percent to 82 percent more than the average African American.
The same is true of the readers of *USA Today* and *The Wall Street Journal,*
who earn, respectively, 55 percent and 110 percent more than the U.S.
median annual income.

The image that *The Advocate* and other magazines presented of how
the "average" gay man lived was representative of some men's lives: usually those with a high level of education, who lived in urban gay neighborhoods and had well-paying jobs and enough disposable income to
purchase nonessential, lifestyle products. But not all the gay men who
identified with the "gay lifestyle" earned at that level. Many gay men, of
course, did not fit the image of the "gay lifestyle" at all—men in rural and
suburban areas, men who were closeted, and men who did not construct
their lives around their sexual identity.

There are also other variables that influence marketing surveys targeting gay populations. More than any other minority, the gay community
is composed of people from differing economic and class backgrounds.
The process of secondary socialization—learning how to fit into a new
environment—often creates a situation in which people with working-
class or lower-middle-class backgrounds attempt to emulate the higher
class status of fellow community members. For gay men, this often manifests itself in spending disproportionately in relation to income in order
to obtain the accoutrements of the "gay lifestyle" and the social position
they symbolize. Such behavior is common enough that gay slang has a

term for it: "piss elegance." Another possible manifestation of this is that gay men may simply lie about income and purchases on marketing surveys in order to portray themselves as more affluent.

Even more of an obstacle than these two problems, is that traditional market research techniques cannot get a clear picture of gay income and spending because the closet prevents researchers from obtaining an accurate, representative sample. Surveys such as those by Simmons Market Research rely on information from self-identified gay men and lesbians. Because economic security is often a factor in the ability to be "out," these samples are, of necessity, not representative. Despite these difficulties, recent, more sophisticated analyses of gay populations have been done. A study by Yankelovich Partners in 1994 showed that heterosexuals and gay people make comparable salaries. Economist Lee Badgett has pioneered new methods of compiling accurate gay income statistics. By surveying gay populations as defined by behavior, not only self-identification, she is able to correlate this information with income statistics for a wide range of occupations. Badgett's study was the first to take into consideration the political and economic realities of workplace discrimination, and she argues convincingly that because of discrimination gay people, as a group, make substantially less than heterosexuals.[11]

However, figures on the economic resources and spending patterns of the gay community are less important than how those figures and the research that underlies them are used. Marketing surveys, no matter how precise, exist to support the economic interests of business and advertising, not to uncover and convey information about the gay community. Overlooked Opinions, for example, estimates that there are 18.5 million gay men and lesbians in the United States, with an estimated combined annual income of $514 billion. These figures were obtained, in part, by using the hotly debated Kinsey estimate that claims that 10 percent of U.S. men are homosexual and multiplying "average" annual income figures. It is unclear how lesbians—who, according to Kinsey, make up less than 10 percent of the female population, *and* who make on the average less money than men—fit into this equation.[12]

As seductive as it is to use market research to determine the gay community's monetary and political resources, such ventures, by their nature, misrepresent economic and social reality. Moreover, they have proven to be influential organizing tools for the right wing. Despite the theories of David Goodstein and others that an image of economic affluence would mitigate the view of gay people as sexual threats to dominant society, the reverse occurred. The new image of gay people as having

higher social and economic standing did not eradicate their threat as dis-
rupters of the sexual and social order, but increased it: now they were
seen as a sexual threat with economic and social power. The image of gay
people as pleasure seekers with little sense of sexual or social responsibility was not erased but reinforced by the image of the well-to-do gay
consumer. Homosexuality, for the dominant culture, was too associated
with sex and pleasure to be recast as economically or politically responsible.

This image of gay pleasure seekers has become firmly embedded in
the popular imagination. The most prominent example of this is that
Supreme Court Justice Antonin Scalia in his dissent in *Romer v. Evans,*
which overturned the Amendment 2 vote, could write, "It is nothing
short of preposterous to call 'politically unpopular' a group [homosexu-
als] which enjoys influence in American media and politics. . . ."

The resentment and hostility these images of an affluent and politically powerful gay community engender in mainstream culture would
not be so powerful were it not for the deep economic and social dissatis-
faction that many heterosexuals experience in their own lives.

The right wing's use of the "gay consumer" image (in conjunction
with the "special rights" argument) was highly effective for raising funds
and rallying support for statewide antigay initiative drives. These campaigns were most effective in cities and areas with depressed economies.
In Colorado, cities such as Aspen, Boulder, Denver, and Vail—all with
relatively high per capita annual incomes—voted solidly against Amendment 2, while poorer areas voted for it. Comparable patterns occurred
in Oregon and Maine. Right-wing organizers understood that the depiction of homosexuals as wealthy and politically powerful would resonate
with voters who felt disenfranchised.

But the "special rights" argument emerged in a nationwide context of
increasing political and economic polarization. An American Civil Liberties Union analysis of why Amendment 2 passed noted that "a significant
portion of the American public increasingly appears to believe that civil
rights protections themselves—not just for gay people—have gone 'too
far.' This was reflected in the lack of public support for affirmative action
programs, particularly for quotas, and in the growing backlash to calls for
racial and gender equality. The feeling that civil rights have gone too far
is also played out in the 'political correctness' debate, where attempts to
address inequalities in American society are ridiculed and dismissed as
mere 'politically correct' reactions to various situations."[13]

The success of Amendment 2 was possible only in a political context

defined, to a large extent, by a national economy that had become increasingly tight for middle- and lower-middle-class people. Since the
early 1970s, a series of economic depressions and inflations forced a reduction in both the white-collar and blue-collar job markets, as well as
increased unemployment. Blue-collar workers were especially hard hit
with factory closings and layoffs. Federal and state job training programs
were also being cut back, as were federally funded child care, health
maintenance, and drug rehabilitation programs. In a downswing economy, such cutbacks placed the nuclear family under even more financial
and emotional stress. This economic context provided rich soil for resentment.

The role of earning level and economic status in shaping social and
cultural attitudes is tremendous. National polling data show that higher
levels of income and education usually correlate positively to more tolerance of homosexuals, as well as to support for laws against antigay discrimination and in favor of decriminalization of gay sexual behavior.
While there are other correlatives that cross-interpret this information,
one simple conclusion to be drawn is that people who are economically
disenfranchised or financially unsteady tend to mistrust and resent those
they see as having more advantages. If they also identify the family unit as
a source of stability and identity, they are likely to be hostile to those they
see as existing outside the structures of heterosexuality and the nuclear
family.[14]

The strong correlations between earning levels and economic status
and tolerance of homosexual behavior can only be understood in the
context of how the national economy over the past three decades has
changed its attitudes regarding gender, children, and family. The economic boom that followed World War II (in which industrial jobs for
men were secured by forcing women out of the workforce) encouraged
and provided a financially stable base for the formation of the traditional
nuclear family. The middle-class norm of two-parent households with a
worker-husband and homemaker-wife was promoted by the mainstream
as the cultural ideal, even though it was not representative of how many
lived—the middle-class career woman and the working-class mother
who held a job were obvious exceptions. The relative economic stability
of the period reinforced traditional gender roles, as well as the idea that
the "family" was a haven of safety for both adults and children.

The social upheavals of the 1960s were accompanied by a spiraling
economic inflation that replaced the family-friendly affluence of the 1950s
and disrupted the stability of the nuclear family. These social and

economic changes affected the status of men and masculinity in the culture, and the role of the husband and father as breadwinner and protector was irrevocably changed.

This shifting in the position of the family in United States society was accompanied by two important developments. As inflation grew, the economy became more difficult for those not solidly in the middle class to negotiate: men had a hard time supporting their families on lower wages; working women were accused of taking jobs away from men; white workers felt injured by affirmative action policies. The middle class was not without problems as well. Having established some economic security in the early-to-mid-1970s, the middle class found that the shaky economy of the next decade placed it in a constant crisis of social and economic instability, a state that social economist Barbara Ehrenreich called "the fear of falling." By the late 1980s this put the middle-class family as well as the lower-class and poor family under stress.

In this context of economic and social crisis, the "family," through the lenses of nostalgia and fear, became a concept that symbolized the stability of a better time. While this image of the family was often patently false, it dovetailed with a rise in conservative politics that conflated "family" with traditional values such as patriotism, established religious practice, tightly defined gender roles, and orthodox sexual morality. The emergence of a conservative, right-wing politics blamed the problems of the family on liberal social policies, liberation movements (especially feminism), the counterculture, and the lack of a strong, traditional masculine presence at home and in the culture. The more that mainstream culture perceived a threat to the traditional family, the more important it became necessary to find a clearly discernible scapegoat. By the late 1970s—with the Anita Bryant campaign and the rise of a strong religious right—homosexuals and the gay movement were targeted as the main enemy of the heterosexual family.[15]

It is easy to see why the "gay consumer" and the "gay constituent," with their alleged disposable income, leisure time, and political clout, would be resented by those who felt that they did not have comparable access or power. But the deep antagonism reflected in right-wing organizing materials toward the gay community is only one manifestation of the mistrust and hostility engendered by perceived economic difference. Often gay bashings are rationalized by the heterosexual bashers in terms of class and economic resentments. Mainstream media reporting on gay men living with AIDS will routinely presume a middle- or upper-middle-class status about their subjects that is not true; often this presumption is used to attack them. Frequently, editorials will complain that too much money is going to AIDS research and services because of gay political and economic clout. But the resentment of, and hostility toward, homosexuals held by mainstream society is so pervasive that it cannot be explained simply by the appearance of economic inequality or the myth of the gay consumer.

The hostility to homosexuality in our society finds much of its basis in the discontent that heterosexuals feel with their lives and the cultural institutions—gender roles, reproductive sexuality, and the family—upon which they are built and have to rely. While much of this is intrinsic to how heterosexuality has been constructed over the centuries, the situation, particularly in relation to the family, has worsened over the past decades. Because of persistent social and economic stress, the biological family unit has become, for many, not a haven in a heartless world, but a problematic institution. As divorce rates climb, births to single mothers among all classes escalate, and the incidence of spousal and child abuse rises, it is clear that the family is not the safe, secure institution it was once proclaimed to be. Even a staunch defender of the traditional nuclear family like Christopher Lasch has admitted that, in its present state and context, the family offers its members little of the support and consolation that have been its alleged hallmark.[16]

The heterosexual nuclear family holds a nearly impossible place in U.S. society now. Its social role is unclear, and it lacks the focus and the moral imperative it had only four decades ago. Most middle- and working-class families struggle financially, at the mercy of trends in the national economy, the job market, and inflation, their difficulties exacerbated by the slashing of federal funds for local schools and support systems for families. As much as people may love and need their families, the traditional family has become an amalgamation of burdens and responsibilities.

Juxtaposed with this, the family is praised by politicians, religious leaders, conservative social commentators, and moralists as the cornerstone of society. It is portrayed in the conservative media as the last outpost of civilization. (And in Freudian terms, the family functions as the most basic social institution that keeps the willful, dangerous id in check and promotes repression in the name of civilization.) To give up or even modify the family seems, to conservatives, unthinkable. As a result, the burdens of the family—economic and emotional self-sacrifice, restricted social activities, mandated sexual restraint—are all recast as virtues that justify the limitations and problems of the family structure. The right's "family values" byword would have none of its potency if the reality of family life were not so much worse than the ideal.

In contrast to the problems of the family, the fantasy of how homosexuals live must *seem* burden free. Childless and unencumbered by the responsibilities of home and family, gay people are viewed by the dominant culture as lacking in obligation and accountability. In this vision, gay lives are defined by leisure time, the heedless pursuit of pleasure, and unearned, privileged access to economic and political opportunity. Homosexuality, viewed through the lens of burdensome institutionalized heterosexuality, becomes not simply a threat to a highly organized, sexually repressive social system, but a personal insult to those who believe or partake in it.

6. The Gay Moment

HETEROSEXUALS are not simply troubled and antagonized by the image of the burden-free homosexual, they are also drawn to it. Over the past two decades, amid many articles that distorted or misrepresented gay people and culture, the mainstream media have also promoted an alternative, seemingly more benign, nonthreatening portrait of gay life. This image has been influential in shaping how mainstream, heterosexual culture views homosexuality.

Essentially urban in its geography, consumer- and arts-focused in its orientation, this image of gay life stands in sharp relief to the harshly homophobic images produced by conservatives and the right wing. In a 1972 article in *Esquire,* gay man are proclaimed to be "the new artisans . . . always on the cutting edge of culture and urban living. Their child-free lives allow them more time to pursue personal . . . and artistic interests." By 1978, gay culture was portrayed in the cosmopolitan media as the cutting edge of sophisticated U.S. nightlife. The disco craze was just beginning and gay-oriented Manhattan nightclubs like Reno Sweeney's and Upstairs were being promoted by the popular media, such as *People* and *New York* magazine, as vital centers of culture. The idea that homosexuals influenced mainstream culture was not a new one; in the 1960s, there was active debate in the media about the power of gay men on Broadway. That influence was always viewed as negative and destructive. By the mid-1980s, however, this had begun to change. The mainstream media were now promoting some gay "influence" in a positive light. In 1987, *New York Times* theater critic Frank Rich noted in *Esquire* that gay male social styles and culture had been not only formative, but welcomed, in shaping how many urban heterosexuals thought about culture and lived their lives.

The image of homosexuals in these articles was closely linked to the "gay lifestyle" and the "gay consumer": white, urban, middle-class, professional men who had the time and money to pursue pleasure rather than responsibility, culture rather than families. Often these men worked in the arts, fashion, or design and were responsible for creating "pleasure." Gay men were presented as cultural trendsetters in their relationships, lives, and artistic endeavors—a positive recasting of the old stereotypes of homosexuals being single and "artistic." The downside of this was not simply that these articles described the lives of only a small segment of the gay community, but that they conflated it with the upscale consumerism of the 1970s and 1980s. Even Frank Rich, in his nonjudgmental *Esquire* piece, noted that the "gay" images of Calvin Klein advertising and the burgeoning gym culture that brought both gay and straight urban singles to the Nautilus machine were "body worship [that] was nothing if not in tune with the moneyed, selfish culture of the Reagan years."[17]

These articles garnered attention because mainstream culture was looking for options beyond the status quo. Gay and lesbian lives were being presented as alternatives not to *heterosexuality* but to its traditional institutions: marriage, strict gender roles, and the two-parent nuclear family. While gay culture did offer a substantial range of alternatives to conventional heterosexual life, the most intriguing and alluring images were, to a large degree, false. By conflating homosexuality with social and economic upward mobility, and promoting the "gay lifestyle" as that of a cultural elite, these articles presented a new fantasy homosexual. On the surface, this was the reverse of the socially destructive fantasy presented by the right wing. Attractive, talented, sophisticated, and artistically productive, this "lifestyle" homosexual was as perfect as a magazine cover.[18]

The social function of this fantasy for heterosexuals was complex. While the "lifestyle" homosexual presented a range of options for heterosexuals looking for alternatives to the restrictions of heterosexuality, it still reinforced the idea of homosexuals as the other: not demonized, but exoticized.

In 1993, both *Newsweek* and *New York* magazine featured cover stories on "lesbian chic." The articles charted lesbian fashion, raised the tantalizing question of Madonna's lesbianism, lauded k.d. lang's androgyny, and explained terms like "lipstick lesbian." *Vanity Fair* explicitly sexualized lesbian chic with a cover photo of butch k.d. lang giving a "shave" to reclining, scantily clad, femme supermodel Cindy Crawford. This marketing of the "new," trendy lesbian had nothing to do with the lives of actual women, or even the influence of feminism or gay liberation on mainstream culture. Not unlike the *Playboy* centerfold of the 1950s, it was a media fantasy of female sexuality. Similarly, two years earlier, *Newsweek* and *Time* had run substantial, sympathetic features on the "new gay male" that promoted the idea of gay men as respectable middle-class consumers. This image was to find its first media apotheosis in March 1994 when IKEA, a Swedish home furnishings chain, broadcast in urban venues a television spot featuring an openly gay male couple shopping for a dining room table. This was labeled the "gay moment" by the mainstream media.[19]

The highly visible, consumer-oriented "gay lifestyle" presented in these articles was a different fantasy of how gay people lived. This fantasy was enjoyed and promoted by some gay people, who felt it elevated the social status of homosexuality and was a welcome relief to many virulently antigay images in mainstream culture. It also flourished in gay publications such as *OUT* and *The Advocate,* whose financial security in an increasing competitive advertising economy depended upon support from corporate advertisers such as Absolut vodka, Kool cigarettes, and American Express. At its roots, however, the exoticized, chic, consumer-oriented homosexual was simply another example of marketing, a false image of homosexuality in the mainstream media.[20]

The presentation of gay men and lesbians in segments of the liberal media as a trendy cultural phenomenon never addressed mainstream culture's long-standing fear and hatred of gay sexuality, or the reality of antigay discrimination and violence against homosexuals. Indeed, the images were predicated on avoiding these issues. The fantasy of the safe, attractive consumer homosexual functioned primarily as an alternative for heterosexuals, but it also helped secure the increasingly fragile heterosexual status quo. Like the "*Playboy* lifestyle" of the 1950s, which provided a fantasy outlet (albeit made possible in a limited degree with consumer goods) while it reaffirmed marriage and family, the "gay moment" offers an alternative paradigm to institutionalized heterosexuality, but consistently avoids dealing with gay sexuality and promotes an inauthentic freedom through consumerism. Ultimately, it mitigates the threat and anxiety that homosexual activity engenders in heterosexuals, and thus reaffirms the social primacy of heterosexuality and removes the possibility of authentic change. In the end, it confuses media visibility with real social legitimacy and power. The homosexuals of the "gay moment" were as nonthreatening as their counterparts in right-wing literature were terrifying.

The fantasy projections of homosexuals of both the right wing and the media hype are opposing reflections. The right wing, at its most extreme, promotes an image of gay people as willful destroyers of gender, family, and cultural standards. The media-hype image of "lifestyle" homosexuals portrays them as cultural elitists and pleasure seekers unencumbered by the everyday realities and burdens that contextualize human existence. Both images—imaginative flights from the reality of institutionalized heterosexuality—have resonance for straight people who understand, on some level, that the traditional structures of marriage and family are inadequate venues for exploring the full potential of their lives.

The reality for gay people is twofold. Most gay men and lesbians lead lives in which they worry about their jobs, paying rent, and making ends meet; some gay people have children and all the responsibilities that come with them. They share, then, many of the same economic anxieties as heterosexuals, although these similarities are almost never addressed or discussed in the mainstream media. Yet as social outsiders, gay people also have a unique vantage point from which to critique mainstream culture, explore new concepts of gender and sexual relationships, and create innovative and liberating social and cultural endeavors. What is most threatening about homosexuals, however, is that their very existence demonstrates not only that there are other options besides heterosexuality, but also that pleasure—emblematically nonreproductive sexual pleasure—needs no justification and can be used to prioritize and evaluate human experience, moral decisions, and the living of life. This is such a daunting and frightening idea that it must be constantly attacked, obscured, disguised, or marketed as something else. This simple truth about homosexuality and gay and lesbian lives is so difficult to state in our society that even homosexuals—hiding behind the temporary and ineffective relief of the "gay moment" or attempting to hide the reality of gay sexuality by insisting, "We are just like everyone else"—are reluctant to speak it.

Ten

Pleasure and the Failure of Privacy

1. Privacy: The Regulation of Pleasure

I N A WORLD in which gay people are constantly harassed, persecuted, and told that they should not exist, privacy has long been a haven, even a necessity. But this retreat to privacy has prevented gay people and the gay community from living openly, from establishing themselves as a distinct and articulate social presence, and from gaining the most basic rights and elements of citizenship that other people and groups enjoy. Historically, for gay people, privacy was a condition of safety and existence. But the safety that privacy offered is only part of its complex relationship to gay freedom.

Western societies have always had a complicated relationship with pleasure, often viewing it as a threat to the social and moral order. Sexual pleasure—especially nonreproductive sexuality and homosexuality—was targeted as very threatening. The evolution and construction of "privacy" has been, to a large extent, an attempt to regulate and contain sexual activity and pleasure. As such, it has had a tremendous impact on homosexuality.

The complicated relationship between privacy and gay freedom is better understood in the context of how our current concept of "privacy" evolved. Contemporary Western societies accept privacy as a given: that it exists as an established, defined social concept; that it is a legal "right"; and that it is, on the whole, a good thing. Privacy, however, is a fairly recent concept whose definition and ramifications are in constant flux. Social and legal concepts of privacy arose in concert with broader changes in human culture. Privacy was most closely tied to the emergence of the idea that people were not simply part of a "class" but had individual identities and personal autonomy as well. This occurred in conjunction with the breakdown of feudalism and the emergence of individual ownership of land, which led to a more democratized concept of private property. This, in turn, encouraged and sustained the rise of the independent, self-sufficient nuclear family.

The concept of privacy was influential in shaping newly evolving ideas about ownership, class, family, gender, and sexuality. As private ownership of property became feasible in the postfeudal era, it created a complicated system of class—social and economic separations predicated on ownership—which in turn created degrees of privacy: the higher the class status, the more privacy was available. This new class structure worked in conjunction with a gender system that granted men legal and cultural privileges not given to women or children, including the power to "own." The concept of ownership extended beyond land to include the family. Men, as heads of households, legally owned their wives and children as "property." The idea that "A man's home is his castle" combined the ideas of property, home, and family as material possessions. This reinforced the position of men and male sexuality in the culture.[1]

The privatization of the individual and the family affected sexuality as well. The relative visibility of sexual display and discourse in the Middle Ages and the Elizabethan era eventually gave way to an increasingly privatized view of sex. Defined as reproductive, sex was now seen as legitimate only within the context of the family. Public discussion about sexuality also became less acceptable; sex was now "private."

The privatization of sexuality dovetailed with the emergence of a middle class in the late sixteenth century. This class became increasingly defined by its access to and desire for personal and family privacy. This, in turn, led to a new code of social behavior about sexuality. The Anglo-Saxon words for the genitals, such as "prick" and "cunt," favored by Chaucer and his contemporaries in the late fourteenth century, were replaced by euphemisms, and finally by "privy members" or "private parts." The rising middle class distinguished itself from the working class by implementing a rigorous social code that downplayed sexual dress, action, and speech. This code of social and sexual propriety—codified as "good taste" and "common decency"—became the prevailing social norm for the middle class and a measure against which the lower classes were judged. By the nineteenth century, this code of proper social convention became an entrenched form of personal and social self-regulation. The pressure to appear socially and sexually proper was so pervasive that the fictional character of Mrs. Grundy, an archetypical guardian of public morals, entered the language, and "What will Mrs. Grundy say?" quickly became a byword for the fear of sexual or social nonconformity.[2]

The idea that sexuality should be "private" did not immediately lead to a "right" to privacy. A theologically based legal system legislated sexual morality and targeted sexual "crimes" committed in private. From the Middle Ages onward, most sexual activities outside of marriage, as well as nonreproductive activity within marriage, were illegal, and perpetrators always ran the risk of punishment.[3]

In the absence of a distinct legal right to privacy, however, there evolved an unwritten social contract that protected sexual behavior as long as it was not discussed publicly. As a function and extension of male privilege and the rights of ownership, this extra-legal protection extended only to adult heterosexual males, not to women or children, who were, legally, property. This "right to privacy" in the male-headed home worked both ways: it insured the "privacy" of the home and it insured that what happened within its confines was not judged by legal standards. Sexual and physical abuse within the family was therefore seen as a "private" matter. It was, for example, legal until the 1970s in many states for a husband to rape his wife. This "privacy" also ensured that the sexual and physical abuse of children was ignored by the legal authorities. The "right to privacy" in domestic and sexual matters reinforced male social and sexual power, and reaffirmed heterosexuality as the norm.

The social contract that permitted sexual privacy concerned heterosexual *activity*. Public display of heterosexual *orientation* was allowed and encouraged. Since heterosexuality informed the most basic social structures, it was, by nature, very public. It was impossible to separate heterosexual orientation from activity; the existence of children, for example, was an indication that sexual activity had occurred. Essentially, this meant that while heterosexual activity was "private," it was still allowed public display. Since homosexual activity was illegal, all indications and display of homosexual orientation had to be hidden.

2. Privacy and Homosexuality

BECAUSE homosexuality was defined over the years as a sin, a crime, and an illness, there has never been a "right" to homosexual privacy; in fact, homosexual behavior has historically been subject to draconian legal measures, including death and life imprisonment. Even the indication of homosexual orientation has been enough to cause ostracism and, often, legally mandated punishment. In the long, complex history of liberal reform to secure greater autonomy and privacy for the individual, there have been, until recently, almost no attempts to decriminalize homosexual behavior. In 1957, a British parliamentary committee, after meeting for four years, issued the Wolfenden Report, which recommended that private, consensual homosexual activities between men be decriminalized; it took ten years for this to be accomplished with the Sexual Offences Act of 1967. At that time every state in the United States with the exception of Illinois had antisodomy laws on its books; some of these laws were so broad and ill-defined that they penalized all forms of homosexual behavior.[4]

The only way to avoid persecution for homosexual activity was to keep it secret. Even this, however, was not enough. In the 1950s and 1960s in the United States, it was not unusual for police to arrest men and women, often in private homes, for actual or suspected homosexual activity. People who frequented more public places, such as bars, clubs, and parks, were routinely arrested and charged under a variety of laws including those against loitering, solicitation, intent to commit an indecent act, and wearing clothing inappropriate to one's gender. These laws were used to regulate public manifestations of homosexuality with the objective of suppressing them completely or, at the very least, driving them underground.[5]

The conflation of orientation and activity, and the prohibitions against both, were part of a larger social scheme to regulate homosexual behavior and identity through the inculcation of fear and the enforcement of laws. While heterosexuals had an extra-legal "right to privacy" and were allowed the public display of orientation, homosexuals had to hide both their activity and their orientation. In the mainstream imagination, homosexual orientation and activity became one and the same. This meant that there was virtually no legal or social concept of privacy for homosexuals. In the absence of a "right to privacy," and in the context of the continued criminalization of all homosexual sexual activity, any public manifestation of homosexual identity—from holding hands to cross-dressing to purchasing homosexually oriented material—could lead to arrest.

It became imperative that homosexuality not be public. This state of nonpublicness, however, cannot strictly be called "privacy" because it was not freely chosen; it is more accurately described as "secrecy." Any authentic notion of privacy is dependent upon choice, and includes the option to be open.

The emergence of the homophile movement in the early 1950s began changing the concept of privacy for homosexuals. The entrenched antihomosexual sentiment of the era forced homophile groups to operate from a position of secrecy; meetings, membership lists, and official documents were often concealed or kept strictly confidential. Because of the harsh antihomosexual sentiment of the times, the political aim of the groups—to create a public space in which homosexuality could exist quietly and unobtrusively—dovetailed neatly with the aims of social regulation of mainstream culture.[6]

One of the goals of the homophile organizations was to convince mainstream culture that homosexuals were "just like everyone else." One aspect of this strategy was to present gay men and lesbians as "normal-looking." Mattachine and Daughters of Bilitis adopted dress codes—suits and ties for men, dresses for women—for public appearances. This attempt at "normalcy," while understandable in the historical context, was a rejection of a more public gay culture manifested by dress, language, or physical affect viewed by the homophile organizations as stigmatizing and unacceptable. The political and social edict to look "normal" was an extension of the code of enforced secrecy that rendered homosexuality invisible. It also played into the tradition that defined "privacy" by "good taste" and "decency." In the 1950s and 1960s, mainstream culture considered any appearance or display of homosexuality indecent and an affront to "good taste." This social regulation of gay appearance and affect was no different from the strictly legal codes that forbade and punished homosexual activity.[7]

Although the homophile groups boldly broke political and social convention by protesting antigay discrimination and police harassment, their main political thrust was to argue for "privacy." This could not be a legal right (which even heterosexuals did not have), but rather inclusion under the unwritten social contract that governed heterosexual behavior. By focusing so intently on the "right to privacy," the homophile groups constructed a false idea of safety. Because display of homosexual orientation was conflated with, and often as illegal as, homosexual activity, "privacy" demanded that there would be no homosexual visibility at all. The safety found in "privacy" was therefore predicated and dependent upon homosexual invisibility, and in the long run did not offer real protection, but only the illusion of it. If anything, this false sense of security hindered additional, effective community and political organizing.

Throughout the 1960s, the idea of privacy became confusing for gay people. Privacy promised a degree of safety that was never secure, and was held as a political ideal that did not exist in the material world. Because it was equated in the social sphere with "good taste" and "decency," it mandated modes of behavior that were antithetical to the existence of a visible gay community. Since the homophile groups supported this false idea of privacy, there was created the image of the "good" homosexual, who was quiet, private, and did not indicate in any speech, manner, or dress that he or she was gay. This, in turn, created the category of the "bad" homosexual, who could be clearly identified as gay. By pinning their political hopes on a concept of assimilation promoted by "privacy," the homophile movement reinforced invisibility as a method to attain tolerance, and created a caste system that stigmatized any gay person who could not or did not adhere to the enforced standards of privacy that required gay people to appear "like everyone else."

The idea of privacy espoused by the homophile movement broke apart with the advent of gay liberation. The very concept of privacy was rejected by the liberation movements of the late 1960s whose politics promoted a new, powerful group identity for the socially disenfranchised, along with the unlimited right to personal autonomy. The first was captured in slogans like "Black is beautiful," "Gay is good," and "Sisterhood is powerful"; the second was expressed in the promotion of sexual freedom, the right to use drugs, and the right to control sexual reproduction.

In this context, and in revolt against the privacy politics of the homophile groups, gay liberation promoted unrestricted gay visibility and the right to express that visibility in any form desired: overt drag, gender-fuck clothing, public affection, unabashed effeminacy or butchness, and open declarations of homosexual desire. Blatant displays of homosexuality, often of a transgressive nature, were common. Heterosexuals also found that they had more freedom to indulge in sexual display and to discuss sexuality. The prevailing politics asserted that sexuality and the reality of sexual activity—for heterosexuals and well as homosexuals— should not be divorced from everyday life, but encouraged and discussed publicly. This new politic treated traditional middle-class notions of decorum, good taste, and decency as old-fashioned and repressive.

The impact of gay liberation politics—as well as other liberation movements—had an enormous effect on social behavior and structures. It was now possible for gay men and lesbians to safely socialize publicly in clubs and bars, to celebrate their sexuality and newfound political power in gay pride marches, and simply to express their affection in public. Within a few short years, police harassment against gay people and bars declined, and some laws such as those against cross-dressing and solicitation went unenforced. Not all harassment against gay people stopped. Many states still had sodomy laws in their penal codes. Non-state-sponsored attempts at suppressing and inhibiting displays of homosexuality also continued, including a widespread social condemnation of public homosexual behavior as being "in bad taste," and systematic antigay violence from individual citizens.

While the homophile movement had helped to create a rudimentary social and political context for the gay liberation movement, its politics of privacy was completely superseded. Gay liberation—in concert with social change movements of the late 1960s—refuted the homophile movement's defensive, assimilationist strategy, and created a political force that demanded attention and acknowledgment. The bold claiming of public space and the assertion of a visible, public identity gained the gay liberation movement more power and ground than was available under the rubric of "privacy."

The goals of complete visibility and sexual freedom promoted by the gay liberation movement could only have come to fruition in a climate of massive cultural change. This did not occur. The more radical segments of the Black Power movement, the civil rights movement, the women's movement, gay liberation, and the counterculture never gained the widespread support they needed to succeed. Their utopian vision of cultural and political change often did not take into account the immediate social reality and material needs of their constituents. It was not possible, for example, for all gay people to "come out" if it meant risking job security. Moreover, gay liberation and other movements found little respect or support in the mainstream media and, as a result, were marginalized. Consequently, these movements never gained enough power to create wide-scale social change; in some cases they adopted more moderate and assimilationist points of view. The gay liberation movement's insistence on visibility, however, influenced all future gay political organizing.

The prominence of the gay liberation movement declined by the mid-1970s, and a more moderate gay rights movement emerged. While the gay rights movement espoused the ideal of visibility, it also reaffirmed the politics of "privacy," which it recast as a political "right." For the gay rights movement, the "right to privacy" meant the right to be let alone: the right not to be harassed, not to lose your job, not to be arrested for nonpublic sexual activity. To this end, it waged political campaigns to decriminalize sodomy and to enact legislation banning antigay discrimination in the workplace and in public accommodations. The aim was to create a world in which it was safe for gay people to live their lives.[8]

As noted earlier, the political stand, and legal tactic, of the gay rights movement was to position homosexuality as an insignificant difference, like left-handedness and color blindness. Homosexuality became only a small part of personal self-definition: We are just like everyone else. In arguing against antigay discrimination, gay rights advocates used the established legal models of gender and race as immutable characteristics that were unrelated to the ability to perform a job, buy a house, or rent an apartment. Gay sexuality, as a unique sexual and social marker, was indistinguishable then from heterosexuality and therefore no impediment to homosexuals' being accepted as active, productive members of society. Thus, if homosexuals only had an acknowledged "right to privacy," they would be safe from discrimination and antigay prejudice.

The problem with this paradigm was that the ideal of visibility directly contradicted the "right to privacy." For mainstream culture, *any* manifestation of homosexual visibility immediately raised the specter of homosexual activity—which was not accepted as morally, socially, or biologically neutral. Because mainstream culture refused to accept homosexual activity, gay sex—and any of its manifestations—had to be hidden to avoid prosecution. Under these conditions, the concept of a "right to privacy" was null, because "privacy" could not be freely chosen. In addition, the constant regulation of homosexuality—enforced by state and social disapproval—made the concept of freely chosen privacy impossible.

The ultimate effect of arguing for a "right to privacy"—even in conjunction with recognizing the need for visibility—was to reinforce the closet. To argue that gay people were "just like everyone else," when gay sexuality was still unacceptable to mainstream culture, was to argue a lie. For gay people to have to hide any evidence of their sexuality—especially since most manifestations of homosexual orientation were seen by mainstream culture as synonymous with activity—was to promote gay invisibility. Like the immigrants who arrived in the United States and discovered that acceptance came only with eradication of any visible "difference," gay people would have to appear not-gay in order to obtain safety and security in the world.

3. Hardwick: *The Failure of Privacy*

THE contradiction and shortsightedness of a "right to privacy" in the fight for gay freedom became overwhelmingly evident in the Supreme Court's 1986 ruling in *Bowers v. Hardwick.*

On the surface *Bowers v. Hardwick* was the ideal case for gay rights advocates to argue for the right of privacy for gay sexual activity. In August 1982 Michael Hardwick was arrested under Georgia's sodomy law for engaging in oral sex with a consenting partner in his own bedroom. The statute forbade contact between the genitals and the mouth or anus for both heterosexuals and homosexuals. Hardwick brought suit in the federal district court, challenging the constitutionality of the law; he lost, but won a reversal from the court of appeals. The State of Georgia then appealed the case to the Supreme Court, which ruled that the Constitution "does not confer a fundamental right upon homosexuals to engage in sodomy." The court's 5–4 decision was based upon a complex history of legislated and common law that dealt with both privacy and sexuality. The Court rejected that idea that the home was a "private" place, outside of the law's jurisdiction, claiming that "victimless crimes, such as the possession and use of illegal drugs, do not escape the law where they are committed at home." The Court then placed prohibitions against sodomy in a historical context, noting that "proscriptions against [it] have ancient roots" and that "decisions of individuals relating to homosexual conduct have been subject to state intervention throughout the history of Western Civilization and the condemnation of those practices is firmly rooted in Judeo-Christian moral and ethical standards." The Court concluded that "to hold that the act of homosexual sodomy is somehow protected as a fundamental right would to be to cast aside a millennia of moral teaching."[9]

The most telling aspect of *Bowers v. Hardwick,* however, is the Court's response to a history of legal precedents that established a "right to privacy" in a range of issues relating to intimate, personal choices, such as family relationships, the raising of children, marriage, procreation, contraception, and abortion—all of which might logically apply in extending the right of privacy to consensual gay sexual activity. The Court declared, however, that "we think it evident that none of the rights announced in those cases bears any resemblance to the claimed constitutional right of homosexuals to engage in acts of sodomy [since] no connection between family, marriage, or procreation on the one hand and homosexual activity on the other has been demonstrated."

Bowers v. Hardwick is predicated on the assumption that homosexuality has been, and continues to be, a serious threat to Western civilization and heterosexuality. This is driven home by the Court's categorization of homosexuality as having "no connection" to "family, marriage, or procreation." In the Court's thinking, homosexual activity is unique in nature—it bears no relation to any form of heterosexual sexual activity. Sexuality, for the Supreme Court, and for mainstream culture, is defined as simply heterosexual and reproductive, even if reproduction does not take place. Within this restrictive definition of homosexual activity, *Bowers v. Hardwick* was impossible to win.

The thinking implicit in *Bowers v. Hardwick* is that homosexual sodomy presents a clear and present danger to the state—an idea reinforced by the Court's de facto acceptance, despite the specific wording and intent of the statute, of heterosexual sodomy. If the Georgia statute were found unconstitutional—thus establishing a sexual "right to privacy" for homosexual activity—homosexual and heterosexual sexual activity would have been placed on equal footing. The Supreme Court was unwilling to do this, deciding that the state had a legitimate interest in regulating homosexual behavior because that behavior was a marked threat to the social and moral status quo. The Court's denial of a "right to privacy" based on homosexuality's conceptualization as a "victimless crime" reemphasizes the idea that homosexuality is an attack on the prevailing cultural norms, since, as with all "victimless crimes," society and the social order are the true victims. This thinking, taken to its logical conclusion, poses the question of whether gay people should be allowed to exist. Because they already do exist, the more pertinent question is, "How can be they be regulated?"

The uniqueness of the Court's view of homosexuality and activity is underscored by Justice Harry A. Blackmun's dissenting opinion, which, quoting an earlier privacy decision, states: "we protect those rights not because they contribute, in some direct and material way, to the general public welfare, but because they form so central a part of an individual's life. [T]he concept of privacy embodies the 'moral fact that a person belongs to himself and not to others or to society as a whole.'" The Court's majority opinion, however, predicated on the perceived destructiveness of homosexual activity, cannot imagine or admit a right to privacy for homosexuals. The homosexual cannot belong "to himself and not to others or to society as a whole" because homosexuality is completely anomalous to human life, sexuality, and culture.[10]

If Michael Hardwick's lawyers had been successful in their arguments, *Bowers v. Hardwick* would have established a right to engage in consensual homosexual activity in private. It is ironic than that the events leading up to Hardwick's arrest were, in reality, quite public.

Michael Hardwick's encounter with the law began a month before his arrest for committing sodomy, when an Atlanta police officer ticketed him for drinking in public outside a gay bar. During the discussion, it was established that Hardwick worked at the bar and was gay himself. Because of a discrepancy between the day and the date on the ticket, Hardwick failed to appear at the specified court hearing. Two hours later, the arresting officer came to Hardwick's house with a warrant for his arrest; Hardwick was not at home. This action was unusual, since it takes forty-eight hours under Georgia law to process a warrant. Upon hearing of the arrest warrant, Hardwick immediately paid his ticket and believed the case resolved. Three weeks later, Hardwick was accosted by three unknown men—whom he describes as "very straight, middle-thirties, civilian clothes"—outside his home; after establishing his identity, they beat him so badly that the cartilage was torn out of his nose and six ribs were broken. He managed to crawl into the house, leaving a trail of blood, and passed out in his bedroom. Hardwick and his lawyers presumed that these men were off-duty police officers—a presumption that, given the lack of any other motive, is consistent with an established pattern of harassment.

Three days after the beating, the police officer who had arrested Hardwick a month earlier appeared at Hardwick's home with a warrant for his arrest that cited the already paid ticket. It was there, after being admitted into the house by a roommate, that he found Hardwick in his bedroom engaging in oral sex with a male partner. Both men were arrested and taken to a holding tank where they were verbally abused as "cocksuckers" by the guards. Later that day, they were moved to another cell, with the guards making it clear to the inmates that Hardwick and his partner were homosexual. After his release, Hardwick arranged with the American Civil Liberties Union to represent him in the state court.[11]

Michael Hardwick's bedroom would not have been invaded by an Atlanta policeman if he had not already been established as having a public gay identity. Viewed in this light, and with the knowledge of the harassment that occurred before the arrest for sodomy, *Bowers v. Hardwick* is much more about the right of gay people to be public about their identity as homosexuals than it is about their right to engage in homosexual activities in private.

With these facts in mind, it is odd that neither Hardwick's lawyer's arguments before the Supreme Court nor the substantial press coverage of the case mentioned the police activities that led to Hardwick's arrest for sodomy. Yet, in the legal record, the press, and the popular imagination, *Bowers v. Hardwick* was repeatedly cast as being about the right to engage in consensual homosexual activity in private.

The continued insistence, despite evidence to the contrary, that *Bow-*

ers v. Hardwick is simply about the "right to privacy" is telling, since it reveals how deeply instilled the idea of privacy is in gay life and culture. While this may be the result of complicated historical circumstance, it is problematic because the idea of privacy and, by extension, the "right to privacy" cannot be argued as an abstract legal concept, divorced from the material reality of the gay body and gay sexuality.

Bowers v. Hardwick argued for the "right" of Hardwick to engage in same-gender sexual activity. Yet, according to legal scholar Kendall Thomas, "Hardwick presents a more fundamental issue. . . . whether the State of Georgia could constitutionally use its police power, specifically its criminalization of homosexual sodomy, to strike at Michael Hardwick's body, that is, at his basic physical existence. . . . Hardwick ought to be understood as a case about Michael Hardwick's right to be protected from state-sanctioned invasion of his corporal integrity, or more fundamentally, his simple bodily existence."[12]

Such an interpretation of Bowers v. Hardwick, and of Hardwick's experience itself, has to take seriously the idea of the gay body and gay sexuality. The prevailing trend in the gay rights movement has been to promote "privacy" as a safety zone for homosexuals. This has been done primarily by way of "Gay people are just like everyone else"—the idea that since there is essentially no difference between heterosexuality and homosexuality, homosexuals deserve the same "right to privacy" granted to heterosexuals. This political conceptualization, by its nature, diminishes and ignores gay sexuality, which is precisely what mainstream culture finds most threatening. The invisibility of gay sexuality in the fight for gay rights has made it difficult to respond to right-wing attacks on gay sex, because the movement has been focused on demanding a "right to privacy" rather than on formulating a strong defense of gay sexuality.

Bowers v. Hardwick did not simply deny gay people the "right to privacy." It stated explicitly that homosexuality has no relationship to any other human or sexual activity or social organization. As Kendall Thomas points out, a fight for the "right to privacy" overlooks the more important question of whether the state has the right to invade and abuse the public gay body. The escalating violence against gay men and lesbians—of which Michael Hardwick's experience is only one example—occurs in the public realm, and cannot be dealt with simply by securing a "right to privacy."

For the gay body and gay sexuality to have the freedom and integrity granted by full citizenship, it must be visible. Full visibility has not been possible within the gay rights movement's strategy to see a right to privacy, because this tactic, while understandable, has historically promoted and sustained gay invisibility. But the question of a right to privacy for gay sexual activity obscures the larger issue that is at the heart of the Supreme Court's ruling in *Bowers v. Hardwick:* How does mainstream culture deal with the enormous threat of gay sexuality? And beneath the myriad social and legal mechanisms to regulate, control, and hide homosexuality, there is a more profound question: If homosexuality is such a threat to culture and civilization, should it be allowed to exist at all?

4. Outing: The Regulation of Public Identity

OUTING—exposing the private gay lives of closeted public figures—erupted as a major political controversy in the early 1990s. Condemned by the mainstream press and hotly debated within the gay community, outing exemplifies the long-standing debates surrounding privacy, sexual identity, public disclosure, and political power that have existed within the gay movement. But the passion and intensity of debate that outing provoked underscored the fact that both the mainstream and the gay community understood the actual and symbolic importance of the issue: Who had the right to regulate gay identity and visibility?

Outing, as a nascent political strategy, first caught the popular imagination after *OutWeek* magazine published "The Secret Gay Life of Malcolm Forbes," by Michelangelo Signorile, its gossip columnist turned AIDS activist, in its March 18, 1990, issue. Signorile's exposé of businessman and socialite Forbes's semisecret gay life was bold, shocking journalism, but the idea of outing, and the politics and reasons behind it, were not new. As early as 1972, writer and gay liberationist John Francis Hunter speculated in his compendium of gay information, *The Gay Insider/USA,* that in the future a group of radical gays (known by various names including "The Lavender Conspiracy," "Operation Empty Closet," and "Mission: Possible") would launch a campaign to bring famous people out of the closet, either by persuasion or by force. Although Hunter's nearly twenty-year-old fantasy was not the blueprint for nineties outing, it spoke to a tension that has always existed between those who live openly lesbian and gay lives and those who remain closeted.[13]

The closet—and the privacy it provides—has been an essential component of gay life. While this "privacy" was often enforced, the emotional pain of the closet was also accompanied, for some, by the privilege of not being harassed for being homosexual. The inequality of this often engendered anger and resentment against people in the closet by those who were "out," and the tension and anger are woven into the very fabric of lesbian and gay life.

Up until the late 1960s, the closet was respected by most homosexuals as an unfortunate but necessary aspect of gay life: secrecy ensured some degree of safety. Gay liberation's mandate to "come out" challenged the need for enforced secrecy. It also redefined and sought "safety" by establishing a public space in which gay men and lesbians could be "out" without fear of punishment or recrimination. In this context, the closet was seen by many gay people as less of a necessity. Post-Stonewall politics articulated the position that, while coming out was a personal decision, more difficult for some than others, leaving the closet was a political and ethical action as well as an individual one. As the need for secrecy decreased, and coming out became easier, the closet was viewed with increasing disdain by those who were out.

This dichotomy was heightened as the gay movement grew more powerful in the 1970s and 1980s. Political conservatives and the religious right, intent on eradicating the public ground claimed by the gay movement, engendered a backlash that attempted to reestablish the closet by making it more difficult and dangerous to be openly gay. Thus, even though the pressure to remain closeted had steadily decreased since the 1950s, the importance and meaning of the closet grew. As homosexuality became more politicized and more visible, the closet took on greater significance; the importance of coming out was countered by increased social pressure to stay in. This created an environment in which men and women who were public figures, or had social and economic privilege, and decided to remain closeted were often seen, by those outside the closet, as remaining there less for safety than for the privileges it granted.

The advent of AIDS in the early 1980s radically changed the closet as a place of safety and privilege. AIDS effectively "outed" many gay men who would have remained closeted. Even popular public figures such as Rock Hudson and Liberace, who had been securely closeted for their entire public and professional lives, were forced out when they became ill. AIDS, as well as the increasing political power of the religious and right-wing political movement, generated a new wave of militant gay activism in groups like ACT UP and Queer Nation. These groups rejected the privacy arguments of the more mainstream gay rights movements, and the debate around "privacy" shifted radically.

When Michelangelo Signorile outed Malcolm Forbes in *OutWeek* magazine, it signaled a full-scale assault on the closet and the outspoken rules about privacy. The fact that Forbes was dead highlights the explosiveness of the issue. The mainstream press, however, which usually ignored gay publications, reported on Signorile's article, and outing suddenly became a hot political topic. It was debated on television talk shows; *L.A. Law* rushed a special episode on outing onto the air; and William Safire explored the term's origins in his *New York Times Magazine* column on language. In New York, OutPost, a guerrilla art collective, plastered New York City billboards and buildings with posters of allegedly closeted celebrities including Jodie Foster and Merv Griffin, with the words "Absolutely Queer" under their photos. The handwriting, as it were, was on the wall. The mainstream press claimed outing was journalistically unethical. Debate also raged within the gay community over the ethics, as well as the political efficacy, of outing public figures.

While outing began as a celebrity phenomenon, it quickly became overtly political. In 1990, direct-action groups like ACT UP targeted elected officials who they felt were betraying the gay community. Governor Jim Thompson of Illinois and Republican Senator Mark Hatfield of Oregon were outed as closeted homosexuals with histories of voting against gay rights and progressive AIDS legislation. ACT UP members in Portland even altered a Hatfield campaign billboard to read: "Hatfield, closeted Gay: Living a Lie—Voting to Oppress." The gay Washington rumor mill buzzed with speculation of who was going to be brought out next. As one outing advocate pointedly put it: "Come out while you are still able to do it yourself."

While the outing of Hollywood celebrities caused tremendous debate within the community—lesbian *Village Voice* columnist C. Carr described outing in general and the outing of Jodie Foster in particular as "gay bashing at its sickest"—the outing of politicians or public figures who enacted or defended antigay stances garnered more support from the gay community. The idea of a homosexual hindering the civil rights of other gay people, or worse, endangering gay men's health by cutting back AIDS programs, seemed so blatantly hypocritical that many gay people were willing to put aside the claim to privacy. Even *The Advocate,* after it had denounced outing as unethical, outed Pete Williams, a gay man who worked for the Pentagon. Michelangelo Signorile's *Advocate* piece focused on the hypocrisy of the Pentagon, which, with full knowledge of Williams's sexuality, continued to employ him while they refused to change the policy that forbade lesbians and gay men from serving in the military. *The Advocate*'s cover displayed Williams's face with the headline: "Did This Man Ruin 2,000 Lives, Know About the Suicides, Waste Taxpayers' Millions on Military Witchhunts?"

The stark juxtaposition of personal responsibility and the ideal of privacy prompted debate within the gay community. While many held fast to privacy as a moral, if not legal, right, they also understood the political power of outing. While Urvashi Vaid, executive director of the National Gay and Lesbian Task Force at the time of the Williams outing, rejected the practice as an attack on "sexual autonomy," she admits that it was instrumental in speeding up the fight to dismantle the military's anti-gay policies.[14]

The outing controversy became a widespread social debate not because of disagreement within the gay community, but because the mainstream media and political establishment were so vehemently against it. Every editorial about outing in a mainstream newspaper or magazine condemned the practice as an infringement on personal privacy.

What caused this vehement reaction in the mainstream media, which had never before evidenced much interest in the rights of gay people? The mainstream press argued that outing was an invasion of privacy and that what people did in bed (or their homes) was their own business. Even public figures, they argued, deserved private lives. These were arguments that the gay rights movement had been making, to little avail, for years. And while the mainstream media's claims had the ring of reason, they were in complete contradiction to the double standard the press had always used with regard to gay people. To understand this double standard and how it functions, it is important to see how the journalistic "right to privacy" is constructed, how it has changed, and what purpose it has served.

The "right to privacy" in the media is a social, not a legal, construction. While there are laws that prohibit spreading lies about a person, and laws that prohibit the unauthorized use of a person's name or image to sell a product, there is no constitutional "right to privacy" that prevents the media from reporting on the lives of public figures, or even private citizens. Historically, journalistic practice has evolved an ethic that, in general, prohibited writing about the "private" lives of public figures (and private citizens) unless there was a compelling reason to do so, thus making the subject newsworthy. The concept of "private life" was loosely defined and has changed over the years. A politician's business or monetary interests were, for instance, considered more private half a century ago than they are now, when financial disclosure is expected. Sexual, domestic, marital, and health situations were always considered private, as long as they did not become a public scandal. This was, in part, because the home was considered a private cultural space, but it was also a response to a general social prohibition against speaking publicly about sexual or personal matters. The past three decades, however, have seen enormous changes in how U.S. culture views the notion of "privacy" and what is newsworthy.[15]

The sanctity of privacy and the expectations about having it have shifted tremendously over this time. This has been primarily a legacy of the social-change movements of the 1960s that placed an enormous, and radically new, emphasis on the relationship between the personal and the public. "The personal is the political" was a hallmark of the civil rights, feminist, gay liberation, and human potential movements; it stated that an individual's "private" life, actions, and thoughts were as important and as influential as public persona and deeds.

The breakdown of the long-standing separation between the "private" and the "public" spheres was a significant disruption of the social order. It emphasized the importance of personal feelings (once considered relatively unimportant in public life) and created criteria by which personal actions could be judged publicly. This shift in how "public" and "private" were viewed was also influenced by a feminist critique of gender and power.

In their idealized, heterosexual conceptions, the public sphere was "masculine," while the private sphere of home and family was the province of the "feminine." "Men," functioning in the world, dealt with power, displayed nonemotional public personae, and exhibited hardness; women, running the home and dealing with children, displayed emotion and softness. Feminists demanded that the distinction between "public" and "private" change, because they limited the potential and actual opportunities for women in the public sphere.

The breakdown of the dichotomy between "public" and "private" spheres led to the belief that people were publicly responsible for their private actions. By the mid-1970s, a racist remark made by a politician in private was accepted as public information. And, by extension, other forms of a public figure's traditional private life—marital problems, domestic violence, adultery, alcohol and drug use, as well as relationships with children—were seen as pertinent and potentially public information. The conceptualization of what was newsworthy had changed dramatically.

Along with these changes, the gay liberation movement insisted on the right of gay men and lesbians to stop being forced into "privacy." This was not a matter of simply "uncloseting" homosexuality, but of maintaining its personal and social importance. Feminism, the human potential movement, and the gay liberation movement all insisted that personal experience and feelings were important, deserving of consideration and acknowledgment in the "public" sphere. Thus, coming out was not simply a social or personal move, but a deeply political one as well.[16]

The mainstream media's attempts to reflect these cultural changes shifted the basic precepts of "the right to privacy." Issues of domestic sexual and physical abuse were addressed with more vigilance by legal authorities and the press. It was now permissible to explore the domestic lives of political figures. This tied in with a larger cultural shift that emphasized the importance of the personal over the private. The increasing popularity of the soft-news media like *People* magazine in the early 1970s, the advent of personal-exposé television talk shows like *Oprah* in the 1980s, and a resurgence of the genre of the memoir in the late 1980s attest to the new cultural importance being attached to the public disclosure and validation of what were once thought of as personal or private areas of life. Tellingly, the process of both serious and frivolous self-revelation is now commonly referred to by the gay term "coming out." Television talk shows will proclaim that a guest is "coming out as an incest survivor," or a pop-personality magazine will describe a movie star as "coming out of the closet as a chocolate fanatic."[17]

While gay liberation's language has been appropriated by the mainstream media, the relationship between the movement and the media has always been problematic. It is in this light that the outing controversy—and in particular the mainstream media's denunciation of outing—has to be viewed. The journalistic "right to privacy," so quickly granted to heterosexuals, has been systematically denied to homosexuals. At the other extreme, the mainstream media have created a blackout, which is just now beginning to end, on honest reporting of gay and lesbian issues. "Privacy" in mainstream journalism has consistently been used to invisibilize, misrepresent, or punish gay people.

The Supreme Court, in *Bowers v. Hardwick,* legally constructed homosexuality as a unique identity and activity, virtually unconnected to any other aspect of human existence. In the same way, the mainstream media historically have defined homosexual behavior and orientation as totally separate from either heterosexual identity or other forms of sexuality. From the mid-twentieth century on, the media routinely presented gay people as criminals and "perverts" who existed outside the accepted moral and social order. It was common practice, before the gay liberation movement protested media coverage, for the mainstream media to refer to homosexuals with derogatory terms such as "fags," "perverts," and "homos"; use of these terms continued in news coverage in various parts of the country until the mid-1980s. The construction of journalistic "privacy" was predicated, historically, upon the privacy of the nuclear family and the heterosexual home; what occurred within those confines was out of the public eye. Because gay people did not fit into that paradigm, they were automatically seen, not as undeserving of privacy, but as simply beyond its reach.[18]

In practical terms, this meant that any indications of homosexuality among public or private figures were not protected by the "right to privacy." Until very recently, even the most staid and respected venues of the mainstream press routinely ran the names and addresses of men who were arrested for sex-related activities, even if performed in the privacy of the home; some small-town newspapers continue this practice today.

This practice both reflected and reinforced the reality that it was not only homosexual activity, but simply the appearance of being homosexual, that was often illegal. Laws that forbade public displays of homosexuality were regularly enforced until the late 1970s, and it was not uncommon for gay men and lesbians to be arrested for these "crimes." While the arrests themselves might be justified as "newsworthy," the printing of the names and addresses was simply punitive. In contrast to this, women arrested for prostitution, an equivalent victimless crime, were rarely named in newspaper stories; and their male customers—equally culpable under the law—were almost never even arrested.[19]

The journalistic "right to privacy" was not denied to all homosexuals, but granted selectively, functioning as a form of protection for those with power, or those who had the approval of mainstream culture. The press consistently covered up two decades of charges against Father Bruce Ritter. They did the same for FBI director J. Edgar Hoover, whose relationship with Clyde Tolson was common knowledge to the press for more than five decades. Both of these men were protected because their conservative political stances positioned them as defenders of the status quo.

Yet the "right to privacy" is waived intermittently by the press when it wants to discredit a public figure. *The New York Times* had editorialized against conservative lawyer and power broker Roy Cohn since his involvement with the Army-McCarthy hearings in 1954. Part of their attack on him was the constant implication that he was a homosexual. Cohn's relationship with G. David Schine, an assistant in his early career, was repeatedly represented, through insinuation, as sexual. These innuendos manifested themselves until Cohn's death. In his 1986 obituary the *Times* again imputed a homosexual identity to him by emphasizing his wearing a toupee and undergoing face-lifts, clear signs of nontraditional masculine vanity.

The attacks on Cohn are placed in perspective by the *Times's* protective coverage of Francis Cardinal Spellman. Knowledge of Spellman's homosexual activities was common throughout the Archdiocese of New York and political circles during his twenty-eight-year tenure as archbishop. These were never reported, even at his death in 1967. When Times Books, then a subsidiary of *The New York Times,* published *The American Pope: The Life and Times of Francis Cardinal Spellman,* by John Cooney, they insisted that the author remove a four-page, completely documented section that detailed Spellman's affairs with "priests, altar boys, and laymen."[20]

The selective granting of the "right to privacy" in journalism is further contextualized by the fact that, historically, the mainstream media simply did not report—or if they did, not accurately—on gay and lesbian life. This blackout on information took several forms. For most of the 1970s and 1980s, the mainstream media would not run a gay news or feature story without quoting, in the interests of "balance," an "expert" critical of homosexuality or the gay community. Large gay and lesbian events were not covered, or when they were, attendance was underreported. Organizers estimated that 650,000 people attended the 1987 national March on Washington for Lesbian and Gay Rights, yet most media reported the much lower police estimate of 200,000; and some papers reduced this to: "Thousands March for Gay Rights." The day after the march, when 3,000 people rallied and sat-in in front of the Supreme Court to protest the *Bowers v. Hardwick* decision, over 600 arrests were made. The protest was the largest act of civil disobedience since actions of the antiwar movement twenty years earlier, yet was not covered by *Time, Newsweek,* or *U.S. News & World Report.* Even in the early 1990s, it was often impossible for direct-action groups like ACT UP, Queer Nation, or the Lesbian Avengers to get press coverage for their protests.[21]

Often, even important stories were not covered because their homosexual content rendered them "unimportant." Within the first nineteen months of the AIDS epidemic, between July 3, 1981, and February 6, 1983, *The New York Times* ran a total of nineteen articles about AIDS. During that time, the number of diagnosed cases of AIDS increased from forty-one to almost one thousand. In comparison, in 1982, after several Manhattan drugstores discovered that random Tylenol containers had been contaminated with poison, *The New York Times* ran fifty-four articles in three months, even though there were only seven cases of poisoning.

Most newspapers in the United States will not identify the gay male survivor of someone who died of AIDS as "lover" in either obituary or paid death notice column.[22]

Many of these practices have changed, or been modified, in the past ten years because of pressure from the gay community. But the reality remains that the mainstream media have never treated homosexuality or the gay community according to the same standards by which others were treated. This mixture of invisibilization and biased reporting in the media has been one of the major ways that mainstream culture has regulated homosexuality. The angry and denunciatory attitude of the mainstream media—*Time* magazine called outing "an outrage"—in response to Michelangelo Signorile's articles on Malcolm Forbes and Pete Williams and the ensuing outing phenomenon was not a response to "unethical" or "unprofessional" behavior, but rather to the reality that it was being done by gay people in the gay press. The question was not about journalistic ethics but about who owned the closet. By forcibly commandeering mainstream culture's primary mechanism to regulate homosexuality, those gay people involved with outing created enormous social disruption and shifting of power. The anti-outing wrath of the mainstream media was less about privacy than the reality of gay people attaining and using their newfound social and political strength.

The power and reality of the closet, however, remained unacknowledged by the mainstream media in their arguments condemning outing, which were almost always positioned as being about privacy. This insistence on framing outing as simply a privacy issue allowed the media to avoid the more pertinent discussion of how entrenched and persistent the closet was in the organization of culture. To even talk about the closet would be to admit its existence, and would necessarily shift the argument from gay people having the right to be invisible to how they were forced to be invisible.

The mainstream media's news and editorial coverage of outing obscured the issue and the reality of "the closet," in often contradictory ways. The most obvious of these was portraying outing as an invasion of the privacy of gay people who "chose to stay in the closet," thus presenting the decision not to come out as a free choice, rather than as part of a broad, socially mandated, strategy of enforced invisibility. Sarah Schulman, in an eloquent letter to *The Village Voice,* stated: "To call [outing] an invasion of privacy is distorting and dishonest. Most people stay in the closet . . . because to do so is a prerequisite for employment. Having to hide the way you live because of fear of punishment isn't a 'right,' nor is it 'privacy.' Being in the closet . . . is maintained by force, not choice."[23]

The mainstream press also presented the closet as a good thing for gay people, a safeguard against antigay sentiments and actions. Refusing to take any responsibility for their role in promoting and perpetuating gay invisibility and harmful attitudes against gay people, the press claimed that gay people would be hurt by outing. The hypocrisy of this was evident in an anti-outing piece by conservative *Chicago Tribune* columnist Mike Royko where, in blatantly antigay tone and language—he refers to homosexuals as "fruits"—he described how people who were outed would face enormous legal, social, and job discrimination.[24]

The mainstream media also portrayed outing as the result of a gay movement—particularly as embodied by ACT UP and Queer Nation— going too far. Editorials frequently pitted "radical and militant gays" against other homosexuals, a rhetorical device that ignored and misrepresented the real intracommunity discussions about outing, and the complicated concerns about privacy and safety. While the gay community was divided on the issue—with a small group of gay people vocally supporting outing, and the majority ranging from confused to highly ambivalent to opposing it—the media's portrayal of anti-outing gay people as the "good gays" was an attempt to actively demonize those gay people who were socially disruptive. This was a replay of the "good" gay–"bad" gay split that occurred in the 1960s homophile movement.

Perhaps most startling in the media's attack on outing was the constant reference to the "unwritten law" in gay life that forbade dragging people out of the closet. While the enforced secrecy of pre-Stonewall life had mandated a stricter code of silence, both gay life and gay politics had changed in three decades. This "unwritten law" was obviously no longer obeyed by all gay people, some of whom had decided that truth and publicness were more important political strategies than enforced secrecy and "privacy." The media's uncritical and self-serving use of this "law" was an attempt to defend its own anti-outing position by attacking homosexuals themselves as being destructive and antigay.

These anti-outing arguments, ironically, gave the impression that the mainstream press was interested in protecting homosexuals—particularly from other homosexuals—and pointed up the double standard that had always defined the relationship of the media to homosexuality. Most obviously, while the mainstream media expressed shock at outing's "invasion of privacy," most of the press had no trouble reporting on the private lives of heterosexual public figures. "Why is it OK," asked Gabriel Rotello, the publisher of *OutWeek,* "to bring out Roseanne Barr as a woman who has had an abortion in her youth and Gary Hart as an adulterer and not OK to bring out gays?"

The double standard of outing homosexuals and heterosexuals has more complicated origins than simply the mainstream media's desire to regulate homosexuals' visibility. When heterosexuals are "outed," it is always for a specific action or activity—the accusation of Bill Clinton's affair with Gennifer Flowers, or Nancy Reagan's alleged dalliance with Frank Sinatra. Straight people are never outed for their sexual orientation. Indeed, the presumption of heterosexuality is so pervasive in our culture that it would be impossible—except in the case of the most self-declared homosexual—to "out" someone as heterosexual. On the other hand, almost all outing of homosexuals is a public declaration of their orientation, rather than specific sexual activity. Sometimes, a specific sexual episode may prompt, or exemplify, the report, but the essence of outing is to make public someone's homosexual orientation.

The double standard in the media would allow specific information about Bill Clinton's sex life to be an exception to the "right to privacy," but would argue that simply saying that Pete Williams is gay is an "invasion" of privacy. This seeming contradiction was explicated by film critic Vito Russo, who countered the argument that a person's sexual activity being a private matter does not even apply to outing: "When we say someone's gay, we're talking about *sexual orientation,* not their sexual activity. It's not our fault that every time someone says *gay,* people think 'sex.' That's *their* twisted problem."[25]

The conflation of sexual activity with sexual identity strikes at the heart of the problems of privacy, gay visibility, and outing. Homosexuals are defined by their sexual activity in a way that heterosexuals are not. The slightest indication of gay visibility immediately implies the overt presence of gay sexuality to mainstream culture. This is why all forms of gay visibility, including simple coming out, are socially disruptive. "I don't mind what gay people do in their own homes," claims a young mother in response to homosexuals on a television talk show. "I just don't want them coming out in my living room." The threat of gay sexuality is so strong that it is not only seen as inseparable from gay sexual activity, but it instills a desire to regulate and control any visible sign of homosexual identity.

Mainstream culture insists upon the constant regulation of homosexual visibility, and the media have been a major enforcer of that regulation.

The press controlled what images of homosexuals and homosexuality were available to the larger culture. It controlled who was able to stay in the closet and who was able to come out. It controlled who had a "right to privacy" and who did not. It controlled who was deemed an appropriate spokesperson for gay rights and who was too "militant."

By the mid-1990s, the political and social parameters of outing began to shift. This occurred for three reasons. The original spate of outings was shocking to both mainstream culture and the gay community. As an act of overt political resistance, outing pushed the boundaries of acceptable behavior; it spoke what was previously considered literally unspeakable. Once outing emerged as a phenomenon, however, its original boldness was tamed; the unspeakable had been spoken. The very act of outing changed how outing was viewed.

As the political climate became more conservative and hostile to gay rights, so did gay and mainstream perceptions of outing. The outings of political figures who had supported antigay political issues—such as cuts in AIDS funding, the military's antigay policy, and the 1996 Defense of Marriage Act (DOMA)—were viewed with sympathy by those in the gay press and community who had once vehemently opposed outing. They were also widely reported in the mainstream press, which had heretofore refused to name an "outed" public figure. This signified an important shift in the conceptualization of outing. Framed no longer as a "privacy" issue, but as one of political and community accountability, information about the private lives of gay politicians now became "newsworthy." Barbara Mikulski, liberal representative from Maryland, was outed by ACT UP members as a lesbian and publicly confronted about her vote in favor of DOMA.

The public perception of outing also changed because the never stable boundaries of "public" and "private" had continued to shift. It was no longer possible to deny—to the gay community or to a broader public—that "private" sexuality had a connection to political action or public persona. This subtle shift made even the threat of outing potent, and some closeted gay public officials began to come out on their own after outing had been threatened. Conservative Republican Congressman Steve Gunderson of Wisconsin gave interviews in 1994 to both *The New York Times Magazine* and *The Advocate* in which he spoke of his sexuality after he had been threatened with outing. The same was true of Arizona Republican Congressman Jim Kolbe. Outing was shocking when it first was used as a political strategy in 1990, but in six years, while still controversial, it become a more accepted part of political discourse and tactics.[26]

The power of outing is that it refuses to let the mainstream media continue to control the terms of privacy. The closet functions as a powerful force in both gay life and the heterosexual world. It protects as well as hides, and the media understand what a powerful force it can be. Beneath the specifics of individual cases and arguments about journalistic ethics, the real meaning of the outing controversy is the intrinsic problem of privacy for homosexuals.

Privacy is socially constructed to regulate not only the visibility of individual sexual acts, but also public manifestations of sexual identity and community. In this way it effectively polices and contains broader discussions about sexual freedom and pleasure. How can gay people find freedom, as well as sexual, psychological, cultural, and physical autonomy, by seeking the right to privacy in a public world that hates them?

Eleven

The Gay Ghetto and the
Creation of Culture

1. Being Visible and Being Public

T HE GAY VISIBILITY that emerged after the Stonewall riots was a relief from the enforced privacy of the pre-Stonewall years. Gay
people insisted that they would no longer be invisible. But while it was
more possible for gay people to fight discrimination from their new position of visibility, the visibility itself did not guarantee acceptance. Often,
the overt presence of homosexuality and more public displays of gay culture engendered a backlash intended to reinforce the closet. This backlash continues today.

Visibility is the ability to be seen, observed, detected; while the decision to become visible is active, being visible is essentially a passive
stance. Being visible is very different from being "public." Historically, for
an individual or a group to be public meant that they were an integral
part of the life of the state—the *res publica*. This public status entitled the
individual to the rights and responsibilities of citizenship. Citizens were
expected to partake in public discourse in a full and open manner, and
their opinions and lives were treated with respect, which included their
not being harassed or abused. In short, they were essential and indispensable members of the body politic.

In the United States gay people are more visible today than ever before, but they are not allowed to be public. They are denied full rights of
citizenship, such as the right to marry and to join the military. In thirty-
nine states, it is still permissible to discriminate against homosexuals in
housing and the workplace; there is no federal law that prevents or re-
dresses discrimination against homosexuals. The Supreme Court has
ruled that there is no constitutional right to privacy for homosexual

sexual activity. In addition, gay man and lesbians frequently are verbally and physically harassed and intimidated. Most journalists and politicians view gay people's opinions as morally suspect or politically limited, or, at best, as special pleading.

Increased visibility for gay people has not ensured for them full rights of citizenship—the right to be "public"—or the social context of safety and respect in which to express themselves fully. Visibility for gay people immediately reinforces their stigmatization by identifying them *as* gay people. By remaining in the closet, gay people can more fully participate as citizens. The irony is that gay people can be *public*—treated as full citizens—as long as they are not *visible* as gay people.

For gay people to be truly public, they would have to be able to display their sexual orientation and discuss their sexuality within the same parameters laid out for heterosexuals. Even if antigay discrimination and harassment were eliminated, gay people would still not be truly public until they were allowed to be as open about their sexuality as heterosexuals. Until gay sexuality is removed from the realm of "privacy," gay people will never be full citizens.

Complete freedom of expression for gay sexuality is the keystone of gay freedom, for it is homosexual sexual activity that makes gay people different. This sexual otherness is at the root of mainstream culture's deep-seated anxiety about homosexuality and its demand that homosexual visibility be regulated by enforcing the closet.

As gay people demanded increasing visibility, mainstream culture responded by creating small exceptions to the closet, social spaces of sanctioned gay visibility. Often these were unspoken truces involving specific social space. It was possible, for example, for gay people to be more visible or honest about their sexuality in certain professions, such as theater or the arts. However, it was equally important for gay people to find material space in the physical world. It would be in this space that they might not only be "visible," but also find the security and the potential social power to become "public" as well. The homosexual demand for visibility and mainstream culture's constant response of regulation manifested themselves in the material world of space and bodies in the formation of the gay ghetto.

2. The Ghetto

San Francisco is a refugee camp for homosexuals. We have fled
here from every part of the nation, and like refugees elsewhere,
we came not because it is so great here, but because it was so bad
there. By tens of thousands, we fled small towns where to be ourselves would endanger our jobs and any hope of a decent life; we
have fled from blackmailing cops, from families who disowned or
tolerated us; we have been drummed out of the armed services,
thrown out of schools, fired from jobs, beaten by punks and po-
licemen.

And we have formed a ghetto, out of self-protection. It is a
ghetto rather than a free territory because it is still theirs. Straight
cops patrol us, straight legislators govern us, straight employers
keep us in line, straight money exploits us. We have pretended
everything is OK, because we haven't been able to see how to
change it—we've been afraid.

—Carl Wittman, "A Gay Manifesto"[1]

The idea of the ghetto—a separate, defined space, within a city, that
houses a specific minority and their culture—has been intrinsic to how
Western culture has defined urban space since the end of the Middle
Ages. Over the past five hundred years, the ghetto has taken a variety of
forms, but one of its major functions has always been to regulate and
control minority culture. The specifics of a ghetto are dictated by historical and social circumstance; they reflect the complex political and psychological relationships between the dominant culture and the minority
cultures. These relationships rest not only upon the power imbalance between dominant cultures and subcultures but also upon the actual and
symbolic threat posed by the subculture to the status quo of the mainstream—a threat that often causes enormous anxiety for the mainstream.

The institution of the ghetto and the associated regulation of public
space in a city perform two important functions. By delineating a circumscribed physical space, the ghetto sets its inhabitants aside as separate
from the proper sphere of city life. That is, ghetto dwellers, while they
may have the right to vote, and may even wield some political power, are
not public or full citizens. Also, the existence of the ghetto defines

citizenship by declaring those who live outside of it as the authentic citizens. The demarcation of who is and isn't a citizen—who is given full rights, including the right to live free from harassment, and who isn't— makes the ghetto a vital part of the definition of city life.

In the past five hundred years, ghettos have taken a variety of forms that manifest enormous differences as well as some similarities. The enforced, restrictive, and at times intentionally genocidal conditions of the Jewish ghettos of Europe (from the end of the Middle Ages to the mid-twentieth century) are obviously somewhat different from the postindustrial social and economic disenfranchisement that reinforces and regulates the black ghettos in the United States. The ghettos of Chinatowns and barrios, defined by cultural differences as well as language, also exhibit tremendous divergence from other ghettos. By definition the material and psychological conditions of the gay ghetto are distinct and unique. Yet even with these differences, each of these ghettos betrays similarities that explicate the complex relationship between dominant culture, minority culture, and the use and regulation of public space.

The Jewish ghetto created in Venice in 1516 is a prototype of the use and meaning of the ghetto in the contemporary world. Most of Europe had forbidden Jews to reside alongside Christians since the anti-Semitic edicts of the Third Lateran Council in 1179. In 1215 by decree of Pope Innocent III, Jews were also mandated to wear an identifying yellow badge or yellow clothing, sometimes embroidered with the Star of David. It was in Venice, however, with its canal-separated islands, that a ghetto, completely isolated from the rest of city life, would be built. In 1516, the Jews of Venice were moved to the Ghetto Nuovo, an old foundry far from the center of the city. (*Ghetto* comes from the old Venetian dialect for "foundry," from *ghetàr,* to cast.) In 1520, there were 1,500 to 2,000 Jews in Venice's population of 120,000.[2]

Only two occupations were open to Jews at this time: medicine and money-lending, both of which were indispensable to the trade city of Venice, but were considered inappropriate professions for Christians. Jews, therefore, were integral to the economic, social, and medical worlds of Venice, and were accepted as such. This understanding of social necessity coexisted with intense anti-Semitism, which frequently erupted in riots during which city officials would raise the drawbridges, sealing off and protecting the ghetto.

While the ghetto was a site of enforced isolation, it was also a place of great learning and culture. The study of history, scripture, and the Talmud flourished inside the ghetto walls. The relationship of the ghetto to the city was not static, but changed to suit the needs of the city. Jewish moneylenders, for example, were allowed more social freedom when they were needed to bolster Venice's failing finances. Even Jewish culture, viewed by both church and state as heretical and dangerous, was promoted and made visible when Venetians thought they might experience pleasure from it. By 1628, the Jewish musical academy was so noted that Venetian nobility would go into the ghetto to hear it perform.

The social relationship between Venetian Jews and Christians was ruled by a complex set of written and unwritten laws, the purpose of which was to allay Christian fears of "the other." Venetian law prohibited any sexual contact between Christians and Jews. Jews were blamed for spreading syphilis and leprosy, both of which were thought to be spread by casual contact. Social formality forbade Christians from touching a Jew's body; business contracts between two Christians were sealed with a kiss or a handshake, but those between a Christian and a Jew with a bow. The fear of the diseased and unclean Jew ran deep, and "proof" of this was seen in Jewish kashruth (dietary laws) and laws mandating cleanliness. A Venetian legislator noted: "These people were so negligent of cleanliness . . . that even their legislators were obliged to make a law to compel them to even wash their hands."[3]

The anxieties of Venice's Christians about sexuality and pleasure were manifested in their view of Jews, and the Jewish body became increasingly sexualized in the Christian imagination. Circumcision was seen as simultaneously a mark of hypersexuality and of feminization and Jewish law was believed to mandate orgies at circumcisions. Even usury was sexualized, since the usurer, it was thought, "puts his money to the unnatural act of generation." Venetian law demanded that Christian prostitutes and pimps wear yellow scarves, making them the only class of people who wore this color besides Jews. Prostitutes were forbidden to wear jewelry, again linking them to Jewish women, who never wore their jewelry outside of the ghetto.

In time, Jews and sexual outsiders became linked in the popular Venetian imagination. Venice enacted laws to regulate the housing and workplaces of prostitutes, in imitation of the Jewish ghetto. Furthermore, because of the stigma of male feminization associated with circumcision, the Jew was symbolically linked with the homosexual. When public manifestations of homosexuality became too prominent—particularly a subculture of cross-dressing and a widespread, visible network of gondolier-hustlers—Venice enacted strict regulatory laws that resembled those governing Jews.[4]

The Jewish ghetto of Venice and the laws regulating Jewish social presence were concrete manifestations of how mainstream culture dealt with anxiety about "the other." Because Venetian Jews contributed to the economic and cultural life of the city, their position as religious and cultural outsiders—and thus a threat to the basic Christian organization of the society—had to be constantly reified. This was done by making them easily identifiable, and by physically isolating them within the broader cityscape. More important, Venetian culture defined Jewish otherness as overtly and dangerously sexual and viewed Jewish bodies as vectors of disease. By conflating sexuality and disease, it used the stigmatization of the Jewish body to further demonize Jewish culture, and to justify regulating it. While the construction and conditions of the Jewish ghetto in Renaissance Venice are specific to their time and place, it is possible to view them as prototypes for the structures and purposes of contemporary ghettos.

The construction of the ghetto serves three material functions: ghettos contain, protect, and display. By separating "the other" in a secure geographic area, they ensure that the minority is "visible" and easy to detect. The ability to identify "the other" is an important mechanism for mainstream culture to allay its fears of cultural difference. While the overt presence of "the other" can be socially disruptive, it is the fear of the undetected "other"—the Jew or the homosexual who passes, and therefore can corrupt from the inside—that engenders even more anxiety. By functioning as a place of visible containment, the ghetto minimizes the fear of the hidden, scary "other."

The ghetto also protects minority groups. Journalist Nat Hentoff has written how, as a Jewish schoolboy in 1940s Boston, he always ran the risk of being beaten up by Irish-Catholic thugs if he ventured out of his own neighborhood. Black residents of urban areas know that they are less likely to be harassed by police or by white people in their own 'hood. The gay ghetto has long been a haven for gay men and lesbians. Even when it may attract violence from outsiders, the gay ghetto creates a space for the possibility of safe public displays of same-gender affection, socializing, and networking. While the protection of the ghetto is never inviolate, other public space is often less safe for gay people.[5]

The ghetto also functions as a place of display; that is, it offers visible evidence of a minority presence and culture. For mainstream culture, this display may be a spectacle of "otherness," in which the ghetto and its inhabitants are viewed as a freak show, or, more patronizingly, as needing help. But the display of ghetto culture also functions as a beacon to minority people who live outside of it. From the early 1920s, African Americans new to Manhattan would gravitate to Harlem, intuiting that they would feel comfortable there. From World War II on, gay men and lesbians understood that New York's Greenwich Village and San Francisco's North Beach neighborhood were gay friendly. Ironically, reports in the national press intending to "expose" and condemn the shocking life of gay ghettos served to promote them to men and women from across the country who otherwise would never have heard of them. By functioning as a visible focal point for minority people, ghettos produce and sustain that minority identity and culture.

The ghetto also generates a third type of display: the presentation of ghetto culture that is produced in a geographic and psychological atmosphere of safety, self-reflection, and support. The accomplishments of the Venetian Jewish musical academy, the literary masterpieces of the Harlem Renaissance, and the birth of off-Broadway theater in Greenwich Village in the 1950s are examples of how culture is made in such a crucible.[6] Because the alternative culture produced in the ghetto appealed to the mainstream, the ghetto became designated as a source of pleasure. The designation of the ghetto as a generator of artistic and cultural pleasure, however, complicated its relationship to mainstream culture. On one hand, mainstream enjoyment of this alternative culture meant that the ghetto was interacting with the broader culture. On the other hand, because ghetto culture often presented visions and ideas that mainstream culture found both pleasurable and threatening, the threat of the ghetto increased.

Beyond these material functions, the ghetto also serves a fourth purpose that is psychological in nature. Because sexuality and pleasure are so strictly repressed and regulated by mainstream culture, the desire for them causes an anxiety that is, in part, alleviated by projecting them onto nonmainstream cultures. For example, there is a long, sustained history of Anglo and European culture viewing nonwhite minorities as exotic, "primitive," and hypersexual. The same process of projection has also influenced how mainstream culture views Jews and homosexuals, and, at times, working-class people as well. This act of projection not only alleviates the anxiety of mainstream culture, but also contributes to the creation, or reinforcement, of the minority's identity as sexual outsiders. The creation and maintenance of the ghetto establishes a distinct space, identified with outsider culture, onto which mainstream culture projects it sexual and emotional ambivalence. While there are enormous differences among specific ghettos, they each become the focus of the mainstream's projection of sexual ambivalence. Just as the Jewish ghetto of Venice became the repository for Christians' fears of sexuality and difference, black ghettos have traditionally fulfilled a similar function for whites. The outsider sexual status of homosexuality, and the more open and honest presentation of sexuality in gay life and culture, have engendered a similar erotic projection that manifests itself in the relationship between the gay ghetto and the city.

The eroticization of the ghetto and its culture creates an "erogenous zone" in the cityscape, easily identifiable as a source of pleasure—sexual and otherwise. While serving the material function of providing outlets for pleasure, this zone also creates and reinforces a cultural and psychological separation of pleasure from everyday life for nonghetto members. Mainstream culture views the pleasures of the ghetto—however they may be defined—as distinctly separate from how "normal" people live their lives. In this way the ghetto takes on an emotional and metaphoric meaning as vital as its geographic importance.[7]

3. Public Gay Spaces: The Invisible Map

ONE of the defining moments in European and U.S. history was the enormous population shift from the rural to the urban that began in the early eighteenth century. This occurred in concert with a move from an agrarian to an industrialized economy, the decline of the biological family as the primary focus of self-identification, the rise of individual identity, and the separation of sexual activity from reproduction. Cities grew as people moved there to find work and an independent life away from their biological families. The rise of urban life promoted the formation of new cultures, including a visible gay and lesbian culture.

The blooming of gay public spaces in urban areas occurred, to a large extent, because the population density of cities ensured a higher percentage of self-identified gay people. As early as 1730, London had clearly defined meeting and cruising places for gay men. As gay communities continued to emerge, gay people found myriad ways to be simultaneously visible and hidden within a complex cityscape. The emergence of public, if not always completely visible, gay space was very important because it encouraged the continued formation of a social community. As important, because only the middle and upper-middle classes had access to private space for socializing, gay use of public space included, and was often defined by, the presence of lower-income and working people. This phenomenon reoccurred continually over the next two centuries.[8]

The emergence of half-hidden gay space—known to homosexuals, obscure to heterosexuals—provided an invisible map for gay men. This map can be conceptualized as a transparent overlay on the official grids and curves, parks and boundaries, of the urban environment. The invisible map was gradually revealed to gay men new to the city by those who already knew its landscape. Many cities sported a "Vaseline Alley" or "Fruited Plain," and certain standard features of the cityscape—the densely wooded park, the waterfront—were commonly known by gay men to be likely meeting places. In 1974, when television talk show host Dick Cavett pointedly asked Tennessee Williams if he was a homosexual, the playwright answered without missing a beat, "I cover the waterfront"—a coded reference to his own cruising habits as well as to a Billie Holiday song of that title that was a gay favorite.

As gay people struggled to find ways to be safely visible, the physical city itself provided a set of templates to accommodate their visibility. City life was structured mainly around the needs of single, working people, and this made the city hospitable to lesbians and gay men. Offices, small factories, and department stores offered plentiful jobs and livable wages. Boardinghouses and apartment buildings allowed men and women to live alone (but provided very little other private space); those that catered to a primarily gay clientele often appeared indistinguishable from those that did not, thus providing a degree of invisibility and safety. The fabric of city life offered gay people a multiplicity of venues to meet, socialize, cruise, and form a community. Reasonably priced restaurants, cafés, and cafeterias provided even the lowest-paid workers a place to eat, and inexpensive entertainment like movies, pool halls, dance halls, and theater were available for socializing and relaxation. Parks, esplanades, and city squares offered free space for solitude or cruising. All of these places existed on both the visible and the invisible map, used by gay people and heterosexuals simultaneously, although perhaps without the knowledge of the latter.[9]

The complexity and diversity of city life suited the needs of the emerging gay community. Density of population ensured that a private person might live his or her life relatively unnoticed and unharassed. This was different from "anonymity"—a word frequently used by sociologists to describe the isolating relationship of the often overwhelming urban population to the individual. Gay people, as a group, were not isolated in urban settings, but had numerous options for personal and communal interaction.[10]

The modern city provided gay people with what urban theorist Richard Sennett calls "multiple contact points": the ability of urban locations to maintain distinct and different identities and functions, often simultaneously, transforming their use and meaning in response to changing needs of inhabitants. This was also true for individuals. It was possible to pass for heterosexual at a job, yet be "gay" when attending the theater with friends or cruising a park. The visible/invisible homosexual world dovetailed neatly with the possibility of multiple use of city locations and the ability to change identities in various public places.

The contours and parameters of the invisible map were formed by needs of the gay community and were always in flux. Geographic features such as streets, parks, and riverbanks, which define a city's physical structure, can change, but that modification usually occurs slowly. Urban populations, however, can shift more rapidly, and these changes often influence how a city is organized, and sometimes even the material structures of a city. Manhattan offers a clear example of this phenomenon. In the early years of the century, New York rapidly became a city of single people: 900,000 single men and 700,000 single women lived within its boundaries. More than 40 percent of men over the age of fifteen were unmarried. *The New York Times Magazine* observed in 1928: "For the Nation's bachelors this city is a Mecca. Not only is it the City of Youth, but it is the City of the Single. It is certain they are not all in a [Madison Square] Garden line-up waiting for admission to the next fight, neither are they all concentrated in speakeasies or along the docks . . . the city has something for every bachelor."[11]

This increase in the unmarried population quickly changed the social and physical structure of the city: the need for boardinghouses and rooming houses increased; taverns and dance halls became places to socialize publicly; inexpensive evening socializing and nightlife grew up to accommodate large numbers of people with low-paying jobs. Historian George Chauncey, in *Gay New York*, has described how, in the early twentieth century, the first clearly defined gay public spaces in New York were working-class neighborhoods, taverns, and entertainment venues. While middle-class gay people had the luxury of socializing and conducting relationships in the privacy of their homes, working-class people—who lived in crowded tenements or boardinghouses—had to socialize, meet sexual partners, and often even have sex in public. This was the beginning of a visible urban gay community.

The emergence of gay public space in a broader framework of working-class culture had three resonant, long-lasting implications. In working-class culture, homosexual visibility occurred in the context of other open sexual displays. Entertainment was more sexually explicit in taverns and bars than in more middle-class venues like theaters. Prostitution, for both women and men, was openly discussed and negotiated, as was abortion. In this context, homosexuality, while still frowned upon by many, secured and maintained a new visibility, its outlaw status on the same par as other illegal or socially unacceptable sexual behavior.[12]

The more open sexuality of working-class neighborhoods caused native-born U.S. citizens to equate these areas and their large immigrant populations—Jews, Italians, Germans, and the Irish—with sexual license. This began an ever-widening cultural gap between middle- and working-class attitudes over the propriety of the displays of sexual orientation and behavior—a disagreement that has shaped contemporary ideas about "public" and "private." Because working-class neighborhoods tolerated a wide range of public and semipublic sexuality, they were frequented by middle- and upper-class men looking for casual sexual or social companionship they could not find in their own social networks.

These neighborhoods illustrate how public space defines, and is defined by, broader social perceptions of gender, class, and sexuality, as well as material use. Women in these neighborhoods often had options for sexual experience and employment denied middle-class women restrained by more sexually repressive social conventions. While many working-class women held jobs to support themselves or their families, they also enjoyed more social freedom than women of higher class status. In turn, it was not uncommon for middle-class people to view poor working women as loose or immoral. Because sexuality was displayed more openly in these neighborhoods, working-class people were thought, by the middle class, to be more sexually active. Displays of masculinity differed in working-class neighborhoods as well, and the images of both the traditional masculine working man and the more effeminate "fairy" or the "queen" were tolerated. This led to toleration of a variety of sexual relationships between men, some of whom identified as homosexuals and others who did not. As a result, working class neighborhoods often had the reputation of being places where gay men might live or socialize, and often such reputations increased over time.

Most of these emerging gay neighborhoods were not distinctly homosexual, but rather were places where gay people lived and socialized with some visibility among heterosexuals. As long as gay people were circumspect—and not very visible—they were not harassed. Often the side room of a hotel bar or the back room of a restaurant would be claimed, by tacit agreement of the management, as a gay public space. The existence of a semipublic, half-acknowledged gay community existing in close proximity to heterosexuals mitigated the hostility gay people faced. For heterosexuals, the presence of gay people provided tangible alternatives to the socially mandated paradigms of heterosexuality, and occasionally provided sexual partners. The places where the invisible map became more visible eased social tensions and provided a mutually beneficial working relationship between the two groups.

Working-class neighborhoods, by nature of their cramped or crowded living space, placed a high value on the use of streets and public or commercial venues such as parks and cafes. This supplied a high level of visibility to all residents and visitors. Visibility was what made, in a material sense, a cohesive neighborhood, and it fit neatly with the needs of an unmarried population whose lives did not center around the biological family or home. Sociologists have traditionally contended that a non-family-based urban presence has a disorganizing effect on cities: that the move away from conventional forms of social regulation—the family, church, school—causes social disruption. George Chauncey, however, argues that this is not a process of disorganization, but of reorganization. Over the past one hundred years, the primary organization of cities has shifted in favor of prioritizing the needs of the single person over the needs of the biological family; a reorganization has effectively changed how contemporary urban life is structured. It has also become the social and physical organization for what is now considered a "gay ghetto" or gay neighborhood.

The reorganization of urban life along nonreproductive, nonbiological family lines changed the mainstream's vision of cities. The increasing number of single women and men, the possibility of sexual activity divorced from reproduction, and the emergence of an urban environment that prioritized the pursuit of pleasure over the comforts (and restraints) of family all combined to promote the image of cities as places of temptation and sin. For those who lived in them, cities were also bastions of freedom. And the large number of single people, both straight and gay, looking for ways to spend their free time changed how mainstream culture viewed leisure time.

Traditionally, the upper classes had their clearly delineated "leisure time"; having time to engage in entertainment, not wage-earning, was one of the conditions that separated them from the working class. The idea that working people might have time devoted simply to pleasure was a fairly new concept. It was also a concept that many in mainstream culture, particularly those who worried about "public morals," saw as potentially problematic. They associated working-class "leisure time" with unchecked, unregulated, and nonreproductive sexuality.[13]

By 1910, over five hundred dance halls had opened in Manhattan, many of them in poorer neighborhoods, adjacent to saloons. The bulk of these establishments were located in highly populated tenement and boardinghouse districts, often in immigrant neighborhoods—the same locations in which gay populations were becoming visible. Many of these venues were noted for their aura of sexual possibility. This sexualization of urban culture was present in other aspects of city life as well. New forms of commercial advertising, and the advent of the electric (and later the neon) light in advertising, often displaying sexual messages, lit up the city at night, promoting an atmosphere of socializing and adventure. Even the newly invented "department stores" (which replaced single-product, utilitarian shops) changed how urban life looked, and by the early 1920s, their elaborate, colorful displays that eroticized clothing, ornamentation, and even undergarments, added to the increasing sexualization of the city. The department stores also made shopping a leisure experience, which it never was before, and large, lavish window displays allowed "window shoppers"—particularly women—new access to public streets. Gay men also found that the ability to "loiter" in front of store windows was a good cover for the often illegal act of cruising.[14]

The increased possibility of public sexual display supported and was supported by enclaves of gay culture. Throughout the 1920s, both Harlem and Greenwich Village became noted centers of gay life and culture. While each was shaped by its specific history and geography, as well as racial and sexual politics, both became vital to the overall social and cultural structure of the entire city.

Harlem, stretching from 114th Street to 159th Street and bordered by the East River and St. Nicholas Avenue, was, in the nineteenth century, a white-middle-class neighborhood of row houses and a thriving commercial district. In 1905, a depression and overbuilding caused a surplus of cheap housing, and black tenants began moving in. White residents fought this integration—one plan was to build a twenty-four-foot-high fence on 136th Street to prevent the spread of black tenancy and ownership—but eventually gave up and left the neighborhood. By 1914, a twenty-four-block area in the center of Harlem was occupied by black residents. Harlem's black population grew as waves of black workers—

more than 250,000 by 1918—fled the overt racist violence and discrimination of the South to Northern cities.[15]

Harlem was made up of apartment buildings, rooming houses, and small sections of owner-occupied buildings. Commercial space was prominent in residential neighborhoods and provided venues for socializing and business; Harlem was a very public neighborhood that afforded its inhabitants a large degree of safety and personal freedom. The freedom that Harlem offered had a sexual component as well. A wide range of sexual behaviors was tolerated, and the social life of Harlem in this period was marked by a sexual openness, both heterosexual and homosexual, that manifested itself in risqué nightclub acts, public drag balls, and an active sex industry. Harlem became a refuge from oppression and a center of black culture and pride. "I'd rather be a lamppost in Harlem than the Governor of Georgia," proclaimed a black folk saying of the time.

The growth of black Harlem as a haven of security and visibility (it was relatively safe in comparison to the South and even other parts of Manhattan), as well as personal freedom, contributed to its becoming a thriving site of black culture. Drawing upon such diverse sources as black folk narratives, expressionism, black nationalism, white bohemian writing, and traditional black secular and religious music, black culture flourished in a movement that was commonly called, by 1920, the Harlem Renaissance. This new, proud black culture was quickly embraced by the mainstream. Black literary writing was published, reviewed, and read by the white establishment, in what poet and novelist Langston Hughes called "the vogue of the Negro." Alfred A. Knopf released novels by Claude McKay, Nella Larsen, and Hughes, among others; these sold well, some even becoming best-sellers.

The flowering of racial pride and artistic production was accompanied, in large part, by a startling new publicness of homosexual identity and culture that informed much of the work that came out of the Harlem Renaissance. While writers like Langston Hughes and Countee Cullen were closeted about their homosexuality, others, like Bruce Nugent and patron of the arts A'lelia Walker, lived more openly. Harlem's acceptance of homosexuality was reinforced by the very public displays of popular culture it supported, such as the Hamilton Lodge Balls, large semiprofessional drag extravaganzas open to the public, and the ability of its performers to be candid about their lives. This influence also spread from Harlem into mainstream culture and, combined with the sexual freedom in Harlem socializing, identified Harlem as having a distinctly gay character.

Black popular entertainment—particularly jazz, blues, and dance—became extraordinarily popular among nonblacks. Blues songs were traditionally sexual in lyrics and spirit, and homosexuality was overtly detailed in songs like "Two Old Maids in a Folding Bed" and "Sissy Man." More important, performers such as Ma Rainey, Bessie Smith, Ethel Waters, and Alberta Hunter were fairly open about their own homosexual activity, and singer Gladys Bentley was famous for performing in drag, singing explicitly sexual songs, and even marrying her lover in a civil ceremony in Atlantic City.

The black popular culture with its open view of sexuality, supported by the Harlem Renaissance, was embraced by mainstream culture, in both the United States and Europe. Noted Harlem performers such as Florence Mills and Mae Barnes became nationally famous when they appeared in *Shuffle Along,* Broadway's first black musical. Josephine Baker's extraordinary success in France, along with the European careers of Bricktop, Alberta Hunter, and Elisabeth Welch (all of whom were known for their lesbian affairs), defined U.S. popular culture, for Europeans, as primarily black and jazz oriented.

While much black art found other venues, Harlem's theaters, nightclubs, and churches remained the place where it originated. In a highly segregated city, it was also the only place that black gay men and lesbians could find any public community. At the height of the Renaissance, Harlem became as famous a place for whites to visit as it was for blacks to live. Harlem's gay life was as much a lure to white gay men and lesbians from other parts of the city. It was there, where the invisible map was less so, that they could find a visible and distinct gay community. The influx of white audiences to Harlem established it, in the mainstream popular imagination, as an important cultural center, as well as a primary source of pleasure within the city.[16]

Like Harlem, Greenwich Village evolved as a site of public gay space in response to changes in New York's social and economic structure. Originally a retreat for wealthy New Yorkers, by 1900 the Village, then called the Ninth Ward, had become a settling place for Italian immigrants. Like other immigrant, working-class neighborhoods, the Village was constructed around inexpensive housing, community-oriented business, and an active public street life. By 1910, an eclectic bohemian population of artists, intellectuals, feminists, and political dissidents began to move to the Village. They were attracted by the neighborhood's small-scale physical and social structure, as well as by its inexpensive rents, conducive to socializing and forming a community. The broader trends in city life toward increased sexualization and public display became more pronounced in the Village. Most of the newcomers held views that were prosex, antimarriage, favorable to birth control, politically progressive, and prioritizing of pleasure over utilitarian production. Political and cultural magazines like *The Masses, Woman Rebel,* and *The Little Review* were published here; experimental theater was presented at the Provincetown Playhouse; and coffeehouses and town meetings became forums for progressive political thought and movements.[17]

This sexually relaxed, profeminist, antiestablishment atmosphere allowed, and at times encouraged, a gay and lesbian presence in the village. By the mid-teens, the gay visibility that had originated in the public saloons and cafés of Manhattan's immigrant communities (usually located around the Bowery and the Lower East Side) now manifested itself in the Village, as gay men and lesbians began to feel enough safety to establish a presence. While there was still some social discomfort about homosexuality among the heterosexual bohemians, and some gay people in the Village saw themselves as individuals rather than part of a "community," the Village was well on its way to becoming a visible location on the invisible map. As the Village became known as a homosexual enclave, more gay people flocked there. This was part of an enormous postwar migration from country to city, but also the direct result of the increasing sexualization of U.S. political movements for personal freedom, including woman suffrage, the fight for birth control, black civil rights, and labor organizing. By the mid-1920s, the Village had a thriving gay community that, for the most part, coexisted peacefully with straight bohemia. Cafés, cafeterias, coffeehouses, and bars catered to a gay clientele, promoting visibility and a sense of community. These establishments were patronized not only by Village residents, but also by out-of-neighborhood gay men and lesbians who saw the Village as a haven.

George Chauncey notes that neither Harlem nor the Village was a "gay neighborhood," because "in neither did homosexuals set the tone." They did, however, fulfill several of the social functions of the traditional ghetto. Both the Village and Harlem were sites of concentrated gay visibility. More important, they functioned as places of display and enticement. As the alternative life of Harlem and the Village became "visible" to the rest of the city, clearly defining them as urban erogenous zones, it brought tourists and slummers who were attracted to the allure of sexual activity, as well as to the artistic accomplishments of the neighbor-hoods. The culture and art produced in these settings was emblematic of (and made possible by) the sexual and political freedom found there.

Harlem and the Village, as concentrated centers of visible gayness, were distinct in the broader cityscape, yet remained clearly connected to the larger urban constellation. But rather than simply containing homo-sexuality, the presence of visible gay life in Harlem and Greenwich Vil-lage highlighted the increased sexuality of the whole city, and this, in turn, engendered various forms of backlash. Since the turn of the cen-tury, reformers and legislators had been attempting to regulate the emer-gence of sexuality in urban life. Laws regulating popular entertainment and "men only" admission policies were enacted to "protect" women. Laws prohibiting certain types of dancing, and limiting contact between dancers, were enforced, especially in dance halls catering to a lower-class and immigrant clientele. The visible gay sexual socializing in both Har-lem and the Village was occasionally affected by these reforms, but, for the most part, these ghettos were viewed as distinctly separate parts of Manhattan.[18]

In 1920, the Eighteenth Amendment and its legal enforcement, the Volstead Act, began thirteen years of Prohibition. Prohibition was a log-ical extension of the middle-class temperance movement, and was a re-action against the perceived threat of working-class immigrant culture. Prohibition had a decidedly ironic effect on social life in Manhattan. By forcing alcohol sales underground, Prohibition thrust most socializing into secrecy. Like homosexuals looking for gay public spaces on the in-visible map, heterosexuals were now forced to navigate their own un-charted social journeys. With no "official" maps, they located speakeasies by talking to cabdrivers and hotel doormen, or watching which buildings certain people entered.

The culture of secretness that Prohibition established fostered a sense of illegal intrigue. The economics of liquor were now unregulated and underground, often the province of gangsters. Speakeasy entertainment was often risqué, the atmosphere highly sexual. Patrons, challenging taboos, frequently socialized across class, gender, sexual-orientation, and sometimes even racial lines. By 1928, the speakeasy had so changed popular moral standards that the Committee of Fourteen, a private morals watchdog group, claimed: "Speakeasies lend an atmosphere of ap-parent respectability to prostitution." Even worse, they complained, was that the strict barriers of middle-class morality were being threatened, since respectable women and men were frequent speakeasy patrons.

Prohibition, by rendering all gay *and* straight nightlife illegal, ironically created an atmosphere that gave it enormous prominence. Existing only underground, speakeasy culture—and its eroticizing effects—became a primary venue for U.S. socializing.[19]

During Prohibition the New York City zoning laws, traditionally concerned with regulating residential and commercial development, were used by neighborhood and business associations to keep "undesirable" venues out of exclusive or wealthy neighborhoods. Electric advertising was viewed by some in city government as a threat to the sexual propriety of city life, not because it changed the aesthetic landscape, but because it encouraged nighttime socializing. A zoning campaign in 1922 banned all "projecting and illuminating signs on Fifth Ave., because they attracted the "wrong sort of people." Brightly colored electric signage was, however, allowed to flourish in Times Square, already established as a highly commercialized and sexualized site for both gay and straight people.[20]

Times Square changed in other substantial ways during Prohibition. Many Times Square restaurants and nightclubs, unable to serve liquor, closed. In turn, this caused a precipitous decline in Broadway theater attendance. When the vacant theaters turned to showing films and booking vaudeville acts, they attracted a less wealthy, more streetwise audience. Illegal liquor sales, prostitution, and gambling all became commonplace in Times Square, which was quickly acquiring a reputation as the center of Manhattan's public sexual life. Gay male culture also thrived here, as theaters and nightclubs began featuring drag shows highlighting gay-themed humor. Cruising and a visible gay male street presence became so commonplace that for decades Times Square was known not by its traditional nickname, the Great White Way, but as the Gay White Way. Along with Harlem and Greenwich Village, Times Square, with its bright lights and carnival atmosphere, was making the invisible map of Manhattan increasingly visible.

This increased visibility began to engender a backlash, similar to those of past decades, against the increasing eroticization of the city. In 1933, Prohibition was repealed, but moral reformers pressured city and state officials to attempt to regulate marginal, "undesirable" social life. George Chauncey notes that the new government agencies, mandated to monitor the sale and distribution of liquor, had another intended purpose: to regulate the public spaces where people drank and socialized. New regulations enforced by the New York State Liquor Authority forbade the licensing of any establishments deemed to be "disorderly"—legally defined as any bar in which prostitution, gambling, or gay socializing could be observed. This was, in part, a response to the emergence of bars catering exclusively to gay patrons, which appeared in the frenzy of post-Prohibition socializing and commerce. In the face of this campaign of legal harassment, the life expectancy of most gay bars was short. The SLA regulations occurred in tandem with efforts by private groups, such as the Committee of Fourteen, to "clean up" Times Square and other parts of the city by banning drag shows and demanding that the police, using antiloitering and antiprostitution laws, crack down on a visible gay street culture. This forced gay people to remain in neighborhoods such as the Village and Harlem.

The enclosure of an openly gay population, beginning in the 1930s, was part of a larger series of changes that were taking place in U.S. society. The Depression changed mainstream perceptions and expectations of gender. Jobs were scarce, and those that were available were more likely to go to men than women; men with families were viewed by employers as more dependable, deserving workers. The prioritization of married men in the job market not only penalized women and single men, but also codified traditional gender roles and the conservative social position of marriage.

In concert with these economic changes came the rise of a new and stable social heterosexual identity, what Jonathan Katz has called "the invention of heterosexuality." It was only in the late nineteenth century that reproductive intercourse, conflated with strictly defined gender identities and a socially sanctioned ideal of sexual pleasure, became a fixed social entity and ideology. By the mid-1920s, heterosexuality was fully established as an identity. The word first appeared in a U.S. dictionary in 1934, defined as "manifestation of passion for one of the opposite sex; normal sexuality." This newly secured identity, in conjunction with tightened economic conditions, solidified traditional gender roles, which, in turn, rendered homosexuality more clearly "the other." The new heterosexual identity was also defined as more clearly reproductive, thus separating it from the nonreproductive, and pleasure-based, homosexuality.[21]

As the "difference" between heterosexuals and homosexuals became increasingly emphasized, the options for mixed straight and gay socializing declined—an ironic turn of events, since gay influence had been instrumental in helping to sexualize urban space, thus expanding freedom for heterosexuals. But as the "difference" between sexual orientations became increasingly apparent, visible homosexuality, as an alternative and a threat, loomed larger than before. As a result, mainstream society placed stricter legal and social regulations on gay visibility and socializing, changing the textures of everyday life by redefining and reorganizing the use of urban space.

Throughout the 1930s, bars and clubs that were found to be "disorderly"—defined, in part, as having an openly gay presence—faced harassment and were frequently forced to close. Throughout the 1920s and early 1930s, the number of men arrested for street cruising yearly were in the hundreds. By the mid-1930s, determined campaigns to stop street cruising were implemented; and in the years after World War II, arrests increased tenfold.[22]

The campaign to remove homosexuality from the public sphere also took other forms. Pressure from religious groups encouraged Manhattan police to enforce existing censorship laws. In 1927, after New York's archbishop called for a purge of "perversion" from the Broadway stage, the police raided and shut down three productions, including Mae West's *Sex,* a play about prostitution that drew on gay and black culture, and *The Captive,* a French play about lesbianism. West's play *The Drag,* which featured actual drag performers in its plot about a closeted gay man, could not open because of political and legal pressure. A letter from "a mother" to *The New York Times* urged the mayor to ban West's play because "perversion is a horror and a social smallpox." West responded angrily to the controversy: "The men who run New York were afraid my play would start a riot."[23]

Explicitly homosexual work by gay artists was also censored or discouraged. Paul Cadmus's 1934 painting *The Fleet's In,* which showed sailors cavorting with homosexuals—identified by styled hair and red ties—was removed from a Washington, D.C., exhibit after the secretary of the navy called it "an unwarranted insult" and said it "evidently originated in [a] sordid, depraved imagination." The outrage against *The Fleet's In* (and other explicitly gay Cadmus works of the 1930s and 1940s) was emblematic of how visible manifestations of gayness were gradually being separated out from mainstream culture. Cadmus's paintings of urban life—realistic tableaux set in the YMCA, public parks, and Greenwich Village cafeterias—always depicted obviously gay figures intermingled with heterosexuals, a reflection of the heterogenous socializing of the times. A straightforward depiction of how sailors socialized was now seen as the product of a "sordid, depraved imagination."[24]

The public space that was once open, if in limited ways, to gay people was now becoming smaller and more contained. After the Depression, Harlem's economy could no longer support the nightlife that sustained gay visibility. Times Square continued to be the well-lit and vibrant heart to Manhattan's sexual pulse, but increased social and legal restrictions now limited the gay presence. Only Greenwich Village remained, to a large extent, a place in which visible gay life might find public space, but even there gay life was more subdued than a decade earlier.

Along with the emergence of a heterosexual identity and the economic hardship of the Depression, it was the growth of the city itself that contributed to the decline of gay presence in public space. As Manhattan had expanded and prospered throughout the 1920s, the city's social and physical organization had become increasingly complex: neighborhoods were in constant flux; ethnic and social identities were changing; economic, class, and gender statuses were protean. Richard Sennett argues that while change and diversity are hallmarks of a healthy city, they can also engender, at times, a lack of psychic and emotional coherence— "disorder"—for city inhabitants. Overwhelmed by intense stimulation, city dwellers may, at certain historical moments, seek to impose order on their lives by attempting to simplify the urban environment. The separation of visible homosexuality and gay culture from public space was an attempt to decomplicate Manhattan's sexual and social complexity, to make it more manageable for heterosexuals. Part of the simplification process was to make homosexuality less present in the general public space and allow it to exist in a secure, but constrained, area: the ghetto.[25]

The institution of the gay ghetto relieved heterosexual anxiety about the semivisible presence of gay people within the city. Throughout the 1930s and 1940s fear of the "hidden homosexual" in U.S. culture continually increased. The 1948 publication of Alfred Kinsey's *Sexual Behavior in the Human Male* gave empirical evidence that homosexuality existed in all strata of society, and that homosexuals could not be identified by stereotypes. This reinforced heterosexuals' fears that homosexuals might lurk anywhere. Popular psychology promoted the idea of the "latent" homosexual—one who was "hidden" within even "normal-looking" men, who might not even realize it themselves. The ghetto alleviated this anxiety, for while it made homosexuality visible, by implication it publicly defined heterosexuality as well.

While the ghetto offered gay people the option of living more open, honest lives, it also signaled a substantive change. For homosexuals, the city no longer offered the multiplicity of identities that it once did—the possibility of being half-visible—and gay people were forced to choose between being more closeted or more open about their sexuality. It was Greenwich Village, with its history of tolerance and its already concentrated gay population, that became Manhattan's unofficially designated gay residential ghetto. While earlier the gay presence had not "set the tone" for the neighborhood, it began to do so more than ever before. The invisible map still existed, but it had been altered. A visible ghetto— a clearly defined place where homosexuals could be seen to exist—had emerged as an indelible mark on the public and private consciousness of the city. For the first time, homosexuality had been granted a public space, and the effects of this on both gay and straight people were unavoidable.

4. Ghettos and Roots: Homosexual Statelessness, or a Crisis in Public Space

IN her essay about European refugees after World War II, philosopher Simone Weil wrote:

> To be rooted is perhaps the most important and least recognized need of the human soul. It is one of the hardest to define. A human being has roots by virtue of his real, active, and natural participation in the life of a community, which preserves in living shape certain particular treasures of the past and certain particular expectations for the future. This participation is a natural one, in the sense that it is automatically brought about by place, conditions of birth, profession, and social surroundings. Every human being needs to have multiple roots. It is necessary for him to draw wellnigh the whole of his moral, intellectual, and spiritual life by way of the environment of which he forms a natural part.[26]

For gay people, a sense of rootedness—which would come, in part, from finding and cultivating lasting public space—is imperative for fostering and creating community. The act of being homosexual is essentially one of displacement and dislocation from the traditional body politic. Gay people stand apart from their nuclear families; their sexual activity is criminalized; their sexual desires are pathologized.

While the situation for gay people is quite different from that of the worldwide diaspora for Jews, their lack of a homeland—in the sense of physical community—is similar. Viewed by both sovereignties and republics as unable, or unwilling, to be part of the prevailing state, Jews were essentially stateless for centuries—without secure citizenship, without rights, and open to all forms of oppression and harassment. Often, even when Jews saw themselves as full-fledged members of a state, their enfranchisement was tenuous and was eventually terminated. The paranoid fantasy of the Jewish traitor—which found its perfect manifestation in France's famous Dreyfus Affair—was predicated not only on the fear of Jewish disloyalty, but on the Jews' presumed, often enforced, condition of statelessness. A contemporary editorial in a right-wing paper "excused" Dreyfus by claiming: "[He] has committed an abuse of confidence, but he has not committed a crime against his country. In order for a man to betray his country, it is necessary first of all that he have a country." The editorial went on to conclude that "the Jews cannot help it" when they betray "their" country.[27]

Richard Sennett notes how this language of anti-Semitism functions not only to denigrate Jews but also to create and reinforce a sense of self-worth for the anti-Semite, and he observes that, "at an ideological level, a language of anti-Semitism . . . arises to expiate the sins of the Anti-Semites of the past." By positing a continuous, universal state of condoned anti-Semitism, this language continually establishes the anti-Semite as the "good citizen" who speaks his mind to protect the good of the republic and the body politic.

The similar exclusion of gay people from the republic—from citizenship—arises from their exclusion from the nuclear family: heterosexuality is a prerequisite for citizenship. The creation of a gay culture and community is an attempt by gay people to find some form of cohesion—a metaphysical, sexual statehood—in spite of the diaspora from what Christopher Isherwood calls "the heterosexual dictatorship."

The simple presence of homosexuals creates a problem for mainstream culture; in a culture in which heterosexuality is the presumed common, shared identity, gay people are automatically suspect. Homosexuals, like the stateless Jews, are by definition outside of full citizenship, and are thus viewed by mainstream culture as having divided loyalties. Just as Dreyfus, defined only by his loyalty to Jews, was said to have betrayed France because "Jews cannot help it," homosexuals, defined only by their antipathy to heterosexual norms, are seen as being unable to control their sexual urges. This sexual traitorousness marks the homosexual as a social and moral pariah whose actions can bring about the moral, political, and—for some evangelical Christians—even physical demise of the state.

This places homosexuals outside of accepted social systems and raises the question of their function in society and, equally important, where they can live. In Venetian culture, Jews were assigned the roles of moneylender and doctor, and they were forced to live in the ghetto. In contemporary Western culture, homosexuals are granted the roles of "artists" and "creators of culture." These are the acceptable gay social "functions" and are, obviously, not as severely mandated as roles for Jews in Renaissance Europe. While these roles or functions make *social* space for the obvious or "out" homosexual to exist in mainstream culture, they do not create a safe *physical* space for homosexuals to live in. The perceived uncleanliness of the homosexual, like that of the Jew—a mixture of sexuality, disease, and contagion—makes him a threat to the moral and physical health of the body politic. The creation of the ghetto—the space that isolates "the other"—solves that problem through the regulation of public space.

The emergence of a distinct urban gay ghetto at mid-century began with the decline of homosexual visibility in public life in the 1930s, but it was the enormous social changes that occurred during and after World War II that allowed it to take root and flourish. The war caused large shifts of population within the United States as, beginning in 1940, more than 16 million men registered for the draft. Many others, women and men, left their hometowns for cities to work for the war effort. In *Coming Out Under Fire: The History of Gay Men and Women in World War II,* Allan Bérubé describes how the complex social and sexual changes engendered by the Second World War allowed large numbers of women and men to come out. The war, and military life, undercut traditional heterosexual expectations by enabling, even encouraging, intimate friendships among people of the same gender. Women outside of the military found new social and personal freedom as they left the home and entered the workforce. After the war, there were many more openly gay women and men than before, with many of them choosing not to return to their homes and biological families and instead settling in large cities.

The visible presence of so large a number of gay people in urban areas occurred in a broader context of social upheaval. After World War II, there was a strong trend in U.S. culture to return to the traditional social structures that had existed before the war, and in particular a reaffirmation of traditional gender roles and the primacy of the family. In the media, men were portrayed as providers and heads of households; women were urged to stay at home, out of the public sphere of the workplace. The nuclear family and the private home were valorized by the media and in the popular imagination, and childhood was idealized as a place of nonsexual innocence. Television shows like *Father Knows Best,* and "women's magazines" such as *Ladies' Home Journal* and *Good Housekeeping,* which flourished after the war, reinforced these ideals. Manufacturers of products ranging from appliances to cleaning products to toys marketed their products to the mythical American family, which was white, suburban, and middle-class and consisted of a working father, at-home mother, and two children. Television became the focal point of home life—between 1948 and 1955 nearly two-thirds of all U.S. families bought one—and this new image of the American family, and its values, was broadcast into millions of living rooms every night.[28]

This conservative social ideology was, in part, a response to the sexual and personal freedoms women and men claimed during the war. It was also greatly shaped by a postwar economic prosperity that promoted a white, heterosexual, middle-class, consumer culture as emblematically "American." This new "America" was, to a large extent, predicated on the idealization and cultivation of "privacy" (and private space) for the nuclear family. As more middle-class families moved to the suburbs, man's place was defined as the public space of the city workplace, but he returned every evening to the woman's private space of the suburban home. Children played in the safe space of the backyard or park. Space became, not only gendered, but also increasingly defined by "safety." The fear of "unsafe" public space became a struggle over the control of public space. This struggle precipitated a series of conflicts, which manifested themselves in a crisis of public space in U.S. culture, a crisis that took many forms.[29]

As young people exhibited discontent with their suburban lives and rebelled in the 1950s, the media and Hollywood promoted fear of their attempts at freedom by conjuring up images of juvenile delinquents and motorcycle gangs taking over city blocks and town squares. As African Americans increasingly demanded basic rights of citizenship, their struggle often centered on the demand that the "public space" of lunch counters and rest rooms be accessible to them. As more gay men and lesbians became visible, their presence was seen as a sign of moral and social decay.

Mainstream culture's anxiety over these conflicts was often projected onto the city itself. Articles in *Life* magazine and more conservative publications like *Reader's Digest* consistently portrayed the city as an unsafe place. In this backlash, cities were no longer perceived as sites of independence and freedom—hallmarks of nontraditional life and culture—but as dangers to families, children, and, increasingly, "Americans." Richard Sennett claims that the exodus of heterosexual families to the suburbs, traditionally viewed by sociologists as a flight from urban crime and disorder, was in actuality a retreat from the diversity of city life to the semiprivate/public space of the suburbs—what he calls the movement into "the new puritanism."

The formation of the gay urban ghetto at this time was a response to the crisis of public space. The gay ghetto was a manifestation of the "dangerous" diversities of city life, but also a public display of difference that helped reinforce the idea of "normal" (i.e., hetero-) sexuality and the importance of the biological family. Just as the Jewish ghetto reinforced the definitions of what it meant to be Christian, the function of the gay ghetto was to make clear not only who was gay but also who was heterosexual. The invention of the gay ghetto was specific in time and place. It could only have happened in the context of postwar U.S. culture and economy, and at a time when the ideas about gender, sexuality, family, and the city were being debated and revised. The emergence of the gay ghetto was a response to the needs of gay people, but also to the enormous changes occurring in mainstream culture.

Greenwich Village in New York is the prototype of gay ghettos—including North Beach in San Francisco, and West Hollywood in Los Angeles—that arose around the country in the late 1940s and the 1950s. Because of its bohemian history Greenwich Village was already known by homosexuals as a "safe" place, and it was a logical place for gay people to relocate after the war. The Village offered cheap rents and a varied housing stock—including tenements, dilapidated row houses, and a few single frame homes—that lent itself to rooming houses, small apartments, and artists' studios.

A gay ghetto emerged in Greenwich Village because the basic social and physical structures established there by the immigrant Italian community matched neatly the needs of the burgeoning homosexual community attempting to establish itself as a visible, public entity. These were similar to the structures that contributed to the formation of a visible public homosexuality at the turn of the century, but now, in the wake of the enormous changes in postwar life, they were paramount in defining the gay ghetto.[30]

Urban immigrant communities in the first half of the century exhibited many of the same characteristics as the emerging postwar gay community: isolation, political disenfranchisement, and cultural hostility from the mainstream culture. The social and physical structures of earlier immigrant communities evolved to suit their emotional, social, and political needs. In this context the ghetto helped form a cohesive community. Public spaces, such as taverns and cafés, promoted a visible social life that allowed people to meet and know one another. Mixed residential and owner-run commercial spaces created a cohesion of daily needs and business that fostered community. Busy daytime and evening use of sidewalks and public areas created an atmosphere of safety and security. This use of public space also encouraged informal information networks—often denigrated by outsiders as "gossip" or "the grapevine"—that helped spread social or political information within communities that could not rely on the mainstream press for accurate information about their lives. The presence of what urban theorist Jane Jacobs calls "street characters" was also vital for community cohesion. Such a character—identifiable to everyone on the neighborhood—might be a store owner, a busybody, a "yenta," or even a priest or rabbi. They provided an important source of information, continuity, and security.[31]

Immigrant culture that would not have been supported by the mainstream was protected and nurtured by the ghetto: the Yiddish theater flourished on New York's Lower East Side; religious feasts and music in Little Italy survive even today. The ghetto also provided a natural, well-structured, and secure political base from which immigrant groups could gain social and political power that allowed them some access and leverage in mainstream culture. The ghetto promoted the continuance of a distinct minority identity.

In the postwar Village, the social and physical structures of immigrant community life were deftly adapted to the needs of the gay community, which, as it demonstrated its commitment to the neighborhood, coexisted peacefully with its heterosexual neighbors. Public spaces, such as bars, cafés, and restaurants, made gay socializing visible. While gay bars were strictly regulated by the city and the police in the 1950s, a network of eating and drinking venues throughout the Village created a very public gay presence. While preexisting small, owner-run businesses, such as produce markets, butcher shops, tailors, and cobblers, provided for everyday needs, gay-owned and -run antique shops and art galleries also flourished in the Village. These provided economic and emotional security for their owners and workers, who could be openly gay without fear of reprisal. Other shops—with wares ranging from theatrical and art supplies to specially designed clothing—found their core clientele in the Village but also drew in non-Village gay people, increasing gay visibility and strengthening the economic viability of the neighborhood.

The social and business life of the gay ghetto promoted an active use of streets and sidewalks by residents and visitors. This was vital for ensuring a climate of safety. Jane Jacobs has demonstrated how active sidewalk use is an essential prerequisite for community safety, and nowhere was this more true than in the gay ghetto. Busy streets—as well as the socializing that took place on front stoops and even fire escapes— created an environment that was well observed and constantly watched. If trouble did break out, residents could deal with it immediately. Jacobs's paradigm that neighborhood residents were communally responsible for shared public space—a variation on the age-old political ideal of "the common"—built a sense of community. This, in turn, encouraged the exchange of social and political information, vital for community coherence. The importance of this type of communication is reflected in gay language and slang. In 1950s Greenwich Village, the phrase "I heard it on the gay-vine" was mirrored by the gay folk wisdom that the three fastest means of communication were "telephone, telegraph, and tell-a-faggot," attesting to the importance of "gossip" as a form of community communication. The existence of street characters—often bartenders, sometimes street hustlers or drag queens—is also a vital aspect of the social world of the gay ghetto.[32]

The two most important differences between the traditional immigrant ghetto and the gay ghetto lie in the fact that gay ghettos are composed of both homosexuals and heterosexuals, and in the role that sexuality plays in the gay ghetto. These two factors shape not only the nature of the gay ghetto, but how gay people interact with the world around them.

While Italian, black, or Jewish ghettos were populated almost entirely by members of the same ethnic group (or if they were mixed, each group had its clearly designated space), gay ghettos were not composed entirely of gay people. The gay ghetto created a safety zone that allowed visibility with fewer fears of reprisal. It is difficult to ascertain the percentage of gay people living in the Village from the mid-1950s to the late 1960s, or for that matter the percentage of gay people living in the gay ghettos of today. Given the political and social climate, the number of visible gay men and lesbians living in Greenwich Village at that time—while higher than in other parts of the city—was certainly a small percentage of the neighborhood's population. How, then, with such a small gay population, did it become a "gay ghetto"?[33]

In U.S. social life, the presence of openly gay people in a public place is so unusual and striking, for both heterosexuals and homosexuals, that the impact resonates far beyond what the small numbers might indicate. Thus, a relatively few gay people can make a clearly defined space "look" much gayer than it actually is. If an increasing number of openly gay people are visible in an area, it will eventually reach a "tipping point," creating the impression that the gay presence is far stronger and more numerous than it is. A "tipping point," in epidemiology and social science, is the critical moment or aggregate number at which the growth of a disease or a phenomenon will increase or decrease. If enough openly gay people live and socialize in a neighborhood, the area may get a reputation for "being gay." If they continue to live there and set up rudimentary social structures, such as businesses and street life—thus making it appealing for more gay people to live or socialize—it may become a "gay neighborhood." The change depends less upon *large* numbers of gay people than upon the perception that the neighborhood is "gay." The more openly gay people live in or visit a neighborhood, the "gayer" it becomes; in this way visibility breeds more visibility. Ironically, this is the reverse of the process in traditional white European immigrant ghettos, which were dependent upon large populations. Those ghettos were enforced areas—albeit safe and nurturing—from which people, once "Americanized," were allowed to move; they were transitional. The gay ghetto, on the other hand, is chosen as a place of safety. It is predicated on encouraging visibility that can be found nowhere else. The gay ghetto values visibility and uses it to attract others and build community.[34]

The peaceful coexistence of gay and straight populations in the gay ghettos of the 1950s and 1960s was similar to how gay life was more integrated into society as a whole in the 1920s and 1930s. That citywide situation ended, in part, because—in Sennett's terms—the "multiplicity of contacts" became too intense and confusing. In the smaller world of the Village, this "multiplicity of contacts" became manageable because all community members saw themselves as participants in their neighborhood. This allowed them to identify with one another—even over the wide cultural chasm of sexual orientation—and work toward the common social goal of creating a community. Furthermore, not only was it possible for gay people to be out, visible, and accepted as members of the community, but the social and financial success of the community depended upon their gay visibility. Here, open gay sexuality is not only possible but necessary; gay freedom is not dependent upon being hidden, but upon being visible—not private, but public.

In many ways the increasing eroticization of the cityscape, which had been occurring since the turn of the century, found its apotheosis in the organization of the sexual subculture of the gay ghetto. The recognition of shared sexual desire, and the identity that emanated from that, was the force that bound the ghetto together. While religion and ethnic custom helped hold the immigrant ghetto together, sexuality is the primary co-hesive force in the gay world. Bars, restaurants, and cafés function as cruising places as well as centers of socializing. Street activity, while en-suring safety, also promotes potential sexual contacts. Even the physical structures and geography—alleyways; access to a waterfront of isolated docks and piers; nonresidential, warehouse areas—all contributed to an urban map that promoted and facilitated easy sexual contact.

The materialization of gay sexuality in the gay ghetto is vital to its health and continuance. Social and physical structures promote cruising and sexual contact as well as encourage a complete range of other sexual expressions. The ability to feel safe enough to hold hands, embrace, or kiss on a street corner, to act "campy" in public, to dress in an effeminate or butch manner are all examples of public displays of sexual orientation permitted in the gay ghetto but forbidden or severely regulated else-where.

The ability to display sexual orientation, and indicate sexual activity, is a prerequisite for visibility of gay people and community. This visibil-ity is, in turn, a prerequisite for organizing and struggling to become public—that is, to have the full responsibilities and privileges of public life and citizenship. Just as the nurturing of minority cultures enabled earlier immigrant groups to organize and eventually function successfully as political entities in the broader context of U.S. politics, gay culture—and sexuality—must also be nurtured. The role that the gay ghetto plays is integral to this process.

In *The Death and Life of Great American Cities,* Jane Jacobs speaks of healthy, functioning neighborhoods as "organs of self-government." That is, they understand the needs of, and provide for the welfare of, the neigh-borhood residents: safety, a social life, communication, self-determination. This can happen in a variety of ways, from supporting local businesses, to setting up social programs that are mutually beneficial to all residents, to simply making sure that the neighborhood functions well. For the gay community, the emergence of the gay ghetto as a functioning social unit was the first step to securing visibility, moving toward a publicness that promoted full citizenship, and discovering the possibility of becoming physically and emotionally rooted.

5. Gay Ghettos as Crucibles of Culture, Change, and Pleasure

WHILE the gay ghetto contains and protects its homosexual residents, it also functions as a place that displays their lives and talents: gay culture. When this culture is acknowledged by the mainstream, the ghetto, as an urban erogenous zone, becomes a lightning rod for the dominant culture's unaccepted or unorthodox feelings and fantasies.

A primary function of art and culture is to evoke pleasure and emotional response in its audience. Culture produced in the ghetto serves other functions as well. It celebrates the lives of its makers and immediate audiences, and can be an expression of selfhood and autonomy. Often it may reflect anger or resentment at the outsider position of the minority culture, even while it takes pride in that outsider status. It can also be a means to communicate information or a communal vision; this often leads to the establishment of a shared artistic or cultural sensibility. The cultural life of the ghetto is also a major link to the dominant culture and to the rest of the city. It is one of the primary ways that nonghetto residents relate to the ghetto and its inhabitants. More important, it is a way that nonghetto residents who share in the sensibility and identity of the ghetto culture can find and partake in ghetto culture.

Nonghetto city dwellers derive enormous pleasure from alternative and minority cultures, from the concerts of Jewish music in the Renaissance ghetto of Venice to the jazz clubs of Harlem to the restaurants of Chinatown. But because mainstream culture has a problematic, paradoxical relationship with pleasure—casting it alternately as a treat, a reward, and a danger—the pleasure of ghetto culture takes on additional meaning. Ghetto culture highlights what is absent from mainstream culture while at the same time reinforcing what is "good" and safe about it. Because of this outsider status, ghetto culture often originates on the fringes of the mainstream's accepted boundaries: the avant garde, the experimental, the "obscene."

The pleasures of ghetto culture also represent, in a visceral way, the allure and the threat of the ghetto itself. To partake in ghetto culture is to partake vicariously in the identity of the ghetto itself. In a positive way, this is seen when musicians like Mick Jagger acknowledge their debt to black music by saying that while their skin is white, their soul is black. The reverse of that is the fear that black-influenced music will, by its "primitive" nature, corrupt the morals of young people.[35]

If ghettos function as erogenous zones for the city, ghetto culture is most often the immediate link to that eroticism. When the pleasure of ghetto culture is appreciated and acknowledged by the dominant culture, it functions as the gateway between the ghetto and the rest of the cityscape. When ghetto culture is disapproved of, or found too threatening, then the gateway has to be controlled or censored.

Gay ghettos have been the birthplace of much of contemporary gay culture (although not all gay culture is produced in the physical space of the ghetto). The creation of culture in the gay ghetto is an actualization of the gay life present there. Often produced for gay audiences, ghetto culture presents truths and visions specific to gay life—insights that come from being cultural and sexual outsiders. When viewed by the mainstream, this culture is often seen as cutting edge or fringe and frequently censored or denounced by critics. Eventually, much art produced in the ghetto is accepted by mainstream culture and often signifies and instigates important cultural or artistic changes. Sometimes its ghetto roots are acknowledged; often they are not. [36]

The emergence of Beat writing and philosophy as a major influence in U.S. culture in the 1950s is a prime example of how the gay ghetto functions as both a generator of art and an instigator of cultural influence and change. While the Beat movement was not primarily homosexual, it owed a great debt to gay ghettos and gay sensibility.

The Beat movement was, at heart, a revolt against the enforced conformity and complacency of the postwar years in U.S. culture. Rejecting the Protestant work ethic, Beat thinkers insisted on the exploration of social, moral, emotional, psychological, and sexual alternatives. Influenced by French existentialism and Eastern religion, they sought to remove themselves from the conventions and materialism of mainstream culture. They embraced drugs as a way of inducing altered states of consciousness, which they felt gave them new insights into what was wrong with mainstream culture. They also admired and appropriated black culture, particularly jazz, and freely adapted ghetto and street slang for their spoken and written speech.

It is not surprising that Beat culture, as a revolution against the status quo, was inextricably bound up with the emergence of the new gay culture and gay ghetto. Underlying the social and literary revolt of the Beat movement was a stand against gender roles, conventional sexual mores, and institutional heterosexuality. Male Beats rejected a masculinity molded by performance in the competitive workplace and the traditional roles of husband and father. Rather, Beat masculinity was determined by writing and performing poetry, painting, and playing music—all non-traditional forms of self-expression for males. While most U.S. white middle-class males had short hair and wore suits, or more formal sports clothes, Beats grew their hair over their collars, sported beards, wore jeans and T-shirts. The "artsy" presentation of the male Beat—from jeans to long hair to sandals—was very similar to the archetypical "gay look" of the 1950s ghetto.

Women Beats revolted against a morality that insisted on female sexual passivity and the limiting roles of wife and mother. (Although, in reality, many women did end up performing those roles.) For the Beats, marriage, family, work, and conventional morality were a trap that limited both life experience and vision. These were precisely the experiences and values of the gay ghettos of Greenwich Village and San Francisco's North Beach, which were also, not coincidentally, enclaves of Beat culture. The social and political threat of Beat culture was enormous. At the 1960 Republican National Convention, J. Edgar Hoover claimed that the three biggest threats to America were "communists, beatniks and eggheads."[37]

While the Village—and, to a lesser degree, North Beach—had a history of bohemian life, it was the emergence of the gay ghetto, particularly juxtaposed with the staunch conformity mandated by postwar U.S. culture, that allowed the Beat movement to flourish there. The lives of gay people in the ghetto—by their nature alternative and renegade—provided both vision and reinforcement for the social structures of Beat living. While there had been precedents for more open and freely defined heterosexual relationships in the past, they were tolerated and acted upon more readily in the gay ghetto. In the 1950s, many landlords would not rent to unmarried couples or tolerate late-night socializing, or even unorthodox dress. This was less problematic in the Village and North Beach, where a secure and sustained gay community had already set less restrictive standards.

Allen Ginsberg and William Burroughs were, along with Jack Kerouac, the most influential writers of the Beat generation. The publication of Kerouac's On the Road in 1957 by Viking Press was a major literary event that defined the "Beat generation" for most Americans. It was, however, the publication of Ginsberg's Howl by City Lights Press in 1956, and an excerpt from Burroughs's Naked Lunch in the Chicago Review in 1957, that made mainstream culture fully aware of exactly how "dangerous" Beat culture was. Ginsberg's explicitly homosexual meditation on the emptiness of contemporary culture and Burroughs's grotesque fantasy vision of a homoerotic, futuristic American dictatorship riddled with violence and boy-rape faced immediate censorship. Copies of *Howl* were seized in San Francisco and distribution halted until a nationally publicized trial deemed the poem "not obscene." After a columnist in the *Chicago Daily News* attacked *Naked Lunch* as "one of the foulest pieces of filth I've ever seen publicly circulated," the University of Chicago, the *Review*'s publisher, censored the magazine. An American edition became available only in 1966, after several highly publicized censorship trials.

The censorship trials of *Howl* and *Naked Lunch* were important breakthroughs for freedom of speech in the United States. They were also clear indications of the limits that mainstream culture was going to place upon the dissemination of gay and Beat culture. While Kerouac's *On the Road* was as antisocial as Ginsberg's or Burroughs's writing in intent, it was the clearly gay content of the latter two authors' writing that called for social and legal regulation. The emergence of the 1950s gay ghetto culture into the mainstream was, by some necessity, interwoven with the advent of Beat writing. The overt presentation of gay culture on its own would have been far too threatening to mainstream culture. The sexualized writings of Ginsberg and Burroughs were viewed and judged as Beat writing with gay content, and thus were afforded some legitimacy; their chances of being published, or legally defended, as specifically gay writing were almost nil.

The coexistence of gay and Beat culture in the gay ghetto reinforced the ghetto's reputation as an urban erogenous zone. The enormous popular fascination with Beat culture—and the sexual, emotional and philosophical freedom it represented—betrayed a widespread discontent within U.S. society. Critics and moralists who attacked the Beats as antisocial and destructive were not wrong: Beat culture *was* a critique of the repressiveness of mainstream culture, and offered alternatives to it. While this was also true of gay culture, the threat of homosexuality was still too great for it to be seen as presenting a possible alternative to the mainstream.[38]

The proliferation of articles on the Beats—complete with photos of coffeehouses, Beat "pads," bongo-playing hipsters, and glossaries of Beat vocabulary—in the mainstream media made Beat communities and culture very visible. The public display of Beat culture reinforced the containment of the culture even as it promoted and glorified it. The media coverage of Beat culture continually hinted at, but never explicitly stated, its overlap with gay culture, by dwelling upon its sexual freedom and nontraditional male gender roles. This enhanced the reputation of

Beat neighborhoods and gay ghettos as urban erogenous zones, and made even clearer the once hidden, invisible map of the city.

If Beat culture and its promotion in the media was an easy, and safe, gateway for gay culture to reach the mainstream, the time was soon coming when the gay ghetto could manifest itself publicly without disguise. By the early 1960s, the mainstream news media had discovered the gay ghetto. At first this discovery manifested itself as the continuation of the crisis over who controlled public space that had begun in the 1950s. In 1963, *The New York Times* ran an article about gay life in Manhattan with the headline "Growth of Overt Homosexuality in City Provokes Wide Concern." The article opened with a tentative note claiming that "the city's most sensitive open secret—the presence of what is probably the greatest homosexual population in the world and its increasing openness—has become the subject of growing concern of psychiatrists, religious leaders and the police." But two columns later the situation is more dire: "[S]ome experts believe the numbers of homosexuals in the city are increasing rapidly. Others contend that, as public attitudes have become more tolerant, the homosexuals have tended to be more overt, less concerned with concealing their deviant conduct."[39]

On June 26, 1964, *Life* magazine published a fourteen-page article on gay male life in the United States, complete with photos of "self-avowed" homosexuals, cruising places, leather bars, and street hustlers. The gay ghetto as a marker on the invisible map was now manifestly visible. This had the immediate effect of making it clear to mainstream culture that gay people existed and that they had claimed, by a conscious act, public space for themselves in the urban landscape. The gay ghetto, now exposed, could function more overtly as an erogenous zone.

Readers of the *Life* magazine article, whether they were appalled or titillated by photos of hustlers and leathermen, were all made aware of the ghetto as a specifically—if unofficially—designated urban space. The ghetto became a place of display, and along with this came the recognition that an increasingly visible gay sexuality was part of urban life. This not only reinforced the heterosexual identity of the rest of the population, but also permitted and encouraged heterosexuals to exhibit a more open interest in gay life and sexuality.

"What do they do in bed?" was the archetypal question asked about homosexuals in the late 1950s and early 1960s. But this question existed not for the answer, which was obvious to most heterosexuals, but as a cloak for a widespread but socially disapproved interest in gay culture and sex. The real question was, "What are we missing?" Heterosexuals viewed gay life, sex, and culture with an ambivalent mixture of envy, anger, and fear. The erogenous zone of the gay ghetto embodied the mainstream's desire to explore new forms of sexuality and sexual organization, their frustration that other people might have more pleasure in their lives, and the trepidation at moving beyond the restrictive boundaries of their own lives.

Life's coverage also affected gay people. The newly visible ghetto became a beacon for homosexuals across the country. *Life* magazine offered concrete proof—with photos—that gay people and gay culture existed. It answered the young homosexual's perennial question—"Am I the only one?"—and it presented clear options to anyone who wanted to find gay community and space. "These brawny young men," began the article, "in their leather caps, shirts, jackets and pants, are practicing homosexuals, men who turn to other men for affection and sexual satisfaction." And while the inevitable "balanced" proviso read, "They are part of what they call the 'gay world,' which is actually a sad and often sordid world," the image of a community, and the materialization of the invisible map, was clear to gay men around the country. The claiming and promotion of the public space of the gay ghetto was a watershed in gay life.

The explosion of a distinct gay art and culture in the 1960s was a direct result of the physical, economic, and social structures of the gay ghetto. The political and artistic milieu of the ghetto promoted experimentation with innovative forms and subject matter, and the abundance of inexpensive space and the willingness of local audiences and business owners to be open to new work created a crucible that encouraged artists. Coffeehouses, cafés, bars, and art galleries were used for impromptu theater spaces and film showings, as were local church halls, union offices, and loft spaces. Art and culture entered a public sphere and was shaped, to a large extent, by an audience that felt involved—as a community—with the artist and the work.

The effect of this upon the broader culture was enormous. Caffè Cino, in the Village, became a center for experimental theater, a birthplace and laboratory for many important playwrights, and the beginning of off-off-Broadway. Filmmakers like Jack Smith, whose "pornographic" camp extravaganza *Flaming Creatures* became the center of a landmark censorship trial, found audiences and defenders for their art in the ghetto culture. Andy Warhol's Factory and much of the art that came out of it was predicated on a gay sensibility and culture that was ghetto based. Even when the art had other cultural roots—Warhol's connections with commercial art and more mainstream galleries—it was the culture, emanating from the ghetto itself, that exerted enormous influence.

Earlier immigrant culture existed as a cohesive entity within the ghetto, but was hardly ever paid attention to by the rest of the city. After dominant culture decided which aspects of immigrant culture it would accept through the process of "assimilation," the subculture moved out of the ghetto and into the mainstream. This was how unique manifestations of minority culture such as Yiddish theater and Italian food were incorporated into mainstream culture. While gay ghetto culture was also a cohesive entity, residents from the rest of the city came into the ghetto to attend and appreciate it. Only after it was nourished and "displayed" in the ghetto did it move into the larger cultural arena. This pattern occurred as well with black culture during the Harlem Renaissance.

The creation of the black and gay ghettos as interactive centers of cultural activity was indicative of the difference between these ghettos and the earlier European immigrant ghettos. Immigrant ghettos were transitional places that encouraged and facilitated their residents to move into American mainstream culture. People came to them after arriving in the United States—often because they had few other options—with the intention of becoming Americans and pursuing the American dream. Told that the streets of America were paved with gold and that prosperity and independence were easily obtainable, immigrants pinned their hopes on moving into the mainstream: if they acted, spoke, dressed, and thought appropriately, they could become Americans.

This was far less true of African Americans, who, while desiring to make a better life for themselves, had already been repeatedly rejected by America. Many migrated to the Northern black ghetto looking for safety and economic independence, leaving behind the horrors of Southern racism and violence. It was, in many ways, a flight *from* America to a place of refuge. While white gay people in the 1950s did not face racial hatred or have the same economic problems as African Americans, they too were fleeing from mainstream America to a place of safety. Both groups understood that, since being white and being heterosexual were prerequisites for full citizenship, "assimilation" was not possible.[40]

When elements of European immigrant ghetto life were accepted— "assimilated"—into the mainstream, it was the result of a diminishment of the original culture, which had been modified to fit acceptable mainstream standards. In stark contrast to this, the cultures of the gay and black ghettos—each in specific ways—emerged in resistance to mainstream

American culture. Their aim was not assimilation but its opposite, cultural independence and the desire to keep and nurture distinct identities. The cultures of these ghettos were, by their very nature, political. As such, they were a threat to the dominant culture, but they also offered enticing alternatives which were as desired as they were feared.

For gay people—refugees fleeing from the hostile world—the ghetto was the beginning of a long process of claiming public space, building an open and self-expressive culture, and fashioning a politics that would not hide who they were through assimilation but make them full citizens in a world that acknowledged and respected their lives and sexuality.

6. From Ghetto to Neighborhood: The Transformation of Public Space and the Homosexual Refugee

In the first place we don't like to be called "refugees." We ourselves call each other "newcomers" or "immigrants." Our newspapers are papers for "Americans of German language"; and, as far as I know, there is not and never was any club founded by Hitler-persecuted people whose name indicated that its members were refugees.

A refugee used to be a person driven to seek refuge because of some act committed or some political opinion held. Well, it was true we have had to seek refuge; but we committed no acts and most of us never dreamt of having any radical political opinion. With us the meaning of the term "refugee" has changed.

—Hannah Arendt, "We Refugees"[41]

I dreamed in a dream of a city where all the men were like
    brothers
O I saw them tenderly love each other. I often saw them in
    numbers walking hand in hand;
I dreamed that that was the city of robust friends—
    Nothing was greater than manly love—it led the rest,
It was seen every hour in the actions of the men of that city;
    and in all their looks and words.

—Walt Whitman, Leaves of Grass[42]

Shortly after midnight on Saturday, June 28, 1969, street riots broke out in Greenwich Village as the New York police executed a routine raid on the Stonewall Inn on Christopher Street. The riots, which were repeated over the next two nights, were not just a spontaneous response to police harassment, but the logical result of the gradual claiming of public space by gay people in Greenwich Village over the past twenty years. This process was part of broader social changes.

The crisis in public space that began in the 1950s provoked the flight of (mostly white) heterosexuals to the suburbs, and was instrumental in the creation and solidification of the black and gay ghettos. But along with this came the wholesale restructuring of cityscape by urban planners that often eliminated established "bad" neighborhoods and replaced them with housing projects or commercial centers. These changes, which significantly reconfigured urban space, alleviated some of the mainstream culture's anxiety about the relationships between space, identity, pleasure, and power.

Simultaneously, the conceptualization of who had access to public space also changed, as progressive political and social movements—predicated on prioritizing the rights of the individual over those of the state or "society"—gained large followings. Black civil rights actions, particularly in the South—lunch counter sit-ins, public transportation boycotts, and marches—were a clear claiming of public space for both actual and political purposes. The movement to protest the war against Vietnam claimed public space with teach-ins and demonstrations. The counterculture—composed of political groups, hippies, rock fans, and drug users—claimed public space with events like outdoor concerts and be-ins, and by their unavoidable presence in public spaces like San Francisco's MacArthur Park; the People's Park in Berkeley, California; and New York's Washington Square. Yet this new claiming of public space by those outside the mainstream was being contested by the dominant culture through the—often illegal—enforcement of Jim Crow laws, laws that required permits for large gatherings, and even vagrancy laws. The crisis over public space was now being fought on overtly political grounds.

The Stonewall riots were a political battle over public space, but they were also, in a broader sense, a fight about the Village itself. For more than a decade, gay and straight life in the village had coexisted without significant tension; the growing number of gay men and lesbians became part of what the Village was. There were, however, tensions between the Village and the rest of the city. Throughout the 1960s, Village street life became more vibrant and active, with musicians, political speakers, and drug culture. Replicating its earlier history as a refuge for bohemians and radicals, the Village was now, as well as a gay ghetto, a hotbed of antiwar resisters, hippies, rockers, and druggies.

By the late 1960s, the Village embodied a series of contradictions in urban space and life. Because it contained openly gay people, artists, and elements of the music and drug counterculture, it was viewed by many in the mainstream as the center of urban pleasure. As a result, it became a popular site of tourism and commerce for people in the mainstream who wanted to partake, if only for an evening, in these alternative cultures. This made the Village vital to the cityscape. At the same time, many in the broader city associated the Village with the most undesirable aspects of urban life: social outcasts, street noise, political troublemakers, street people, crime, illegal drugs, and homosexuality. Frequently, conservative politicians called for police "clean-ups" of the Village, cracking down on street life, sexual activity, and gay bars. The Village was thus what Richard Sennett calls a "zone of transition": an urban space whose use, contested by opposing political forces, prompts not only social discord but change—what he refers to as "the uses of disorder."[43]

And, indeed, the Stonewall riots were a declaration that the Village was a gay public space being publicly claimed by its inhabitants. During the riots, the gay people involved made it clear that this was a battle about space, with cries of "Liberate Christopher Street" and "Christopher Street belongs to the queens." Emboldened by their rebellion, gay people held hands, hugged, and kissed in public without the usual fear of reprisal. On Sunday evening, Allen Ginsberg came to the Stonewall Inn and noted of the crowd: "You know the guys there were so beautiful—they lost that wounded look that fags all had ten years ago."[44]

The effect of the riots on the entire gay community was immediate. Up to this point, the Mattachine Society had professed a politics of privacy, with rare exceptions (most notably the 1965 picketing in Washington, D.C., to protest the federal government's refusal to employ homosexuals). New York Mattachine members were outraged by the riots, viewing such open rebellion as trashy behavior, destructive to their tradition of political organizing. The morning following the first night of riots, Mattachine members placed a neatly printed sign on the boarded-up Stonewall Inn:

WE HOMOSEXUALS PLEAD WITH
OUR PEOPLE TO PLEASE HELP
MAINTAIN PEACEFUL AND QUIET
CONDUCT ON THE STREETS OF
THE VILLAGE—MATTACHINE

The simple act of posting a placard addressed to the gay community—a public act antithetical to Mattachine's politics of privacy—was made possible, literally overnight, by the rioters' claiming of public space. The irony was that while Mattachine acted upon the new permission to use public space, its message was that the homosexuals of the Village should be less public.

This claiming of public space led the way for the birth of a new wave of homosexual activism. Within weeks, the Gay Liberation Front was born. In contrast to the homophile groups, the Gay Liberation Front eschewed a privacy-based politics and contended that gay people take their place in the public sphere. Integral to this demand was the insistence that gay sexuality no longer be hidden under the double-standard rubric of "privacy." Their nondeferential approach and confrontational tactics were reflected in their chant: "Out of the closets and into the streets." Homosexual politics had moved from the realm of the private and joined the overt display and claiming of public space that characterized other social-change movements of the 1960s with which GLF saw itself working in coalition. This radical departure ushered in new ways of political organizing, and reconceptualized how homosexuals thought of themselves and were perceived by mainstream culture.

One of the major tenets of this new political theory was that all homosexuals—whether they admitted it or not—were oppressed and, as such, were "refugees" from mainstream culture. Gay Liberation Front members saw themselves as political activists whose sexual "difference" marked them as outcasts. This was a marked deviation from homophile groups, whose constituency thought themselves, except for their sexuality, as "just like everyone else." The new Gay Liberation Front ideology insisted, however, that the "We are just like everyone else" position was untenable in contemporary society. Aside from denying the importance of sexuality in people's lives this position did not take into account that no matter how individuals defined themselves, anyone perceived by the dominant culture to be homosexual was likely to be harassed and penalized by strictly enforced antihomosexual laws and attitudes. Like Hannah Arendt's Jewish refugees who "committed no acts and . . . never dreamt of having any radical political opinion" but who finally had to accept that the simple fact of their Jewishness made them refugees, these nonpolitical gay people were oppressed simply by their "being" homosexual. The assertion that all gay people were oppressed as a class—and therefore criminals and outcasts—was a major shift in traditional political thought about homosexuality, and, more importantly, politicized the importance of personal identity. The first step in acknowledging and actualizing this politics was the public claiming of identity and space: coming out.

The threat of this politics—a rejection of the mandate of enforced personal and sexual privacy—was that it claimed every homosexual as a potential refugee from mainstream culture, and every refugee as a potential political rebel and dissident. Even more so, this rebel status, predicated on an identity defined by a nonreproductive sexual pleasure, threatened the basic structures of mainstream culture.

The claiming of public space by gay people that began with the Stonewall riots was part of a complex process that made the invisible gay map increasingly visible. Like Whitman's "dream of a city," the map now offered a place of visibility, freedom, and potential citizenship. The emergence of the new, visible map of the gay city posed this important question: How do homosexuals become visible in our culture? As Whitman indicates in his depiction of the sexualized city of Eros and pleasure, homosexuals can only become visible through manifesting their "difference"—that is, their sexuality. The regulation of homosexual behavior and affect—the closet—has been the major obstacle to gay people gaining freedom and citizenship.

In *The Human Condition,* Hannah Arendt speaks of the importance of "natality"—the beginning of a public presence through action, particularly *political* action: "If action as beginning corresponds to the fact of birth, if it is the actualization of the human condition of natality, then speech corresponds to the fact of distinctness and is the actualization of the human condition of plurality . . . living as a distinct and unique being among equals." It is in this sense that the Stonewall Riots and the gay liberation movement constitute the beginnings of a cohesive move to make homosexuality public and give homosexuals personal, social, and political freedom. It is the act of coming out—of political speech—that is a prerequisite for freedom and citizenship for all gay people.[45]

Arendt's definition of natality—political action and speech that begin the "actualization of the human condition of plurality"—can be applied not only to coming out but also to sexual activity as well. The equation of homosexual activity with political action is at the root of how gay people become visible. Public manifestations of homosexual identity and affect, both of which are indicative of sexuality, proclaim and secure space in the material world: coming out becomes political speech, sexual activity a political act. The threat of these actions, for mainstream culture, is that they are the embodiment of a subversive concept of pleasure that runs counter to the basic social organization. The visible map marked not only homosexuality, but pleasure as well.

The growth of the gay ghetto and the Stonewall Riots marked points at which refugees became active dissidents by refusing to continue to hide, and by publicly displaying the "difference" that marked them out from heterosexuals. It was by making the invisible map visible that gay people began taking their place in the city and the world in the struggle to gain full citizenship. The ultimate irony is that only by being obviously and openly gay and public can gay people be just like everyone else.

Conclusion

The World Turned Upside Down

1. Pleasure and Misrule

Civilization and Misrule

PLEASURE THREATENS HOW society is organized. This is understood by the child who realizes the possibility of forbidden pleasures (from taking that extra cookie to masturbation); by the factory worker who knows that an unpaid "personal" day will hurt the family budget; and by the politician who supports laws that attempt to regulate or prohibit "unacceptable" sexual activity. Humans have accepted as inevitable—even morally beneficial—the repression of pleasure in exchange for an orderly world.

While Freud's *Civilization and Its Discontents* rearticulated this deeply held belief, the language he used to describe this paradigm—the pleasure principle and the reality principle—has become common usage. Freud's theory affirmed the necessity of repression in creating civilization; "happiness," he explained, "has no cultural value." But Freud was also insistent in examining and exploring the importance of pleasure and sexuality in human existence. The pursuit of Eros—pleasure in its broadest sense: physical, emotional, artistic, sexual—was a primary drive that informed all human activity even as it was in direct conflict with "civilization."

"Civilization" is structured and supported by the mechanisms that regulate and contain the human capacity for pleasure: laws, customs, standards, manners, social and moral codes. But the human instinct to pursue pleasure is so persistent, and the codes that mandate repression so resented, that "civilization" has constructed socially acceptable spaces for the pleasure principle to manifest itself. These controlled events and periods of time—known as "Misrule" in European societies—are part of everyday contemporary life. Today they take many forms, some nearly imperceptibly woven into the fabric of everyday living: the annual office party, where getting drunk and acting out is expected; a group of women friends going to a male strip bar and loudly vocalizing their appreciation of the naked male form; the Sadie Hawkins Day dance, where gender roles are reversed. But other, more established manifestations of Misrule such as Mardi Gras, Halloween, and April Fools' Day are manifestations of centuries-old conventions and customs.

While some scholars trace the antecedents of these events as far back as the Eleusinian Mystery cults of Attic Greece, their earliest forms in European societies are found in the Saturnalia of ancient Rome and the rural-based, pagan holidays that celebrated the changing of seasons and the planting and harvesting of crops. The forms these celebrations take today are often watered down, and desexualized, versions of the more elaborate social and religious celebrations of medieval Europe. In some societies Misrule has been highly institutionalized. During the seven days of Saturnalia, Roman government and public business were shut down, schools closed, and criminals went unpunished. In medieval and Tudor England, mayors would hand over the keys of the city to the King (or Abbot) of Misrule during the Christmas season so that the revels—often overtly sexual and blasphemous—could take place. The pre-Lenten festivals of France, as well as the carnivals of Venice and Florence, were established social events of Misrule. The popular masquerades of 18th-century London provided Misrule in an increasingly regimented society.

Today these traditional forms of Misrule are less integrated into the fabric of everyday life, their manifestations not as intense, and their celebrations usually more commercialized. Yet the impulse behind them is the same. They are a time of emotional and physical release in which the repressive rules and regulations of "civilization" are not simply ignored, but reversed. Play replaces work, masks replace faces, fantasy replaces reality, cheerful rudeness replaces good manners, ribaldry replaces social decorum, emotion replaces rationality. In medieval Scotland the Abbot of Misrule was called the Abbot of Unreason, and at heart Misrule is about the triumph of the pleasure principle over the reality principle. This is—in language taken from the Prophet Isaiah and traditionally used to describe Misrule—the world turned upside down.

The loosening of sexual restraints and the encouragement of sexual activity, as well as various forms of transvestism and atypical gender behavior, have always been integral to Misrule. The regulation of sexuality and gender affect are two of the most stringently monitored bulwarks of civilization, and the subversive freedom of Misrule directly undercuts and contradicts them. Sex itself—its loss of control and its prioritization of pleasure over reason, satisfaction over sense—is one of the most basic manifestations of Misrule.

Misrule presents the possibility of a more egalitarian world. Under Misrule, power structures are reversed and demolished, granting power to people and groups who are generally denied them.

One of the most powerful forms of social regulation is privacy. There are two primary methods by which this occurs: the legal concept of private ownership, which grants to individuals control over aspects of the material world, and the social codes of civility, manners, and decorum, which relegate sexual (and other) behavior to the private sphere. Misrule challenges and undercuts both of these regulatory apparatuses. Private ownership—of land, of social privileges, and of people, such as the rights men have over women and children, or owners over slaves—has been traditionally reversed and negated by Misrule. Privately held property was frequently opened to the public during the carnivals and festivals of feudal and medieval Europe. British ceremonies of Misrule in the sixteenth and seventeenth centuries often focused on the enormous tension between property owners and "commoners" that was being exacerbated by the dismantlement of the commons. The role of ownership in personal relations was also contested during traditional celebrations, when women often had the right to beat their husbands, children to disobey their parents, and serfs to keep the fruit of their labor. In the pre–Civil War American South ceremonies of Misrule at Christmas reversed, for a period of time, the roles of master and slave.[1]

The frank sexual atmosphere encouraged by Misrule is an overt challenge to the concept of privacy that mandates that sexual behavior (and even discussion) is permissible only "in private." This attempt to regulate sexuality by removing it from the public sphere and consigning it to a restricted private one is enacted through social codes of manners and civility that define acceptable public behavior. By making sex public, Misrule not only promotes and exalts public life and behavior over the regulatory concept of privacy, but questions the very nature and value of this distinction. By imagining and implementing a new social organization that contests existing repressive regulations and grants more freedom to everyone, Misrule offers a critique of what is wrong with the world and a utopian vision of a new world.

The most obvious and established forms of Misrule are public events such as Mardi Gras. But the impulse behind Misrule—the reversal or rejection of rationality and ordered civilization—takes other forms. Riddles and paradoxes, often associated with the wisdom of fools and jesters, contain aspects of Misrule. Freud, in *Jokes and Their Relation to the Unconscious,* explores the subversive nature of humor and its ability to challenge authority and social order. Manifestations of the supernatural such as witches, ghosts, fairies, magic, and voodoo, which invoke a mixture of fascination and fear in the dominant culture, are often associated with Misrule. This association has historical resonance and precedent since many traditional ceremonies of Misrule grew out of the principal pagan and witch cult festivals. The underlying precepts of Misrule are also found in myriad forms of entertainment that transport us—for short periods of time—out of the ordered, rational everyday world and into one created by the imagination.

One of the most complicated cultural variations on the concept of Misrule is found in the ambivalent relationship of adults to children and the world of childhood. The unfettered world of children's imagination and desire—dress-up, nonsense rhymes, and many children's games are examples of modified Misrule—presents a bracing challenge to the adult world of reason and regulation. While the imagination of children is often praised by adults, it can also be a source of irritation or embarrassment and result in strict punishment. Until they are taught to behave in socially appropriate ways—until they are civilized—children represent, and often act upon, the unchecked pleasure principle of Misrule.[2]

The prevalence of Misrule throughout history suggests that it is a fundamental expression of a human and social need to experience pleasure and freedom in the context of a rigidly structured social organization. Thus, as important—and enjoyable—as Misrule may be, it is equally important for society to insure that it remain a contained event: Mardi Gras only lasts three days, riddles and jokes are often deemed inappropriate forms of expression, and even popular entertainment may need to be controlled through censorship. The exhilaration and freedom of Misrule always carries with it the threat of loss of control, of chaos.

Anthropologists and cultural historians have traditionally described Misrule as a safety valve that exists to reinforce the established social order by creating specific outlets for the limited pursuit of prohibited freedoms. But an alternative theory articulated in the late nineteenth century by Karl Marx, and now held by many contemporary scholars as well, characterizes Misrule as a manifestation of popular *revolt* against the existing social order. This theory is substantiated by a long history of political and social rebellions against repressive authority that have taken place during Carnival and other Misrule ceremonies: peasant uprisings in sixteenth-century Germany, rural insurrections in pre-Revolutionary

France, slave rebellions in the American South. The limited freedom of Misrule sparked in those with severely restricted freedom the ability to fight for more. Understood this way, Misrule is not only the pursuit of pleasure but a fundamental desire to challenge social inequities and to re-shape society.

It is important not to conflate the impulse of Misrule with all politi-cal actions or movements that challenge authoritarian rule or seek pro-gressive social change. Yet even when ceremonies of Misrule are not the immediate impetus for political action, the language of Misrule is often used to describe periods of conflictive social change. Radical religious and political dissenter groups formed during the English Civil War such as Ranters, Levellers, and Diggers—many of whom promoted a vision of a classless society, the restoration of the common, the abolition of private property, equality for women, and various forms of sexual freedom—consciously referred to their goal as "the world turned upside down." This phrase was also used by critics of the French Revolution in 1789 and by supporters of the Paris Commune in 1871.[3]

Similar language was also used to describe more recent periods of so-cial upheaval. Zelda Fitzgerald, in her writings about the 1920s and the Jazz Age, frequently claims "the world has been stood on its head" and Cole Porter's sprightly 1934 hymn to sexual freedom, "Anything Goes," explicitly charts the reversals of traditional Misrule, in which the world has gone mad and basic concepts like black and white, day and night, are reversed. In the 1960s critics of the counterculture repeatedly claimed that "every thing is turned upside down" or "the world has gone crazy," a perception that the counterculture agreed with and celebrated. The Doors urged their listeners to "break on through to the other side," and the Rolling Stones' "Sympathy for the Devil" claimed that Satan—an epitom-ical Lord of Misrule—was the primary architect of human events.

The drug culture, prompted by the anti-rationalist tenor of the times, encouraged explorations of alternate realities. The Jefferson Airplane's "White Rabbit" instructed young people to "go ask Alice" about the pleasures found down the rabbit hole of altered consciousness. Political liberation movements demanded new freedoms and an end to institu-tionalized discrimination: "power to the people" succinctly reflects Mis-rule's antiauthoritarian populism. Specific references to Misrule also appeared at this time. In 1965 Allen Ginsberg was crowned Kral Majales (King of the May)—a traditional medieval Lord of Misrule—by Czecho-slovakian students who were agitating against Soviet control of their country. Ginsberg, aware of the historical links between Misrule and pleasure, began his poem celebrating the event: "And I am the King of May which is the power of sexual youth." In the mid-1960s a San Francisco counterculture collective that fed and clothed street people and runaways called themselves Diggers in homage to the social revolutionaries of the seventeenth century.

The social changes of the 1920s and 1960s focused, to a large degree, on relaxing strict gender roles and prohibitions on sexual behavior. Rudolph Valentino's sensuous masculinity and the boyish look of flappers redefined masculinity and femininity, and increased access to birth control allowed sexual activity to be separated from reproduction. By the 1960s the sexual revolution, the birth control pill, and the beginning of the women's movement began changing how people thought about sex and gender. "You can't tell if it's a boy or a girl" ran the complaint about long hair in the dominant culture. By 1969 the traditional transvestism of Misrule became the stabilizing norm in The Kinks' hit song, "Lola," in which girls are boys and boys are girls in a "mixed up, muddled up, shook up world," except, of course, for Lola.

When Misrule remains contained, it operates as a safety valve releasing the tensions that accumulate when people—either voluntarily following the rules of civilization, or forcibly kept in line by the power structures of their society—cannot experience the freedoms and pleasures they seek. But the threat of contained Misrule is that the limited freedom it offers may alert individuals and groups to what they are missing and encourage them to seek it in their everyday lives. Controlled Misrule may grant a temporary relief of frustration, but it also challenges the status quo and provides people with the possibility of new visions and new freedoms. As such, it has the potential to radically change and restructure society.

When these new possibilities of freedom are pursued, the potency of Misrule's threat—the ascendancy of the pleasure principle over the reality principle—increases. No longer contained, Misrule threatens to become permanent and undermines many of the laws, codes, and established authoritarian relationships that construct civilization as we know it. These social controls have traditionally been understood—by those with or without power—to be the only method by which humans can secure stability and safety in the material world. The idea of permanently overturning, changing, or even questioning these structures instills in many people the fear that civilization will collapse into chaos. This specter of chaos has, historically, been a strong argument against social change and against the possibility of allowing or encouraging more individual freedom and pleasure. Thus the "family values" mantra of today.

Yet civilization does not crumble when repressive laws, standards, and customs—institutionalized slavery, the divine right of kings, denying women the vote and labor the right to organize—once thought indispensable for social stability, are repealed or overthrown. The reality is that societies ultimately function more smoothly and fairly because of progressive reform. The ongoing project known as civilization is an endless process of refining and how individual freedom and liberty—including, or perhaps, especially the pursuit of pleasure—can be broadened.

Freud warned that the reality principle must be ever-vigilant in containing the inherent excesses—and destructive potential—of the pleasure principle. Humans have invested enormous time and energy in curtailing pleasure and freedom. This effort betrays not only how deeply suspicious and wary we are of pleasure, but how deeply we understand its power. The fear that unlimited—or too much or, in some people's minds, even a little more—pleasure and freedom would destroy the world is groundless. If history has shown us anything, it is that blind and often selfish adherence to the overtly repressive regulations of the reality principle has caused more destruction of human life and culture than pleasure or freedom ever would.

The ongoing negotiation between the reality principle and the pleasure principle is the struggle to create a productive, workable society and support and encourage individual pleasure and freedom. Misrule—in all of its many manifestations—is the resurgence of the pleasure principle in the context of an overly stifling reality principle. It is simultaneously a revolt and a call for change. Most important, it offers a vision of a more just and equitable world in which freedom and pleasure, and not fear and repression, guide our lives.

Homosexuality as Misrule

Homosexuality has always been intrinsic to manifestations of Misrule. The celebratory sexuality of Misrule, predicated on pleasure and repudiating reproduction, consistently presented the possibility, and often the reality, of homosexuality. The prevalence of same-gender activities such as male morris dancing and mummery, all female harvest celebrations, as well as same-gender secret societies explicitly countered the entrenched heterosexuality of social organization. The prominence of a symbolic phallus (and at times more faithfully reproduced representations) like the maypole or suggestively carved scepter for the King or Abbot indicated an underlying male homoeroticism in many of the celebrations. The transvestism integral to Misrule ceremonies is a rejection of proscribed gender roles and their buttressing of heterosexual social and power structures.

The hiddenness of homosexuality that has been conflated with the mythos of the unseen and supernatural, is also associated with Misrule. Since the Middle Ages, homosexuality has been associated with witchcraft, the magical, and the fantastic: from fairies (a word that continues to be associated with homosexuality) to the gothic. Folklorists have noted strong connections between pagan-based rural folk beliefs, acceptance of homosexual activity, and traditional ceremonies of Misrule. Significantly, the fool and jester—emblematic of Misrule—who speak the truth through riddles are figures long associated with homosexuality. This tradition was perpetuated by Harry Hay when he chose Mattachine—a word associated with masked court jesters of the Italian Renaissance and secret societies of unmarried men in medieval France—as the name of the United States' first major gay liberation group.[4]

The historical evidence linking homosexuality and Misrule indicates a more than a casual connection between the two. On a profound level, homosexuality—metaphorically and in actual practice—is the embodiment of Misrule. It is the world turned upside down. Even the language used to describe homosexuality reflects the perverse reversals of Misrule: invert, unnatural, immoral, illegal, she/male, bull dyke, nancy boy. Homosexuality even reverses accepted anatomical functions as exits become entrances. The most essential cultural reversal, however, is that homosexuality is evidence that sexual activity can exist independent from reproduction. Without the mandate (or necessity) of reproduction, the need for tightly constructed gender norms disappears, allowing men to act like women and women like men. The threat of homosexuality is the threat of Misrule: by providing viable, pleasurable alternatives to rigidly organized social structures, the basic tenets of civilization are contested.

Gay culture—the claiming of public space by gay people by simply living their lives openly or expressing themselves through art and literature—is one of the most visible social manifestations of homosexuality. The dominant culture, fearful of public homosexuality, attempts to regulate it through laws, moral prohibitions, social codes, and even the threat of punishment. Sometimes, however, the dominant culture allows, even encourages, aspects of gay culture—art produced by openly gay or

closeted artists, drag shows, representations of gay lives on stage, or simply increased visibility of gay life—to enter the public sphere. This relaxation of repression occurs when the dominant culture perceives that
the pleasure provided by gay culture outweighs its threat. Like contained
Misrule, regulated public displays of homosexuality and gay culture allow the dominant culture a sanctioned release from its own repressive
standards. But as with Misrule, these manifestations of gay culture function both as a safety valve and a potential engine of social change.

Displays of contained gay culture depend on a context in which homosexuality has little possibility of an authentic, sustained public presence. In this framework they function as an outlet, albeit limited, for gay
expression as well as a safe place for the dominant culture to experience
new pleasures and freedoms. When homosexuals began demanding the
right to be public and have full citizenship—early European gay rights organizing, the formation of U.S. homophile groups in the 1950s, and most
significantly the liberation movement that sprang up after the Stonewall
riots—the social fabric that allowed and encouraged regulated manifestations of gay culture was ripped apart. Homosexuality was no longer
contained; instead, it threatened to become part of everyday life.

The gay liberation movement, in the context of other political and
countercultural movements of the 1960s, attempted to establish a state
of public, uncontained Misrule by demolishing prohibitions against homosexual identity and activity, as well as traditional gender roles. This attack on institutionalized heterosexuality struck at the heart of how
civilization was ordered, presenting a radical revision of how human lives
and sexuality might exist in the world.

It was now impossible for those in the mainstream to enjoy gay culture—in various stages of closeting—without having to admit the social
and political presence of an open homosexuality. This politicization profoundly altered the position of homosexuality in the culture. Once seen
as a matter of personal psychology or pathology, homosexuality was essentially a private matter with potential public ramifications. Now politicized homosexuality became unavoidably public and as such threatened
the stability of the world, turning it upside down.

2. Pleasure Envy

Who Is an American?

Identifying homosexuality as a manifestation of Misrule places it in a historical and social context that illuminates its power to entice and threaten. But abstract discussions do not address the very real question of how gay people live in the world.

Full citizenship in a democracy carries with it the right and the responsibility of the individual to help shape the policies of the state. Yet often this ideal of full citizenship has been denied some groups in spite of their standing as citizens. Women did not have the right to vote until the ratification of the Nineteenth Amendment in 1920. African-American men and women were granted freedom under the Thirteenth Amendment of 1865, but only the men had the right to vote, and not until the ratification of the Fifteenth Amendment in 1870. It took the Voting Rights Act of 1965 to ensure that all African Americans could vote safely, and even after that, white majorities in some parts of the country continued to prevent full participation of African Americans in the electoral process by enacting measures, such as redistricting and reapportionment, that limited African-American electoral clout.[5]

Throughout U.S. history, certain groups—women, African Americans, Asian immigrants, Latinos, some European immigrant groups, Native Americans—were denied full citizenship by the dominant culture, mostly of Anglo descent. Most often, the stated reason for this was the alleged biological or cultural inferiority of the minority group, but the real resistance to granting them full citizenship was the dominant culture's overwhelming fear that the enfranchisement of these groups would radically change U.S. society and, more important, that the balance of power would shift when these groups—with their own needs, opinions, agendas—had a voice in governance.

The question of who gets to set the national political agenda, or who has full citizenship, has at its roots the more important question of who gets to be an American. Being an "American" is a category that exists apart from having full citizenship, or even, in varying degrees, political power. It is a mythic category whose parameters are set by tradition and bigotry. The United States was founded, essentially, on the assumption that its citizens would be male, property-owning, white, Protestant

Christian, Anglo, and heterosexual. This is the mythic American citizen, a prototype that has been both enshrined and attacked since before the signing of the Declaration of Independence. From Abigail Adams's sharp letters to her husband demanding that John "remember the ladies" while attending the Continental Congress in Philadelphia, through the efforts of immigrant groups to find economic security and respect in the United States, to the continued battles of African Americans to overcome racial discrimination in jobs and housing, there has been a struggle by those outside the limited definition of "American" to be included in it.[6]

This struggle has met with continued resistance from those who were already considered "Americans." White women were denied full citizenship but were, because of their race, considered "Americans." This was not true of most minority groups unless they could, through "assimilation," become "American" by emulating the Anglo ideal, while in the process losing most of their national character. This process of assimilation worked only for "white" European groups who were able to conform and, to a large extent, "pass." There were, to be sure, variations on acceptability. Jews and Roman Catholics, for example, managed to "assimilate," in the years after World War II, and after much struggle gained social power and prominence. Even after achieving legal citizenship, many groups—especially those who barely managed to conform to the ever-changing parameters of "whiteness"—did not become "Americans."[7]

The process of assimilation—as ineffective as it sometimes was for whites—did not work at all for most nonwhite people. Whiteness continues to be one of the most enduring determinants of being an "American." Skin color and ethnic cultural affect—language and hairstyle, as well as taste in music, food, and dress—present a decisive deterrent for nonwhites seeking to become "Americans." Even after the long-established image of the melting pot was replaced by the "gorgeous mosaic," or the more homely "salad bowl," to describe the multiracial and multicultural nature of U.S. society, the mythic notion that the American character was defined by whiteness, Anglo heritage, and Protestant Christianity did not change.

In 1990, the General Social Survey conducted by the National Opinion Research Center at the University of Chicago found that more than 50 percent of white Americans did not favor laws banning racial discrimination in housing; 78 percent believed that African Americans enjoyed living on welfare; 56 percent thought them more prone to violence than white Americans; and 53 percent considered them of less-than-average intelligence. Comparable numbers were reported when white attitudes toward the U.S. Latino/Latina population were measured. Such entrenched attitudes are fed by, and in turn feed, the firmly established belief that an "American" is defined primarily by whiteness. Today's culture wars—over bilingual education, Ebonics, Afrocentrism, immigrant rights, how ethnicity should be measured on the national census, and other topics—embody the fight over who is, or can be, an American.

"Democracy" is often conceptualized as a joint effort of rule by citizens in which the majority opinion holds sway. This is not its true meaning. The government of the United States is designed, in theory, so that the majority does not get to make all of the decisions. Federal and state constitutions provide safeguards against what legal scholar Lani Guinier calls "the tyranny of the majority." Responding to James Madison's worry that "[I]f a majority be united by a common interest, the rights of the minority will be insecure," Guinier has approached this problem of "fundamental fairness" in a democracy and has postulated what she calls Madisonian democracy: "a situation in which the majority rules but does not dominate." Fundamental fairness is difficult to achieve in a society in which not all members are treated with equal respect.

It is ironic that Lani Guinier's argument for "fundamental fairness"— which emerges from a solidly mainstream liberal tradition—is now, in our contemporary political culture, labeled by conservatives as unsettlingly radical. But in a sense the right's reaction to her arguments is correct, for, in its essence, her critique of "majority rule" is profoundly disruptive to the political and cultural status quo. Underlying Guinier's assessment is the understanding—again in the liberal tradition—that difference can be accommodated in a democracy, that difference is nonthreatening. This attitude reflects a utopian idealism that posits a generosity, empathy, and mutability of the human spirit rarely evident in human history.

The reality is that difference is threatening. The white majority in the United States is extraordinarily threatened by racial difference, which is why African Americans and other nonwhite racial groups have had to fight hard to gain even the most basic freedoms.

The questions of why a majority should not act tyrannically to preserve its own interest and why it should allow a "difference" that might substantially alter the cultural, social, and political system have been answered and elaborated upon by political philosophers from Thomas Paine, Mary Wollstonecraft, and Toussaint-Louverture to Margaret Fuller, John Stuart Mill, and Sojourner Truth. The Enlightenment's belief that all humans are equal, and that a higher social order follows from the implementation of that equality, is integral to our Western heritage. Yet, as firmly embedded—or self-evident—as these beliefs might be, they are ignored, avoided, and curtailed in myriad ways. This happens not simply to suit the needs and desires of a "majority" which wishes to eliminate or dominate a "minority" (often for economic or territorial reasons) but, most important, to bolster basic construct of "civilization": the repression of pleasure.

Heterosexuality, along with whiteness, Anglo heritage, and Protestant Christianity, has been a primary defining characteristic of the "American" identity. Like whiteness, it is a nonnegotiable standard, and there is little question of the dominant heterosexual culture's hostile attitudes toward homosexuality. The National Opinion Research Center's 1992 General Social Survey found that between 70 and 77 percent of U.S. heterosexuals think that homosexuality is always "morally wrong." These attitudes profoundly place homosexuality and homosexuals out of the mainstream of U.S. life and the definition of an authentic "American" character. While homosexuals—as a group—have never been denied the right to vote, and so have been able to take part in setting the political agenda, they have been denied full citizenship. In the recent past, homosexuals have been denied the right to public assembly, freedom of the press, and sexual expression. Even now, they are denied the right to marry; to serve openly in the military; and often to engage in certain civil contracts like joint adoption. In most states, homosexuals lack legal safeguards against discrimination in employment and housing. And, in twenty states, homosexual sexual activity is still illegal.[8]

Gay people's quest for full citizenship aptly illustrates Lani Guinier's astute political assessment of the "tyranny of the majority." Because the majority of people in our society identify as heterosexual (although some of them may indulge in covert homosexual behavior), and because they may view homosexuality as an abomination, a crime, an illness, a social problem, or a not-particularly-useful personal quirk, there is little reason for the majority to grant full citizenship or even basic civil rights to homosexuals. Until now, the usual venues for seeking equality—state and federal law and court adjudication—have resulted in important but limited success in winning homosexual rights.

In the absence of legal protections, and in the face of legal discrimination, gay people have sought safety in the concept of privacy.

Constitutional privacy is conceptualized by most Americans as a good thing. It is defined as the ability to be let alone. In a democracy, it is defined as a "right" and a basic safeguard of individual liberty: to be able to worship, vote, work, and live as one chooses. This ideal of privacy is hardly a reality. Our democratic system has developed a complex, evolving definition of legal "privacy" that has shaped, and been shaped by, the changing parameters of social acceptability. The right to private worship, for example, does not include the right to practice polygamy. The right to sexual privacy does not include the right to commit sodomy.

Perhaps the most obvious protections offered by privacy is the right to not be intruded upon in "private" space.

In U.S. culture, personal freedom is defined largely by the capability to control space and own goods: the ability to have privacy. In the colonial period, citizenship was predicated on owning private property. Now, the more money you have, the more privacy you can buy. This means, in everyday, material terms, that the wealthy who own homes in exclusive neighborhoods (that may even have their own security force) have more privacy than middle-class people who rent their apartments in nice neighborhoods (but are dependent upon a landlord and a lease). In turn, middle-class renters have more privacy than working-class people who live in a city-owned housing project (in which they may be subject to state surveillance or intrusion), who, in turn, have more privacy than homeless people, who have none at all. Under this system, privacy becomes, in essence, a commodity, not a right. Privacy is not available to everyone because privacy is not free.[9]

This has two implications for gay people. The first is that the fight for privacy is, in our society, dependent on being able to buy and own "space" or property in which to be let alone. The right to engage in consensual sex, therefore, can only be enjoyed by those people who have access to private space, and then only when it is not prohibited by law. When personal freedom is defined under the rubric of privacy, it is not available to everyone. But, more important, its very definition as "private" makes it non–community-based. Thus, fighting for the right to privacy completely reinforces the dominant culture's mandate that gay people are acceptable only when they are private, not when they are public or a community. To fight for the right to privacy, under the current definition of privacy, is to fight for the right to the closet.

In addition to ownership, a more fundamental definition of privacy is the basis for the construction of such regulatory concepts as decorum, manners, and civility. These regulations, which change year by year, are the basis of "civilization," the development of which has essentially been a process of deciding what can be done in public and what must be done in private.

In the Middle Ages, forms of public nudity, public discussions of sexuality, and frankness about bodily functions were completely acceptable. The rise of a middle class, the codification of private property, and the gradual cohesion of the "home" (and nuclear family) as a legally defined realm of privacy radically altered "manners" and "decorum." These new social structures—in conjunction with an increasingly strict patriarchal mind-set and an emerging capitalist system that prioritized production over pleasure—denied women social autonomy, relegated children to the status of "property," and established the heterosexual marriage as the only accepted site of sexual activity. Privacy was now the bulwark of respectability and manners, the primary regulatory device of sex and pleasure.

The regulation of sexuality was not simply about "privacy." The rise of the state, which was quickly replacing the more diffusely organized feudal system throughout Europe, established legal codes to regulate sex and pleasure. The installation of strictly enforced codes of social and sexual behaviors, in conjunction with "privacy," was the foundation for *civilité*—that is, civility, or civilized behavior. The state, having the power to encourage or punish a wide range of human activities (particularly sexual activity), set standards of acceptable private and public behavior, by, for example, defining appropriate dress, licensing or banning entertainment and drinking establishments, and regulating sexual activity and reproduction. Because the state had vested interests in promoting the nuclear family, reproduction, and gender roles that contributed to economic growth and stability, deviant sexual behavior was outlawed. Gay sexuality had no right to privacy, indeed, no right to exist. Under these laws and codes of manners, to be civilized meant to be heterosexual.[10]

These legal and social codes function in a remarkably similar way today. Even when homosexual behavior is legal, the lives of gay men and lesbians are constantly curtailed by codes of social behavior and decorum. For example, public gay behavior, such as holding hands, wearing drag, acting too butch or too fem, showing affection, or even giving the appearance of being a couple, is still defined, by the dominant culture, as "bad taste," improper, or lacking in decorum. This continues to be a primary mechanism that regulates and confines gay life to the private sphere. These social codes, which function as efficiently as explicit legal statutes, mandate the standard of enforced privacy and secrecy for gay people today.

Civilized behavior—what the dominant culture deems permissible in public—is a standard by which gay people are constantly judged and found

lacking. Only by blending in—appearing "straight"—can gay people secure a modicum of safety in public, but this cannot be confused with acceptance. The reality is that disguised homosexuality is being rewarded
for its ability to "pass," to be "civilized." Any public manifestation of homosexuality remains, therefore, improper or distasteful: uncivilized.

The dominant culture's impulse to enforce, through manners and
decorum, "civilized" behavior in subcultures is more than a desire to promote superficial cultural conformity. The efforts of a dominant culture
to "civilize" the "uncivilized" obscure the real intent to colonize: to subju-
gate a subculture.

Pleasure and the Other

The role of the pleasure principle in culture is complex and often contradictory. While humans have an instinctual drive toward pleasure, they
also realize that there is a need for order and stability—civilization in the
best sense. A basic tension in human existence—within the individual,
between the individual and the state, and within the state itself—is the
need to find a balance between pursuing pleasure and creating structures
that provide for the material necessities of living and survival: what
Freud calls the reality principle. This tension has been mediated in various ways in different societies throughout history. While some societies
have organized themselves in such a way that pleasure (including personal and sexual freedom) was prioritized or celebrated and others have
organized themselves using more repressive structures, all have had to
negotiate this balancing act. In almost all Western societies, a constant, in
dealing with the anxiety generated by the pleasure principle has been the
projection, by the dominant culture, of fantasies and myths associated
with pleasure and sexuality onto subcultures—particularly sexual, racial,
and ethnic subcultures that did not already conform to the dominant culture's "civilized" image of itself.

This projection of pleasure and sexuality is neatly expressed by Edward Said in his theory of Orientalism. Said argues that European societies manufactured enormous fantasies and myths about "the Orient" that
had little to do with the reality of Asian cultures, but were reflections of
European preoccupations and anxieties about sexuality and power. Orientalism envisioned Asian cultures as both mysterious and dangerous—
filled with incredible beauty and sexual allure, yet fraught with cruelty
and punishment. The reality of Asia and its numerous countries and distinct cultures became, for the European, collapsed into "the Orient."

It became "exotic"—literally "outside," or "the other." Orientalism managed, within a neat, closed system, to encapsulate both the desire for pleasure and its projected dire consequences: pleasure and danger, beauty and cruelty.

The subjugation of minorities and subcultures, and the projection of anxiety-based pleasure fantasies onto them, are integral to the nation-state power politics that have ruled the Western world for centuries. Both are at the heart of colonialism, and the construction of the world into "civilized" and "uncivilized" countries and people. The inability of individuals and societies to deal with the anxiety engendered by the plea-sure principle has been profoundly formative in constructing and implementing the harsh realities of power abuses and social injustices that exist in the world.

The dynamic of creating the exotic as a way of dealing with pleasure ambivalence is replicated in the way the dominant culture in the United States has viewed many European immigrant cultures, African-American cultures, and gay culture. In the nineteenth century, Italian immigrants were seen by the majority of "Americans" as a threat to the United States' moral and social order, and, at the same time, as sexually alluring. African-American culture, particularly as manifested in music, dance, and speech, has always been viewed by white mainstream culture as both corruptive and liberating. Following the same pattern, the dominant cul-ture has seen gay culture as embodying both social decay and sexual free-dom, and gay people have been exoticized and eroticized into the dangerous and desirous "other."

This complicated relationship places gay culture in a unique position. The traditional paradigm of assimilation has never worked for gay people, in part because the nonreproductive nature of gay sexuality, which goes so deeply against the grain of "civilization," sets homosexuals intractably apart. (The dominant culture's fear and distrust of homosexuals [rooted in the nonreproductive nature of gay sexuality] is so deeply entrenched that even when gay men and lesbians become biological or adoptive par-ents, it does not abate. Often, because there is such a taboo on gay people relating to children, the antagonism toward homosexuals becomes more intense. While this appears, on the surface, to be paradoxical it simply reaffirms how strong mainstream culture's fear of homosexuality is.)

More important, gay people and gay culture cannot "assimilate" into the dominant culture because for the past one hundred years the domi-nant culture has been steadily "assimilating" into gay culture. Contrary to popular belief, and even some gay rights rhetoric, gay people have not been patterning their lives on the structures of heterosexuality; rather, the opposite has occurred. Heterosexuals have increasingly been rejecting traditional structures of sexuality and gender and have been reorganizing in ways pioneered by gay men and lesbians.

During the past century, as gay culture established itself as a vital public entity, dominant culture has changed. As gay people became more secure in this increasingly open gay culture, heterosexuals were actively exhibiting their discontents with traditional social and sexual arrangements—"civilization." While some gay people opted for more "private" lives, often because such arrangements provided safety, heterosexuals began to discard the moral and social regulations that limited their personal and sexual freedom.

Over the past one hundred years, it has become apparent to heterosexual women and men that the once secure structures of institutionalized heterosexuality are, at best, failing to meet their emotional and sexual needs. As individuals have discovered the importance of personal freedom and sexual pleasure they have revolted against these structures. Gender roles, the bulwark of many social and sexual regulations, have radically shifted. Strictly defined ideas about how a "man" or "woman" acts or is allowed to act have undergone drastic revisions granting women more personal autonomy and allowing men more emotional freedom. Marriage and the traditional biological nuclear family unit have also changed. The assault on marriage came from many directions: divorce law reform, feminists' battles for married women's rights, and the increased freedom of children and young adults broke down the male-centered power dynamic in the family. With the U.S. divorce rate now hovering at 50 percent, and the traditional two-parent–wife-at-home family in the minority, it is clear that traditional marriage no longer meet the needs of adults or children.

An important factor in changing mainstream opinion was the growing realization that sexual activity does not need to be justified by reproduction.

The battle to separate sex from reproduction was also intricately interwoven with the struggle for sexual liberation that began in the 1950s. As women and men began to feel permission to explore their sexual desires and rebelled against traditional social and sexual restrictions, the foundation of institutionalized heterosexuality began to crack. Sexual intercourse relieved of the burden of pregnancy, in conjunction with more independence for women and young people, encouraged a new sense of sexual freedom.

All of the important shifts in the structures of institutionalized heterosexuality came about because women and men demanded more personal and sexual freedom. This quest for freedom was, however, complicated. While new freedom engendered more sexual pleasure, it profoundly upset the basic social structures upon which people built their lives, thus limited the scope of the changes people were willing—or able—to make. Women, for example, frequently demanded changes that granted them new freedom, but made life more difficult for men. When men sought more sexual freedom, it was often at the expense of women's autonomy. Broader experiments in social change, such as communal or cooperative living, found little economic support in a society predicated on the biological family unit.

As more women and men incorporated these new freedoms into their lives, and the institutions traditionally viewed as the foundations of society were radically altered, a backlash occurred. The social and sexual changes were so extensive that those invested in maintaining the status quo felt that the world was turned upside down, that Misrule was uncontained and was threatening to destroy civilization. This fear of unrestrained Misrule was often shared by women and men who, while enjoying more freedom in their lives, missed the security that a more ordered, repressive society offered.

The rise of conservative politics has brought about a defense of marriage and the family based on the claim that the violence and dysfunction in the home and the public sphere stemmed from changes wrought by feminists, liberal social reformers, and the gay movement. Consequently, the right has called for the repeal of many of the progressive changes that occurred in the past three decades. The federal and state programs attacked have been those that conservatives viewed as part of the decades-long dismantling of traditional structures and moral codes: programs that helped provide day care for working mothers, supplied birth control information to teens, offered abortion referrals to married and unmarried women, introduced sex education in public schools, taught about homosexuality in a nonjudgmental manner, or provided nonmoralistic AIDS and safe-sex education. The attacks were carried out under the rubric of a return to "family values."

The term "family values" is most commonly used by the right in discussions of sexual and moral issues—particularly as a buzzword against homosexuality—but its implications are more comprehensive. The right's promotion of the "family" as the fundamental unit in U.S. society is predicated on a deeply conservative vision of America as a primarily white, Anglo, Protestant, heterosexual society grounded in a patriarchal view of maleness. The "family values" argument is not simply a defense of traditional sexual morality but also a platform for reinforcing racial, ethnic, and religious hierarchies. At its heart, the call for "family values" is a call for the enforcement of traditional conservative standards of who is and who isn't an American.

The appeal of "family values" is strong for many people, particularly if they already feel a lack of social stability. Yet it is important to note that the right has been unwilling to address the material needs of individuals and families. Legislative measures, including tax breaks for low-income working families, job-training programs, low-interest mortgages, food stamp programs, raising the minimum wage, and a negative income tax, which would all help promote the stability of the family, were routinely opposed by conservatives.

The right's "family values" politics has had several results. One has helped establish a culture of resentment that targets everyone who does not fit into the prescriptive mold of an authentic "American." The culture of resentment encompasses many aspects of society: race, gender, class, sexuality. Anger toward affirmative action programs, welfare, open admissions in colleges, and bilingual education programs for immigrants is voiced by many white people; resentment has been expressed by many men and even some conservative women toward affirmative action for women, feminist demands of equal pay for equal work, legal battles by women to enter all-male organizations, and charges of date rape and sexual harassment.

The threat of affirmative action, or having to worry about sexual harassment, or legal mandates that women be admitted to military academies was the threat of being forced to give up the ideal—the fantasy—of a mythic "America." This image of a cohesive white, Protestant, Anglo America has never been true; it has no basis in historical reality. It is a lie promoted and sustained by people with social and political power for their own advantage.

Over the past three decades this culture of resentment has flourished. At the most extreme levels, it is visible in the far-right militia movements and their mistrust of any organized form of U.S. democratic government. It is also manifested in the widespread anger at legal and illegal immigration, bilingual education, affirmative action programs aimed at nonwhites and women, state-subsidized birth control and abortion programs, multicultural programs in schools, government funding for the arts, and, most particularly, issues surrounding gay rights and homosexuality.

The rhetoric of political conservatives and the religious right against gay rights and homosexuality is inseparable from campaigns against other targets in the culture of resentment. The argument that gay rights are special rights is almost identical to arguments against affirmation action for racial and ethnic minorities. The specter of homosexuality and gay culture as a morally corrupting influence recalls the dominant culture's attacks on aspects of African-American music and culture. Yet the right-wing attacks on homosexuality are unique, not so much in their intensity—although some far-right leaders do call for death to homosexuals—but in their claim that it is homosexuality *itself* that is the problem: that there is something inherently disordered and morally wrong with homosexuality *per se*. This is not to say that other minorities are not persecuted by the dominant culture, but that the attacks on homosexuality are distinguished by the assertion that it is not only what homosexuals do but what they are that is culturally dangerous. While such extreme views may be held by some neo-Nazi fringe groups about Jews and African Americans, homosexuals are the only group to be conceptualized in this way by the mainstream.[11]

The Liberation of Pleasure

To the dominant culture, organized around the containment of pleasure, homosexuality has come to represent unrestrained pleasure. While other minority cultures are experienced as threatening by the dominant culture—in part because of the way they manifest pleasure—homosexuality has come to symbolize pleasure itself. And it is the dominant culture's conflicted relationship to pleasure that has created a paradoxical, even contradictory, response to a more visible gay culture and to the concurrent movement for gay rights.

In the three decades since the Stonewall Riots, the dominant culture has continued to enjoy and learn from gay culture. Yet as gay culture has become more accepted by the dominant culture, the fight for gay civil rights has engendered a different response. Although some basic civil rights and antidiscrimination protections have been secured for gay people, there has been an enormous backlash against the drive for gay rights. This backlash, while an inextricable part of the culture of resentment, is directly related to the increased acceptance and visibility of gay and lesbian culture. Rather than paving the way for an acceptance of gay rights, a wider acceptance of gay culture has, ironically, reinforced in the dominant culture a determined antipathy to the idea of full citizenship for gay people.

This is, in part, a fearful reaction to the direct challenge posed to the social order by a highly organized political campaign. But this simple backlash reaction is only a partial explanation. The strength of the support this backlash has elicited is indicative of its emotional power for heterosexuals. While individual antigay political campaigns waged by the right may be mounted or funded by specific political groups, they have the tacit approval of the majority of Americans. The swift passage of the Defense of Marriage Act in 1996 by an astounding majority of legislators, and its enormous popular approval rating, show the depth and fervor of Americans' approval for legally limiting the rights of gay people.

The gay rights movement is a threat to the social and political structures that maintain heterosexuality as a dominant social institution. Yet even when civil rights or antidiscrimination laws are passed (usually by slim margins), they do not necessarily change, or even challenge, deep-seated prejudices and fears. Ultimately, the threat posed by gay rights activism is—despite the enormous efforts of conservatives that go into countering it—a fragile one.

The threat posed by gay culture and art is, on the other hand, far more complex and potent. Gay culture engenders ambivalent emotions in heterosexuals about pleasure, sexuality, and personal autonomy. Caught between the longing for more freedom and the fear of breaking from the comforting, if repressive, restraints of civilization, heterosexuals are often profoundly troubled by their disparate reactions to gay culture and need to find a way to mitigate them. Because an outright rejection of gay culture would deprive heterosexuals of pleasures they want, they have to find another solution.

Refusing to grant homosexuals full citizenship, basic civil liberties, or minimal respect for their personal and sexual integrity is a primary way for heterosexuals to feel more comfortable in their enjoyment of gay culture. Individual heterosexuals don't have to invent this dynamic personally; it is offered to them—already formulated in explicitly political language—by conservative politicians and political groups. Right-wing campaigns that claim gay rights are special rights, or that seek to prohibit the "promotion" of homosexuality in schools or public life, are engineered not only to regulate public displays of homosexuality but to provide constituents (as well as potential converts) with a simple resolution of their own ambivalence toward gay culture.

So deep is this ambivalence that even mainstream and liberal political and social groups employ variations of it. The desire to avoid or downplay gay concerns and sexuality is at the root of much liberal policy. The Defense Department's "don't ask, don't tell" military policy, which acknowledged the existence of gay people in the armed services and then instituted an official method of closeting them is a clear example of this thinking. This kinder, gentler version of the closet underlies a wide range of liberal political positions: the lack of sustained support for gay teachers and gay curricula in middle and high schools, the media's outrage over "outing" and their use of "privacy" to reinforce the closet, the prioritization of other minority groups' rights as "more important" than gay rights, the repackaging of homosexuals as socially productive consumers, and the constant promotion in the media of a "good image" of gay people—that is, not visibly gay, political, angry, or openly sexual. Many of these variations of the closet are subsumed under the larger social tenets of decent or tasteful behavior that, while ostensibly calling for "good manners" or "civility," actually implement the invisibilization of homosexuality.

The fight to gain equal rights for homosexuals is a vital one that will not only make U.S. democracy more just, but will help fulfill the idealistic dream of America as a land of freedom for everyone. But this project cannot happen in a vacuum. Just as the repeal of Jim Crow laws and the enactment of civil rights legislation did not eradicate racism, the repeal of antigay laws and the passing of equal protection and nondiscrimination legislation for homosexuals will not bring about freedom for gay people. Changing or enacting a law will not change heterosexuals' hearts and minds or speak to their deepest fears.

Traditional western political theory views culture and politics as separate entities, having little to do with one another. The reality is that they are intimately connected, and in the struggle for gay freedom they are inseparable. Complete freedom for gay people will only happen when the repression of sexuality and pleasure, now perceived to be the bulwark of civilization, is replaced by more humane visions of freedom and sexuality, pleasure and responsibility.

This process has been happening—slowly and painstakingly—for centuries. It is evident in the struggles of women to find autonomy and freedom, and in the rebellions by women and men against stifling gender roles. It is evident in the emergence of a new understanding of the importance of sexuality and the self that has emerged in the last one hundred years. It is evident in changing attitudes about children and sexuality and in the nascent changes occurring in the restructuring of traditional arrangements of, and sometimes the very idea of, the family.

Paradoxically, the freedom of gay people will only come when heterosexuals reject "civilization" to seek and realize more freedom in their own lives. Until now many of the profound changes in the defining paradigms of society have come, largely, through the influence of gay culture. This is what has made it a beacon of freedom and a decisive threat.

It will never be possible for gay people to assimilate, because civilization—as it is now defined and structured—does not, cannot, admit the value and worth of homosexuality. This negates the argument that gay people will achieve full rights as citizens when they begin to act like heterosexuals. The reality is that only when those in the dominant culture realize that *they* are better off acting like gay people will the world change and be a better, safer, and more pleasurable place for everyone.

"We are your worst fear. We are your best fantasy" is as valid today as it was in 1971. But it is not a solution. The truth is that fears and fantasies are terrible—even destructive—means of organizing civilization. In the end, the freedom of gay people will signal the beginning of freedom for heterosexuals as well. Only after freedom and sexuality are valued and prioritized by the dominant culture will we all be able to live lives that are not only fully human, but also filled with pleasure.

Notes

One: The Making of Americans

1. "Becoming American" has been linked, historically, to being a "productive" worker. Shulamith Firestone's *The Dialectic of Sex* is perceptive on women and capitalism; Jeffrey Escoffier's "The Political Economy of the Closet," in Amy Gluckman and Betsy Reed's *Homo Economics,* and John D'Emilio's "Capitalism and Gay Identity," in his *Making Trouble,* address the complicated relationship between homosexual identity, community, and capitalism.

2. The politics of woman suffrage campaigns have striking parallels to the current fight for gay rights. Ellen Carol DuBois's *Feminism and Suffrage* and Christine A. Lunardini's *From Equal Suffrage to Equal Rights* both detail how social "assimilationists" were pitted against political "activists." Eleanor Flexner's *Century of Struggle* is astute in its analysis of the tensions between a predominantly white suffrage movement and the fight for the black male vote, a situation similar to the gay rights movement and the African-American community today. Illuminating discussions of the complicated histories of Asian and Native American struggles for citizenship are found in Howard Zinn's *A People's History of the United States* and David H. Bennett's *The Party of Fear:*

3. "Homophobia" as a rational fear is a difficult idea for gay rights advocates to accept, since it is counter to the historical model of assimilation. George Weinberg coined the term "homophobia" in 1972 in his *Society and the Healthy Homosexual;* that work's now-simplistic analysis has been supplemented by works like Suzanne Pharr's feminist *Homophobia: A Weapon of Sexism,* and writings by people of color, such as James Baldwin's "Here Be Dragons," in *The Price of the Ticket,* and Barbara Smith's anthology *Home Girls.*

4. While the hatred of gay people reinforces male privilege, it also serves to unite, across a wide gender gap, heterosexual women and men. The idea that "heterosexuality" might function as a "nationalist" identity remains largely unexplored, but is touched upon in Jonathan Ned Katz's *The Invention of Heterosexuality* and George Mosse's *Nationalism and Sexuality.*

5. Weinberg's concept of "homophobia" does not address the complex interactions of gay culture with mainstream culture. Sartre's "ethnic" cultural/psychological model is reflected in Sander Gilman's *The Jew's Body.* Gilman's claim that anti-Semitism is fueled by sexual paranoia resonates with the psychological construction of the hatred of homosexuality.

6. Edmund White skewers the canon in his essay "The Personal Is Political," in *The Burning Library*: "the canon is for people who don't like to read, people who want to know the bare number of titles they must consume in order to be considered polished, well rounded, civilized. Any real reader seeks the names of more and more books, not fewer and fewer."

7. Mirta Ojito's "Bias Over English-Only Rules" detailed the extent of the discrim-

ination against Spanish-speaking workers in the United States (*The New York Times,* April 23, 1997).

8. Although "race" is a construct, most people identify as being a member of a specific "race." Recent discussions of the history and construction of "whiteness" include Richard Dyer's *White,* Theodore W. Allen's *The Invention of the White Race,* Alexander Saxton's *The Rise and Fall of the White Republic,* and David Roediger's *The Wages of Whiteness.*

9. For many politicians the culture wars are clearly just a political football, yet these battles often reflect real confusions over shifting moral and social values. William Bennett's *The Book of Virtues* and Gertrude Himmelfarb's *The De-Moralization of Society* are examples of marketing traditional "virtues" and "values" as conservative solutions to complicated social realities.

Two: The Pleasure Principle

1. Despite the Third Reich's persecution of homosexuals, the linkage between male homosexuality and Nazism remains firmly rooted in the popular imagination. Films like Luchino Visconti's *The Damned* (1969) and Lina Wertmuller's *Seven Beauties* (1975) promote the idea of homosexuality and gender nonconformity as Nazi "decadence."

2. The biblical prohibitions against homosexuality are reinterpreted in Derrick Bailey's 1955 *Homosexuality and the Western Christian Tradition,* and that reinterpretation was refined in John Boswell's *Christianity, Social Tolerance, and Homosexuality.* Neither book addresses the Bible's profound antipleasure underpinnings.

3. Justinian's edicts are discussed by Bailey (pp. 73–78). Both edicts are mild in their moral condemnation, fueled more by the fear that homosexual behavior causes destruction of the city. The image of Sodom destroyed—usually by AIDS—is present today, even in such "reasonable" right-wing tracts as George Grant and Mark A. Horn's *Legislating Immorality.*

4. The relationship between women's independence and social conceptions of pleasure has received little attention. Women's history, because pleasure has traditionally been understood as a masculine prerogative, often ignores it. Sarah B. Pomeroy's *Goddesses, Whores, Wives, and Slaves* discusses the freedoms Roman women enjoyed; Vera Lee's *The Reign of Women in Eighteenth-century France* and Dorothy Anne Liot Backer's *Precious Women* do the same for eighteenth-century France. Lillian Faderman's collection of primary documents, *Lesbian-Feminism in Turn-of-the-Century Germany* shows pleasure as valued more highly in societies that promote individual freedom.

5. Much feminist critiquing locates in Freud an essential justification of misogyny. Juliet Mitchell's *Psychoanalysis and Feminism* attempts to read Freudian theory as a description of women's lives under patriarchy, not an explanation of their experience.

6. Freud's comments, from *General Introduction to Psychoanalysis,* are quoted in Norman O. Brown's *Life Against Death,* p. 138.

7. Herbert Marcuse's critique of Freud's theory of repression is from *Eros and Civilization,* p. 3.

8. Freud argued that the rights of the individual played little part in civilization, but he was not naïve: "The first requisite of civilization, therefore, is that of justice—that is, the assurance that a law once made will not be broken in favour of an individual. This implies nothing as to the ethical value of such a law."

9. Efforts to "protect" women and children from male abuse have, historically, focused upon sex. The relationship between nineteenth-century social purity movements and the changing position of U.S. women is explored in John Money's *The Destroying Angel,* William Leach's *True Love and Perfect Union,* Ann Douglas's *The Feminization of American Culture* and Lucy Bland's *Banishing the Beast.*

10. Marcuse's comments on the pleasure principle appear in *Eros and Civilization,* p. 15.

11. The interplay between sexual instincts and fantasy runs through much of Freud's writing. Of particular relevance are *Beyond the Pleasure Principle, The Sexual Enlightenment of Children,* and *Sexuality and the Psychology of Love.*

12. Schiller's arguments reflect the antirationalist impulses of Romanticism, which by prioritizing art and emotion over reason attacked social and moral codes. Alice A. Kuzniar's *Outing Goethe and His Age* details the period's homoeroticism; Alex Potts's *Flesh and the Ideal: Winckelmann and the Origins of Art History* explores how the critic's homosexuality and aesthetic theories radically transformed perceptions of art. Schiller's *Letters on the Aesthetic Education of Man* is quoted in *Eros and Civilization.*

13. Primary documents on U.S. utopian and communitarian movements can be found in Charles Nordhoff's 1875 *The Communistic Societies of the United States.* Carol Weisbrod's *The Boundaries of Utopia* discusses the legal issues that arose regarding unorthodox sexuality; Louis J. Kern's *An Ordered Love* discusses the conflicted role of homosexuality in Shakerism. Emma Goldman's *Living My Life* includes a clear defense of pleasure and sexuality.

14. Thorstein Veblen, usually considered a critic of consumerism, has much to say in *The Theory of the Leisure Class* about how gender, family, and "home" are constructed under capitalism. Veblen demonstrates how "leisure"—a class-based commercialization of pleasure—bolsters institutional heterosexuality.

Three: Popular Culture

1. Brigid Brophy, in the first five chapters in *Prancing Novelist,* defends all manifestations of the imagination as the pleasure principle's revolt against "civilization." Pornography—"simply a masturbation fantasy written down"—she claims is censored because it is the clearest example of creativity's sexual nature.

2. Subversive affect, if not intent, can be seen even in conservative examples of popular culture. Lynda Hart argues in *Fatal Women* that the "evil" or fallen women in nineteenth-century British novels and plays, while ostensibly replicating stereotypes, presented audiences with a clear critique of patriarchal heterosexuality.

3. Popular culture's ability to challenge social norms is kept in check by "social standards" and censorship. While the threat (and pleasure) of cross-dressing is often contained by the accepted "conventions" of theater, its potential for disruption remains enormous. Peter Ackroyd's *Dressing Up* provides succinct examples of this. The theater program note claiming "intent to civilize our stage" is from page 96 of the book.

4. James M. Barrie's *Peter Pan,* one of the best known and beloved vehicles for female cross-dressing, offers several subversive messages. The androgynous Peter's refusal to participate in the enforced conventions of male heterosexuality is both emphasized and undercut by his being played by a woman. Peter is "doomed" to eternal childhood (a common negative image of gay men), yet the play celebrates his freedom and voices a sharp critique of gender and "civilization."

5. Puritan condemnation of the stage was based on more than its association with homosexuality. In an attempt to clarify the individual's relationship to God, Puritanism

scorned luxury and comfort as well as manifestations of the imagination. (More than the theater, this included the pomp and symbolism of the Anglican service.) The quote about the sodomite theatergoer is from Nicholas De Jongh's *Not in Front of the Audience*.

6. The best information on Charlotte Charke is found in Fidelis Morgan's *The Well-Known Troublemaker,* which includes Charke's own autobiography and extensive commentary by Morgan. Morgan's *The Female Wits: Women Playwrights of the Restoration* also documents the freedom many women found in the theater.

7. Because carnival and misrule have always been associated with gender nonconformity, sexual dissidents, and rebellion, they are—like homosexuality—simultaneously alluring to the individual and threatening to the social order. Mikhail Bakhtin's *Rabelais and His World* is a key text for understanding "carnival," and Terry Castle's *Masquerade and Civilization,* from which the material on British masquerades comes, explores the sexual politics and the implicit homosexual sensibility of masquerade.

8. Castle, in *Masquerade and Civilization,* notes that in the early eighteenth century cross-dressing became so strongly identified with homosexuality as to often define it—a situation, she argues, that exemplifies Michel Foucault's concept, in *The History of Sexuality,* of the "invention" of the modern homosexual.

9. Woolsey's decision, reprinted in the Random House edition of *Ulysses,* also sets up an implicit legal distinction between high and low art, and thus a difference in how obscenity laws are implemented. For decades after, the presence of primary gay content ensured that suspected "obscene" material would be considered "low art" and more easily censored.

10. The culture wars, while actual political battles, are also symbolic fights over the reassertion of traditional "values" in the face of newly established, less repressive mores. The question of who "controls" popular culture is, however, misleading, for it posits that culture can exist independent of the market. Conservative political groups may want to "control"—ban—Calvin Klein ads, but the Calvin Klein corporation already "controls" them, deciding which images are created and displayed. Commodified popular culture, while still potentially disruptive, now has little to do with individual artists or the emotional desires of an audience.

Four: Subculture and Dominant Culture: The Limits of Assimilation

1. David H. Bennett's *The Party of Fear* gives a good overview of the hostility and violence that immigrants faced. Alan M. Kraut's *Silent Travelers,* a study of myths surrounding immigration and disease, focuses on how in anti-immigrant sentiment contagion became a metaphor not only for physical but for social and moral disorder.

2. See Charles Hamm's *Irving Berlin* for information on Israel Zangwill's 1908 drama *The Melting Pot,* one of the earliest celebrations of the concept. Joseph H. Udelson's biography, *Dreamer of the Ghetto: The Life and Works of Israel Zangwill,* not only details the writer's life and work, but is a fine analysis of the role of assimilation (and Zionism) in turn-of-the-century Jewish culture.

3. Noel Ignatiev's *How the Irish Became White* is a fine examination of the process of "becoming white." European Jews were listed on nineteenth-century immigration forms as "oriental."

4. The complexities of Asian immigration policies are documented in David H. Bennett's *The Party of Fear.* Kraut's *Silent Travelers* gives a frightening account of how public health regulations were used against Asian immigrants. Maxine Hong Kingston's *The Woman Warrior* and *China Men* explore the effects of these policies.

5. Stirling Stuckey's *Slave Culture* details how disparate slave cultures coalesced in

the United States. Ronald Segal's *The Black Diaspora* is a good source on the magnitude of the slave trade, as well on the methods slave owners used to suppress slaves' African cultures and identity. He also argues that slave revolts were a direct product of a new, distinct slave culture.

6. All of the material on the corn-shucking festivals comes from Roger D. Abrahams's *Singing the Master*. Supplementary materials on the complexity of master-slave relationships can be found in Mel Watkins's *On the Real Side*. The inversion, albeit temporary, of slaves and masters is in the tradition of Misrule. Stephen Nissenbaum's *The Battle for Christmas* discusses these cultural patterns in plantation Christmas customs and their relationship to slave escapes and revolts.

7. The Oxford English Dictionary first notes that "integration" was used in South Africa in 1940. During the Harlem Renaissance the artist Romare Bearden referred to "amalgamation," and the author and editor Alain Locke used "initiation into America," notes *The Portable Harlem Renaissance Reader,* edited by David Levering Lewis.

8. For more thinking on the role of black cultural influence, see Alain Locke's "Harlem as Zion" and Langston Hughes's "The Negro Artist and the Racial Mountain" in *The Portable Harlem Renaissance Reader.*

9. Sarah Schulman's "Freedom Summer" in *10 Percent* (June 1994) discusses the ways "fake tolerance" functions to obscure and suppress production of authentic minority art.

10. The most obvious examples of this cultural appropriation are Elvis Presley's recording of Big Mama Thornton's "Hound Dog" and Pat Boone's recording of "Blueberry Hill." See also Alice Walker's "Nineteen Fifty-five" in *You Can't Keep a Good Woman Down,* for Thornton's side of the story.

11. Joseph Breen's anti-Semitic comments are documented in Frank Walsh's *Sin and Censorship: The Catholic Church and the Motion Picture Industry*. Walsh also gives a detailed analysis of how conservative religious and political groups in the United States responded to what they perceived to be the serious moral threat of Hollywood and the movies.

12. The best information on Jews in Hollywood is found in Neal Gabler's *An Empire of Their Own*. Cecil Beaton's anti-Semitism is documented in A. Scott Berg's biography, *Goldwyn,* and in Hugo Vickers's *Cecil Beaton*. The quote concerning John Garfield is from Gabler, page 301.

13. The fear of Jewish power in the entertainment business is present even today. In a column entitled "Sin City: What Kind of Priest Is This Anyway?" Walter Goodman reported that William A. Donohue, the president of the Catholic League for Religious and Civil Rights, claimed that the ABC television series *Nothing Sacred* was "pure propaganda . . . [by] those that have animus against Catholicism." Donohue also noted that the show's producers are Jews (*The New York Times,* October 29, 1997).

14. This "comic" dialogue is found in Mel Watkins's *On the Real Side* (p. 32). Watkins also provides a historical and social context for subversive African-American humor, as well as a plethora of examples.

15. The complicated use of stereotypes and their potential for subversion is discussed in Watkins, as well as in Joseph Boskin's *Sambo*. George Wolfe's *The Colored Museum* is a clear contemporary example of the radical subversion of stereotypes.

16. Information on the use of blackface and "ethnic" musical traditions can be found in Ian Whitcomb's *Irving Berlin and Ragtime America* as well as Charles Hamm's *Irving Berlin,* which also provides lyrics for "Becky's Got a Job in a Musical Show" and other songs.

17. Material on Fanny Brice's life and career, as well as a detailed account of the

nose bob can be found in Barbara Grossman's *Funny Woman*. Interestingly, almost none of the media coverage surrounding Barbra Streisand's portrayal of Brice in *Funny Girl* mentions the nose bob, although Streisand herself is known and praised for "keeping" her nose.

Five: Gay Culture

1. Material on the early formation of community, particularly the molly-houses, can be found in Alan Bray's *Homosexuality in Renaissance England* and David E. Greenberg's *The Construction of Homosexuality*. Documentation of lesbian life is more difficult to obtain; Greenberg has passing references to lesbian clubs, but Emma Donoghue's *Passions Between Women* is the best source.

2. Visibility of lesbian culture is more difficult to chart than that of gay male culture. Donoghue's *Passions Between Women* charts visible lesbian identity, partly through cross-dressing, whereas Lillian Faderman's *Surpassing the Love of Men* uses "intimate friendships" as a signifier of lesbianism (which may not necessarily have a sexual component). Blanche Wiesen Cook's *Women and Support Networks* examines lesbian visibility in circles of political activism.

3. Discussions of the root of "Mattachine" can be found in Harry Hay's interview in Jonathan Ned Katz's *Gay American History*, Stuart Timmons's *The Trouble with Harry Hay*, Urvashi Vaid's *Virtual Equality*, and Harry Hay's *Radically Gay*, edited by Will Roscoe. The cultural roles of jester and fool are discussed in Bakhtin's *Rabelais and His World*.

4. Feminist responses to drag have varied. Robin Morgan, in *Going Too Far*, condemns drag as antiwoman "blackface." Pamela Robertson's *Guilty Pleasures* views it as highly subversive, and, in *Transgender Warriors*, Leslie Feinberg describes a history of cross-dressing and drag in revolutionary political movements.

5. Variants of this monologue have been performed by professional and amateur drag performers since the mid-1940s. Although the piece could be read in Mae West's voice, there is no evidence connecting it to her. Charles Pierce renders an updated version of it on *Charles Pierce: Recorded Live at Bimbo's San Francisco*, a undated recording probably from the late 1960s.

6. The specter of a gay male cultural conspiracy preoccupies much antihomosexual writing; see Edmund Bergler's *Fashion and the Unconscious* and William Goldman's *The Season*. Interestingly, while paranoia about the hidden homosexual is rampant in 1950s McCarthyism, psychoanalysts such as Irving Bieber and Charles Socarides named paranoia as a defining characteristic of the gay male personality.

7. John D'Emilio's *Sexual Politics, Sexual Communities* notes that the gay community is always growing. While ethnic communities tend to become small, Margaret Mead notes, in *The Third Generation*, that as assimilation continues, younger generations will often reclaim some aspects of earlier ethnic culture.

8. This argument relies on a notion of idealized cultural production, since most low and even high art is a product of consumer culture. See Patrick Brantlinger's *Bread and Circuses* and Debora Silverman's *Selling Culture*.

9. Edmund Bergler's *Homosexuality: Disease or Way of Life?* using a complicated but ludicrous argument, attacks Proust, Melville, and Maugham as inauthentic artists because of their homosexuality.

10. These arguments about gay playwrights can be found in Goldman's *The Season*, Kaier Curtin's *"We Can Always Call Them Bulgarians,"* and Michael Bronski's *Culture Clash*. See also Benjamin DeMott's essay "But He's a Homosexual . . ." in *New American Review* 1 (1967).

11. Methods of suppressing and negating minority writing are discussed in Joanna Russ's *How to Suppress Women's Writing* and Toni Morrison's *Playing in the Dark.*

Six: Gay Freedom, Gay Movement, Backlash

1. Kertbeny's arguments, which can be found in John Lauritsen and David Thorstad's *The Early Homosexual Rights Movement,* are remarkably similar to psychologist Irving Goffman's "scapegoat arguments."

2. Henke's text is found in Richard Plant's *The Pink Triangle,* along with a detailed history of early German and Third Reich laws against homosexual behavior.

3. Historically, German laws regulating sexuality were predicated on containing "degenerate sexuality." Thus, under many circumstances, Christians were forbidden to have sex with Jews. For attitudes and penal codes about "degenerate" Jewish sexuality, see Plant, as well as Daniel Jonah Goldhagen's *Hitler's Willing Executioners,* Saul Friedlander's *Nazi Germany and the Jews,* vol. 1, and Deborah Dwork and Robert Jay van Pelt's *Auschwitz.*

4. Huey Newton's letter in support of gay liberation is found in Len Richmond and Gary Noguera's *The Gay Liberation Book.* Newton's letter highlights the lack of support from other leftist groups and feminist groups.

5. Carl Wittman's manifesto (1969) is found in Karla Jay and Allen Young's *Out of the Closets.* Wittman died of complications from AIDS on January 22, 1986. See Michael Bronski, "A Tribute," in "Gay Community Notes," *Z Magazine,* January 1988.

6. For more thought on the process of social containment through consumer capitalism, see Victoria De Grazia and Ellen Furlough's *The Sex of Things: Gender and Consumption in Historical Perspective* and Emily Apter and William Piltz's *Fetishism as Cultural Discourse.*

7. The pervasive gay content of underground films in the 1960s is discussed in Juan Suarez's *Bike Boys, Drag Queens, and Superstars.* Parker Tyler's *Screening the Sexes* discussion of "sensibility" presents an interesting argument, to which Vito Russo responded in his discussion of "representation" in *The Celluloid Closet.*

8. For a critique of the effect of consumerism on AIDS, see Sarah Schulman's *Stagestruck: Theater, AIDS, and the Marketing of Gay America* and Joshua Oppenheimer's essay "Movements, Markets, and the Mainstream: Gay Activism and Assimilation in the Age of AIDS" in his and Helena Reckitt's anthology *Acting on AIDS.*

9. The enormous influence of gay culture on pop music, and consequently on mainstream culture, is detailed in Richard Smith's *Seduced and Abandoned.*

10. The best discussions of gay male sexual behavior, and by extension institutions of gay culture like bathhouses and back rooms, are still Alan M. Kraut's *Silent Travelers* and Allan M. Brandt's *No Magic Bullet,* which provide good background on the interconnections between sexuality, health, and social issues. Randy Shilts, in *And the Band Played On,* gives an account of San Francisco bathhouse closings, which is challenged by Allan Bérubé's "The History of Gay Bathhouses," in Dangerous Bedfellows' *Policing Public Sex.*

11. The social evolution and varying effectiveness of safe-sex campaigns is charted in Cindy Patton's *Sex and Germs, Inventing AIDS,* and *Fatal Advice.* Also informative are the essays in Oppenheimer and Reckitt's *Acting on AIDS* and Steven Epstein's *Impure Science.*

12. Douglas Crimp's *AIDS Demo Graphics* reproduces many ACT UP safe-sex posters and discusses both theory and production.

13. Sarah Schulman's *My American History* gives a detailed account of the formation

and political theory and goals of the Lesbian Avengers, as well as astute comments on direct-action politics in the 1980s and early 1990s.

14. Barbara Ehrenreich's fine critique of middle-class anxiety in *Fear of Falling* provides a clear background to the Briggs and Bryant campaigns. Also, discussions of nineteenth-century anti-immigrant movements in David H. Bennett's *The Party of Fear* shed light on the antigay backlash of the 1980s.

15. Lani Guinier's treatment of the problems of attaining full citizenship for minorities in *The Tyranny of the Majority* is illuminating for discussions of gay rights.

Seven: The Eroticized Male Body

1. Perceptions of the body change with custom, politics, and science. Bernard Rudofsky's *The Unfashionable Human Body* charts changes in body presentation; John Berger's *Ways of Seeing* analyzes how social attitudes affect the ways bodies are viewed and understood.

2. Exceptions to the unadorned male body symbolizing strength include, for example, that in France before the Revolution, the "State" was embodied in the adorned body of the king, later in the plainly dressed "citizen." See Dorinda Outram's *The Body and the French Revolution*.

3. Margaret Walters's *The Nude Male* notes that erect posture symbolizes the phallus. Alex Potts's *Flesh and the Ideal* examines changing interpretations of Greek representation of the male body.

4. James Saslow's *The Poetry of Michelangelo* is the best source of accurate translations. The Anthony Burgess quote appears in Walters's *The Nude Male*. Eve Kosofsky Sedgwick, in *The Epistemology of the Closet*, discusses how "critical praise" can be used by the dominant culture to reinforce the closet (i.e., if art is great it can't be homosexual).

5. Edward Said's *Orientalism* discusses the "feminization" of Eastern clothing in the West. In Western art the unclothed body of both the "savage" and the "noble savage" elicited an erotic response. Even abolitionist literature used nakedness to elicit an erotic, if sentimental, response from white viewers.

6. Anne Hollander's *Sex and Suits* and John Harvey's *Men in Black* are the best works on the construction of masculinity through clothing and deportment.

7. Ellen Moers's *The Dandy* is the best study of the phenomenon; Alan Sinfield's *The Wilde Century* discusses the homosexual implication of nonreproductive masculinity, the "immorality of idleness."

8. The progressive politics of dress reform are discussed in Rudofsky's *The Unfashionable Human Body*, Hollander's *Seeing Through Clothes*, Jonathan Miller's *The Human Body*, Joel Kaplan's *Theatre and Fashion*, Edward Carpenter's *Selected Writings*, vol. 1, as well as in the autobiographies of Amelia Bloomer and Isadora Duncan.

9. Richard Ellmann's *Oscar Wilde* is the standard biography; Neil Bartlett's *Who Was That Man* and Sinfield's *The Wilde Century* are essential in explicating the homosexual, class, and aesthetic politics surrounding Wilde and his trials.

10. The new social conflicts over masculinity are described fully in Martin Green's *The Children of the Sun*. Martin Taylor's *Lads* charts this material through the poetry of the time. Philip Hoare's biography *Serious Pleasures: The Life of Stephen Tennant* also provides details on the revolt against British manhood and empire.

11. Presentations of lesbianism are discussed in Esther Newton's essay "The Mythic Mannish Lesbian" in *Hidden from History*, edited by Martin Duberman et al. Terry Castle's *Noel Coward and Radclyffe Hall* is an important, perceptive study of the intersection between gay male and lesbian styles and spheres.

12. Donald Bogle's *Toms, Coons, Mulattoes, Mammies, and Bucks* is a good survey of black male images in film. Richard Dyer's *Heavenly Bodies* contains astute commentary on Paul Robeson's screen image, and Martin Duberman's *Paul Robeson* discusses his film career in depth.

13. Detailed information about USO shows, drag, and homosexuals can be found in C. Tyler Carpenter and Edward H. Yeatts's *Stars Without Garters!*

14. Allan Bérubé notes in *Coming Out Under Fire* that the large number of dishonorable discharges mandated that many gay people find alternative work situations. For the lives of people of color in the new gay ghettos, see James Baldwin's essay "Here Be Dragons," as well as his novel *Another Country,* and Audre Lorde's autobiographical *Zami.*

15. Michael Malone's *Heroes of Eros,* Joan Mellen's *Big Bad Wolves,* and Donald Spoto's *Camerado* detail the evolution and changing meaning of the male body in Hollywood films.

16. Robert W. Wood's *Christ and the Homosexual* contains a detailed chapter on gay men's clothing after World War II. Postwar novels such as Michael De Forrest's *The Gay Year,* Edwin Fey's *Summer in Sodom,* and Harrison Dowd's *The Night Air* all contain descriptions of gay styles and fashion.

17. Robert W. Wood's *Christ and the Homosexual* contains a rare analysis of the origins of post-war gay male clothing and fashions. This excerpt appears on page 43. Paul Goodman's *Growing Up Absurd* contains lengthy discussions of the influence of gay male fashion (identified as being "invented in Cherry Grove") on the clothing fads of teenage boys.

18. Photographs of patrons in leather and military clothing at a San Francisco leather bar appear in *Life,* June 26, 1964.

19. Edmund Bergler's *Counterfeit-Sex* refers to gay men as "frightened fugitives." Juan A. Suarez's *Bike Boys, Drag Queens, and Superstars* makes clear the artistic and social connections between *The Wild One* and the films of Kenneth Anger. Suarez does not deal with film images of the lesbian outlaw like Anybody's in *West Side Story* or the unnamed motorcycle member played by Mercedes McCambridge in *Touch of Evil.* Paul Goodman's *Growing Up Absurd* and Robert W. Wood's *Christ and the Homosexual* examine some of the origins of the social and psychoanalytic conflation of homosexuality and juvenile delinquency.

20. Philip Wylie's *Generation of Vipers* labeled the stereotype of the castrating, narcissistic mother "momism." Robert Lindner's 1956 *Must You Conform?* takes, for its time, a more radical view of gender and social revolt.

21. The details of James Dean's life and homosexuality are found in John Gilmore's *The Real James Dean* and Paul Alexander's *Boulevard of Broken Dreams.* Walter Ross's bestselling *The Immortal,* a 1958 novel based on Dean's life, portrays him as a homosexual.

22. The Charles Atlas ad is reprinted in Kenneth R. Dutton's *The Perfectible Body.* Some media images of nonmasculine men in the 1950s, like roles played by Wally Cox and Tony Randall, existed to reinforce the leading man's masculinity.

23. Sandow's life and career are detailed in David L. Chapman's *Sandow the Magnificent,* which also hints at a homoerotic side to his personal life.

24. Physique photography in the 1950s is now available in collections such as *Bruce of Los Angeles, Lon of New York, The Art of George Quaintance, Beefcake,* and *The Complete Physique Pictorial.*

25. Bruce Rodgers's *The Queen's Vernacular* lists a whole set of terms referring to homosexuals and hairstyling. Joe Orton's unpublished novel (written with Kenneth Halliwell) was entitled *The Boy Hairdresser.*

26. Miller's essay was reconfigured in book form as *On Being Different;* its earlier history is recounted in Edward Alwood's *Straight News.*

27. Disco was a key transition point of gay culture entering the mainstream. Andrew Kopkind's essay "The Dialectic of Disco," in his *The Thirty Years' War,* charts this moment.

28. Leslie Fiedler's *Love and Death in the American Novel* locates the erotics of the male "flight from civilization" as a core theme of U.S. literature. Richard Amory's classic porn novel, *Song of the Loon,* casts this in blatantly sexual terms.

29. Michael Schau's *J. C. Leyendecker* reprints most of the artist's work and describes his life with his lover, Charles Beach, who was also his main model.

30. Decter's "The Boys on the Beach" ran in *Commentary,* September 1981. Gore Vidal's rebuttal, "Pink Triangle and Yellow Star," is reprinted in his *The Second American Revolution.* Norman Podhoretz's "The Culture of Appeasement" (*Harper's Magazine,* March 1978) accused homosexuals of undermining national identity and security. He reprised this theme almost twenty years later in "How the Gay Rights Movement Won" (*Commentary,* December 1996).

31. *Drummer* ran its first "daddy" piece in December 1980 (issue 42) and its first *Drummer Daddy* supplement in May 1982.

32. An account of the Calvin Klein controversy appeared in *The New York Times,* November 8, 1995.

33. Frank Rich's essay "Gay Decades" in *Esquire* (November 1987) was one of the first in the mainstream to note gay influence in advertising. Marky Mark was interviewed in *The Advocate* (January 25, 1994); the discussion included the burning of Calvin Klein underwear by the Gay and Lesbian Alliance Against Defamation (GLAAD) to protest allegedly homophobic remarks by Mark.

34. Mapplethorpe's life and career are detailed in Patricia Morrisroe's *Mapplethorpe,* Jack Fritscher's *Mapplethorpe: Assault with a Deadly Camera,* and Arthur C. Danto's *Playing with the Edge.*

35. Mapplethorpe's images of black men have been criticized as racist by such writers as Essex Hemphill, in *Ceremonies,* and defended by Ntozake Shange in her introduction to Mapplethorpe's *The Black Book.*

36. The Bruce Bawer quote is from his *A Place at the Table,* page 160.

Eight: Suffer the Little Children

1. The Pied Piper legend is known mostly through children's books and the Browning poem (with its sentimentalized Kate Greenaway illustrations). Sabine Baring-Gould discusses it in *Curious Myths of the Middle Ages.* That the Piper usually appears on Saint John's Eve (June 23) is notable, as this important summer festival (and carnival) has roots in both wicca (witch) and pagan culture. Pennethorne Hughes's *Witchcraft* supplies context for the sexual connotations of this festival. The Piper story later informs J. M. Barrie's *Peter Pan.*

2. Ann Douglas's *The Feminization of American Culture* discusses sentimental literature and child mortality. *The Bad Seed,* first a novel and then a play, is best known as the 1956 film. Joel Best's *Threatened Children* analyzes the rhetoric of child-victim hysteria. Both Best and Carol Clover's *Men, Women, and Chain Saws* offer insightful observations on children in horror films.

3. Anthony Hecht's essay on *The Merchant of Venice* in *Obbligati* is an astute overview of the blood libel and children. Jeffrey Richards's *Sex, Dissidence, and Damnation* discusses myths of the Jewish molester and poisoner. George K. Anderson's *The Legend of*

the Wandering Jew charts the history of the Jew as stateless pariah. David I. Kertzer's *The Kidnapping of Edgardo Mortara* explores anti-Semitic fears of Jews in relation to children in the late nineteenth century. Claudine Fabre-Vassas's *The Singular Beast: Jews, Christians, and the Pig* contains detailed information on several anti-Jewish pogroms that began with charges of child murder as well as exploring the history of Christian myths about Jews and children.

4. Sexual abuse in anti-Catholic-immigrant propaganda is documented in Peter Gardelia's *Innocent Ecstasy*. David H. Bennett's *The Party of Fear* discusses white fears of Asian and black sexuality. D. W. Griffith's *Birth of a Nation* (1915) and the Fu Manchu films of the 1930s are popular depictions of, respectively, African-American and Asian men as rapists.

5. Philippe Aries's *Centuries of Childhood* is the best work on the social construction of childhood. His discussions of children, the invention of privacy, and the patriarchal home are reflected in Lawrence Stone's *Family, Sex and Marriage in England, 1500–1800*.

6. Freud's *Three Contributions to the Theory of Sex* and Norman O. Brown's reformulation of polymorphous perversity in *Life Against Death* inform this discussion.

7. Antimasturbation campaigns are discussed in Paula Bennett and Vernon A. Rosario's *Solitary Pleasures* and John Money's *The Destroying Angel*. Blanche Wiesen Cook notes in *Eleanor Roosevelt,* vol. 1 (p. 179) that E. R. would tie her daughter's hands to the crib to stop her from masturbating.

8. The eroticized child is discussed in Steven Marcus's *The Other Victorians*. James R. Kincaid's *Child-Loving* gives an insightful overview of the topic, and Leslie Fiedler's *Love and Death in the American Novel* and his essay "Come Back to the Raft Ag'in, Huck Honey!" in *An End to Innocence,* explore the image of the erotized, and homosexual, child in U.S. literature.

9. Most of the material on Father Ritter and Covenant House comes from Charles M. Sennott's *Broken Covenant*. The first quote here is in Sennott (p. 157), taken from a Ritter newsletter; the second is from Ritter's *Sometimes God Has a Kid's Face*. This section is based upon my article "At Play in the Fields of the Lord," which appeared in *Gay Community News,* February 18, 1990.

10. Ritter's fund-raising reflected then-President Bush's rhetoric of "a thousand points of light," a Victorian view of charity also espoused in Gertrude Himmelfarb's conservative *The De-Moralization of Society*. The debate over the number of missing children is detailed in Joel Best's *Threatened Children*. Best completely discounts the NCMEC figures, but is also wary of accepting the F.B.I. figures at face value. He argues that, because of a variety of problems in reporting, it is very difficult to obtain completely accurate numbers.

11. Because pedophilia is such a potent antigay weapon, much of the gay press felt it was in a no-win situation. If Ritter was innocent, his homophobia stood even stronger; if guilty, he was a gay child molester.

12. Much of the discussion of Pee-wee Herman is a substantial revision of my article "'I Know You Are, but What Am I?': How the Mainstream Media Is Out to Get Pee-wee Herman," which appeared in *Gay Community News,* August 4, 1991.

13. It is impossible to use current statistics, or even devise a sound method of generating new ones, to obtain accurate information on "heterosexual" and "gay" child abusers. Much abuse, especially in the home, goes unreported and the labeling of a suspected abuser's sexual orientation (even when self-identified) may not be accurate.

14. Feminist critiques of heterosexuality and the family (as opposed to patriarchy) are rare; Shulamith Firestone's *The Dialectic of Sex* and Ti-Grace Atkinson's *Amazon Odyssey* are good examples. The nineteenth-century writings of Charlotte Perkins

Gilman and Catherine Beecher suggest collectivizing cooking, homemaking, and child care as ways to make the home a better place for women and children.

15. The commodification of family and home is not new. Since the 1950s, when women's power was redefined as buying power, not only have the family and home been constructed by consumer goods, but their very security has rested on the ability to buy the accouterments of a middle-class life. Jane Davison's *The Fall of a Doll's House*, Joan Kron's *Home-Psych*, and Ruth Schwartz Cowan's *More Work for Mother* all discuss the ramifications of this.

16. Books for gay families stand in sharp contrast to the freer, multitracial and parentless world of *Pee-wee's Playhouse*. Indeed, some of the most resonant children's books in mainstream literature portray families in which parents are dead or absent: *Peter Pan, Mary Poppins, The Wizard of Oz, Winnie the Pooh, Pippi Longstocking, Alice in Wonderland, Madeleine, Boxcar Children*, and the Narnia series. The same is even true of the popular television show *Party of Five*.

17. In 1996 and 1997 *The New York Times* ran five feature articles on gay and lesbian families; none discussed sexuality. Cindy Rizzo's "What's That" appeared in *Gay Community News*, Summer, 1994.

18. Laura Benkov's *Reinventing the Family* relies on very traditional ideas about "family." Daniel Mendelsohn's "Suburban Life" (*OUT*, March 1996) charts a movement of gay people from the city to the suburbs, as does *Life Outside* by Michelangelo Signorile. See Richard Sennett's *The Uses of Disorder* and *The Conscience of the Eye* for the argument that the postwar flight from the city was an essentially conservative, privatizing flight from the complexity of contemporary life.

19. The fear of recruitment is also a replay of 1950s McCarthyite paranoia. Normal citizens "recruited" to be Communist agents, human beings "recruited" to be space aliens, women "recruited" to be prostitutes. Leslie Fiedler's *An End to Innocence* examines the specter of the hidden communist, and Peter Biskind's *Seeing Is Believing* examines paranoia in science fiction films.

20. N'Tanya's "Whose Kids? Our Kids! Race, Sexuality and the Right in New York City's Curriculum Battles" is a perceptive analysis of the Rainbow Curriculum fight (*Radical America*, vol. 25, no. 1, p. 11).

21. Popular nonfiction titles for gay teens such as Michael Thomas Ford's *The World Out There*, Brian McNaught's *Now That I'm Out, What Do I Do?* and Rachel Pollack and Cheryl Schwartz's *The Journey Out* either downplay sexuality or deal with it in very circumspect fashion. Sex manuals for gay adults, such as Charles Silverstein's and Felice Picano's *The New Joy of Gay Sex* or Peter Tatchell's *Safer Sexy*, do not specifically address the concerns of gay teens.

22. Richard J. Gelles's 1988 *Intimate Violence* details the magnitude and extent of violence—including spousal, parental, and between siblings—within the home. Recent studies show that both the amount and the severity of the violence have increased. Elizabeth Pleck's *Domestic Tyranny* details, historically, how public and social policies to deal with family violence have failed because they are predicated on "keeping the family together."

Nine: The Construction of a Pleasure Class and the Marketing of Homosexuality

1. The language of antigay initiatives has become more sophisticated over the past decade. Oregon's original 1988 bill (others followed in 1992 and 1994) was a moral condemnation of homosexuality that alienated voters. Later anti–gay rights referenda

in Idaho, Maine, and Colorado (drawing from anti–affirmative action sentiment) focused the idea of "no special rights," which became a catchphrase in Colorado in 1992. *The Colorado Model: A Practical Workbook,* by Colorado for Family Values, details, step by step, the group's organizing tactics. John Gallagher and Chris Bull's *Perfect Enemies* provides a clear report on all of these campaigns.

2. The marketing of minority identity is not new. Madam C. J. Walker amassed a fortune in the 1920s after inventing and marketing beauty products for African-American women. Her daughter, A'lelia Walker, was a lesbian and a patron of the Harlem Renaissance.

3. Barbara Ehrenreich's *Hearts of Men* examines how *Playboy* addressed 1950s male anxieties. Sarah Schulman has pointed out that *Playboy*'s popularity also marked a new concept of "leisure" by presenting an alternative to home-oriented men's magazines like *Popular Mechanics,* thus turning the workroom into the rec room.

4. Jeb Alexander's *Jeb and Dash,* edited by Ina Russell, illustrates that even in the 1920s and 1930s gay men's personal and social identities were being informed by what they bought. Esther Newton's *Cherry Grove, Fire Island* demonstrates how vacation-oriented consumerism was integral to a newly forming gay and lesbian social identity.

5. "Gay lifestyle" was an urban-based male phenomenon that was accessed by men across the country. Lesbian magazines and papers (*Big Mama Rag, Majority Report, Amazon Quarterly, off our backs*) remained community based.

6. Details of the *After Dark* advertising policy, and the Donald Embinder quote, appear in "Homosexual Magazines in Bids," *The New York Times,* July 13, 1976, p. 20. The *Wall Street Journal* quote appears in Grant Lukenbill's *Untold Millions.*

7. Some of the data of the 1968 *Advocate* survey appear in Lukenbill's *Untold Millions.*

8. Consumer surveys of any kind present problems in interpretation. Some respondents may lie, particularly if they feel that consumer status is equated with social standing. Also, these surveys don't measure debt level, an important factor in evaluating a financial portrait accurately.

9. David Goodstein's "desleazification" quote appeared in "Homosexual Periodicals Are Proliferating," *The New York Times,* August 1, 1978.

10. The ambiguous influence of gay voters on policy is discussed in Urvashi Vaid's *Virtual Equality* and Gallagher and Bull's *Perfect Enemies.*

11. Lee Badgett's "Beyond Biased Samples" argues that studies that are constructed to measure homosexual behavior (and don't require a declaration of homosexual identity) obtain more accurate representative samples of a homosexual population. Badgett's study appears in Amy Gluckman and Betsy Reed's *Homo Economics.*

12. Lukenbill's *Untold Millions* critiques the Kinsey 10 percent figure for women. But the 10 percent is wrong for both genders, since it measured the percentage of men who had engaged in homosexual behavior sometime during their life, not men who self-identified as "gay," or whose sexual behavior was primarily with other men.

13. The right wing's use of "special rights" arguments—pitting "authentic" racial minorities against an "inauthentic" gay minority—was an attempt to gain credibility in communities of color. It also implies that the gay minority is all white. "Oppressed Minorities or Counterfeits?" by Tony Marco (founder of Colorado for Family Values) articulates this position (*Citizen,* April 20, 1992). The ACLU's *Briefing Book on Anti-gay Ballot Initiatives* provides in-depth analysis of the right's attempt to win over communities of color. The quote on page 150 is from that document.

14. Badgett's study "Lesbian and Gay Occupational Strategies," examines anti-gay discrimination in the workplace and its effect on gay income. The study is reprinted in

Gluckman and Reed's *Homo Economics*. The ACLU's *Briefing Book on Anti-gay Ballot Initiatives* also examines antigay discrimination.

15. Stephanie Coontz's *The Way We Never Were* demonstrates that the "crisis of the family" is not new, but that a media-driven, politically expedient revisionism—nostalgia for good old days—erases knowledge of past tensions and problems.

16. The family has never been what its defenders have claimed. Lawrence Stone's *The Family, Sex, and Marriage in England, 1500–1800* details the complicated history of the family. Christopher Lasch's *Haven in a Heartless World,* while bemoaning the intrusion of the public sphere into the private life of the family, documents the family's failings.

17. The positioning of homosexuality as a positive cultural force began as early as February 1972 with "The Pleasure Seekers" in *Esquire.* Andrew Kopkind's 1970s and 1980s articles on gay influence, which appeared in *The Village Voice,* are collected in *The Thirty Years' War.* Frank Rich's "The Gay Decades" appeared in *Esquire,* November 1987.

18. Theater and film have always offered imaginative alternatives to the burdens of heterosexuality. George S. Kaufman and Moss Hart's unconventional, "unproductive" family in *You Can't Take It With You* (1936) leads into the drag queens and anti–right-wing sentiment of *La Cage aux Folles* (1978). The cult of high society and the aesthete is embodied in the very public careers, and coded work, of barely closeted gay men like Noël Coward and Cole Porter. In England and the United States, the popularization of an artistic, leisure class has always relied upon the concurrent idealization of homosexuality.

19. The lesbian chic phenomena was not seamless hype. The *Newsweek* cover (June 21, 1993) indicated some ambivalence with its "Lesbians, Coming Out Strong: What Are the Limits of Tolerance?" tag line. *New York*'s "Lesbian Chic: the Bold, Brave New World of Gay Women" (May 10, 1993) put a more positive spin on the topic. James Wolcott's "Lover Girls" *Vanity Fair* piece (June, 1997) perceptively observes: "But who made gay women into the media culture's sexiest new properties? Straight white men." Amy Gluckman and Betsy Reed's "The Gay Marketing Moment" and Dan Baker's "A History in Ads: The Growth of a Gay and Lesbian Market" are both informative; they appear in Gluckman and Reed's *Homo Economics* .

20. The advertising base in most gay magazines is a mix of general luxury consumer items (liquor, cars, vacations) and AIDS drugs and viatical companies. Little work has been done on the ultimate effect of AIDS products on the image of the "gay consumer."

Ten: Pleasure and the Failure of Privacy

1. "A man's house is his castle, *et domus sua cuique est tutissimum refugium*" was articulated by jurist Sir Edward Coke in *Institutes: Commentary upon Littleton,* in 1628. In his later commentary on "Semayne's case," Coke noted: "The house of everyone is to him as his castle and fortress."

2. Jamake Highwater's *The Mythology of Transgression* provides an overview of how replacing the "dirty words" of the Anglo-Saxon vulgate with proper Latin was part of a larger social attempt at controlling sexual activity. Mrs. Grundy appears as a character in Thomas Morton's 1798 play *Speed the Plough.* In the mid–nineteenth century the indoor toilet became a symbol of middle-class status and cleanliness and further privatized bodily functions and "civilized" the language that described them.

3. Although nonreproductive sexual behavior was clearly proscribed at this time, some sexual freedom also existed in the social contract. Chaucer's *The Canterbury Tales,* and even some mystery and morality plays, attest to this.

4. Sodomy law reform is not a recent movement. Louis Crompton's *Byron and Greek Love* details Jeremy Bentham's thoughts on legal reform in 1785. Emma Goldman attacked laws that criminalized sexual behaviors in the late nineteenth century. Jonathan Ned Katz's *Gay American History* gives a historical overview of U.S. sodomy laws.

5. Boston's *Mid-town Journal,* a popular weekly scandal sheet that published from 1938 to 1966, documents numerous cases of arrests in private homes. Often individual gay men and lesbians were placed under surveillance by morality groups like the Watch and Ward Society, and their actions reported to the police. The March 13, 1953, issue featured such a raid with the headline: "Wild Stag Bags Drag Lads: Copenhagen Kids' Odd Birthday Party Features Sex Orgy."

6. The Mattachine Society's original vision, articulated by Harry Hay, was explicitly progressive. Changing membership and the repression of the time shifted its focus and philosophy. Both John D'Emilio's *Sexual Politics, Sexual Communities* and Will Roscoe's *Radically Gay* chart this evolution.

7. The homophile groups' stand on "privacy," dress codes, and "good taste" were in stark juxtaposition to their participation in such public events as picketing the White House. Penny Sparke's *As Long as It's Pink* explores the effectiveness of "good taste" as a method of social control.

8. The idea that privacy provided a legal, or even constitutional, safety net was not unique to the gay rights movement. *Roe v. Wade* secured women the right to have an abortion based on a "right to privacy." Rosalind Petchesky, "Giving Women a Real Choice," in *The Nation* (May 28, 1990, p. 732), critiques the legal efficacy of a "right to privacy" argument.

9. Before a penal code revision in 1977, only homosexual behavior was included under Georgia's sodomy law. The revision applied the law to heterosexual activity as well. Some of the most moralistic language quoted here comes from Chief Justice Warren E. Burger's concurring opinion.

10. Historically, in U.S. law, a right to privacy has often been predetermined by preexisting connections to marriage or family. *Griswold v. Connecticut* (1964) secured the right to use contraceptives within marriage; *Loving v. Virginia* (1969) struck down anti-miscegenation marriage laws; *Moore v. East Cleveland* (1976) stated that the welfare of a family took precedence over local zoning laws. This position was modified in *Eisenstadt v. Baird* (1972), which gave unmarried couples the right to use contraceptives, and *Roe v. Wade* (1973), which claimed abortion as a matter of personal privacy. Moreover, Judge Merhige's dissent in *Doe v. Commonwealth's Attorney* (1976) explicitly articulated a "right to privacy" for homosexual activity. The *Bowers v. Hardwick* decision did not view these as precedents because homosexuality stood apart from marriage, reproduction, and family. John Gordon's "Process, Privacy, and the Supreme Court" gives a concise overview of the topic (*Boston Law Review* 28:691).

11. Kendall Thomas's "Beyond the Privacy Principle" (*Columbia Law Review,* Vol. 92, October 1992) is invaluable in understanding *Bowers v. Hardwick* and has informed much of this chapter. More information on Hardwick's arrest can be found in Laurence Tribe's *American Constitutional Law* and Peter Irons's *The Courage of Their Convictions.*

12. Kendall Thomas, "Beyond the Privacy Principle," p. 1463.

13. John Francis Hunter (who also published under John Paul Hudson) wrote for the gay press and was involved in the early gay movement. The "outing" fantasy in *The Gay Insider/USA* reflects the antiprivacy politics of the Gay Liberation Front; the soon-to-emerge, more moderate, gay rights groups took a more conservative stand. Larry Gross's *Contested Closets* is an invaluable source of primary documents and analysis

about outing. Many of the arguments in this section appeared in an earlier form in my "Outing: The Power of the Closet" in *Gay Community News,* June 3, 1990.

14. Vaid argues in *Virtual Equality* that her opposition to outing is based on a feminist perspective that prioritizes the need for complete sexual and reproductive autonomy. See also footnote on C. Carr in Gross, p. 274; Signorile in *The Advocate,* August 27, 1991 and Richard Rouilard, same issue.

15. Cultural and social contexts surrounding privacy change constantly. *Robertson v. Rochester Folding Box Co.* (1902), one of the first "right to privacy" decisions, concerned the unauthorized use of photographic images: technology forced the court to make common law without precedent. Outing has been both the result of and a catalyst for radical changes in the configuration of privacy. See Gordon's "Process, Privacy, and the Supreme Court" for more on Robertson and the origins of privacy law.

16. The gay liberation movement mandate to "come out" radically changed perceptions of "privacy" for both homosexuals and heterosexuals. Andrew Hodges and David Hutter's pamphlet "With Downcast Gays" was one of the first articulations of the ethics of coming out and self-oppression, as was Carl Wittman's "A Gay Manifesto."

17. The current popularity of the personal memoir is a good example of the culture of self-disclosure. While gay and lesbian writing has always emphasized the importance of writing about the personal, it is only recently that heterosexual authors have acted on that permission.

18. Antigay language remained common in some of the mainstream press until the mid-1980s. Edward Alwood's *Straight News* notes, among other examples, that only after community protests in 1981 did the *Philadelphia Daily News* stop using the word "faggot."

19. It is now more common for the police to also release the names of "johns" in prostitution arrests. This is the result of feminist protests against a double standard, more determined attempts to "clean up" cities in the wake of gentrification and development, and renewed social and moral campaigns against "quality of life" crimes.

20. The censorship of the Cooney biography never became big news. A thorough account of it is given in "The New York Times v. Gay America," by George DeStephano, in *The Advocate,* December 9, 1986. Spellman's homosexuality was an open secret, as was Boston's Richard Cardinal Cushing's, and the two prelates were referred to as "Fanny Spellman" and "Kitty Cushing" both within and outside the gay community.

21. Lack of coverage for ACT UP and other direct-action groups is documented in Alwood's *Straight News* and Sarah Schulman's *My American History.*

22. *The New York Times'* coverage of AIDS and of the Tylenol scare is discussed, along with other problems with AIDS coverage, in Rodger Streitmatter's *Unspeakable* and Alwood's *Straight News.*

23. Sarah Schulman's letter appeared in *The Village Voice,* April 24, 1990, and is printed in its entirety in Gross's *Contested Closets.*

24. Mike Royko's "Antsy Closet Crowd Should Think Twice" appeared in the *Chicago Tribune,* April 2, 1990, and is reprinted in its entirety in Gross's *Contested Closets.*

25. Vito Russo's letter appeared in *The Village Voice,* April 24, 1990, and is reprinted in its entirety in Gross's *Contested Closets.*

26. Gunderson's view of his threatened outing and his coming out interviews are recounted in his autobiography, *House and Home.* Gross's *Contested Closets* contains material on earlier Gunderson outings, including a court case in which he was accused of transmitting anal warts to a sexual partner.

Eleven: The Gay Ghetto and the Creation of Culture

1. Wittman's "A Gay Manifesto" is reprinted in Karla Jay and Allen Young's *Out of the Closets*.

2. Richard Sennett's *Flesh and Stone*, in particular chapter 7, "Fear of Touching," informed my discussion of the Jewish Ghetto and position of Jewish culture and sexuality in Christian Europe. David Kertzer's *The Kidnapping of Edgardo Mortara* contains historical information on Jewish ghettos in Italy, as well as a detailed look at the role of the ghetto in the mid–nineteenth century. Deborah Dwork and Robert Jan van Pelt's *Auschwitz: 1270 to the Present*, while focusing on the Holocaust, demonstrates the evolution of this ghetto into a death camp.

3. Sennett details Christian fears of Jewish uncleanliness and disease. Sander Gilman's *The Jew's Body* examines these fears in relation to Jewish male sexuality.

4. Gilman's *The Jew's Body* discusses the symbolic meaning of circumcision for Christians. The influence of the "feminized Jew" on Freud's theories about women is discussed in Gilman's *The Case of Sigmund Freud*. Guido Ruggiero's *The Boundaries of Eros* details information about sexual relationships between Jews and Christians, as well as similarities between legal restrictions on Jews, prostitutes, and homosexuals.

5. Nat Hentoff's memoir *Boston Boy* paints a vivid portrait of growing up Jewish in an Irish-Catholic city.

6. Eva Le Gallienne's Civic Repertory Theater, which revitalized U.S. theater in the 1930s, was largely the product of an ongoing and thriving lesbian culture. Helen Sheehy's *Eva Le Gallienne* is a complete record of her life and career.

7. Discussions of the eroticization of the gay ghetto have traditionally focused on gay men. *Queers in Space*, edited by Gordon Brent Ingram et al., contains several good discussions of lesbian visibility, in particular Maxine Wolfe's "Invisible Women in Invisible Places," Carrie Moyer's "Do You Love the Dyke in Your Face," and Elsie Jay's "Domestic Dykes: The Politics of In-Difference."

8. Christopher Hill's *The World Turned Upside Down* provides a firm basis for understanding the rural to urban shift in British culture. Alan Bray's *Homosexuality in Renaissance England* and Rictor Norton's *Mother Clap's Molly House* detail the early formations of a gay subculture.

9. The discussion of gay public space in New York in this section is informed by George Chauncey's indispensable *Gay New York*. Kathy Peiss's *Cheap Amusements* provides detailed information not only on how and where working people relaxed in turn-of-the-century New York, but how leisure time was constructed.

10. In *The Uses of Disorder*, Richard Sennett elucidates the paradox of how crowded urban centers offer more privacy than rural settings.

11. *The New York Times Magazine* quote appears in Chauncey's *Gay New York*, p. 135.

12. Timothy J. Gilfoyle's *City of Eros* is a comprehensive study of prostitution and sexual subcultures in New York in the nineteenth and early twentieth centuries.

13. Elizabeth Ewen's *Immigrant Women in the Land of Dollars*, a study of turn-of-the-century women's lives on the Lower East Side, makes clear the threat that working class leisure posed to the dominant culture.

14. Peiss's *Cheap Amusements* discusses the role of the dance hall and saloon in city life. William Leach's fascinating *Land of Desire* examines not only the role that neon and department stores played in eroticizing the city, but how the new consumer culture profoundly altered urban life. Chauncey's *Gay New York* examines urban gay male cruising habits.

15. The material on the history of Harlem and the Renaissance was drawn from, among other sources, Bruce Kellner's *The Harlem Renaissance: A Historical Dictionary of the Era,* Steven Watson's informative *The Harlem Renaissance,* and David Levering Lewis's *The Portable Harlem Renaissance Reader.* The Harlem Renaissance was not only a crucible of black culture but a conduit into the mainstream, where its influence radically changed the underpinnings of "American" art and culture. Houston A. Baker's *Modernism and the Harlem Renaissance,* James de Jongh's *Vicious Modernism,* and Ann Douglas's *A Terrible Honesty: Mongrel Manhattan in the 1920s,* are all perceptive studies of this influence.

16. The impact of Harlem's theatrical and musical culture on U.S. and European culture is immeasurable. Eric Garber's "A Spectacle in Color: The Lesbian and Gay Subculture of Jazz Age Harlem" in *Hidden from History,* edited by Martin Duberman et al., is a good primer on the topic. Bruce Kellner's *The Harlem Renaissance* provides detailed descriptions of many artists, venues, and specific shows. My "Harlem on Her Mind: Rediscovering the Legendary Josephine Baker" (*Gay Community News,* February 28, 1988, p. 16) examines the prevalence of lesbian performers in 1920s black popular music. Also informative are autobiographies and biographies of performers like Alberta Hunter, Bricktop, and Josephine Baker. Ted Vincent's *Keep Cool: The Black Activists Who Built the Jazz Age* is the best study of the direct connections between jazz, black culture, and political activism.

17. June Shochen's *The New Woman* and Anne Cheney's *Millay in Greenwich Village* sketch a portrait of Village feminism, bohemianism, and sexual politics. Margaret Sanger's *An Autobiography* discusses the censorship of *Woman Rebel.* Sanger also writes of how important it is for feminism to offer working women "leisure" as well as the vote and safe working conditions.

18. The legal regulation of dance halls and other public entertainments is discussed in Peiss's *Cheap Amusements.*

19. John Kobler's *Ardent Spirits* is a popular but comprehensive history of Prohibition. The effect of Prohibition on gay people is discussed in Chauncey's *Gay New York.* Peiss, in *Cheap Amusements,* examines middle-class campaigns to curb drinking in working-class communities.

20. William Leach's *Land of Desire: Merchants, Power, and the Rise of a New American Culture* details how the advent of electric and neon lighting and commercial signage that turned New York into a "city of color and light" affected not only urban nightlife but economics, zoning laws, and population shifts.

21. Jonathan Katz's *The Invention of Heterosexuality* is the best work available about the political and social ramifications of the evolution of a public heterosexual identity.

22. Cruising locations and arrest patterns for public cruising are discussed in Chauncey's *Gay New York.*

23. Emily Wortis Leider's *Becoming Mae West* contains information on not only the performer's career and legal troubles, but the influence of gay male culture on her style and persona. *Three Plays by Mae West,* edited by Lillian Schlissel, brings into print for the first time Mae West's dramatic work. Kaier Curtin's *"We Can Always Call Them Bulgarians"* places West's plays, and the censorship of them, in a comprehensive history of gay theater.

24. Lincoln Kirstein's *Paul Cadmus* collects most of the artist's work and supplies a detailed history and an informed commentary.

25. Sennett's theories of urban upheaval and reorganization in *The Uses of Disorder* are historically specific; as a paradigm they are extraordinarily useful in understanding and evaluating urban history.

26. Although Simone Weil's *The Need for Roots* is an examination of the moral responsibilities of nationhood and citizenship in postwar France, it remains provocative in discussing issues of citizenship and dominant culture today.

27. Richard Sennett's *The Fall of Public Man* contains a perceptive analysis of the Dreyfus Affair, subcultures, nationalism, and citizenship. The anti-Dreyfus editorial quoted here is from this book. While Rebecca West, writing of the English spy Guy Burgess in *The New Meaning of Treason,* does not dwell on Burgess's homosexuality, it informs her whole discussion of the case and raises the issue of the "homosexual traitor" and national loyalty. Alan Bennett's duo of plays, *Single Spies* (about Burgess and Anthony Blunt), also treats this, as does the film *Another Country* (1984).

28. The enormous impact of popular culture's reinforcement of the social and moral importance of the family in U.S. life is detailed in Lynn Spigel's *Make Room for TV* and Gerard Jones's *Honey I'm Home.*

29. The vision of a happy, contented postwar America was often contested at the time, even in popular culture. Elizabeth Long's *The American Dream and the Popular Novel* examines both the promotion and the critique of the family in best-selling novels of the period. Popular studies like David Riesman's *The Lonely Crowd* and C. Wright Mills's *The Power Elite* and *White Collar* offered harsh critiques of the work ethic, family life, and the suburbs.

30. The formation of postwar gay ghettos and gay public spaces followed similar organizational patterns across the country: Susan Stryker and Jim Van Bushkirk's *Gay by the Bay* discusses San Francisco's North Beach; Elizabeth Kennedy and Madeline Davis's *Boots of Leather, Slippers of Gold* looks at working-class neighborhoods in Buffalo, N.Y.; and the History Project's *Improper Bostonians: Lesbian and Gay History from the Puritans to Playland* examines Boston's Beacon Hill and Scully Square. Post-Stonewall ghettos such as San Francisco's the Castro, Boston's South End, and New York's East Village also follow this pattern.

31. Jane Jacobs's *The Death and Life of Great American Cities* informs much of this chapter and is invaluable in understanding the relationship of the city to contemporary culture. A staunch defender of "the common," Jacobs contrasts the Village to other, more privatized, New York neighborhoods and declares as false the popular notion that urban privacy ensures personal safety; she argues that visibility and an aware, cohesive neighborhood are more likely to cut down on crime. Garrett Hardin's "The Tragedy of the Commons" (*Science* 162, 1968) is the classic analysis of the effect of enclosure (privacy) on contemporary society.

32. The most famous example of a "street character" in the gay ghetto is Harvey Milk. Randy Shilts's *The Mayor of Castro Street* details his role as a community personality and leader.

33. It is very difficult to ascertain the percentage of gay people who live in a "gay neighborhood." There are no records of, or even reliable methods of measuring, the gay population of the Village in the 1950s. George Chauncey, who has done extensive work on the topic, conjectured that the gay population in the 1950s was probably a small percentage of the Village's total population. Stephen O. Murray's *American Gay* contains some preliminary statistics on Toronto's Yonge Street neighborhood, and an article in the *San Francisco Examiner* (September 12, 1993) uses the U.S. census to count same-sex households in the city's neighborhoods.

34. Malcolm Gladwell's article "The Tipping Point," in *The New Yorker,* June 3, 1996, succinctly explains how "tipping" occurs. The emergence of New York's Chelsea as a gay ghetto is an example of "tipping" and is discussed in Jesse Green's "Where the Boys Went," in *The New York Times Magazine,* October 19, 1997. Tracking neighborhood "tip-

ping" can have explicitly political purposes and has been used by real estate development companies and white community groups to monitor and prevent a neighborhood from "going black."

35. Robert Pattison's *The Triumph of Vulgarity* and Linda Martin's *Anti-Rock: The Opposition to Rock and Roll* examine racist underpinnings of attacks on rock music. Richard Wagner's anti-Semitic essay "Jews and Music," from the 1850s, is the prototype of attacks on the moral and social corruptiveness of "degenerate" subcultures.

36. While ghetto and underground culture often begins as authentic expression of a subculture, it can quickly become commodified and marketed. Sarah Schulman's *Stagestruck: Theater, AIDS, and the Marketing of Gay America* charts how this has happened to gay and lesbian theater.

37. The interconnected growth of gay and Beat culture was replicated twenty years later when gay culture, evolving again, merged with and out of the countercultures of the 1960s and early 1970s. Carl Wittman's "A Gay Manifesto," and many other pieces in Karla Jay and Allen Young's *Out of the Closets,* depict this evolution. Paul Goodman's *Growing Up Absurd* noted and analyzed in the 1960s the connections between Beat culture and the growing visibility and influence of the newly emerging urban culture.

38. Beat culture's threat was quickly countered by commodification (marketing the "beatnik" look) and mainstreamed in the media. Films like *The Beat Generation* (1959) "exposed" the immorality of the Beats, and the "beatnik" dance sequence in *Funny Face* (1957) simultaneously mocked and celebrated the freedom of Beat culture.

39. Robert Doty's "Growth of Overt Homosexuality in City Provokes Wide Concern" ran December 17, 1963, in *The New York Times.* Doty quoted some Mattachine Society members for the sake of balance, but the article dwelt single-mindedly on the new visibility of homosexuals, reflecting the dominant culture's fear that public space was increasingly "unsafe."

40. The quest for assimilation and the use of the ghetto can cause rifts within groups. Robert Orsi's *The Madonna of 115th Street* charts bitter conflicts between Irish and Italian Catholics in New York over the public presentation of Italian Catholicism, particularly street festivals and other forms of public devotion, in contrast to the more private, and acceptable, Irish-Catholic traditions.

41. "We Refugees" appears in Hannah Arendt's *The Jew as Pariah.*

42. The effect of Whitman's sexuality on his work is examined in Charley Shively's *Calamus Lovers* and *Drum Beats,* as well as in Gary Schmidgall's *Walt Whitman: A Gay Life.* This version of "I dreamed in a dream . . ." was removed by Whitman from the 1860 edition of *Leaves of Grass* before publication and does not appear in any of the standard editions of the work. It can found in *Whitman Manuscripts: "Leaves of Grass" (1860): A Parallel Text,* edited by Fredson Thayer Bowers. In an effort to reconstruct a more complete view of Whitman's homosexuality, Shively has restored this version to the Calamus poems in *Calamus Lovers* (page 206).

43. Richard Sennett argues in *The Conscience of the Eye* that "zones of transition" (which often arise with changes in personal and social identities) are not only inevitable, and sometimes dangerous, but vital for the growth of the city, the maturation of urban life, and the evolution of a more just democracy.

44. The Allen Ginsberg quote appears in Donn Teal's *The Gay Militants.*

45. Hannah Arendt speaks of "natality" in *The Human Condition* and describes it as "the central category of political thought" because it mandates a reinvention of the self, usually from a position of exile and often in conjunction with other people in similar situations. Sennett, in *The Conscience of the Eye,* discusses Arendt's concept in relation to the ever-changing social and political life of the city.

Conclusion: The World Turned Upside Down

1. Mikhail Bakhtin's *Rabelais and His World* is the standard analysis of the role of Carnival in Europe and the function of literature as social disruption. Barbara Babcock's anthology *The Reversible World* contains invaluable information about a wide range of Misrule throughout the world; Terry Castle's *Masquerade and Civilization* focuses specifically on manifestations of Misrule in eighteenth-century British culture. Stephen Nissenbaum's *The Battle for Christmas* traces the history of Christmas from its origins as a near-violent time of Misrule to its current sentimental incarnation and is a good analysis of how Misrule is regulated. Roger D. Abrahams's *Singing the Master* describes and analyzes Christmas Misrule ceremonies on plantations.

2. The impulses of Misrule are evident in much of children's literature. Alison Laurie's *Don't Tell the Grown-ups* delineates how "uncivilized" and anti-social classic children's books are and why this is what makes them popular. Jacqueline Rose's *The Case of Peter Pan* uses a psychoanalytic approach to James M. Barrie's work (as well as children's literature in general) and arrives at similar conclusions. Roger Sale's *Fairy Tales and After* is a less rigorous analysis but contains insights into the role that fairy tales and children's books play in helping children deal with social repression. While Maureen Duffy's *The Erotic World of Faery* does not deal specifically with children's literature, it contains invaluable information about the role of the imagination, Misrule, and writing.

3. Christopher Hill's *The World Turned Upside Down,* while it does not deal specifically with Misrule, makes clear the connections between social revolution and popularism in sixteenth-century England. The outlaw and bandit have always been central to Misrule and J. C. Holt's *Robin Hood* charts the beginnings of the Robin Hood legend and its connections to popular social revolt. Margaret A. Murray's *The Witch-Cult in Western Europe* is a fine analysis of the anti-authoritarian social and political role of witchcraft in European society. She is particularly insightful on how elements of the witch-cults became incorporated into more popular forms of Misrule.

4. Specific connections between witchcraft, Misrule, and homosexuality can be found in Arthur Evans's *Witchcraft and the Gay Counterculture* and *The God of Ecstasy* and Judy Grahn's *Another Mother Tongue*. Will Roscoe's collection *Radically Gay: Gay Liberation in the Words of Its Founder Harry Hay,* contains Hay's research and thinking about homosexuality, social change, and traditional manifestations of Misrule.

5. New York State passed the Married Women's Property Act in 1848, the first in the nation. Miriam Schneir's *Feminism: The Essential Historical Writings* and June Sochen's *Herstory* contain information on women's unfolding access to citizenship.

6. The Abigail and John Adams letters are found in Alice Rossi's *The Feminist Papers* and Schneir's *Feminism: The Essential Historical Writings.*

7. David H. Bennett's *The Party of Fear* makes explicit the resonances of anti-Semitic and anti-Catholic prejudice of the 1880 anti-Nativist movements in the New Right today.

8. Urvashi Vaid's *Virtual Equality* contains extensive survey information on how homosexuals are viewed.

9. Melvin Wulf's "Constitutional Practice: On the Origins of Privacy" in *The Nation* (May 27, 1991, page 700) is an interesting analysis on the construction of citizenship through private property.

10. Norbert Elias's *The Civilizing Process* details not only the historical methods of "civilizing" but notes the evolution of the language describing it.

11. Daniel Jonah Goldhagen's *Hitler's Willing Executioners* details the complex history of how European anti-Semitism became, in his words, "eliminationist anti-Semitism."

Bibliography

Abrahams, Roger D. *Singing the Master: The Emergence of African-American Culture in the Plantation South.* New York: Pantheon Books, 1992.

Ackroyd, Peter. *Dressing Up: Transvestism and Drag; The History of an Obsession.* New York: Simon & Schuster, 1979.

Alexander, Jeb. *Jeb and Dash: A Diary of Gay Life, 1918–1945.* Edited by Ina Russell. Boston: Faber and Faber, 1993.

Alexander, Paul. *Boulevard of Broken Dreams: The Life, Times, and Legend of James Dean.* New York: Viking, 1994.

Allen, Theodore W. *The Invention of the White Race.* London: Verso, 1994.

Alwood, Edward. *Straight News: Gays, Lesbians, and the News Media.* New York: Columbia University Press, 1996.

Anderson, George K. *The Legend of the Wandering Jew.* Hanover, N.H.: University Press of New England, 1991.

Apter, Emily, and William Pietz, eds. *Fetishism as Cultural Discourse.* Ithaca, N.Y.: Cornell University Press, 1993.

Arendt, Hannah. *Eichmann in Jerusalem: A Report on the Banality of Evil.* rev. and enl. ed. New York: Viking, 1964.

———. *The Human Condition: A Study of the Central Dilemmas Facing Modern Man.* Garden City, N.Y.: Doubleday Anchor, 1959.

———. *The Jew as Pariah: Jewish Identity and Politics in the Modern Age.* New York: Grove Press, 1978.

Aries, Philippe. *Centuries of Childhood: A Social History of Family Life.* New York: Knopf, 1962.

Atkinson, Ti-Grace. *Amazon Odyssey.* New York: Links Books, 1974.

Atlas, James. *Battle of the Books: The Curriculum Debate in America.* New York: W. W. Norton, 1992.

Babcock, Barbara, ed. *The Reversible World: Symbolic Inversions in Art and Society.* Ithaca, N.Y.: Cornell University Press, 1978.

Backer, Dorothy Anne Liot. *Precious Women: A Feminist Phenomenon in the Age of Louis XIV.* New York: Basic Books, 1974.

Bailey, Derrick Sherwin. *Homosexuality and the Western Christian Tradition.* 1955. Reprint, Hamden, Conn.: Archon Books, 1975.

Baker, Houston A., Jr. *Modernism and the Harlem Renaissance.* Chicago: University of Chicago Press, 1987.

Bakhtin, Mikhail. *Rabelais and His World.* Translated by Helene Iswolsky. Bloomington: Indiana University Press, 1984.

Baldwin, James. *The Price of the Ticket: Collected Nonfiction, 1948–1985.* New York: St. Martin's Press, 1985.

Baring-Gould, Sabine. *Curious Myths of the Middle Ages.* Edited by Edward Hardy. New York: Oxford University Press, 1978.

Barthes, Roland. *The Pleasure of the Text*. Translated by Richard Miller. New York: Hill & Wang, 1975.

Bartlett, Neil. *Who Was That Man?: A Present for Mr. Oscar Wilde*. London: Serpent's Tail, 1988.

Bawer, Bruce. *A Place at the Table: The Gay Individual in American Society*. New York: Poseidon Press, 1993.

Bell, David, and Gill Valentine, eds. *Mapping Desire: Geographies of Sexuality*. New York: Routledge, 1995.

Benkov, Laura. *Reinventing the Family: The Emerging Story of Lesbian and Gay Parents*. New York: Crown, 1994.

Bennett, Alan. *Single Spies: Two Plays about Guy Burgess and Anthony Blunt; Talking Heads: Six Monologues*. New York: Summit Books, 1990.

Bennett, David H. *The Party of Fear: From Nativist Movements to the New-Right in American History*. Chapel Hill: University of North Carolina Press, 1988.

Bennett, Paula, and Vernon Rosario II, eds. *Solitary Pleasures: The Historical, Literary, and Artistic Discourses of Autoeroticism*. New York: Routledge, 1995.

Bennett, William. *The Book of Virtues: A Treasury of Great Moral Stories*. New York: Simon & Schuster, 1993.

Berg, A. Scott. *Goldwyn: A Biography*. New York: Knopf, 1989.

Berger, John. *Ways of Seeing*. London: British Broadcasting Corporation; Harmondsworth: Penguin, 1972.

Bergler, Edmund. *Counterfeit-Sex: Homosexuality, Impotence, Frigidity*. 2d, enl. ed. New York: Grove Press, 1961.

———. *Fashion and the Unconscious*. New York: R. Brunner, 1953.

———. *Homosexuality: Disease or Way of Life?* New York: Collins Books, 1967.

Berman, Paul, ed. *Debating P. C.: The Controversy over Political Correctness on College Campuses*. New York: Dell, 1992.

Bernstein, Richard. *Dictatorship of Virtue: Multiculturalism and the Battle for America's Future*. New York: Knopf, 1994.

Bérubé, Allan. *Coming Out Under Fire: The History of Gay Men and Women in World War II*. New York: Free Press, 1990.

Best, Joel. *Threatened Children: Rhetoric and Concern about Child-Victims*. Chicago: University of Chicago Press, 1990.

Biskind, Peter. *Seeing Is Believing: How Hollywood Told Us to Stop Worrying and Love the Fifties*. New York: Pantheon Books, 1983.

Bland, Lucy. *Banishing the Beast: Sexuality and the Early Feminists*. New York: New Press, 1995.

Boogle, Donald. *Toms, Coons, Mulattoes, Mammies, and Bucks: An Interpretative History of Blacks in American Films* (3rd ed.) New York: Continuum, 1994.

Boskin, Joseph. *Sambo: The Rise and Demise of an American Jester*. New York: Oxford University Press, 1986.

Boswell, John. *Christianity, Social Tolerance, and Homosexuality: Gay People in Western Europe from the Beginning of the Christian Era to the Fourteenth Century*. Chicago: University of Chicago Press, 1980.

Bowers, Fredson Thayer, ed., *Whitman's Manuscripts:"Leaves of Grass" (1860): A Parallel Text*. Chicago: University of Chicago Press, 1955.

Brandt, Allan M. *No Magic Bullet: A Social History of Venereal Disease in the United States Since 1880*. New York: Oxford University Press, 1985.

Brantlinger, Patrick. *Bread and Circuses: Theories of Mass Culture as Social Decay*. Ithaca, N.Y.: Cornell University Press, 1983.

Bray, Alan. *Homosexuality in Renaissance England*. London: Gay Men's Press, 1982.

Bronski, Michael. *Culture Clash: The Making of Gay Sensibility.* Boston: South End Press, 1984.

Brophy, Brigid. *Black Ship to Hell.* New York: Harcourt, Brace & World, 1962.

————. *Prancing Novelist: A Defense of Fiction in the Form of a Critical Biography in Praise of Ronald Firbank.* New York: Barnes & Noble, 1973.

Brown, Norman O. *Life Against Death: The Psychoanalytic Meaning of History.* New York: Vintage, 1959.

Bull, Chris, and John Gallagher. *Perfect Enemies: The Religious Right, the Gay Movement, and the Politics of the 1990s.* New York: Crown, 1996.

Cantor, Eddie, with Jane Kesner Ardmore. *Take My Life.* Garden City, N.Y.: Doubleday, 1957.

Carpenter, C. Tyler, and Edward H. Yeatts. *Stars Without Garters! The Memoirs of Two Gay GI's in WWII.* San Francisco: Alamo Square Press, 1996.

Carpenter, Edward. *Selected Writings.* Vol. 1, *Sex.* London: Gay Men's Press, 1984.

Carpenter, Humphrey, and Mari Prichard. *The Oxford Companion to Children's Literature.* New York: Oxford University Press, 1984.

Castle, Terry. *The Female Thermometer: Eighteenth-Century Culture and the Invention of the Uncanny.* New York: Oxford University Press, 1995.

————. *Masquerade and Civilization: The Carnivalesque in Eighteenth-Century English Culture and Fiction.* Stanford, Calif.: Stanford University Press, 1986.

————. *Noel Coward and Radclyffe Hall: Kindred Spirits.* New York: Columbia University Press, 1996.

Chandler, Kurt. *Passages of Pride: Lesbian and Gay Youth Come of Age.* New York: Times Books, 1995.

Chapman, David. *Adonis: The Male Physique Pin-Up, 1870–1940.* London: Gay Men's Press, 1989.

————. *Sandow the Magnificent: Eugen Sandow and the Beginnings of Bodybuilding.* Urbana: University of Illinois Press, 1994.

Chauncey, George. *Gay New York: Gender, Urban Culture, and the Making of the Gay Male World, 1890–1940.* New York: BasicBooks, 1994.

Chen, Constance M. *"The Sex Side of Life": Mary Ware Dennett's Pioneering Battle for Birth Control and Sex Education.* New York: New Press, 1996.

Cheney, Anne. *Millay in Greenwich Village.* University: University of Alabama Press, 1975.

Clover, Carol J. *Men, Women, and Chain Saws: Gender in the Modern Horror Film.* Princeton, N.J.: Princeton University Press, 1992.

Clum, John. *Acting Gay: Male Homosexuality in Modern Drama.* New York: Columbia University Press, 1992.

Cober, Robert J. *Homosexuality in Cold War America: Resistance and the Crisis of Masculinity.* Durham, N.C.: Duke University Press, 1997.

Cook, Blanche Wiesen. *Eleanor Roosevelt.* Vol. 1, *1884–1933.* New York: Viking, 1992.

————. *Women and Support Networks.* New York: Out & Out Books, 1979.

Cooney, John. *The American Pope: The Life and Times of Francis Cardinal Spellman.* New York: Times Books, 1984.

Coontz, Stephanie. *The Way We Never Were: American Families and the Nostalgia Trap.* New York: Basic Books, 1992.

Cowan, Ruth Schwartz. *More Work for Mother: The Ironies of Household Technology from the Open Hearth to the Microwave.* New York: Basic Books, 1983.

Crompton, Louis. *Byron and Greek Love: Homophobia in 19th-Century England.* Berkeley: University of California Press, 1985.

Curtin, Kaier. *"We Can Always Call Them Bulgarians": Emergence of Lesbians and Gay Men on the American Stage.* Boston: Alyson, 1987.

Dangerous Bedfellows, eds. *Policing Public Sex: Queer Politics and the Future of AIDS Activism.* Boston: South End Press, 1996.

Danto, Arthur C. *Playing with the Edge: The Photographic Achievement of Robert Mapplethorpe.* Berkeley: University of California Press, 1996.

Davison, Jane. *The Fall of a Doll's House: Three Generations of American Women and the Houses They Lived In.* New York: Holt, Rinehart & Winston, 1980.

de Beauvoir, Simone. *The Second Sex.* New York: Knopf, 1952.

De Grazia, Edward. *Girls Lean Back Everywhere: The Law of Obscenity and the Assault on Genius.* New York: Random House, 1992.

De Grazia, Victoria, and Ellen Furlough, eds. *The Sex of Things: Gender and Consumption in Historical Perspective.* Berkeley: University of California Press, 1996.

D'Emilio, John. *Making Trouble: Essays on Gay History, Politics, and the University.* New York: Routledge, 1992.

————. *Sexual Politics, Sexual Communities: The Making of a Homosexual Minority in the United States, 1940–1970.* Chicago: University of Chicago Press, 1983.

De Forrest, Michael. *The Gay Year.* 1949. Reprint, New York: Lancer Books, 1968.

De Jongh, James. *Vicious Modernism: Black Harlem and the Literary Imagination.* New York: Cambridge University Press, 1990.

De Jongh, Nicholas. *Not in Front of the Audience: Homosexuality on Stage.* London: Routledge, 1992.

Dolinsky, Jim, ed. *Bruce of Los Angeles.* Berlin: Bruno Gmunder, 1990.

Donoghue, Emma. *Passions Between Women: British Lesbian Culture, 1668–1801.* New York: HarperCollins, 1995.

Douglas, Ann. *The Feminization of American Culture.* New York: Knopf, 1977.

————. *A Terrible Honesty: Mongrel Manhattan in the 1920s.* New York: Farrar, Straus & Giroux, 1995.

Dowd, Harrison. *The Night Air.* New York: Dial Press, 1950.

Duberman, Martin Bauml. *Paul Robeson: A Biography.* New York: Knopf, 1988.

————, Martha Vicinus, and George Chauncey Jr., eds. *Hidden from History: Reclaiming the Gay and Lesbian Past.* New York: New American Library, 1989.

DuBois, Ellen Carol. *Feminism and Suffrage: The Emergence of an Independent Women's Movement in America, 1848–1869.* Ithaca, N.Y.: Cornell University Press, 1978.

Duffy, Maureen. *The Erotic World of Faery.* New York: Avon Books, 1972.

Dutton, Kenneth R. *The Perfectible Body: The Western Ideal of Male Physical Development.* New York: Continuum, 1995.

Dwork, Deborah, and Robert Jan van Pelt. *Auschwitz: 1270 to the Present.* New York: W. W. Norton, 1996.

Dyer, Richard. *Heavenly Bodies: Film Stars and Society.* New York: St. Martin's Press, 1986.

————. *White.* New York: Routledge, 1997.

Ehrenreich, Barbara. *Fear of Falling: The Inner Life of the Middle Class.* New York: Pantheon Books, 1989.

————. *The Hearts of Men: American Dreams and the Flight from Commitment.* Garden City, N.Y.: Doubleday Anchor, 1983.

Elias, Norbert. *The Civilizing Process: The Development of Manners.* Translated by Edmund Jephcott. New York: Urizen Books, 1978.

Ellmann, Richard. *Oscar Wilde.* New York: Knopf, 1988.

Emerson, Ken. *Doo-dah!: Stephen Foster and the Rise of American Popular Culture.* New York: Simon & Schuster, 1997.

Epstein, Steven. *Impure Science: AIDS, Activism, and the Politics of Knowledge.* Berkeley: University of California Press, 1996.

Evans, Arthur. *The God of Ecstasy: Sex Roles and the Madness of Dionysos.* New York: St. Martin's Press, 1988.

————. *Witchcraft and the Gay Counterculture.* Boston: Fag Rag Books, 1978.

Ewen, Elizabeth. *Immigrant Women in the Land of Dollars: Life and Culture on the Lower East Side, 1890–1925.* New York: Monthly Review Press, 1985.

Fabre-Vassas, Claudine. *The Singular Beast: Jews, Christians, and the Pig.* Translated by Carol Volk. New York: Columbia University Press, 1997.

Faderman, Lillian. *Surpassing the Love of Men: Romantic Friendship and Love Between Women from the Renaissance to the Present.* New York: William Morrow and Company, 1981.

Faderman, Lillian, and Brigitte Eriksson, eds. *Lesbian-Feminism in Turn-of-the-Century Germany.* Weatherby Lake, Mo.: Naiad Press, 1980.

Fey, Edwin. *Summer in Sodom.* New York: Paperback Library, 1965.

Fiedler, Leslie. *An End to Innocence.* Boston: Beacon Press, 1955.

————. *Love and Death in the American Novel.* rev. ed. New York: Dell, 1962.

————. *The Stranger in Shakespeare.* New York: Stein and Day, 1973.

Firestone, Shulamith. *The Dialectic of Sex: The Case for Feminist Revolution.* New York: William Morrow and Company, 1970.

Fischer, Hal. *Gay Semiotics: A Photographic Study of Visual Coding Among Homosexual Men.* San Francisco: NFS Press, 1977.

FitzGerald, Frances. *America Revised: History Schoolbooks in the Twentieth Century.* Boston: Little, Brown, 1979.

Flexner, Eleanor. *Century of Struggle: The Woman's Rights Movement in the United States.* New York: Atheneum, 1973.

Ford, Michael Thomas. *The World Out There: Becoming Part of the Lesbian and Gay Community.* New York: New Press, 1996.

Foucault, Michel. *The History of Sexuality.* Vol. 1, *An Introduction.* Translated by Robert Hurley. New York: Pantheon Books, 1978.

Frazer, Sir James George. *The Golden Bough: A Study in Magic and Religion.* abridged ed. New York: Macmillan, 1922.

Freud, Sigmund. *Beyond the Pleasure Principle.* Translated and edited by James Strachey. New York: Norton, 1961.

————. *Civilization and Its Discontents.* Translated by James Strachey. New York: W. W. Norton, 1961.

————. *The Sexual Enlightenment of Children.* New York: Collier Books, 1963.

————. *Sexuality and the Psychology of Love.* New York: Collier Books, 1963.

————. *Three Contributions to the Theory of Sex.* Translated by A. A. Brill. New York: Dutton, 1962.

Friedlander, Saul. *Nazi Germany and the Jews: Volume I, The Years of Persecution, 1933–1939.* New York: HarperCollins, 1997.

Fritscher, Jack. *Mapplethorpe: Assault with a Deadly Camera.* Mamaroneck, N.Y.: Hastings House, 1994.

Gabler, Neal. *An Empire of Their Own: How the Jews Invented Hollywood.* New York: Crown, 1988.

Gardelia, Peter. *Innocent Ecstasy: How Christianity Gave America an Ethic of Sexual Pleasure.* New York: Oxford University Press, 1985.

Gates, Henry Louis, Jr. *Loose Canons: Notes on the Culture Wars.* New York: Oxford University Press, 1992.

Gelles, Richard J., and Murray A. Straus. *Intimate Violence: The Definitive Study of Causes and Consequences in the American Family.* New York: Simon & Schuster, 1988.

Gilfoyle, Timothy J. *City of Eros: New York City, Prostitution, and the Commercialization of Sex, 1790–1920.* New York: W. W. Norton, 1992.

Gilman, Sander. *The Case of Sigmund Freud: Medicine and Identity at the Fin de Siècle.* Baltimore: Johns Hopkins University Press, 1993.

———. *The Jew's Body.* New York: Routledge, 1991.

Gilmore, John. *The Real James Dean.* New York: Pyramid Books, 1975.

Gluckman, Amy, and Betsy Reed. *Homo Economics: Capitalism, Community, and Lesbian and Gay Life.* New York: Routledge, 1997.

Golby, J. M., and A. W. Purdue. *The Civilisation of the Crowd: Popular Culture in England, 1750–1900.* New York: Schocken Books, 1985.

Goldhagen, Daniel Jonah. *Hitler's Willing Executioners: Ordinary Germans and the Holocaust.* New York: Knopf, 1996.

Goldman, Emma. *Living My Life* (two volumes). New York: Dover Publications, 1970.

Goldman, William. *The Season: A Candid Look at Broadway.* New York: Harcourt, Brace & World, 1969.

Goodman, Paul. *Growing Up Absurd: Problems of Youth in the Organized Society.* New York: Vintage, 1960.

Grahn, Judy. *Another Mother Tongue: Gay Words, Gay Worlds.* Boston: Beacon Press, 1984.

Grant, George, and Mark A. Horne. *Legislating Immorality: The Homosexual Movement Comes Out of the Closet.* Chicago: Moody Press, 1993.

Greenberg, David E. *The Construction of Homosexuality.* Chicago: University of Chicago Press, 1988.

Greene, Graham. *Graham Greene on Film: Collected Film Criticism, 1935–1940.* Edited by John Russell Taylor. New York: Simon & Schuster, 1972.

Gross, John. *Shylock: A Legend and Its Legacy.* New York: Simon & Schuster, 1992.

Gross, Larry. *Contested Closets: The Politics and Ethics of Outing.* Minneapolis: University of Minnesota Press, 1993.

Grossman, Barbara. *Funny Woman: The Life and Times of Fanny Brice.* Bloomington: Indiana University Press, 1991.

Grover, Kathryn, ed. *Hard at Play: Leisure in America, 1840–1940.* Amherst: University of Massachusetts Press, 1992.

Guinier, Lani. *The Tyranny of the Majority: Fundamental Fairness in Representative Democracy.* New York: Free Press, 1994.

Gunderson, Steve, and Rob Morris with Bruce Bawer. *House and Home.* New York: Dutton, 1996.

Hamm, Charles. *Irving Berlin: Songs from the Melting Pot; The Formative Years, 1907–1914.* New York: Oxford University Press, 1997.

Hart, Lynda. *Fatal Women: Lesbian Sexuality and the Mark of Aggression.* Princeton, N.J.: Princeton University Press, 1994.

Harvey, John. *Men in Black.* Chicago: University of Chicago Press, 1995.

Hay, Harry. *Radically Gay: Gay Liberation in the Words of Its Founder Harry Hay.* Edited by Will Roscoe. Boston: Beacon Press, 1996.

Hecht, Anthony. *Obbligati: Essays in Criticism.* New York: Atheneum, 1986.

Hemphill, Essex. *Ceremonies: Prose and Poetry.* New York: Plume, 1992.

Hentoff, Nat. *Boston Boy.* New York: Knopf, 1986.

Hichens, Robert. *The Green Carnation.* 1894. Reprint, New York: Dover, 1970.

Highwater, Jamake. *The Mythology of Transgression: Homosexuality as Metaphor.* New York: Oxford University Press, 1997.

Hill, Christopher. *The World Turned Upside Down: Radical Ideas during the English Revolution.* New York: Viking, 1972; Penguin Books, 1975.

Himmelfarb, Gertrude. *The De-Moralization of Society: From Victorian Virtues to Modern Values.* New York: Knopf, 1995.

The History Project: *Improper Bostonians: Lesbian and Gay History from the Puritans to Playland.* Boston: Beacon Press, 1998.

Hoare, Philip. *Serious Pleasures: The Life of Stephen Tennant.* London: Hamish Hamilton, 1990.

Hodges, Andrew, and David Hutter. *With Downcast Gays: Aspects of Homosexual Self-Oppression.* London: Pomegranate Press, 1974.

Hollander, Anne. *Seeing Through Clothes.* New York: Viking, 1978.

———. *Sex and Suits: The Evolution of Modern Dress.* New York: Knopf, 1994.

Holt, J. C. *Robin Hood.* London: Thames & Hudson, 1982.

Hooven, F. Valentine, III. *Beefcake: The Muscle Magazines of America, 1950–1970.* Cologne: Taschen, 1995.

Hughes, Pennethorne. *Witchcraft.* Baltimore: Penguin Books, 1965.

Hunter, John Francis. *The Gay Insider/USA.* New York: Stonehill, 1972.

Hyde, H. Montgomery. *The Other Love: An Historical and Contemporary Survey of Homosexuality in Britain.* London: Heinemann, 1970.

Ignatiev, Noel. *How the Irish Became White.* New York: Routledge, 1995.

Ingram, Gordon Brent, Anne-Marie Bouthillette, and Yolanda Retter, eds. *Queers in Space: Communities/Public Places/ Sites of Resistance.* Seattle, Wash.: Bay Press, 1997.

Irons, Peter. *The Courage of Their Convictions: Sixteen Americans Who Fought Their Way to the Supreme Court.* New York: Penguin Books, 1990.

Jacobs, Jane. *The Death and Life of Great American Cities.* New York: Random House, 1961.

Jannsen, Volker. *American Photography of the Male Nude 1940–1970.* Vol. 1, *Bruce of Los Angeles.* Vol. 2, *Lon of New York.* Berlin: Janssen Verlag, 1996.

Jones, Gerard. *Honey, I'm Home!: Sitcoms, Selling the American Dream.* New York: Grove Weidenfeld, 1992.

Kaplan, Joel H., and Sheila Stowell. *Theater and Fashion: Oscar Wilde to the Suffragettes.* Cambridge: Cambridge University Press, 1994.

Katz, Jonathan Ned. *Gay American History: Lesbians and Gay Men in the U.S.A.* New York: Thomas Y. Crowell, 1976.

———. *The Invention of Heterosexuality.* New York: Dutton, 1995.

Kellner, Bruce, ed. *The Harlem Renaissance: A Historical Dictionary for the Era.* New York: Methuen, 1984.

Kennedy, Elizabeth Lapovsky, and Madeline D. Davis. *Boots of Leather, Slippers of Gold: The History of a Lesbian Community.* New York: Routledge, 1993.

Kern, Louis J. *An Ordered Love: Sex Roles and Sexuality in Victorian Utopias: The Shakers, the Mormons, and the Oneida Community.* Chapel Hill: University of North Carolina Press, 1981.

Kertzer, David I. *The Kidnapping of Edgardo Mortara.* New York: Knopf, 1997.

Kincaid, James R. *Child-Loving: The Erotic Child and Victorian Culture.* New York: Routledge, 1992.

Kingston, Maxine Hong. *China Men.* New York: Vintage, 1989.

———. *The Warrior Woman: Memoirs of a Girlhood Among Ghosts.* New York: Knopf, 1976; Vintage, 1977.

Kirstein, Lincoln. *Paul Cadmus.* New York: Imago, 1984.

Kobler, John. *Ardent Spirits: The Rise and Fall of Prohibition.* New York: Putnam, 1973.

Kopkind, Andrew. *The Thirty Years' War: Dispatches and Diversions of a Radical Journalist, 1965–1994.* Edited by JoAnn Wypijewski. London: Verso, 1995.

Kraut, Alan M. *Silent Travelers: Germs, Genes, and the "Immigrant Menace."* New York: BasicBooks, 1994.

Kron, Joan. *Home-Psych: The Social Psychology of Home and Decoration.* New York: Potter, 1983.

Kuzniar, Alice A., ed. *Outing Goethe and His Age*. Stanford, Calif.: Stanford University Press, 1996.

Laing, R. D. *The Politics of Experience*. New York: Pantheon Books, 1963.

Lasch, Christopher. *Haven in a Heartless World: The Family Besieged*. New York: Basic Books, 1977.

Laurie, Alison. *Don't Tell the Grown-ups: Subversive Children's Literature*. Boston: Little, Brown, 1990.

Lauritsen, John, and David Thorstad. *The Early Homosexual Rights Movement (1864–1935)*. rev. ed. Ojai, Calif.: Times Change Press, 1995.

Leach, William. *Land of Desire: Merchants, Power, and the Rise of a New American Culture*. New York: Pantheon Books, 1993.

Lee, Vera. *The Reign of Women in Eighteenth-Century France*. Cambridge, Mass.: Schenkman Publishing Company, 1975.

Leider, Emily Wortis. *Becoming Mae West*. New York: Farrar, Straus & Giroux, 1997.

Lewis, David Levering, ed. *The Portable Harlem Renaissance Reader*. New York: Viking, 1994.

Lindner, Robert. *Must You Conform?* New York: Rinehart, 1956.

Long, Elizabeth. *The American Dream and the Popular Novel*. Boston: Routledge & Kegan Paul, 1985.

Lorde, Audre. *Zami: A New Spelling of My Name*. Freedom, Calif.: Crossing Press, 1982.

Lukenbill, Grant. *Untold Millions: Positioning Your Business for the Gay and Lesbian Consumer Revolution*. New York: HarperCollins, 1996.

Lunardini, Christine A. *From Equal Suffrage to Equal Rights: Alice Paul and the National Woman's Party, 1910–1928*. New York: New York University Press, 1986.

Malone, Michael. *Heroes of Eros: Male Sexuality in the Movies*. New York: Dutton, 1979.

Mapplethorpe, Robert. *The Black Book*. New York: St. Martin's Press, 1986.

Marcus, Steven. *The Other Victorians: A Study of Sexuality and Pornography in Mid-Nineteenth Century England*. New York: Basic Books, 1966.

Marcuse, Herbert. *Eros and Civilization: A Philosophical Inquiry into Freud*. New York, Vintage Books, 1962.

Marshall, Richard, and Robert Mapplethorpe. *Robert Mapplethorpe*. Boston: Bullfinch Press, 1990.

Martin, Linda, and Kerry Segrave. *Anti-Rock: The Opposition to Rock 'n' Roll*. Hamden, Conn.: Archon Books, 1988.

McNaught, Brian. *Now That I'm Out, What Do I Do?* New York: St. Martin's Press, 1997.

Meyer, Leisa D. *Creating GI Jane: Sexuality and Power in the Women's Army Corps During World War II*. New York: Columbia University Press, 1996.

Miller, Jonathan. *The Body in Question*. New York: Random House, 1987.

Miller, Merle. *On Being Different: What It Means to Be a Homosexual*. New York: Random House, 1971.

Mitchell, Juliet. *Psychoanalysis and Feminism: Freud, Reich, Laing, and Women*. New York: Pantheon, 1974; Vintage, 1975.

Moers, Ellen. *The Dandy: Brummell to Beerbohm*. New York: Viking, 1960.

Money, John. *The Destroying Angel: Sex, Fitness & Food in the Legacy of Degeneracy Theory; Graham Crackers, Kellogg's Corn Flakes & American Health History*. Buffalo, N.Y.: Prometheus Books, 1985.

Morgan, Fidelis. *The Female Wits: Women Playwrights of the Restoration*. London: Virago, 1981.

Morgan, Fidelis, with Charlotte Charke. *The Well-Known Trouble-Maker: A Life of Charlotte Charke*. London: Faber & Faber, 1988.

Morgan, Robin. *Going Too Far: The Personal Chronicle of a Feminist*. New York: Random House, 1977.

Morrison, Toni. *Playing in the Dark: Whiteness and the Literary Imagination.* Cambridge, Mass.: Harvard University Press, 1992.

Morrisroe, Patricia. *Mapplethorpe: A Biography.* New York: Random House, 1995.

Mosse, George L. *Nationalism and Sexuality: Respectability and Abnormal Sexuality in Modern Europe.* New York: Howard Fertig, 1985.

Murray, Margaret A. *The Witch-Cult in Western Europe.* New York: Oxford University Press, 1921.

Murray, Stephen O. *American Gay.* Chicago: University of Chicago Press, 1996.

Newton, Esther. *Cherry Grove, Fire Island: Sixty Years in America's First Gay and Lesbian Town.* Boston: Beacon Press, 1993.

Nissenbaum, Stephen. *The Battle for Christmas.* New York: Knopf, 1996.

Nordhoff, Charles. *The Communistic Societies of the United States from Personal Visit and Observation.* 1875. Reprint, New York: Dover, 1966.

Norton, Rictor. *Mother Clap's Molly House: The Gay Subculture in England, 1700–1830.* London: Gay Men's Press, 1992.

O'Carroll, Tom. *Paedophilia: The Radical Case.* London: Peter Owen, 1980.

Oppenheimer, Joshua, and Helena Reckitt, eds. *Acting on AIDS: Sex, Drugs, and Politics.* London: Serpent's Tail, 1997.

Orsi, Robert Anthony. *The Madonna of 115th Street: Faith and Community in Italian Harlem, 1880–1950.* New Haven: Yale University Press, 1985.

Outram, Dorinda. *The Body and the French Revolution: Sex, Class, and Political Culture.* New Haven: Yale University Press, 1989.

Pattison, Robert. *The Triumph of Vulgarity: Rock Music in the Mirror of Romanticism.* New York: Oxford University Press, 1987.

Patton, Cindy. *Fatal Advice: How Safe-Sex Education Went Wrong.* Durham, N.C.: Duke University Press, 1996.

———. *Inventing AIDS.* New York: Routledge, 1990.

———. *Sex and Germs: The Politics of AIDS.* Boston: South End Press, 1985.

Peiss, Kathy. *Cheap Amusements: Working Women and Leisure in Turn-of-the-Century New York.* Philadelphia: Temple University Press, 1986.

Pharr, Suzanne. *Homophobia: A Weapon of Sexism.* New York: Chardon Press, 1988.

Plant, Richard. *The Pink Triangle: The Nazi War Against Homosexuals.* New York: Henry Holt, 1986.

Pleck, Elizabeth. *Domestic Tyranny: The Making of Social Policy Against Family Violence from Colonial Times to the Present.* New York: Oxford University Press, 1987.

Pollack, Rachel, and Cheryl Schwartz. *The Journey Out: A Guide for and about Lesbian, Gay, and Bisexual Teens.* New York: Puffin, 1995.

Pomeroy, Sarah B. *Goddesses, Whores, Wives, and Slaves: Women in Classical Antiquity.* New York: Schocken Books, 1975.

Potts, Alex. *Flesh and the Ideal: Winckelmann and the Origins of Art History.* New Haven: Yale University Press, 1994.

Quaintance, George. *The Art of George Quaintance.* Edited by Volker Janssen. Berlin: Janssen Verlag, 1990.

Rector, Frank. *The Nazi Extermination of Homosexuals.* New York: Stein & Day, 1981.

Rich, Andrienne. *Blood, Bread, and Poetry: Selected Prose, 1979–1985.* New York: W. W. Norton, 1986.

Richards, Jeffrey. *Sex, Dissidence, and Damnation: Minority Groups in the Middle Ages.* New York: Routledge, 1990.

Richmond, Len, and Gary Noguera. *The Gay Liberation Book.* San Francisco: Ramparts Press, 1973.

Ritter, Bruce. *Sometimes God Has a Kid's Face: The Story of America's Exploited Street Kids*. New York: Covenant House, 1988.

Robertson, Pamela. *Guilty Pleasures: Feminist Camp from Mae West to Madonna*. Durham, N.C.: Duke University Press, 1996.

Rodgers, Bruce. *The Queens' Vernacular: A Gay Lexicon*. San Francisco: Straight Arrow Books, 1972.

Roediger, David R. *The Wages of Whiteness: Race and the Making of the American Working Class*. London: Verso, 1991.

Rose, Jacqueline. *The Case of Peter Pan, or the Impossibility of Children's Fiction*. London: Macmillan Press, 1984.

Ross, Walter. *The Immortal*. New York: Simon & Schuster, 1958.

Rossi, Alice S., ed. *The Feminist Papers: From Adams to de Beauvoir*. Boston: Northeastern University Press, 1988.

Roszak, Theodore. *The Making of a Counter Culture: Reflections on the Technocratic Society and Its Youthful Opposition*. Garden City, N.Y.: Doubleday, 1969.

Rudofsky, Bernard. *The Unfashionable Human Body*. Garden City, N.Y.: Doubleday, 1971.

Ruggiero, Guido. *The Boundaries of Eros: Sex Crime and Sexuality in Renaissance Venice*. New York: Oxford University Press, 1985.

Russ, Joanna. *How to Suppress Women's Writing*. Austin: University of Texas Press, 1983.

Russo, Vito. *The Celluloid Closet: Homosexuality in the Movies* (Revised edition). New York: Harper & Row, 1987.

Said, Edward. *Culture and Imperialism*. New York: Knopf, 1993.

———. *Orientalism*. New York: Pantheon Books, 1978.

Sale, Roger. *Fairy Tales and After: From Snow White to E. B. White*. Cambridge, Mass.: Harvard University Press, 1978.

Sanger, Margaret. *An Autobiography*. 1938. Reprint. New York: Dover, 1971.

Saslow, James M. *The Poetry of Michelangelo: An Annotated Translation*. New Haven: Yale University Press, 1991.

Schau, Michael. *J. C. Leyendecker*. New York: Watson-Guptill, 1974.

Schmidgall, Gary. *Walt Whitman: A Gay Life*. New York: Dutton, 1997.

Schneir, Miriam. *Feminism: The Essential Historical Writings*. New York: Vintage Books, 1972.

Schor, Juliet B. *The Overworked American: The Unexpected Decline of Leisure*. New York: Basic Books, 1991.

Schulman, Sarah. *My American History: Lesbian and Gay Life During the Reagan/Bush Years*. New York: Routledge, 1994.

———. *Stagestruck: Theater, AIDS, and the Marketing of Gay America*. Chapel Hill, N.C.: Duke University Press, 1998.

Schumacher, Michael. *Dharma Lion: A Biography of Allen Ginsberg*. New York: St. Martin's Press, 1992.

Sedgwick, Eve Kosofsky. *Epistemology of the Closet*. Berkeley: University of California Press, 1990.

Segal, Ronald. *The Black Diaspora: Five Centuries of the Black Experience Outside Africa*. New York: Farrar, Straus & Giroux, 1995.

Sennett, Richard. *The Conscience of the Eye: The Design and Social Life of Cities*. New York: Knopf, 1990.

———. *The Fall of Public Man*. New York: Knopf, 1977.

———. *Families Against the City: Middle-Class Homes of Industrial Chicago, 1872–1890*. New York: Vintage, 1974.

———. *Flesh and Stone: The Body and the City in Western Civilization*. New York: W. W. Norton, 1994.

————. *The Uses of Disorder: Personal Identity and City Life.* New York: Knopf, 1970.

Sennott, Charles M. *Broken Covenant.* New York: Simon & Schuster, 1992.

Shange, Ntozake. Foreword and "irrepressibly bronze, beautiful & mine," in Robert Mapplethorpe, *The Black Book.* New York: St. Martin's Press, 1986.

Sheehy, Helen. *Eva Le Gallienne.* New York: Knopf, 1996.

Shilts, Randy. *And the Band Played On: Politics, People, and the AIDS Epidemic.* New York: St. Martin's Press, 1987.

————. *The Mayor of Castro Street: The Life and Times of Harvey Milk.* New York: St. Martin's Press. 1982.

Shively, Charley, ed. *Calamus Lovers: Walt Whitman's Working-Class Camerados.* San Francisco: Gay Sunshine Press, 1987.

————. *Drum Beats: Walt Whitman's Civil War Boy Lovers.* San Francisco: Gay Sunshine Press, 1989.

Silverman, Debora. *Selling Culture: Bloomingdale's, Diana Vreeland, and the New Aristocracy of Taste in Reagan's America.* New York: Pantheon Books, 1986.

Silverstein, Charles, and Felice Picano. *The New Joy of Gay Sex.* New York: HarperCollins, 1992.

Sinfield, Allan. *The Wilde Century: Effeminacy, Oscar Wilde, and the Queer Moment.* New York: Columbia University Press, 1994.

Smith, Barbara. *Home Girls: A Black Feminist Anthology.* Albany, NY: Kitchen Table—Women of Color Press, 1983.

Smith, Richard. *Seduced and Abandoned: Essays on Gay Men and Popular Music.* London: Cassell, 1995.

Sochen, June. *Herstory: A Woman's View of American History.* New York: Alfred Publishing Company, 1974.

————. *The New Woman: Feminism in Greenwich Village, 1910–1920.* New York: Quadrangle Books, 1972.

Sontag, Susan. *Against Interpretation: and Other Essays.* New York: Farrar, Straus & Giroux, 1966; Dell, 1969.

Sparke, Penny. *As Long as It's Pink: The Sexual Politics of Taste.* London: Pandora, 1995.

Spigel, Lynn. *Make Room for TV: Television and the Family Ideal in Postwar America.* Chicago: University of Chicago Press, 1992.

Spoto, Donald. *Camerado: Hollywood and the American Man.* New York: New American Library, 1978.

Stone, Lawrence. *The Family, Sex, and Marriage in England, 1500–1800.* New York: Harper & Row, 1977.

Streitmatter, Rodger. *Unspeakable: The Rise of the Gay and Lesbian Press in America.* Boston: Faber & Faber, 1995.

Stryker, Susan, and Jim Van Buskirk. *Gay by the Bay: A History of Queer Culture in the San Francisco Bay Area.* San Francisco: Chronicle Books, 1996.

Stuckey, Stirling. *Slave Culture: Nationalist Theory and the Foundations of Black America.* New York: Oxford University Press, 1987.

Suarez, Juan A. *Bike Boys, Drag Queens, and Superstars: Avant-Garde, Mass Culture, and Gay Identities in the 1960s Underground Cinema.* Bloomington: University of Indiana Press, 1996.

Tatchell, Peter. *Safer Sexy: The Guide to Gay Sex Safely.* London: Cassell, 1994.

Taylor, Gordon Rattray. *Sex in History: Society's Changing Attitudes to Sex Throughout the Ages.* New York: Ballantine Books, 1954.

Taylor, Martin. *Lads: Love Poetry of the Trenches.* London: Constable, 1989.

Teal, Donn. *The Gay Militants.* New York: Stein & Day, 1971.

Timmons, Stuart. *The Trouble with Harry Hay: Founder of the Modern Gay Movement.* Boston: Alyson, 1990.

Tribe, Laurence. *American Constitutional Law,* 2nd ed. New York: Foundation Press, 1988.

Tyler, Parker. *Screening the Sexes: Homosexuality in the Movies.* New York: Holt, Rinehart and Winston, 1972.

Udelson, Joseph H. *Dreamer of the Ghetto: The Life and Works of Israel Zangwill.* Tuscaloosa: University of Alabama Press, 1990.

Vaid, Urvashi. *Virtual Equality: The Mainstreaming of Gay and Lesbian Liberation.* New York: Anchor Books, 1995.

Vickers, Hugo. *Cecil Beaton: A Biography.* New York: Little, Brown, 1985.

Vidal, Gore. *The Second American Revolution and Other Essays (1976–1982).* New York: Random House, 1982.

Vincent, Ted. *Keep Cool: The Black Activists Who Built the Jazz Age.* London: Pluto Press, 1995.

Walker, Alice. *You Can't Keep a Good Woman Down.* New York: Harcourt Brace Jovanovich, 1981.

Walsh, Frank. *Sin and Censorship: The Catholic Church and the Motion Picture Industry.* New Haven: Yale University Press, 1996.

Walters, Margaret. *The Nude Male: A New Perspective.* New York: Paddington Press, 1978.

Watkins, Mel. *On the Real Side: Laughing, Lying, and Signifying—The Underground Tradition of African-American Humor That Transformed American Culture, from Slavery to Richard Pryor.* New York: Simon & Schuster, 1994.

Watson, Steven. *The Birth of the Beat Generation: Visionaries, Rebels, and Hipsters, 1944–1960.* New York: Pantheon Books, 1995.

———. *The Harlem Renaissance: Hub of African-American Culture, 1920–1930.* New York: Pantheon Books, 1995.

Weil, Simone. *The Need for Roots: Prelude to a Declaration of Duties Toward Mankind.* New York: Putnam, 1952.

Weinberg, George. *Society and the Healthy Homosexual.* New York: St. Martin's Press, 1972; Doubleday Anchor, 1973.

Weisbrod, Carol. *The Boundaries of Utopia.* New York: Pantheon Books, 1980.

West, Mae. *Three Plays by Mae West: Sex, The Drag, The Pleasure Man.* Edited by Lillian Schlissel. New York: Routledge, 1997.

West, Rebecca. *The New Meaning of Treason.* New York: Viking, 1964.

Whitcomb, Ian. *Irving Berlin and Ragtime America.* New York: Limelight Editions, 1988.

White, Edmund. *The Burning Library: Essays.* New York: Knopf, 1994.

Willis, Ellen. *Beginning to See the Light: Pieces of a Decade.* New York: Knopf, 1981.

Wittman, Carl. "A Gay Manifesto." In *Out of the Closets: Voices of Gay Liberation,* edited by Karla Jay and Allen Young. New York: World Publishing, 1972.

Wolfe, George. *The Colored Museum.* New York: Grove Press, 1988.

Wood, Robert W. *Christ and the Homosexual: Some Observations.* New York: Vantage Press, 1960.

Zinn, Howard. *Declarations of Independence: Cross-Examining American Ideology.* New York: HarperCollins, 1990.

———. *A People's History of the United States.* New York: Harper & Row, 1980.

Index